THE CRISIS IN AMERICAN EDUCATION

REVOLUTION

AT

BERKELEY

Edited by
MICHAEL V. MILLER and SUSAN GILMORE

With an Introduction by IRVING HOWE

THE DIAL PRESS, NEW YORK, 1965

First Printing, September 1965
Second Printing, November 1965

ACKNOWLEDGMENTS

041597

JOHN BOLER, "Behind the Protest at Berkeley" reprinted with the permission of Commonweal Publishing Co. Inc. and the author.

HAL DRAPER, "The Mind of Clark Kerr" reprinted by permission of the author from the Independent Socialist Club pamphlet.

NATHAN GLAZER, "What Happened at Berkeley" © 1965 by the American Jewish Committee. Reprinted by permission of *Commentary* and the author.

NATHAN GLAZER and PAUL GOODMAN, "An Exchange on Berkeley" reprinted by permission of the authors and *The New York Review of Books*. Copyright © 1965 New York Review, Inc.

NATHAN GLAZER and PHILIP SELZNICK, "Berkeley" © 1965 by the American Jewish Committee. Reprinted by permission of *Commentary* and the authors.

PAUL GOODMAN, "Thoughts on Berkeley" reprinted by permission of the author and *The New York Review of Books*. Copyright © 1965 New York Review, Inc.

PAUL GOODMAN, "Berkeley in February" reprinted, with permission from *Dissent* and by permission of the author.

SIDNEY HOOK, "Academic Freedom and the Rights of Students" (formerly "Freedom to Learn But Not to Riot") © 1965 by The New York Times Company. Reprinted by permission, and by permission of the author.

SIDNEY HOOK, "Second Thoughts on Berkeley" reprinted by permission of the author.

CLARK KERR, "The Frantic Race to Remain Contemporary" reprinted from *Daedalus*, Fall 1964, and from THE USES OF A UNIVERSITY © 1963 by the President and Harvard University Press. Reprinted by permission of Harvard University Press, *Daedalus*, and the author.

PAUL KRASSNER, "The Naked Emperor" reprinted by permission of *Cavalier* Magazine, copyright © 1965 by Fawcett Publications, Inc., and by permission of the author.

COLIN MILLER, "The Press and the Student Revolt, 1964" reprinted by permission of the author. Parts of this article were published and copyrighted by *Frontier Magazine*.

MICHAEL V. MILLER, "The Student State of Mind" reprinted, with permission, from *Dissent* and by permission of the author.

A. H. RASKIN, "The Berkeley Affair: Mr. Kerr vs. Mr. Savio & Co." © 1965 by The New York Times Company. Reprinted by permission, and by permission of the author.

KEN SANDERSON, "Multiversity Lost" reprinted by permission of the author, and *Spider*.

MARIO SAVIO, "An End to History" reprinted by permission of the author and *Humanity*.

JOHN SEARLE, "Faculty Resolution" reprinted by permission of the author.

JOHN R. SEELEY, *"Quo Warranto:* The 'Berkeley Issue' " reprinted by permission of the author. To appear in a forthcoming issue of *Ramparts*.

MICHAEL SHUTE and JAMES PETRAS, "Berkeley '65" © 1965 by *Partisan Review*. Reprinted by permission of *Partisan Review* and the authors.

LARRY D. SPENCE, "Berkeley: What It Demonstrates" reprinted by permission of *Studies on the Left* and the author.

SOL STERN, "A Deeper Disenchantment," reprinted by permission of *Liberation* and the author.

CALVIN TRILLIN, "Letter from Berkeley." Reprinted by permission; © 1965 The New Yorker Magazine, Inc.

TABLE OF CONTENTS

Introduction by IRVING HOWE
Berkeley and Beyond
xi

Chronology of Major and Controversial Events
xxiv

I
IMAGES OF A UNIVERSITY
3

CLARK KERR
The Frantic Race to Remain Contemporary
5

PAUL GOODMAN
Thoughts on Berkeley
27

SIDNEY HOOK
Academic Freedom and the Rights of Students
32

JOHN R. SEELEY
Quo Warranto: The "Berkeley Issue"
42

II
A CAMPUS DIVIDED
51

MICHAEL V. MILLER
The Student State of Mind
53

HAL DRAPER
The Mind of Clark Kerr
62

A. H. RASKIN
The Berkeley Affair: Mr. Kerr vs. Mr. Savio & Co.
78

JOHN SEARLE
The Faculty Resolution
92

III
AFFIRMATIONS AND ADMONITIONS
105

JOHN F. BOLER
Behind the Protests at Berkeley
107

SIDNEY HOOK
Second Thoughts on Berkeley
116

NATHAN GLAZER
What Happened at Berkeley
160

PHILIP SELZNICK and NATHAN GLAZER
Berkeley: Two Comments
182

NATHAN GLAZER and PAUL GOODMAN
Berkeley: An Exchange
198

IV
THE STUDENT SPOKESMEN
205

JAMES F. PETRAS and MICHAEL SHUTE
Berkeley '65
207

LARRY D. SPENCE
Berkeley: What It Demonstrates
217

SOL STERN
A Deeper Disenchantment
225

MARIO SAVIO
An End to History
239

PAUL KRASSNER
The Naked Emperor
244

V
THE NEW RADICAL SPIRIT
251

CALVIN TRILLIN
Letter from Berkeley
253

PAUL GOODMAN
Berkeley in February
285

APPENDICES
Two Perspectives on Berkeley
303

KEN SANDERSON
Multiversity Lost
305

COLIN MILLER
The Press and the Student Revolt, 1964
313

Introduction by IRVING HOWE

Berkeley and Beyond

Let's start with a happening—or, more precisely, an imagining. Somewhere in Berkeley a group of students (veterans of "the action") is beginning to discuss the December uprising; perhaps one or two young professors, of the kind the students trust and admire, are there too, joining in the reminiscence. As if by common need, they find themselves moving toward the one question that for them requires notable courage to ask—for it must be painful even to admit that it is a question. *Did it really matter?* At first it might have struck them as outrageous, a kind of self-betrayal, even to hint at such a question, but now, as the weeks and months slip away, it becomes a question hard to avoid. After all the excitement, after the thrill of victory, after the speeches and negotiations and policy-making: *did it really matter?*

In one obvious sense, yes. There were student grievances concerning freedom of speech; these grievances were fought to a climax dramatic beyond anyone's anticipation; the immediate results look good. Such actions, though smaller in scope, have been fought through before, and they will have to be fought through again. Academic freedom, never a permanent conquest, must frequently be regained.

So far, so good. But when my imaginary students ask themselves *did it really matter?* they are obviously thinking about more than immediate reforms on the campus; they are worrying about long-range repercussions and possibilities. To ask whether the Berkeley uprising marked a mere colorful incident in their lives or was a milestone toward some encompassing commitment; to wonder whether it was a flareup of youthful energy and rebelliousness or the beginning of a sustained inquiry by American students into the nature and purpose of the education they receive—these are the more enduring, difficult, and important questions. And they do not yet permit of any certain answer.

I think (perhaps it would be more accurate to say I hope) that out of the Berkeley struggle and the turmoil that has since occurred at such schools as St. John's, Brooklyn and Fairleigh Dickinson there will come a persistent series of questionings, by students and teachers alike, directed to problems such as these: (1) Can the idea of the university as a center of learning and free intellect survive in the age of bureaucratic structure, the age of the "multiversity"? (2) At a time when young people spend more and more of their lives in universities, is there not a need for new definitions of their rights, freedoms and responsibilities as students? (3) Will the rebellious students be able to provide a new social energy for this country, will they come to be a new source of ideas and commitment for a revitalized democratic radicalism? Only if they, and we, now turn our attention to questions such as these, will the Berkeley events really have mattered.

The Idea of the University. At the risk of seeming naïve or utopian, I want to posit the idea that almost every student who comes to an American university has somewhere in the back of his mind a true vision of what a university is supposed to be. He may be hostile or confused, he may already be cynical about it, but somewhere, however dimly, he knows—for it is an idea that has been with us for a long time—what a university should be.

The language I use is not his, but some glimpse of the following he does have: that the university should serve as a center for disinterested learning; that it should be quick with the passions of controversy yet dedicated to those studies which the outer world may dismiss as esoteric; that it should be a sanctuary for opinion; and that in its precincts he should be able to encounter men who will serve as models of intellectual discipline and enthusiasm.

Now there are some American universities in which the student can find all of these, though it takes a bit of looking; but only rarely can he find them as the dominant voice of a university or find them uncontaminated by the grossness of utilitarian measurement and the calculations of the business ethic. What has been happening to the American university is a gradual and all-too-cheerful adaptation to the surrounding social landscape: It has become too absorbed with weapon-producing research, too subject to the creed of material growth and power, too caught up in the mystique of quantification. Here is testimony from Clark Kerr, president of the University of California, who speaks as the agent of the prevailing drift:

> The university has become a prime instrument of national purpose. . . . This is the essence of the transformation now engulfing our universities. Basic to this transformation is the growth of the "knowledge industry," which is coming to permeate government and business. . . . What the railroads did for the second half of the nineteenth century and the automobile for the first half of this century, the knowledge industry may do for the second half of this century: that is, to serve as the focal point for national growth. And the university is at the center of the knowledge process.

There is the voice of dominant America, knowledge as "industry." And its style too, "the knowledge process." How old fashioned, by contrast, is the view of Cardinal Newman that "knowledge is capable of being its own end," and how characteristically utopian of Lewis Mumford to write: "As the cloister of the monastery might be termed a passive university, so the university might be called an active cloister; its function is the critical reappraisal and renewal of the cultural heritage." Between the crude utilitarianism of Kerr and the intellectual seriousness of Mumford there can be no compromise.

Part of the trouble with the American university is endemic to our style of life. We have always, in our lust for self-congratulation, deluded ourselves as to the quality of American education, and we have never properly realized how deep is the conflict between the values of the free mind and the values of the market place. But partly the trouble has to do with something new in our society, the growth of "mass education" during the last twenty or thirty years.

By "mass education" we have in mind an historically new situation in which it is commonly assumed that all members of society have a right to receive as much learning as they wish to or can absorb; we may also be pointing to what follows from this assumption, namely, the problems inherent in the effort to give a growing segment of the population at least some sort—often it's a pretty sad sort—of college education.

"Mass education" is here to stay, historically irreversible. Only a small number of reactionaries oppose it on principle, though an alarming number of liberals, their liberalism increasingly diluted, begin to conclude that it must fatally corrupt educational standards. Whether more American boys and girls will go to college each year is no longer a question. The question is, what will happen to them once they arrive? For "mass education" is one of the more significant democratic experiments of our time: an experiment barely begun, and under circumstances that work heavily against its realization. Our society has stumbled into the possibilities of "mass education"—perhaps more accurately, it has been forced to confront these possibilities because of military and technological pressures. But it has not yet appropriated a small fraction of the talent, energy and resources needed to make "mass education" a success. Whether *this* society can do that is, to my mind, an open question; perhaps here, as in other areas of social life, we shall have to suffer the results of an uncompleted revolution.

Even if the circumstances for introducing "mass education" were entirely favorable, even if the whole country were to throw itself heart-and-soul into the work of serious education, there would still be severe difficulties. For we would be trying to cope with the heritage of centuries of neglect, we would have to break through those thick deposits of inertia and resistance which have settled onto the consciousness of millions of people. To do this would be highly meaningful work, for we would be facing real problems, not the pseudo-problems thrown up by weaponry and advertising. We would be trying to fulfill the democratic revolution of the past 150 years, which for the first time in history stirred the masses into the possibility of consciousness.

The difficulties, I repeat, would be staggering. Consider, for example, the recent expansion of our colleges and the consequent pressure to appoint to our faculties men who lack the necessary training and more important, the spirit of devotion and austerity which, at least occasionally, ought to characterize the scholar and intellectual. I do not wish to be misunderstood: I quite agree that thousands of college teachers are decent human beings trying to do a decent job. But perhaps that is just the trouble. Fifty or sixty years ago, when the American university had a relatively well-defined role as the cultural training-ground for the country's upper strata, a decently mediocre professor was not likely to do much damage. As a carrier of the received culture, he might even do some good. Today, in an atmosphere of fevered expansion, lucrative busy-work and harsh uncertainty as to what a university should be, the decently mediocre professor tends all too often to be a disaster. Tradition could carry him, in the past; now he must float, or sink, on his own. He is a disaster because he cannot cope with the staggering task of convincing thousands of ill-prepared and poorly-motivated students that, quite apart from utilitarian or national ends, there is a value to the life of the mind. And he cannot persuade his students that there is such a value because, more often than not, he does not know what the life of the mind is.

Inevitably then, "mass education" brings with it severe and unprecedented problems. But the truth is that the turn to "mass education" has not occurred under favorable circumstances: it has not been planned or thought through, and frequently has been the result of drift, panic and national egotism. Coming in a society characterized by misshapen values and economic injustice, racial prejudice and political evasiveness, "mass education" is contaminated from the very moment of its birth. To make high claims for the life of the mind in a world devoted to accumulating money and bombs is either to indulge in a pious hypocrisy or to indicate to one's students that if they are to become serious intellectuals they must be ready to accept a measure of estrangement and perhaps deprivation.

Yet all of these problems thrown up by the sudden turn to "mass education" might be manageable if only there were present in our universities a firm and self-assured intellectual leadership which understood and was prepared to fight for the values of an "active cloister," a leadership which knew what Cardinal Newman meant when he wrote that the university is "the high protecting power of all knowledge . . . it maps out the territory of the intellect, and sees that . . . there is neither encroachment nor surrender on any side." Of how many university administrations in America, indeed, of how many faculties, could one say that they live or try to live by this standard?

Neither encroachment nor surrender . . . The reality is closer to the opposite. There are steady encroachments by the spirit of hucksterdom, the blight of weaponry, the disease of tainted research. There is a steady surrender to educational gimmickry which short-changes the students and educational big-enterprise which seduces the professors. (Students sometimes complain about professors who lack social awareness and continue to do their own abstruse research. In the present circumstances, this complaint seems to me misdirected. The old-fashioned traditional scholar sticking by his narrow specialty no matter who gets bombed or what freedom march occurs, may not be an intellectual hero nor an inspiring model for the young; but at least he sustains the values of disinterested scholarship which are essential for the survival of a true university. Much more menacing, as it seems to me, is the professor-entrepreneur busy with a mess of grants, textbooks, institutes, conferences, consultations, indeed, with everything but serious teaching and intellectual work.)

Lest all this seem exaggerated, I quote at some length from two quite moderate professors at the University of California at Berkeley, Sheldin Wolin and John Schaar:

For some time now, the students, especially the undergraduates, have felt themselves to be an alien presence within the multiversity, an "Other Academia" analogous to the "Other America," ill fed, ill housed and ill clothed not in the material sense, but in the intellectual and spiritual senses. As the multiversity has climbed to higher and higher peaks of research productivity, material riches, and bureaucratic complexity, the students have fallen into deeper and deeper abysses of hostility and estrangement. The students' own favorite word for their condition is "alienation," by which they mean . . . a sense of not being valued members of a genuine intellectual and moral community. Their feeling is grounded in reality.

The architects of the multiversity simply have not solved the problem of how to build an institution which not only produces knowledge and knowledgeable people with useful skills, but which also enriches and enlightens the lives of its students—informing them with the values of the intellect, preparing them to serve as the guardians of the society's intellectual honesty and political health, arming them with the vision by which society seeks its own better future. It is the performance of these latter tasks that distinguishes a genuine educational community from a mere research factory and training institution. . . .

By any reasonable standard, the multiversity has not taken its students seriously. At Berkeley, the educational environment of the undergraduate is bleak. He is confronted throughout his entire first two years with indifferent advising, endless bureaucratic routines, gigantic lecture courses, and a deadening succession of textbook assignments, and bluebook examinations testing his grasp of bits and pieces of knowledge. . . . It is possible to take a B.A. at Berkeley and never talk with a professor. To many of the students, the whole system seems a perversion of an educational community into a factory designed for the mass processing of men into machines.

This indictment is severe, but not, I am prepared to testify, excessive. Nor is it complete. A diagnosis of the malaise afflicting the American university would have to say a good deal about the increase in the size and power of administrative bureaucracies which regard the university as essentially "their" institution to be spared the troubles of restlessness and innovation. Something would have to be said about that prime vulgarity known as "publish or perish," a travesty of scholarship and common sense. And something more would have to be said, as I am glad the Berkeley students did, about the pressures faced by state universities from boards of regents heavily weighted toward conservative and business ideologies and almost always without faculty or student representation.

In short: the future of the American university, insofar as it will remain a university, is severely problematic; the ideal of the "active cloister" put forward by Mumford remains to be clarified and defended; and no one can do this as well as teachers and students together, for their interests, while not identical, are at least congruent.

The Place of the Student. Partly because the university has come to play a larger role in the socio-economic life of the country than ever before, hundreds of thousands of young people now spend larger portions of their lives in the universities than ever before. And not merely their lives as minors subject to institutional control, but also as young adults usually able to vote, expected to pay taxes, and liable to military service.

One consequence ought to be a serious effort to reconsider the relationship between university and student, the terms of which were originally set under radically different conditions. In regard to public discussion and the rights of political minorities, the American university remains, by and large, a stronghold of democratic freedom; but its inner life as an institution is usually far from democratic. The system of authority governing the American university ranges from the outright dictatorship of the "strong" president to academic control by a faculty conscious of its traditional privileges; in most cases there is an uneasy compromise between top administration and faculty, with an intervening bureaucracy slowly accumulating more and more power.

But as far as students are concerned, they are supposed to remain in and be content with a state of almost complete dependence. University administrators, brimming with rectitude, presume to supervise the private lives of students. Decisions concerning academic standards and procedures are generally made without so much as consulting students. This is not, I think, a healthy situation, and without indulging in any mystique about the spontaneous wisdom or virtue of the young, we ought to recognize the appropriateness of student consultation in academic affairs.

The doctrine by which administrators justify their supervision of student life is called *in loco parentis,* the institution acting in place of parents. Concerning this dubious rationale Dean Kathryn Hopwood of Hunter College has written that it is "quite at variance with the genesis of the European universities, such as the ones at Bologna and Paris, where the students employed visiting scholars to teach them." And here is the testimony of a young man recently self-removed from graduate school, Thomas Hayden, who writes with understandable bitterness about *in loco parentis:*

> To go to college involves a partial surrender of the freedoms of speech, press, and assembly, and often the freedom of privacy. It means arbitrary hours for women students and compulsory functions for both sexes. It means the "double jeopardy" of receiving punishments from the university for crimes committed in and adjudicated by the city. It means tolerating personal dossiers and students who spy for the dean of men or con-

gressional investigating committees. It means the supervision
and regulation of privacy. It means living under threat of
punishment for "conduct unbecoming a student" or "inability
to adjust to the university pattern." Margaret Mead has commented forcefully on the distinction between the work force
and student force in the same age range:

> A handful of tugboat employees or flight engineers, because
> of their admitted rights in a complex system in which they are
> working members, can hold up a city or a country until their
> demands are met, but in some states students are not even
> allowed to vote.

And, unlike parents of students not in college,

> parents of studying children must both support them and,
> correlatively, retain control of their conduct or delegate
> comparable control to some quasi-parental educational insti-
> tution. In either case the student is treated like a dependent
> child.

Needless to say, student extracurricular activities are organized
with this dependent status clearly in mind. The philosophy of
student activities is articulated by most universities as either the
"preparation" theory or the "privilege" theory. The first and
most important of these goes like this: college is a "preparatory"
period when the student, through incubation, is equipped with
the skills he will need later in life. "Preparation" means involving the students in a make-believe laboratory world of student
activities where they can safely practise being a citizen.

Is this, asks the writer, a serious educational philosophy? Surely the answer must be that it is not. All that can be
said in behalf of *in loco parentis* is that it is a convenience for
deans.

The usual attitude toward students in the American university
is that they constitute a mixture of necessary consumer and irk-
some dependent. They pay their money (or receive their fellowships) and must then submit to whatever disciplines and routines
the university proposes. Now there is a sense in which this seems
quite proper: the student, being a novice, has come to learn from
his superiors, and before the latter admit him to their ranks they
have the obligation to test his competence. Yet this hardly justifies
the present systematic refusal to consider seriously student opinion

concerning such matters as teaching procedures, curriculum, course requirements, etc. (Actually, student opinion *is* taken into account, even about such sacrosanct matters as faculty tenure; but this happens in the worst possible way, through gossip, hearsay, comparison of class sizes, etc.)

At the graduate level the situation becomes still more galling. The graduate student, though presumed to be a serious person and often one who makes notable sacrifices to pursue his studies, is placed in a condition of dependency far more severe than that of the undergraduate. The whole career of the graduate student can be at the mercy or whim of a few professors, sometimes only one professor. Anyone who has taught in an American university knows how often the bright and lively undergraduate undergoes a depressing change in style soon after entering graduate school: he becomes professionally cautious, intellectually timid, concerned to please and adapt to professors. This is hardly a system calculated to encourage manliness and independence of spirit. Surely, without challenging the authority of the faculty or creating that state of "anarchy" which is said to haunt the dreams of educational administrators, it should be possible to consult systematically with our graduate students concerning a wide range of educational policies.

Even to raise such a possibility is to provoke outcries from certain professors about the danger of reducing our universities to "banana republics" where overpoliticized students would establish a terrorist reign of laxness. How far-fetched a fantasy this seems in the actual context of American university life! And besides, such fears would seem a bit more worthy if American professors had shown themselves proudly resistant against the real danger to their authority, which comes from the steady encroachments of academic bureaucracies.

What our more thoughtful and restless students are requesting is not that academic decisions be turned over to "student mobs," but that they be allowed, through democratic channels, to express their views about matters of the greatest concern to them. Often enough students are wrong in their opinions about academic life and educational policy, but then so too are the rest of us; and a supply of fresh mistakes might be invigorating. We professors ought to appreciate the value of constructive—even not-so-constructive—restlessness: for while it might make our lives less comfortable, it would surely make them more interesting.

Students and Politics. In one crucial sense, what happened at Berkeley must be considered apart from the political views, real or alleged, of the student leaders. For the grievances of the Free Speech Movement had an intrinsic weight and meaning; they required satisfaction and settlement, no matter what anyone might have felt about the political opinions of this or the other FSM leader; and at the height of the struggle, the students were right to insist that questions about the leaders' politics could only distract attention from the urgencies of their campaign.

Yet, in any larger perspective, it is obviously important to consider the motivating ideas of the student leaders; and while these do range, as they insist, across the entire political spectrum, it would be disingenuous to deny that a number of them think of themselves as radicals. Their radicalism is vague and non-ideological; it places a heavy stress upon individual integrity, perhaps more than upon collective action; it seldom follows from any coherent theory of modern society. The campus radicals respond most strongly to immediate and morally unambiguous issues, such as Negro rights, free speech, etc., yet they also feel strongly that they are "alienated" from the prevalent norms and values of the society. Suspicious of older radicals, tending to dismiss (a little too casually, I think) the experience of the last forty years, properly hostile to what Orwell once called "smelly little orthodoxies," and sometimes a bit impatient with systematic thought, they cast about for a mode of socio-cultural criticism which will express their strong ethical revulsion from the outrages, deceits and vulgarities of our society. Frequently, their radicalism tends to be more a matter of personal life-style than a program for common activity; they react violently against the hypocrisies of "success" and worry about finding kinds of work and ways of life that seem to them authentic.

It is an encouraging development. One reason for the dullness of American political and intellectual life these past fifteen years has been the absence of a new generation of campus radicals who could stir things up a little. We have badly needed such young people—devoted, passionate, educated—who will not be content with "the given," but will set to work patiently to reconstruct American society along democratic lines. Now it appears that such a generation is beginning to make itself heard.

But the question must always arise in regard to student politics: how long, how deeply will this new generation persist? We are all familiar with the rhythm of a certain kind of campus radicalism. A sudden flare of political interest; a fury of activism, sometimes accompanied by premature ideological hardening and an impatience with those outside the campus who are regarded as insufficiently "revolutionary"; and then, often because the original commitment was not well thought out, a slide into disillusionment, leading to the frenetic weariness of careerism, or the cautions of official liberalism, or literary reflections on the tragic limitations of mankind. Now this is, of course, a caricature, but it is a caricature based on more than a little reality. And the question must inevitably arise whether the radicalism of the students at Berkeley and elsewhere rests upon serious thought or is the kind of one-shot affair which in the past has often paved the way for a later adjustment to the status quo.

The question cannot yet be answered, but it seems to me of great importance. For it leads us to a larger problem concerning the possibilities of new social and intellectual energy in our country. Previous social movements, like the CIO in the thirties, and even the Negro liberation movement of our own day, can largely be seen as drawing their strength from the justified grievances of particular classes and groups. Radical intellectuals hoped that expressions of working class discontent would lead to a larger effort toward social change; those under the influence of Marxism spoke of the proletariat's "historical mission" and its "inherent revolutionary potential." Right now, it is hard to think in these terms. We find ourselves, instead, wondering whether some new impulse toward democratic radicalism might emerge in the United States which would rest not merely on the demands of oppressed classes and mistreated groups but also on a commonly apprehended need for a better society. That is, we wonder whether intelligent people, on various levels of the economic scale, can be drawn into a new politics based on their sense of responsibility, a vision of idealism, a wish to remake the world. If anything of the sort is ever to happen in the United States, it may well begin on the campus.

We can end only with questions. Will the energy of student rebellion be frittered away or will it grow into something stable, enduring and reflective? It is so hard for young people to wrench themselves away from our sticky world of "success" that when now and again they do become radicals, they tend to think of their commitment mainly as an extreme posture—a rebellion against the middle class, a nose-thumbing at the world of their fathers—rather than an effort to initiate a serious politics. And sometimes this difficulty leads to an unearned impatience, or even contempt, for the procedures of democracy and an accompanying submission to the allure of charismatic leaders and authoritarian ideologies.

The student rebels will have to work their ideas out for themselves, and there is little reason why they should repeat the experience of an older generation, even that segment of an older generation which may have learned something from its experience. Yet it may be useful to stress what it is we believe we have learned: that for a radical (or any other) politics ever to make a deep and lasting impact upon American society, it must be rooted in democratic values and be committed to democratic procedures. Anything else would serve merely to illustrate Santayana's remark that those who refuse to learn from the mistakes of the past are doomed to repeat them.

Meanwhile, as at least a minority of American students begins to stir to a new consciousness and activity, we look on with hope and interest.

CHRONOLOGY OF MAJOR
AND CONTROVERSIAL EVENTS

September 14: Dean of Students, Katherine Towle, sends a letter to all student organizations to inform them that the sidewalk area in front of the campus at Bancroft and Telegraph will no longer be available for setting up tables, raising funds, recruiting members, and giving speeches for off-campus political and social action. Previously, this property was thought to belong to the city of Berkeley. It is now revealed, however, that the property belonged to the University, and henceforth all University rules restricting political activities would apply to this area.

September 17: The leadership of student organizations, including political groups ranging from the far left to the far right, form a united front to request that the administration restore the area to its traditional role as a center of student political activity and expression.

September 21: The first day of classes. Dean Towle, after meeting with representatives from the united front, modifies the previous ruling. Students would be allowed to set up tables and distribute informational material, but they would still not be allowed to engage in the essential stuff of politics. After the students' request to resume traditional political activities is turned down, the united front holds its first rally on the steps of Sproul Hall (Berkeley Administration Building).

September 28: Chancellor Edward Strong modifies the ban to permit campaigning for candidates and propositions on ballots.

Dean Arleigh Williams warns that students persisting in what has now been defined as "illegal politics" may be expelled. Meanwhile, several political organizations continue setting up tables and engaging in pre-ban activities.

September 30: Five students are cited for violating the newly-formed regulations against manning tables and are asked to appear at 3:00 PM before the deans. Over 400 students sign statements that they are equally responsible for manning the tables and appear in Sproul Hall requesting that they too be given disciplinary hearings. All are refused access to the deans except the original five students and the three leaders of this protest group who are now scheduled to meet with Dean Williams at 4:00 PM. The general student protest continues and continues to be ignored; finally even the meeting with the eight students' leaders is cancelled. As evening approaches, the hundreds of students remain outside the dean's offices; at 11:45 Chancellor Strong announces the indefinite suspension of the eight students; the assembly of students remains at Sproul Hall until the following morning.

October 1: Students set up tables on steps of Sproul Hall and plan noon rally to protest rules and to demand equal treatment for all students subject to these rules. Police arrest Jack Weinberg for operating a CORE table on Sproul steps, and crowds of students spontaneously surround the police car and prohibit it from carrying away Mr. Weinberg. Individual speakers—among them, Mario Savio who soon distinguishes himself as the major spokesman of the Free Speech Movement (FSM)—then begin addressing the more than 2,000 assembled students. The protest is extended when students enter Sproul Hall for a second major sit-in. Meanwhile a group of faculty members attempts to mediate; however, the administration announces that the rules are not negotiable. The student protesters remain.

October 2: The administration calls in several hundred policemen who assemble around the demonstrators. University officials, including President Kerr, members of the faculty, and student leaders meet and discuss issues. At the last minute, they reach a six-point agreement which includes the University's dropping charges against Mr. Weinberg. The police leave and demonstrators disperse.

October 3–4: The Free Speech Movement is formed out of the united front and subsequently an executive committee representing the various political and religious organizations is established, as well as a twelve-man steering committee to plan interim policy and to choose students to serve on the student-faculty-administration study committee.

October 5: Chancellor Strong, pursuant to the agreement of October 2, appoints ten members to the Campus Committee on Political Activity (CCPA) to investigate and suggest solutions to the campus political problems. The FSM is first given two delegates to the committee; it is later granted two more.

October 13: The Academic Senate passes a motion for "maximum freedom for student political activity" and agrees to participate actively in the faculty-student-administration committee. The CCPA holds its first meeting at which fifty of the approximate 300 students in attendance testify against the illegal formation of that committee. Meanwhile graduate students meet to select seven members to the FSM Executive Committee.

October 15: President Kerr agrees to reconstitute the CCPA, adding six more members to the original twelve. He also requests the Academic Senate to establish an *ad hoc* committee to advise on the September 30 suspension of eight students.

November 7: The CCPA reaches an impasse on the question of University discipline of students and organizations engaging in activities that "directly result" in "unlawful acts" off campus.

November 9: FSM demonstrates its position by again setting up tables, thus ending the self-imposed six-week moratorium on such activities. As a result, Chancellor Strong dissolves the CCPA.

November 10: Seventy students receive letters from the Dean's office citing them for violating the rules in manning tables. Hundreds of graduate students sign statements declaring that they are equally responsible for manning tables.

November 12: Faculty *ad hoc* committee (The Heyman Committee) recommends that six of the eight students—all of whom had been out of school since September 30—be immediately re-instated and charges expunged from their records and that Mario Savio and Art Goldberg be officially suspended for six weeks, beginning September 30. Chancellor Strong refuses to act on the findings of the committee before the meeting of the Academic Senate on December 8.

November 20: Regents meet and approve suggestions made by President Kerr and Chancellor Strong concerning the suspension to date of the eight students and the one semester probation of Savio and Goldberg. They also agree to modify their policy on political activity; however they maintain that organizations and individuals be disciplined for what they called "illegal advocacy." Meanwhile a rally of over 3,000 students that had assembled at Sproul Hall marches first to the west gate of the campus to hear Joan Baez and then across the street to University Hall where the regents were meeting, to await the results.

November 23: FSM holds mass rally after which three hundred students sit in for three hours in Sproul Hall over issue of University discipline for off-campus activities.

November 24: Chancellor Strong issues a statement of new rules following the decisions of the regents in their November 20 meeting. FSM resumes setting up tables; and a welcome Thanksgiving recess intervenes.

November 28: Mario Savio and Art Goldberg receive letters from Chancellor Strong initiating new disciplinary action against them for acts allegedly committed October 1 and 2.

November 30: Chancellor Strong rejects FSM demands that charges against Savio and Goldberg be dropped.

December 1: FSM issues ultimatum. Teaching assistants and Graduate Coordinating Council agree to strike on December 4 "if conditions warrant."

December 2: University ignores ultimatum. FSM holds rally that attracts thousands, after which approximately one thousand persons move into Sproul Hall. More than eight hundred students remain for the night.

December 3: At 3:05 AM, Chancellor Strong urges students to leave Sproul Hall; at 3:45 AM, Governor Edmund G. Brown announces that he has dispatched police (about 635 of them) to arrest the students. The arrest of about 814 students continues for twelve hours, during which time graduate students picket University buildings in protest of police action. Simultaneously, faculty members meet to consider the crisis, to protest the regents' policy of November 20 and the governor's summoning police, and to establish an Academic Senate Committee to which students could appeal regarding the penalties imposed by the administration for political action. Faculty members raise bail for the arrested students. During the day a strike is called and many classes are cancelled.

December 4: Students released on bail, and the strike continues.

December 5–6: Council of Department Chairmen meet during the weekend to work out agreements to be presented at a student-faculty-administration convocation at the Greek theater Monday, December 7. On Sunday, Professor Robert A. Scalapino, chairman of the Council meets with President Kerr to work out agreement. Two hundred faculty members meet to consider the resolutions made at impromptu faculty meeting of December 3.

December 7: Departmental chairmen call off all classes between 9:00 AM and 2:00 PM. At 11:00 AM Professor Scalapino and President Kerr address faculty members and students gathered at the Greek theater for this "extraordinary convocation." The meeting is adjourned, and Mario Savio attempts to make an announcement, but is removed by police. He is then released and allowed to speak. At noon rally, FSM condemns the inadequacy of the proposals announced by President Kerr; graduate students call off picketing and the strike is suspended until after the meeting of the Academic Senate.

December 8: Academic Senate meets and votes 824 to 115 for the five-point proposal made by the Committee on Academic Freedom against control of student speech and political advocacy. FSM states full support for the faculty position.

December 15: The Associated Students of the University of California (ASUC, the students' government) approves motion that the regents accept the five-point Academic Senate proposal to end the "free speech" controversy.

December 18: The University board of regents do not accept the proposal made by the Academic Senate. They appoint a committee of regents to examine the issues and consult with students, faculty and "other interested persons" in order to make recommendations to the board.

January 2: At an emergency meeting, the board of regents names Martin Meyerson, Dean of the College of Environmental Design, as acting chancellor, replacing Edward W. Strong.

January 3: The new acting chancellor delivers his first address to the campus community in which he set down provisional rules for political activity on the Berkeley campus: the Sproul Hall steps are designated as an open discussion area during certain hours of the day; tables are permitted.

REVOLUTION
AT
BERKELEY

I

IMAGES OF
A UNIVERSITY

The Berkeley students have made vehement demands on their University to revise a system which they feel has both restricted their freedoms as citizens of society at large and denied them sufficient autonomy as members of an academic community. The force of their protest has jarred the public into an awareness of the need for analysis and reappraisal of the university's nature and purpose in a rapidly changing society.

About a year and a half before the crisis on his campus, University of California President Clark Kerr delivered a series of lectures at Harvard—later published as The Uses of the University—*in which he attempted to describe systematically the evolution of the modern university under the impact of a bureaucratic, technological society. In his article "The Frantic Race to Remain Contemporary," which we have included here, Kerr presents an abbreviated version of the theories in his book.*

According to Kerr, the university Newman extolled has become fragmented into a maze of disparate and specialized faculties seldom in communication with each other and more involved in research than teaching. Kerr has added a new term, "multiversity," to the language of higher education. The role of the president and his staff is to mediate among the elements of this multiversity—the departments, the student body, and the administration itself. This conception places administrators at the center of the system and firmly in control of major decisions.

In the modern multiversity, which not surprisingly resembles in

3

*structure the big corporations and highly centralized federal govern-
ment that help support it, what happens to its only paying members,
the students? Caught in a paternalistic yet impersonal machine, are
they destined to become molded, like products on an assembly line?
Social critic Paul Goodman, who is continuously anxious about the
state of American youth, has in recent years been asking questions
of this kind. In his "Thoughts on Berkeley," he regards students
as the group most exploited by the ruling class in modern society;
and he implies that they are the major hope for revolutionary improvement of that society. Goodman wants to redesign the university so that the framework permissive of exploitation is replaced by
one in which students and faculty work together as an autonomous
community of scholars.*

*Sidney Hook, professor of philosophy at New York University,
is much less willing than Goodman to trust students with autonomy.
In "Academic Freedom and The Rights of Students," he builds his
university on a kind of argument-from-whippersnapper. Hook implies that a chain of authority should exist within the university
system which reserves the chief decisions in matters of policy and
discipline for professors with tenure.*

*Sociologist John R. Seeley in "Quo Warranto: the 'Berkeley
Issue'" refuses to take for granted any of the traditional reasons
for conferring authority on a particular body in the university community. After the manner of the classical political theorist, he
questions the moral bases for the legitimacy of those who would
govern the campus, and he finds none of the readymade answers
acceptable. Yet he feels that the Berkeley students have raised precisely this crucial issue.*

CLARK KERR

The Frantic Race
to Remain Contemporary*

"The true American University," David Starr Jordan once observed, "lies in the future." It still does; for American universities have not yet developed their full identity, their unique theory of purpose and function. They still look to older and to foreign models, although less and less; and the day is coming when these models will no longer serve at all.

The American university is currently undergoing its second great transformation. The first occurred during roughly the last quarter of the nineteenth century, when the land grant movement and German intellectualism were together bringing extraordinary change. The current transformation will cover roughly the quarter century after World War II. The university is being called upon to educate previously unimagined numbers of students; to respond to the expanding claims of government and industry and other segments of society as never before; to adapt to and channel new intellectual currents. By the end of this period, there will be a truly American university, an institution unique in world history, an institution not looking to other models but itself serving as a model for universities in other parts of the globe. This is not said in boast. It is simply that the imperatives that are molding the American university are also at work around the world.

* This article is adapted in substantial part from the author's Godkin Lectures delivered at Harvard University in 1963, which were published by the Harvard University Press in 1963 under the title, *The Uses of the University*. This article is from *Daedalus*, Fall 1964.

Each nation, as it has become influential, has tended to develop the leading intellectual institutions of its world—Greece, the Italian cities, France, Spain, England, Germany, and now the United States. The great universities have developed in the great periods of the great political entities of history. Today, more than ever, education is inextricably involved in the quality of a nation. And the university, in particular, has become in America, and in other nations as well, a prime instrument of national purpose. This is new. This is the essence of the transformation now engulfing our universities.

American universities are currently facing four great areas of related adjustments: (1) growth, (2) shifting academic emphases, (3) involvement in the life of society, and (4) response to the new federal involvement. The direction of adjustment in each of these areas is reasonably clear; the detailed arrangements and the timing are not. There are several other areas where adjustments will be necessary but where the direction of adjustment is as yet by no means clear; and four such areas will also be noted below.

Growth. The number of university and college students in the United States will almost double during the sixties. This addition of three million will duplicate in one decade the growth of the three centuries since Harvard was founded. The proportion of graduate students will rise considerably, and there are already 25,000 post-doctoral students.

Existing university campuses are being enlarged and many new ones founded. The University of California, for example, now has seven campuses and a total enrollment of 65,000 students. Four of those campuses will triple or more in size in the next decade. One campus admitting undergraduates for the first time this fall, and two entirely new campuses admitting students for the first time in 1965, are being planned to accommodate ultimate enrollments of 27,500 each.

But university expansion alone cannot begin to meet the demand for some kind of education beyond the high-school level. In the years before World War II, post-high-school study was the exception; it is rapidly becoming the norm. In California today four out of every five high-school graduates seek further education; soon it will be even more. This great shift in the pattern of American education will call for many more four-year colleges, both public and private. And a particularly large number of junior colleges will be formed as the community college movement becomes nationwide. Problems of differentiation of function will arise among public sectors of higher education—junior colleges, four-year colleges, and universities—as they compete for state support. The State of California has already met that problem through legislative adoption of a Master Plan for Higher Education, and other states are working along similar lines. However the total demand for higher education may be parceled out among the public and private institutions of varying types, one fact is clear: this will be the most unprecedented period of campus development in American history, or indeed in the history of the entire world.

To accommodate the great increase in enrollments, many academic calendars are being rearranged, particularly in state-supported institutions, to permit more nearly year-round use of physical facilities. Students will be able to accelerate their work if they wish, and general students will come and go with less reference to their "class"; more of them will drop in and drop out as suits their particular schedules and needs.

There will be some further mechanization of instruction (television, language laboratories, programmed learning) to improve quality and to save faculty time for other endeavors, including more individual work with students. The sciences will almost eagerly embrace these aids to learning. The foreign language departments will be rather reluctant, because these devices can threaten their structure of faculty employment and the recruitment and utilization of graduate students.

Because of the competition for faculty members, salaries will continue to rise; fringe benefits of all sorts will be devised to tie professors to a particular campus. In addition to competition among universities, there is also intensified competition with industry and government. This competition has obvious advantages in raising faculty income, but it has its negative aspects. As the market becomes more active, internal equity will be injured, for some disciplines are much more in demand in the market than others. Teaching loads will be competitively reduced, sometimes to zero, although more teachers are needed and students are complaining about lack of attention. The identification of the professor with his university will be generally loosened—he will become more a member of a free-floating profession. The rules regarding how much time a professor can spend away from his university assignments, and those affecting the sources of his income within the university, will continue to be in great flux.

This current phenomenon of rising salaries and benefits, however, may be of relatively short duration, lasting, perhaps, for the remainder of this decade. Faculty salaries have been catching up with incomes in other professions after a historical lag. By 1970, also, the personnel deficit of today may be turning into the surplus of tomorrow as all the new Ph.D.s roll into the market. A new plateau of compensation may be reached in the seventies.

In addition to the great expansion of individual institutions of higher learning, there will be an increasing tendency for university centers to cooperate and even coalesce for added strength, particularly in their graduate and research programs. Allan Nevins has put it this way: "Observers of higher education can now foresee the inexorable emergence of an entirely new landscape. It will no longer show us a nation dotted by high academic peaks with lesser hills between; it will be a landscape dominated by mountain ranges." The highest peaks of the future will rise from the highest plateaus.

One such plateau runs from Boston to Washington. At the universities and laboratories situated along this range are found forty-six per cent of the American Nobel Prize winners in the sciences and forty per cent of the members of the National Academy of Sciences. A second range with its peaks runs along the California coast. C. P. Snow has written:

And now the scientific achievement of the United States is moving at a rate we all ought to marvel at. Think of the astonishing constellation of talent, particularly in the physical sciences, all down the California coast, from Berkeley and Stanford to Pasadena and Los Angeles. There is nothing like that concentration of talent anywhere in the world. It sometimes surprises Europeans to realize how much of the pure science of the entire West is being carried out in the United States. Curiously enough, it often surprises Americans too. At a guess, the figure is something like eighty per cent, and might easily be higher.

The California mountain range has thirty-six per cent of the Nobel laureates in science and twenty per cent of the members of the National Academy of Sciences. The Big Ten and Chicago constitute a third range of academic peaks, with ten per cent of the Nobel laureates and fourteen per cent of the members of the National Academy of Sciences. These three groupings of universities—the East Coast, California, and the Big Ten and Chicago—currently produce over three quarters of the doctorates conferred in the United States. Another range may be in the process of developing in the Texas-Louisiana area.

This concentration of talent partly follows history—the location of the older private and public universities. Partly it follows industrial strengths and population centers. But it also has its own logic. No one university can cover all specialties, or cover them well enough so that there is a sufficient cluster of close intellectual colleagues. The scholar dislikes intellectual isolation, and good scholars tend to swarm together. These swarms are extraordinarily productive environments. No library can be complete, nor any graduate curriculum. Some laboratories, to be well used, must be used by more than one university. Thus the Big Ten and Chicago, through their Committee on Institutional Cooperation, are merging their library resources, creating a "common market" for graduate students, diversifying their research laboratories on a common-use basis, and parceling out foreign language specializations. Something similar is happening in the University of California system, and between Berkeley and Stanford. Harvard and MIT, Princeton and Pennsylvania, among others, run joint research enterprises. These clustering universities in turn have clustering around them scientifically oriented industrial and governmental enterprises. To match the drawing power of the great metropolis, there now arrives the Ideopolis. The isolated mountain can no longer dominate the landscape; the constellation is greater than the single star and adds to the brightness of the sky.

The rate of growth being forced upon American universities and colleges by the surging enrollment wave will present difficult problems. As President Johnson said in his 1964 commencement address at the University of Michigan: ". . . more classrooms and more teachers are not enough. We must seek an educational system which grows in excellence as it grows in size." A period of rapid growth is necessarily a period of both flexibility and ingenuity. Institutions can readily adopt on new campuses ideas and programs that would require costly reorganization on older campuses. The University of California, for example, is building its new Santa Cruz campus as a series of small residential colleges, each with its own subject field orientation. The University's new Irvine campus will explore ways of involving organized research units in the formal process of instruction. The new San Diego campus of the university will subdivide its ultimate enrollment of 27,500 students into a series of smaller colleges, with groups of four such colleges constituting largely self-contained sub-campuses of varying academic emphases. The University of the Pacific, in Stockton, California, has established a new residential college in which the entire curriculum is conducted in Spanish. Thus the enrollment explosion may bring unusual opportunities for colleges and universities, along with the heavy burden of numbers.

The current surge in higher education is not, of course, unique to the United States. In Canada the proportion of eighteen- to twenty-one-year olds in higher education is expected to double in the decade from 1962 to 1972. In France the total enrollment in higher education is expected to soar from around 200,000 now to 500,000 by 1970. In Britain, the much-discussed Robbins Committee Report recommends doubling the number of universities by 1980. These figures reflect the rapidly growing pressures resulting from a vast increase in secondary enrollments throughout much of the world. The decade of the fifties has seen a world increase of eighty-one per cent in secondary enrollments and an increase of seventy-one per cent in college enrollments.

The data both from this country and abroad clearly indicate that we are witnessing everywhere the demise of two long-held notions: that higher education ought to be restricted to a small élite minority, and that only a small percentage of a country's population is capable of benefiting from some kind of higher education. Growth is having quite uneven impacts on American universities. Some, and they are almost always private, are building walls around themselves as aristocratic enclaves protected from the swirling currents of the population explosion. Others, and they are mostly public, are engulfed with more than their share of accommodation to the new hordes, that do not wish to be bar-

barous, advancing through their gates. The aristocratic enclave offers refuge to the faculty member who wishes protection from the new invasion, and many do; but it will become a more and more isolated element within the society of the future. The university with the open door will suffer the pangs of adjustment, but it will become in the process a more central element in a dynamic society. The one will be a pleasant place to be but increasingly out of tune with the surrounding society. The other will be a less pleasant place to live but will provide a more challenging and exciting environment, and will be more a part of the evolving life around it. Each will have its place, but the places they occupy will grow farther and farther apart.

Shifting Academic Emphases. A second major factor in the changing scene for American higher education is that knowledge is exploding along with population. There is also an explosion in the need for certain skills. The university is responding to all these explosions.

The vastly increased needs for engineers, scientists, and physicians will draw great resources to these areas of the university. Also, some new professions are being born. Others are becoming more formally professional, for example, business administration and social work. The university becomes the chief port of entry for these professions. In fact a profession gains its identity by making the university the port of entry. This creates new roles for education; but it is also part of the process of freezing the structure of the occupational pyramid and assuring that the well-behaved do advance, even if the geniuses do not. The university is used as an egg-candling device; and it is, perhaps, a better one than any other that can be devised, but the process takes some of the adventure out of occupational survival, and does for some professions what the closed shop has done for some unions. The life of the universities for a thousand years has been tied into the recognized professions in the surrounding society, and the universities will continue to respond as new professions arise.

The fastest-growing intellectual field today is biology. Here there is a veritable revolution where the doctrine of evolution once reigned supreme. To the classifying efforts of the past are being added the new analytical methods of the present, often drawn from chemistry and physics. There are levels of complexity to be explored in all living structures. The "code of life" can now be read; soon it will be understood, and soon after that, used. It is an intellectual discovery of unique and staggering proportions. The secrets of the atom, much as they have changed and are changing human activity on this planet, may hold no greater significance than the secrets still hidden in the genetic code. If the first half of the twentieth century may be said to have belonged to the physical sciences, the second half may well belong to the biological. Resources within the universities will be poured into the new biology and into the resulting new medicine and agriculture, well supported though medicine and agriculture already are. Medical education and research may be, in particular, on the threshold of revolutionary change.

Another field ready to bloom is that of the creative arts, hitherto the ugly duckling or Cinderella of the academic world. America is bursting with creativity in painting, music, literature, the theater, with a vigor equaled in few other parts of the world today. Italy, France, Spain, Germany, Russia, England, the Low Countries have had great periods of cultural flowering. America is having one now. In the arts the universities have been more hospitable to the historian and the critic than to the creator; the latter has found his havens elsewhere. Yet it is the creativity of science that has given the sciences their prestige in the university. Perhaps creativity will do the same again for the humanities, though there may be less new to create than has recently been true in science, and though the tests of value are far less precise. A very important role remains for the historian of past ages of creativity and for the critic of the current productions. But the universities need to find ways also to accommodate pure creative effort if they are to have places on stage as well as in the wings and in the audience in the great drama of cultural growth now playing on the American stage.

These possibilities for expansion—in the training of engineers, scientists, physicians, and the newer professionals, in biology, and in the creative arts, among various others—raise the problem of balance. As James Bryant Conant has noted, the Western world has had for a thousand years a continuing problem of "keeping a balance between the advancement of knowledge, professional education, general education, and the demands of student life."

But the balance is always changing; this is the unbalancing reality. The balance is not equal treatment, the provision of equal time in some mechanical and eternal way between teaching and research, or between the humanities and science. The dynamics of balance did not give equal treatment to the available scientist in Padua in 1300 when Giotto was painting his chapel, or to the available artist in Padua in 1600 when Galileo was lecturing from his crude platform. Balance cannot be determined on the scales by blind justice, field versus field and activity versus activity.

The essence of balance is to match support with the intellectual creativity of subject fields; with the need for skills of the highest level; with the kinds of expert service that society currently most requires. None of these measures is constant. Balance requires, therefore, a shifting set of judgments which relates facilities and attention to the possibilities inherent in each field, each skill, each activity at that moment of time in that environment, yet preserves for all fields their essential integrity. To know balance is to know the potential creativity, the potential productivity, the potential contribution of each competing activity in an unfolding pattern of time and an evolving landscape of environment. To know balance is to know more than anyone can ever know in advance. But decisions must nevertheless be made, and time will tell how well. The only certainly wrong decision is that the balance of today must be preserved for tomorrow. Where will the world's work and the university's work best be done? The answer to that question is the true definition of balance.

Involvement in the Life of Society. The third great change affecting the contemporary university is its thorough-going involvement in the nation's daily life. At the heart of this involvement is the growth of the "knowledge industry," which is coming to permeate government and business and to draw into it more and more people raised to higher and higher levels of skill. The production, distribution, and consumption of "knowledge" in all its forms is said to account for twenty-nine per cent of the gross national product, according to Fritz Machlup's calculations; and "knowledge production" is growing at about twice the rate of the rest of the economy. Knowledge has certainly never in history been so central to the conduct of an entire society. What the railroads did for the second half of the last century and the automobile for the first half of this century may be done for the second half of this century by the knowledge industry: that is, to serve as the focal point for national growth. And the university is at the center of the knowledge process.

So the campus and society are undergoing a somewhat reluctant and cautious merger, already well advanced in some fields. MIT is at least as closely related to industry and government as Iowa State ever was to agriculture. Indeed, universities have become "bait" to be dangled in front of industry, with drawing power greater than low taxes or cheap labor. Route 128 around Boston and the great developing industrial complexes in the San Francisco Bay area and Southern California reflect the universities in these areas. The Gilpatric report for the Department of Defense explained that forty-one per cent of defense contracts for research in the fiscal year 1961 were concentrated in California, twelve per cent in New York, and six per cent in Massachusetts, for a total of nearly sixty per cent, in part because these were also "centers of learning." Sterling Forest outside New York City seeks to attract industry by location next to a new university campus. In California, new industrial laboratories were located next to two new university campuses before the first building was built on either of these campuses. Sometimes industry will reach into a university laboratory to extract the newest ideas almost before they are born. Instead of waiting outside the gates, agents are working the corridors. They also work the placement offices. And the university, in turn, reaches into industry, as through the Stanford Research Institute.

The university and segments of industry are becoming more alike. As the university becomes tied into the world of work, the professor—at least in the natural and some of the social sciences—takes on the characteristics of an entrepreneur. Industry, with its scientists and technicians, learns an uncomfortable bit about academic freedom and the handling of intellectual personnel. The two worlds are merging physically and psychologically.

The rapid production of new knowledge has given new significance to university extension slogans about "life-long learning." Television makes it possible for extension to reach into literally every home; the boundaries of the university are stretched to embrace all of society. The student becomes alumnus and the alumnus continues as student; the graduate enters the outside world and the public enters the classroom and the laboratory. Knowledge has the terrifying potential of becoming popular, opening a Pandora's box.

Extension divisions are proving to be increasingly effective administrative devices for linking campus and community in the further pursuit of knowledge. Freer of traditions and rules than regular university academic departments, extension units can respond quickly and in a variety of patterns to meet society's needs for current information and training. Professional schools and colleges, in particular, are making widespread use of extension programs for "refresher" and "continuing education" courses for the active practitioners in their fields. University of California Extension, for example, now enrolls in its courses one of every three lawyers and one of every six physicians in the state. Its total enrollment now numbers some 200,000 students, and it sponsors a remarkably wide range of academic activities including workshops, resident seminars and conferences, theater groups, symposia attracting participants of world renown, and even, recently, a notable scientific expedition to the Galapagos Islands. During the summer of 1964, in response to the growing concern with problems of school integration, University Extension was able to present several short-term workshops and courses on this urgent subject. The new role for knowledge is bringing a new and potentially quite exciting role for extension divisions in American higher education.

The campus becomes a center for cultural life; it has a ready-made audience in its students and faculty and it has the physical facilities. Persons attracted by the performing and visual arts and the lectures come to live around the campus—also assorted crackpots. As the downtown area in some cities decays, the campus takes its place as the cultural center of the community. A new dimension has been added to the land grant idea of service.

The New Deal took professors to Washington from many campuses, the New Frontier from more than just one. In Wisconsin before World War I, the campus and the state house in Madison were exceptionally close. Today the campus is being drawn to the city hall and the state capitol as never before. The politicians need new ideas to meet the new problems; the agencies need expert advice on how to handle the old. The professor can supply both. Keynes concluded his *General Theory* as follows: ". . . the ideas of economists and political philosophers, both when they are right and when they are wrong, are more powerful than is commonly understood. Indeed the world is ruled by little else. Practical men, who believe themselves to be quite exempt from any intellectual influences, are usually the slaves of some defunct economist. Madmen in authority, who hear voices in the air, are distilling their frenzy from some academic scribbler of a few years back. I am sure that the power of vested interests is vastly exaggerated compared with the gradual encroachment of ideas." As, for example, the ideas of Keynes.

The university must range itself on the side of intelligent solutions to sometimes unintelligent questions. These questions more and more arise from abroad as well as at home; and the quality of the answers has been made all the more crucial in a world swept by communist and nationalist revolutions.

There are those who fear the further involvement of the university in the life of society. They fear that the university will lose its objectivity and its freedom. But society is more desirous of objectivity and more tolerant of freedom than it used to be. The university can be further ahead of the times and further behind the times, further to the left of the public and further to the right of the public—and still keep its equilibrium—than was ever the case before, although problems in this regard are not yet entirely unknown. There are those who fear that the university will be drawn too far from basic to applied research and from applied research to application itself. But the lines dividing these never have been entirely clear, and much new knowledge has been generated at the borders of basic and applied research, and even of applied knowledge and its application. Whitehead once wrote of the creative margin when the "adventure of thought" met "the adventure of action."

Involvement with the Federal Government. Growth and shifting emphases and involvement in society all take money; and which

universities get it in the largest quantities will help determine
which of them excel a decade or two hence. Will federal support
be spent according to merit or according to political power? Will
private donors continue to do as well as they recently have done
for those universities that have done well already? Will the states
find new sources of revenue or will their expenditures be
held under a lid of no new taxes? The answers to these questions will help predict the standings on the next rating scale of
universities.

Of key importance to American universities is the role of the
federal government, particularly through federal support of scientific research. This support, which received its great impetus during
and after World War II, has already changed the face of the leading
American universities almost as much as did the land grant program a century earlier. Federal support has today become a major
factor in the total performance of many universities, and the sums
involved are substantial. Higher education in 1960 received about
$1.5 billion from the federal government—a hundredfold increase
in twenty years. About one third of this $1.5 billion was for
university-affiliated research centers; about one third for project
research within universities; and about one third for other things,
such as residence hall loans, scholarships, and teaching programs.
This last third was expended at colleges as well as universities, but
the first two thirds almost exclusively at universities, and at relatively few of them.

The billion dollars for research, though only ten per cent of
total federal support for research and development, accounted for
seventy-five per cent of all university expenditures on research and
fifteen per cent of total university budgets. Clearly the shape and
nature of university research are profoundly affected by federal
monies. The effects of this extensive federal aid and the new problems that have arisen as a consequence are many and varied, but
the more important of them might be grouped under the two general headings of "federal influence" and "balance."

(1) Federal control as a substantive issue is, as Sidney Hook
has said, a "red herring." With a few exceptions—the generally
necessary exception of secrecy in certain types of work, and the
unnecessary exception of the disclaimer affidavit once required by
the National Defense Education Act—there has been no control

in any deleterious sense. The real problem is not one of federal
control but of federal influence. A federal agency offers a project.
A university need not accept—but, as a practical matter, it usually
does. Out of this reality have followed many of the consequences
of federal aid for the universities; and they have been substantial.
That they are subtle, slowly cumulative and gentlemanly makes
them all the more potent.

A university's control over its own destiny has thus been substantially reduced. University funds from tuition and fees, gifts and
endowments, and state sources go through the usual budget-mak-
ing procedures and their assignment is subject to review in accordance with internal policy. Federal research funds, however, are
usually negotiated by the individual scholar with the particular
agency, and so bypass the usual review process. Thus twenty to
fifty to eighty per cent of a university's expenditures may be
handled outside the normal channels. These funds in turn commit
some of the university's own funds; they influence the assignment
of space; they determine the distribution of time between teaching
and research; to a large extent they establish the areas in which
the university grows the fastest. Almost imperceptibly, a university
is changed.

The authority of the department chairman, the dean, the president is thereby reduced; so also is the role of faculty government.
This may have its advantages. The university's internal process of
distributing funds would be generally less selective and less flexible
than the federal research project approach. Within a university,
the tendency is to give each faculty member about the same opportunity and once having given it to keep giving it thereafter; but
the project method allows more attention to exceptional merit and
has the advantage that all projects may end sometime. Additionally, federal agencies are more responsive to particular national
needs than the universities would be, given the same amount of
money to spend according to their own priority system.

There are, however, clearly detrimental effects. Some faculty
members come to use the pressure of their agency contacts against
their university. They may try to force the establishment of a new
administrative unit or the assignment of land for their own special
building, in defiance of general university policy or priorities.
These pressures, of course, should be withstood; they speak well

neither of the professor nor of the agency. Also, some faculty members tend to shift their identification and loyalty from their university to the agency in Washington. The agency becomes the new alma mater. There are especially acute problems when the agency insists on the tie-in sale (if we do this for you, then you must do that for us) or when it requires frequent and detailed progress reports. Then the university really is less than a free agent. It all becomes a kind of "putting-out" system with the agency taking the place of the merchant-capitalist of old.

(2) The question of "balance" in federal aid arises in relation both to support of specific fields within an institution and to distribution of support among institutions of higher learning. Among the totality of university functions, federal support has been heavily concentrated on research and on graduate and postdoctoral training in fields of national interest. Expenditures have been largely restricted to the physical and biomedical sciences, and to engineering, with only about 3 per cent for the social sciences and hardly any support for the humanities.

All this is said to have destroyed the "balance" among fields, and it is generally concluded that something should be done about it. The balance among fields, however, has never been a static thing. If it were, philosophy, theology, and the classics would still be the dominant areas of study, as they have not been for a long time. Assuming that the balance of 1942, say, was appropriate for 1942, this does not mean it would have been appropriate for 1962. It is not enough to say that the old "balance" has been destroyed. The real question is what should be the proper balance today. It is clear that the flowering of the Renaissance should have affected the "balance" in the sixteenth century. It would seem likely that the splitting of the atom and the deciphering of the genetic code should in their turn affect the balance of the twentieth century. We should expect the most money and the brightest students and the greatest prestige to follow the most exciting new ideas. By and large they have done so, and this is one way of defining the nature of balance.

The real question, it seems to me, is not one of balance in any historical or monetary sense, but rather what is most appropriate to each field in each period. "All fields are equal, only some are more equal than others." There should be no effort to do the same things in the same amounts for each field. Each should receive support in accordance with its current potentialities, and potentialities vary. There are no timeless priorities.

Federal research expenditures have also been heavily focused on relatively few institutions. If both project research and large research centers are included, six universities received fifty-seven per cent of the funds in a recent fiscal year, and twenty universities received seventy-nine per cent. If project research alone is considered, the figures are twenty-eight and fifty-four per cent. As a percentage of total university expenditures for all purposes among the leading twenty recipients, federal funds have amounted to twenty to fifty per cent when project research alone is counted, and from twenty to over eighty per cent when the research centers are added. These twenty universities are only about one tenth of all universities in the United States. They constitute the primary "federal grant" universities.

The project approach almost automatically led to concentration of federal research effort in a relatively few universities. The universities best equipped to undertake the research were also those with the faculty and facilities to provide for the training of Ph.D.s. It is no coincidence that the six universities with a little more than twenty-five per cent of project funds graduated about twenty-five per cent of the Ph.D.s; and a similar situation prevails for the top twenty universities. If "only the best will do," this concentration of effort is inevitable. A different result would have been quite surprising.

The concentration of effort has undoubtedly strengthened the facilities and improved the quality of faculties of universities already in the front rank. It has probably widened the gap between those of the first and those of the second and third ranks. It may in fact, have actually injured universities of the second and third ranks and some colleges by turning their potential faculty members into research personnel in the front-rank universities. The good are better; the poor may well be worse. And it has greatly accentuated the differences between colleges and universities.

The general policy of federal agencies in allocating research grants to universities for the last two decades has been one of "seeking excellence wherever it is." The period has been one of what I have called "intuitive imbalance." We are now clearly entering a new phase of federal support policy, one that might be called "bureaucratic balance."

The new balance calls for developing a larger number of outstanding centers of graduate instruction and research. The Seaborg report of 1960 suggested expansion from the present fifteen or twenty centers to thirty or forty over a fifteen-year period. The National Education Improvement Act of 1963 envisaged expansion from twenty to seventy. Teaching is being emphasized along with research. Summer refresher courses for teachers of science, improvement of science textbooks, and language laboratories are programs already established. The National Science Foundation has a large effort under way to improve and renovate equipment for undergraduate teaching in the physical sciences. Undergraduates, as well as graduate students, are being assisted by loans and scholarships. The social sciences are receiving increasing sums of money. More funds are being granted to colleges as well as to universities, and to universities of all ranks.

A particularly significant step in the direction of broadening institutional support is the new science development program announced in the spring of 1964 by the National Science Foundation. This program is specifically designed to raise the overall quality of science programs in good institutions to the level of excellent. Distinguished institutions are excluded: "institutions already recognized as being outstanding in science should continue to depend on existing programs for assistance."

Undergraduate as well as graduate institutions will be eligible, and the grants (up to five million dollars per institution) may be used in any way the institution chooses to strengthen single departments or related departments, to create new departments, or to improve the entire science program. *Science* magazine, commenting on the NSF plan, said, "it is probably safe to say that the success or failure of this program is going to have a far-reaching influence on the evolution of higher education in the United States."

The approach to a university "as an institution" has interesting implications. If additional universities are to be selected to become centers of strength in research and graduate instruction, then it will be necessary for the federal government to be concerned with the "general health of the institution." This will be a notable departure from historical practice, except in agriculture. If we are to move toward federal orientation to the "total function of the university," then the University Grants Committee in Great Britain is the outstanding precedent, and one that has received some support in the United States. However, there are only about thirty universities in Great Britain, and it is clear what is and what is not a university. Additionally, the University Grants Committee has come to exercise more influence over the establishment of new programs, the cost and size and even the appearance of new buildings, the equalization of faculty salaries among institutions, and the determination of admission policies than would currently be acceptable if it came from the federal government in this country.

Some hard choices must be faced. The decentralized project approach of the last two decades has much to recommend it. It is selective on merit, flexible in accordance with quality of performance, and responsive to national goals. The universities and their scholars retain substantial freedom. But such dominant reliance on the project approach is no longer likely. It is said that support to institutions as such will "give a university the necessary autonomy" and will permit dispersion of effort and better balance in several directions. It is difficult, however, to assess the merit of a total institution as complex as a modern university. One alternative is to rely on a formula, as in the case of agriculture in the land grant institutions. Another is to be guided by political influence; and this is increasingly happening. Inter-university competition is being taken from the quasi-academic arena of the agency committee to the legislative halls.

The partnership of the federal government with higher education and particularly with the federal grant universities over the last two decades has been enormously productive in enlarging the pool of scientific ideas and skills. Now we are entering a new phase of widening and deepening relationships. This new phase can carry the American commitment to education to new heights of endeavor. It can also preserve the traditional freedom of higher education from excessive control. It can enlarge the horizons of equality of opportunity. It can maintain and even increase the margin for excellence. The challenge is to make certain it does all these things.

However this turns out, the scene of American higher education will continue to be marked by great variety, and this is one of its great strengths. The large and the small, the private and the public, the general and the specialized all add their share to overall excellence. The total system is extraordinarily flexible, decentralized, competitive—and productive. The new can be tried, the old tested with considerable skill and alacrity. Pluralism in higher education matches the pluralistic American society. The general test of higher education is not how much is done poorly, and some is; rather it is how much is done superbly, and a great deal is, to the nation's great benefit.

Changes Still to Come. But there are some problems still to be fully faced; and they are problems of consequence.

(1) One is the improvement of undergraduate instruction in the university. The much-advertised conflict between teaching and research puts the problem the wrong way. The teaching of graduate students is so closely tied to research that if research is improved, graduate instruction is almost bound to be improved also. And the almost universal experience seems to be that federal research support has improved graduate instruction. At the undergraduate level, however, a "subtle discounting of the teaching process" has been aided and abetted.

The reasons for the general deterioration of undergraduate teaching are several. Teaching loads and student contact hours have been reduced. Faculty members are more frequently on leave or temporarily away from the campus; some are never more than temporarily on campus. More of the instruction falls to teachers who are not members of the regular faculty. The best graduate students prefer fellowships and research assistantships to teaching assistantships. Post-doctoral fellows who might fill the gap usually do not teach. Average class size has been increasing.

There seems to be a "point of no return" after which research, consulting, graduate instruction become so absorbing that faculty efforts can no longer be concentrated on undergraduate instruction as they once were. This process has been going on for a long time; federal research funds have intensified it. As a consequence, undergraduate education in the large university is more likely to be acceptable than outstanding; educational policy from the undergraduate point of view is largely neglected.

Improvement of undergraduate instruction will require the solution of many sub-problems: how to give adequate recognition to the teaching skill as well as to the research performance of the faculty; how to create a curriculum that serves the needs of the student as well as the research interests of the teacher; how to prepare the generalist as well as the specialist in an age of specialization looking for better generalizations; how to treat the individual student as a unique human being in the mass student body; how to make the university seem smaller even as it grows larger; how to establish a range of contact between faculty and students broader than the one-way route across the lectern or through the television screen; how to raise educational policy again to the forefront of faculty concerns.

(2) Another major task is to create a more unified intellectual world. We need to make contact between the two, the three, the many cultures; to open channels of intelligent conversation across the disciplines and divisions; to close the gap between C. P. Snow's "Luddites" and scientists; to answer fragmentation with general theories and sensitivities. Even philosophy, which once was the hub of the intellectual universe, is now itself fragmented into such diverse specialities as mathematics and semantics. However, the physical sciences are drawing together as new discoveries create more basic general theories; the biological sciences may be pulled together in the process now going on; the social sciences might be unified around the study of organizations and the relations of individuals to and within them. Biochemistry and social psychology may come to be central focalizing fields. As knowledge is drawn together, if in fact it is, a faculty may again become a community of masters; but "a sense of the unity . . . of all knowledge" is still a very long way off.

(3) A third problem is to relate administration more directly to individual faculty and students in the massive institution. We need to decentralize below the campus level to the operating agencies; to make the collective faculty a more vital, dynamic, progressive force as it now is only at the departmental level; to bridge the growing chasm between the department that does the teaching and the institute that does the research, with the faculty member torn between; to make the old departments and divisions more compatible with the new divisions of knowledge; to make it possible

for an institution to see itself in totality rather than just piecemeal and in the sweep of history rather than just at a moment of time; to bring an understanding of both internal and external realities to all those intimately related to the process, so that there may be greater understanding; to see to it that administration serves and stimulates rather than rules the institution, that it is expendable when necessary and flexible all the time; to assure that the university can do better what it does best; to solve the whole range of governmental problems within the university.

(4) Additionally, there is the urgent issue of how to preserve a margin for excellence in a populist society, when more and more of the money is being spent on behalf of all of the people. The great university is of necessity élitist—the élite of merit—but it operates in an environment dedicated to an egalitarian philosophy. How may the contribution of the élite be made clear to the egalitarians, and how may an aristocracy of intellect justify itself to a democracy of all men? It was equality of opportunity, not equality *per se,* that animated the founding fathers and the progress of the American system; but the forces of populist equality have never been silent, the battle between Jeffersonianism and Jacksonianism never finally settled.

George Beadle, president of the University of Chicago, once implied that the very large American university (but not his own) might be like the dinosaur which "became extinct because he grew larger and larger and then sacrificed the evolutionary flexibility he needed to meet changing conditions"; its body became too large for its brain. David Riesman has said that the leading American universities are "directionless . . . as far as major innovations are concerned"; they have run out of foreign models to imitate; they have lost their "ferment." The fact is that they are not directionless; they have been moving in clear directions and with considerable speed. These directions, however, have not been set as much by the university's visions of its destiny as by the external environment including the federal government, the foundations, the surrounding and sometimes engulfing industry.

But the really new problems of today and tomorrow may lend themselves less to solutions by external authority; they may be inherently problems for internal resolution. And these solutions, if they are to come, are more likely to emerge on the campuses of those old, private universities which have prided themselves on control of their own destiny, and on the totally new campuses of the state universities in America (and the new public universities in Britain). The university for the twenty-first century is more likely to emerge from these environments than from any others. Out of the pride of the old and the vacuum of the new may come the means to make undergraduate life more exciting, intellectual discourse more meaningful, administration more human. And perhaps there will arise a more dynamic demonstration of how excellence makes democracy more vital and its survival more assured. Then the contemporary American university may indeed rise to "the heights of the times." Then it may demonstrate that it has a mind as well as a body.

PAUL GOODMAN

Thoughts on Berkeley*

The function of administration is to expedite the essential academic business of teaching and learning, e.g., as secretary and janitor; and protectively to represent the academic community in its external relations, e.g., in court or as fund-raiser. When administration becomes the dominant force in the community, however, it is a sign that extra-mural powers are in control—State, Church, or Economy—and the administration is their agent. Notoriously, image-burnishing and fund-raising disregard or even prevent teaching and learning.

At Berkeley, the students griped that the University of California has become a "factory, disregarding faculty and students," a factory to process professional licences and apprentices for technological corporations, and to do extra-mural contracted research. The particular bone of contention, the Free Speech ban, seems also to have been extra-murally instigated, by backlash elements, persons like Senator Knowland, etc. The administration certainly acted with panic, under outside pressure and out of touch with its own community.

At present in the United States, students—middle-class youths —are the major exploited class. (Negroes, small farmers, the aged are rather out-caste groups; their labor is not needed and they are not wanted.) The labor of intelligent youth *is* needed and they are accordingly subjected to tight scheduling, speedup, and other factory methods. Then it is not surprising if they organize their CIO. It is frivolous to tell them to go elsewhere if they don't like the rules, for they have no choice but to go to college, and one factory is like another.

* From *The New York Review of Books,* January 14, 1965.

Thus far in the Berkeley revolt, two new factors have emerged:
(1) The students want to extend the concept of academic freedom
from *Lehrfreiheit* (freedom of professors to teach according to
their lights) to include *Lernfreiheit* (freedom of students to ask for
what they need to be taught, and if necessary to invite teachers,
including advocates of causes). I shall return to this later. (2) The
faculty energized by the students, wants to resume prerogatives
that it had given up to the administration, e.g., discipline. This is
probably the more important issue; but in my opinion the administration can not agree (and the regents have so voted) to the
faculty resumption of prerogatives, because this could go very far
and entirely unmake the academic-factory; e.g., the faculty might
hire or teach in disregard of image, endowments, or research
grants; they might resist huge classes or abolish grading. The question, then, will be whether there are enough professors who are
concerned for the academic community to fight it out, rather than
pursuing their grants and independent research.

It is useful to recall the important student strike, a few years
ago, at New York State University at Oyster Bay (now Stony
Brook). Here the state tried to impose a new president, to turn
the liberal arts school into an engineering institute. The students
were angered by disregard of their physical and social needs; the
faculty was indignant at the attempt to fragment the divisional
system into departments that could be administratively subjugated.
Backed by the faculty, many students struck and the new president
had to go.

Generally speaking, student efforts to get an education befitting
free men rather than slaves can succeed only with strong faculty
backing, for the students are transient, they do not *definitely* know
what they want, they do not know the score behind the scenes and
thus they can be abashed by administrative double-talk. On the
other hand, given the supine history of American faculties in our
sectarian and trustee-ridden colleges, and given the present extra-
mural careerism of the important professors, the students must
lead if there is to be any change.

The extension of academic freedom to the claim to freedom-
to-learn implies a revolutionary change in the status of American
college-going. Up to now, American collegians have been re-

garded, and have regarded themselves, as late-adolescents; but the claim to *Lernfreiheit* means that they are young adults who are capable of knowing what they ought to get.

This is, of course, the (non-English) European and Latin tradition. It goes with early sexual maturity, with economic independence (often in bohemian poverty), and with active involvement in politics. Classically, in Europe, it has also involved drawn-out education, many moratoria, much changing of schools and career plans, and "being a student" as itself a kind of profession of young adults, especially of the upper class.

Some of these changes are evident in this country. Whatever parents and administrators may say about extended sexual tutelage and *in loco parentis,* the young are practicing earlier sexual maturity without apologies. The past ten years have witnessed a remarkable resurgence of youthful political engagement. And since the selective service, it becomes far-fetched to deny the eighteen-year-old vote. It is hard to see how the university can welcome recruiters for Peace Corps or Army and disallow CORE or SNCC. (Incidentally, since the Supreme Court's "abatement" decision the illegal activity has turned out to be legal after all!) Administration itself has dealt a mortal blow to the notion of late-adolescence by its persistent attempts to abolish the fraternity system, which was a bulwark of youth house and social life ideology (leading, for instance, to trivial student governments). I do not think the aim of administration has been to treat the students as young adults; rather, the abolition of fraternities seems to be an attempt to tighten control, increase academic performance, and to gouge rent (since dormitories are built with federal funds). Nevertheless, the effect of abolition must be student maturation, demands to live off-campus or to liberalize dormitory rules, to lower rents and improve food, and to be represented by a government that is not otiose.

On the other hand, there are strong American influences to prevent student maturation and independence. First, the frantic career-drive, spurred by the anxiety of middle-class parents, leading to conformism, and willingness to submit to scheduled miseducation, credits, and grading, in order to get a diploma quick. Secondly, the students are not financially independent; tuition is exceedingly high, so that it is impossible to opt for independent poverty; scholarships and loans put the student under administration control. Probably most important, the universal compulsory school-going without alternative choices, is infantile. In 1900, only six per cent graduated from high school. We thus have conflict: the direct and evident need for the students as a working class of the economy would tend to make the students more mature; but the conditions of their collegiate exploitation tend to make them insecure and immature.

The evolution of both faculty and student organizations in the United States has been different from the communities of scholars in Europe. We do not have community guilds but rather national unions. The faculty unions—e.g., The American Association of University Professors or the Teachers Union—were first formed as defensive leagues; my guess is that they will now begin to take the offensive. I can conceive of them declining to take graduate students from Ole Miss; or defending the principles of the original Mobilization for Youth, as a committee of the American Sociological Association has done; or attacking the entrenched boards of education with new ideas for the public schools. On the other hand, the student unions—e.g., the Student Peace Union, the Students for a Democratic Society—started largely for extra-mural political reasons; but my guess is that they will now, as at Berkeley, look to improve the academic community. In this the National Students Association could be a leader. Hopefully, as I have said, the student activity will revive the dormant community of the faculty.

In my opinion, the chief *political* action of students would, at present, be intra-mural—humanizing and making cultural the academic community—for the colleges and universities have become so tightly interlocked with the dominant tightly interlocked system of society that any *intra-mural* improvement will be a profound shock to the system. Also, in these matters the students can really know what they are talking about.

What is the role of a student government? In our contemporary conditions, it is interesting to hark back to the "nations," the powerful student government of medieval universities.

The medieval student government was a band to bargain collectively on rent with the townspeople, on food prices with the tavern-keepers. Our present governments could bargain this way with both the town and the administration, the bookstores, the co-op.

In medieval conditions, the nations bargained with the faculty on tuition. With us this is wholly an administrative matter. One thinks of the students of City College in New York going to Albany on the tuition fight. A related issue is class size and immature section men. The tuition mounts, but the student gets less and less for his money. A few years ago there was a strike on this issue (I think successful) at Rochester.

A purpose of the nations was to regulate morals and keep the peace, in order to prevent outside sanctions; and if need be to get the faculty to rescue students in trouble with the secular arm. They were also a *conjuratio,* a sworn league for mutual aid in sickness and other troubles, a kind of lodge.

Besides these medieval functions, our modern situation requires some new student government powers. In the frantic expansion, there is a vast amount of building. On visits to eighty colleges around the country, however, I have seen scarcely a single new dormitory that shows any thought (or concern) for the student users. And there are fancy façades but lousy food. The students certainly ought to have an advisory role from the beginning in any plans for new physical plant. (The faculty, let me say, should have more than an advisory role, instead of being routinely consulted and disregarded.) Further, in the present lockstep grading and scheduling, students should have a say in rules of moratoria and transfer, so that they can shape their educations to their own current powers and concerns, and not be short-changed on "credits." Ultimately, faculty must and will control what it teaches and how it teaches, but the students must come to their studies voluntarily, when they are ready; they cannot be force-fed.

I submit that all these matters could be better dealt with by concerted self-interest than by paternalistic administrators and guidance counselors. Further, I think that professors would be delighted to be teaching mature young persons who can take care of themselves. The GI-bill without shell-shock.

SIDNEY HOOK

Academic Freedom and
the Rights of Students*

Americans are accustomed to reading about universities as storm centers of political disturbance in Latin and Asiatic countries. In a country like the United States, however, most criticism of student bodies in the past has been directed against their political apathy. The fact, therefore, that a building was seized by students at the Berkeley campus of the University of California, bringing all administrative activities to a halt, that a strike was declared, paralyzing teaching, and that the governor of the most populous state in the union, after the arrest of some 800 students, felt it necessary to appeal for problems to be solved "by evolution not revolution," should give not only educators but all reflective citizens pause. It has focused attention upon a question of considerable complexity —the rights, and the responsibilities, of students.

Since so much of the controversy and agitation swirls around the slogans of freedom, the first question to be asked is: Do students enjoy the right of academic freedom? This depends on what is meant by academic freedom. Perhaps the best short definition was offered by Arthur O. Lovejoy, founder, together with John Dewey, of the American Association of University Professors.

"Academic freedom," he wrote, "is the freedom of the teacher or research worker in higher institutions of learning to investigate and discuss the problems of his science and to express his conclu-

* From *The New York Times Magazine,* January 3, 1965, and originally titled "Freedom to Learn but not Freedom to Riot."

sions, whether through publications or the instruction of students, without interference from political or ecclesiastical authority, or from the administrative officials of the institution in which he is employed, unless his methods are found by qualified bodies of his own profession to be clearly incompetent or contrary to professional ethics."

A number of interesting implications may be drawn from this definition. First, academic freedom exists primarily for "teachers" —in the most comprehensive sense of that term. Strictly speaking, it makes no sense to talk of "academic freedom" for students. Students have a right to freedom to learn. The best guarantee of freedom to learn is academic freedom for those who teach them. Where teachers are deprived of academic freedom, students are *ipso facto* deprived of the freedom to learn.

The converse, however, is not true. It is simply false both in logic and in fact to assert that freedom to teach and freedom to learn are indivisible. Many things may interfere with the student's freedom to learn—poverty, racial discrimination, inadequate transportation—which have no direct relevance to academic freedom. The latter may flourish in institutions to which students are unjustly denied the opportunity to enter. The movement to abolish poverty, discrimination and other social evils in order to give students access to education and to effective freedom to learn flows from their *moral* rights as persons and from their *civil* rights as citizens. They are not corollaries of academic freedom. To deny this would make the university responsible for the entire state of society and its reform.

Second, academic freedom is not a civil right like freedom of speech. A teacher who is dropped or refused a post on grounds of incompetence, because, say, he indoctrinates his students with the belief that the earth is flat, or that the Elders of Zion are engaged in a conspiracy to destroy America, or that Communists are twentieth-century Jeffersonian democrats, is not being deprived of freedom of speech. He can still proclaim his discovery from the house tops. As a citizen he can talk nonsense without let or hindrance. But in order to talk "nonsense" in the academy with impunity—and strange things *can* be heard within it!—a teacher must win the right to do so by certification from his peers that he is competent and by having acquired tenure. What may sound like nonsense to the plain citizen may be the birth of a revolutionary discovery.

The same consideration applies to the student.

There is no direct connection between the student's freedom to learn and his freedom of speech. The controlling consideration must be his freedom to learn. If restrictions are placed on freedom of speech—aside from those which exist on the freedom of *all* citizens —they must be justified by the educational needs of the student and reasonable institutional provisions for its expression. It is one thing to set up a miniature Hyde Park on some corner of the campus and encourage students to use it; it is another to allow them to call a mass meeting on Prexy's lawn at dawn.

Third, responsibilty for the certification of a teacher's competence, and for interpreting and applying the rules of tenure, must ultimately lie in the hands of the faculty. The faculty should also set the educational standards which students are required to measure up to. Students may be free to learn but sometimes they don't learn enough. Students too, therefore, must earn the right to continue as students. Higher education is not a civil right like the right to a fair trial or other Bill of Rights freedoms that do not have to be earned.

Fourth, an important aspect of the faculty's responsibility for the entire educational enterprise is ultimate control over the classrooms, meeting halls and other educational facilities of the campus and over the conditions of their use. This has a bearing, as we shall see, on some crucial questions.

The extent to which these principles are applied is affected by the fact that legal authority in American higher institutions of learning is vested either in boards of regents or in corporate boards of laymen. While there is no practicable way of reversing this historical trend, immense progress has been made in winning over those with legal authority to the acceptance of enlightened principles of academic freedom which in effect entrust educational policy to the faculties. This has been a gradual and sometimes painful development, but today academic freedom is in a more flourishing state than ever before in its history. It is only when one remembers how many and onerous were the religious, political and social restrictions upon the teacher's freedom in the past that one can grasp the remarkable progress that has been made.

What is true of the teacher's academic freedom is also true of the student's freedom to learn. My own lifetime spans a period from relative tyranny in the classroom to open inquiry. During my freshman year in college, I gave two reports in a class in political science. In the first, I defended Charles A. Beard's approach to the Constitution—to the manifest disapproval of the teacher. In the second, I argued that Calhoun's logic was superior to Webster's in their famous debates. This was too much for the instructor who ejected me from the class with the indignant observation: "When you aren't preaching sedition you are preaching secession!" That could hardly happen today. Although conditions are not uniform, almost everywhere the climate of opinion and practice is healthier than it used to be.

The issues that agitate campuses today are more likely to arise from the behavior of students than from actions of the faculty. Of these, some stem from rules governing the students' personal and social behavior, and some from efforts to regulate their extracurricular political activities both on and off campus.

Confusion, and sometimes needless controversy, arise from a failure to distinguish between the area of conduct in which students may justifiably exercise their rights as individual citizens and that which is related to the specific function of the college and to the business which presumably brings the student to school. To indicate the relevance of this distinction, let us examine some of the concrete issues that have provoked controversy in recent years.

The first concerns the personal morality of students. Unfortunately, personal morality for many people refers exclusively to sexual behavior, but, properly understood, it embraces every form of individual conduct whose consequences have some bearing on the welfare of others. On the assumption that in institutions of higher learning we are not dealing with children, standards of personal deportment should initially be left to the students themselves. In the interests of safety, however, it is necessary to establish rules and regulations governing the use of cars, liquor, smoking and visits to dormitories, but, wherever possible, these rules should be administered by the students themselves. Anything students can properly do for themselves as adults should be left to them. To student self-government, broad-based and representative, can be entrusted many of the functions incidental to organized student life in the college community—although the faculty cannot forgo exercising some oversight as a kind of appeals body to see that fair play is done.

Should students be permitted to organize political groups on campus or invite speakers of extremist political views to address them? This kind of problem has occasioned far more bitter controversy than problems of purely personal behavior. And failure to define the issue properly has prevented the right kind of questions from being asked and the relevant considerations brought to bear.

A student request which may have considerable *educational* validity may be wrongfully denied because it is mistakenly put forward as a political demand. This is particularly true with respect to who should be allowed to speak on a university campus. This has nothing to do with questions of free speech or academic freedom. Political speakers can reach students in many ways. If the faculties do not permit the use of college facilities to individuals outside of the academic community, they are not denying the civil right of freedom of speech to speakers, who can easily address students off-campus, or the civil right of freedom to listen to students, who can attend their meetings off-campus. This is a false issue.

The genuine issue is the *educational* one. It is on educational, not political, grounds that a valid case can be made for permitting recognized student organizations to invite speakers of their choice to the campus to discuss any topic, no matter how controversial. The educational process cannot and should not be confined merely to the classroom. Students should be encouraged to pursue their educational interests on their own initiative, and contemporary issues which convulse society are legitimate subjects of inquiry.

Faculties and administrations often suffer from educational timidity. They are unduly fearful when a speaker of extremist views is invited to the campus. If a college is doing its job properly, it doesn't require Fascists or Communists to instruct its students about Fascism or Communism. But so long as students want to hear such speakers—often to see them in the flesh and to find out how they tick mentally—there can be no reasonable educational objection to their appearance—particularly if it is made clear that such speakers do not represent the views of the student body or faculty.

If students and faculty cannot cope with the "arguments" of the Lincoln Rockwells and Gus Halls, then the college is failing badly in its educational task. In an open and honest forum, the cause of freedom and democracy can triumph over all challengers. And as for the vaunted "public image" (horrid phrase!) of the college, the prolonged controversy and newspaper publicity attendant upon banning a speaker is usually far more damaging than the one-day sensation provided by his appearance. For one thing seems assured by experience. A prolonged controversy over an invitation to an extremist almost always guarantees him an overflow audience when he does finally appear.

In the rare cases in which the need for control of student activities does arise, failure on the part of the faculty to draw the line means that it has abdicated from its educational responsibilities. For example, students, sometimes unfortunately abetted by junior faculty personnel, will occasionally try to break up meetings of speakers with whom they disagree. A self-respecting faculty cannot tolerate such activities. Similarly, if outside groups send professional organizers onto the campuses of large metropolitan universities to recruit students or to provoke incidents with the administration or faculties, they should be barred from access.

Then, too, small groups of students, zealots in some cause, will occasionally violate the rules of fair discussion and honest advocacy. I could fill a volume describing stratagems of this kind I have observed over a lifetime. A few students, for example, will organize a "Free Speech Forum" or something else with a libertarian flavor. Their first speaker will be Lincoln Rockwell or someone of his kidney. Thereafter, featured as "a reply" to Fascism, will come a succession of Communist speakers, sometimes paid from general student or school funds. The "educational" point of the forum is to build up Communism in its various disguises as the only real answer to Fascism.

Complaints about the absence of liberal speakers are met with the statement that liberals have been invited but refused to come. The evidence? A carbon copy of a letter to a liberal figure 2,000 miles or more distant, the original of which he may never have received. Where representatives of the student body are unable to prevent dishonest practices of this kind, the faculty is justified in stepping in.

The same general principles should govern student publications. On educational grounds, students should be encouraged to publish their own newspapers, periodicals and pamphlets, exchanging ideas, commenting on great issues, testing and challenging their teachers' views. But it would be ridiculous to say that this freedom is absolute and exempts them from restraints against slander and libel. Particularly obnoxious is the circulation of anonymous literature on campus defaming members of the student body or faculty.

Only those who believe it is possible to be liberal without being intelligent will affirm that the content of speech is always privileged, irrespective of its effects.

The very fact that speech can be used not only for advocacy —which is permissible—but for incitement, defamation and slander —which is not—shows how absurd it is to hold that speech should never be restricted. There should be no prior censorship, of course, unless there is convincing evidence that a speaker plans to incite to violence. We do not have to wait for a mob actually to move to lynch someone before we stop the agitator inciting it.

The irony of the situation is that students in our mass institutions of learning suffer today far more from the failure of faculties to attend to the students' individual educational needs than from alleged suppressions of their freedom of speech. The students' freedom to learn is frustrated by crowding, inferior staffing and by the indifference of many faculties to the best methods of classroom teaching. Colleges still operate on the absurd assumption that anyone who knows anything can teach it properly. It is an open scandal that the worst teaching in the American system of education takes place at the college level.

In some universities, large introductory courses where skillful teaching is of critical importance in arousing student interest are turned over to young, inexperienced graduate assistants at the outset of their careers who stumble along by trial and error and groping imitation of the models of teaching they vaguely remember. No wonder they sometimes play up to students, joining them in their vague resentments against the educational establishment in a kind of compensatory camaraderie. Some observers believe that unless conditions change the real revolt on campus will some day be directed against the shoddy educational treatment to which students have been subjected. As the numbers of students grow the situation deteriorates.

A sense of proportion, a pinch of humor and a draft of common sense are wonderful specifics against friction, but they vanish when either students or faculty resort to ultimatums. Both sides have a mutual interest in keeping the educational enterprise going. When problems and difficulties arise they must be routed through recognized channels of petition, complaint and protest. The officially elected representatives of the student body should meet periodically with representatives of the faculty which, when grave issues are at stake, should sit as a committee of the whole.

Attempts by any group, even when it feels it has a legitimate grievance, to short-circuit official channels, to appeal over the heads of the representative student body for mass demonstrations or strikes, to threaten force and violence or to resort to so-called passive resistance should be condemned by both students and faculty Such tactics are not only destructive of the atmosphere in which teaching and learning can take place, they prejudice the chances for reaching mutually satisfactory settlements.

The student "Free Speech Movement" at the University of California had every right to press for a modification of university rules governing campus and off-campus activities. What was shocking, however, was its deliberate boycott and by-passing of the Associated Students, the elected representative organization of the student body. It neither used all the existing channels of protest nor sought to avail itself of the remedies open to it.

Even more shocking was the demagogic and odious comparison drawn by some students between the situation at the University, which, despite its restrictions, is still far more liberal than most, and the situation in Mississippi. And worst of all was the resort to tactics of mass civil disobedience which could only be justified in extreme situations in behalf of basic principles of freedom. Except in such situations, changes in the laws of a democratic community must be urged by practices within the law.

Almost as shocking as the action of the students in seizing University property was the failure of the faculty at Berkeley to condemn the action. Indeed, by failing to couple its call for an amnesty for students with a sharp rebuke for their actions, the faculty seemed to condone indirectly the students' behavior. Apparently those who wanted to be heroes were to be spared the consequerces of their heroism.

The administration of the University also seems at fault in not anticipating developments on campus. Signs of student unrest and dissatisfaction were apparent many months ago. The faculty, therefore, should have been brought into the picture much earlier and entrusted with the formulation of rules of conduct, in consultation with official representatives of the student body, and with their subsequent enforcement.

The really disquieting aspect of the situation at the University of California, however, was the extremism of the student leaders, the lengths to which they were willing to go—at one point, bloodshed and possible loss of life seemed imminent—and the contemptuous and disingenuous account they gave of their behavior. One of them described their activities as "controversial measures to begin a dialogue." Student concern with the content and method of their education is sure to grow and should be encouraged. But if they are going to lie down, seize buildings and call strikes whenever their demands are not granted by faculty and administration, it bodes ill for the future.

Even before the events at Berkeley, I read literature distributed by a strong student group at the University of California calling for "the total elimination of course, grade and unit system of undergraduate learning" and urging other proposals—not all of them as silly. But what was definitely not silly or funny in the light of what has happened was the injunction to students to resort ultimately to "civil disobedience" to get their way! It is a safe bet to anyone who knows the psychology of students that once they get away with the tactic of civil disobedience in protesting a minor rule, their demands —and their conduct—will grow wilder and more unreasonable.

No service is done to students by flattering them or by giving them the impression they can acquire an education in any other way than by hard intellectual discipline—by accepting the logic of ideas and events. They cannot be encouraged too much to broaden their intellectual interests, and they certainly must not be discouraged from giving expression to their generous enthusiasms for civil rights, for human welfare, for peace with freedom. But good works off campus cannot be a substitute for good work on campus. Ultimately, the good causes our society always needs have a better chance of triumphing if their servitors equip themselves with the best education our colleges and universities can give them.

JOHN R. SEELEY

Quo Warranto:
The "Berkeley Issue"

The events of the last few months at Berkeley—which are reaching toward a new crisis even as I write—have one curious character: they evoke a "response" in nearly everyone; and in everyone who makes any response, that response is likely to be passionate to say the least.

In the midst of dramatic confrontations—in outer space, in Selma, in Vietnam—"Berkeley" as a conversational topic or a subject of vivid reporting and heated debate, holds its own, when it does not dominate. And not just on the West Coast, but equally in Washington, Boston or New York; and not merely among the young or the academic; and not only at home but abroad. It is not just that a specter is stalking academia, but that a tremor, which may well portend an earthquake, is rightly felt to have passed over the academic and nonacademic world.

The sense of seismic shock was evident even before some of the more dramatic manifestations came clear: one chancellor already dismissed his office; another chancellor and his president flip-flopping into resignation and out; the mighty governor of the mighty State of California summoning his patrol from the highway and his sheriff from the hunt to support by naked force the tottering moral authority of a great university's "administration." And now once again—as with Charles James Fox's insistence on calling magistrate or king "thou"—the desperate question of right time, place and use of a four-letter word confounds the populace and shakes the realm. No more in the one case than the other can the argument, taken at face value, be judged capable of shaking the souls of men and the props of kingdoms. It must then be what the argument "represents"—or foreshadows—that causes the fascinated attention of an ever-widening public, the escalation, the "mounting action" of the students, the increasing output of low statements from high places, and, in general, the spectacle of a government in desperate moral and political straits, striking out in every direction and in many cases inadvertently striking itself.

Of course, as part of the dispute itself, there has been no want of "interpretation" as to what the argument "really represents." It really represents, allegedly, spoiled children crying for more because they already have too much. Or, it represents the justifiable complaint of perspicacious students who, neglected by an over-specializing and over-ambitious faculty, simply mistook the enemy and made the administration the scapegoat for real wrongs—committed by others. Or, it represents a mere protest against the general and inevitable "alienation" that, of course, infects the university as it infects all other institutions. Or, it is essentially a communist (or anarchist) conspiracy, or the students are the dupes and servants of such aims. Or it is a kind of accidental spill-over from the more legitimate confrontations of feeble right with forceful wrong in Mississippi, Alabama and the like. Or it is a motiveless—or rationally motiveless—plot to destroy the great university, to "bring it to a grinding halt" for the sheer joy of doing so.

The lines of explanation are almost as various as the analysts at work. They have, for the most part, however, one thing in common. They exculpate the administration, and they trivialize, patronize or otherwise detract from the dignity of the students; and they do so mostly by claiming that "the cause" is other than it seems. And by "other than it seems," they mean not deeper or more general, but *different,* different in such a sense that the alleged grievance is a *mask* for motives of less respectability or none.

Such unmasking is a dangerous game: for the participants, because it can be played two ways; for the onlookers, because their moral sense and their power to judge and act is weakened by a general belief that "everything is only a cover for something else," or by the mistaken supposition that this is true in a particular case where it is untrue—or true but immaterial. Every court in the land knows that, in general, it had better try the issues as presented, and only at utmost need "look behind them"—to the greed of attorneys, or the cleanness of the hands of the adversaries, let alone to motives which are always mixed, and none the worst for that. It is a sound rule.

Let us, therefore, at least begin by taking the matter at its plain and manifest face-value. It is clear that the students are indicting the administration (and the government) of their university: not, or not primarily, their fellow-students, professors, the surrounding society, or the city of Berkeley or State of California, or the police or the courts of either.

It should be plain that the primary target is the government of the university in the generic sense of that term and not with special reference to momentary incumbents of office, i.e., the attack is on monarchy, not the monarch (except incidentally), on despotism, not any particular despot. Despite the wry current comment "to Kerr is human; to be Strong, divine," hardly anyone—at least until very recently—wanted Kerr to go and few, if any, wanted any particular other person to go. Nor has there been any great talk of replacing one or more "bad" regent with one or more better one: it is the regency that is at stake, not this or that regent.

The structure of the sequence of events taken as a whole is classic. It begins with the minor act of a minor official: the tired Negro lady in Montgomery is asked or told to go to the back of the bus; a minor University official, seemingly, attempts to restrict in a minor way the minor use of a minor bit of University property. There is non-compliance with the order issued—with no lively or clear sense at that moment of the underlying or over-arching moral issues. There is action against the lawbreakers and explanation for the action. But the action, far from intimidating, provokes, and the accompanying explanation heightens the antagonism to the issuing authority because it generalizes and reveals the moral foundations for an act that might otherwise have been written off as error or inadvertence. Action and explanation call forth a wider protest, and in turn meet with a "response." The response is now under review, and if it represents duress or deception (or an attempted mixture of both) it is taken as a revelation, an exposure of the real character and animating motives and thought system of the authority in question. And so to some sort of moral climax. From a set of sore feet in Montgomery to the president of this nation reluctantly sending in his troops to fill the void left by the withering of the august authority of the sovereign State of Alabama. From an ostensible spat over the location of the activity of "advocacy," to the questioning and perhaps the determination by trial of whether a university so constituted and so governed can long survive. The words "a university" are well advised; for, given the spread of effect due to the mass media and given the conditions at numberless universities, the question is no longer "this University" (Berkeley) but *any* university, at least in North America. Hence—as with the American Revolution and its prodromal struggles—the bated breath and trembling limb in every capital and cabal. The fear is that like the sound of the shot at Lexington, so the sound of heads, being bumped down the stone stairs of Sproul Hall, may be heard around the world.

For this is what we are come to: the questioning of the legitimacy of a long-standing form of authority. Again, first in a particular, (though by then very broad) matter; and then in utter generality. When Berkeley students denied the authority of the regents and their administration to intervene in any way between them and the Constitutional protections of the First and Fourteenth Amendments, they were *in that sphere* sweeping away the existence of a university authority altogether. When the students in the heat of that battle began to question the provenance of the regents and the source of their authority to govern a university at all, they had raised the question of legitimacy.

And this is what is happening, or appears to be happening, at every university where there is "trouble." Whether the "arbitrary act of arbitrary authority" first complained of has to do with panty-raids or marijuana, deans who sow sexual suspicion, the double standard of dormitory hours for men and women, dress-regulations or food, the place of the student council or this or that regulation —in every confrontation students are asking: *Who* says? And by what right? They ask the historic question that free men have timelessly asked of authority grown arbitrary, big and careless: *Quo Warranto?*

And the answers they receive are somewhat wondrous. Because they, the governors or regents or board members, have, or give or get the money. "Because the law empowers them to." "Because attendance here is a privilege, not a right." "Because, like it or not, this is part of the power structure and they have the power." "It isn't right, but there it is." "Because this is a private institution and you are lucky to be here." "Because *someone* must govern!" "Because this is a public institution and they 'represent' the public interest."

These, and like answers culled from my correspondence and experience, go to the heart of every question, except the question of legitimacy. And it is now only, or almost only, about legitimacy that the students are asking. Not, what is so?; they already know or can soon find out. Not, what makes it work?; they are already acquainted with power and its workings. But *what justifies it? What commands or ought to command my loyalty and obedience?* And to this there seems no instant answer. And in the awful silence, souls shake, and otherwise good men look to their weapons, whether verbal as in Kerr's responses or violent as in Brown's.

Is the question that the students ask improper? Or improper as coming from them? Or is it insufficiently precise to be capable of answer? Or is it proper but unimportant?

We might turn to sacred or to secular authority for an answer —or we might content ourselves with the empirical observation that no government that lacks a legitimation does in actuality long endure. Indeed, it would not be misleading to say that a government shorn of legitimacy in the eyes of the governed is already in process of dissolution: as with a fatal illness, the question is merely how long?

In the realm of the secular, there is perhaps no greater authority on authority and its legitimation than Max Weber. He too regards it as a continuing and universal necessity of all government. He sees, in effect, three and only three sources of sanctification given among men: legitimation rests always on traditional grounds or rational grounds or on "charismatic" ones, or some mixture of these.

Traditional grounds invoke the hallowing effect of time, of the sacredness men are willing to impute to "what was ever thus," or "so from time immemorial." Little in America normally claims this ground, and it is particularly difficult for the modern "multiversity," bristling with its modernity, to appeal to it. "Charismatic" grounds depend on the quality of one extraordinary figure whose very char-

acter—his exemplification or incarnation of the numinous or heroic
—"calls" others to him in what is really a common obedience to
that high and holy principle that he only "represents." Few American university presidents so appear; and where and if they do,
there would be free consent—and hence no question of enforcing
authority. So we are left with "rational grounds" as a possible
source for the indispensable mantle of authority.

By "rational grounds" cannot, of course, be meant calculations
of self-interest or mere fear of consequences. (It is precisely out of
and because of these that the *occasion* of dispute has arisen.) What
is meant is an established belief in the "legality" of the pattern of
rules and "the right of those elevated to authority under such
rules to issue commands." "Legality" here means *morally valid*
law; not just any law as it happens to be. And valid means
rationally and truly defensible in terms of still more deeply held
beliefs.

We are driven back a further stage. Since university presidents
are generally appointed, in fact if not in form, by governors or
regents, such moral power as they have (except negligibly by
charisma) must be derivative from their boards. And how are these
board members (or equivalent) "elevated to authority under such
rules" as would authenticate or morally validate their "commands?"
By public election, so that the will of all is involved? Not that. By a
show of certified competence, endorsed by a government and watch-
dogged by an organized profession, as judges in Britain? Not that
either. By competitive examination, like civil servants? No. By the
consent of the governed scholars generally, or faculty-and-students
locally? Not exactly. By exhibited moral leadership, either before
or after appointment, so that the gubernatorial pudding is justified
in the eating? Neither their provenance nor their performance suggest so. Then what? Perhaps the capacity to define, interpret and
convey in a superior fashion the "purpose of the organization."
Perhaps.

If so, it is most crucial, for as Chester Barnard (sometime
president of New Jersey Bell Telephone) points out, this is at issue
not only in general but with the issue, even in a privately held corporation, of any and every command. Having established that "in
principle and in fact the determination of authority lies with the
subordinate individual," and that the necessity of such assent "to

establish authority *for him* is inescapable," he lays down four simultaneous conditions, failing any one of which a "communication"
will lack authority: understandability; compatibility with (recipient's view of) the purpose of the organization; compatibility with
"his interest as a whole"; ability to comply. It is the second and
third, the compatibility conditions—with the organization's purpose
and the recipient's "interest as a whole"—that are in all the University disputes at issue. The conflict of interest may motivate the
dispute; but it is to the quarrel about the organization's purpose
that we must look for justification. The very existence of the disputes, and their acrimony, denies that boards may claim legitimacy
because of unusual success in securing and maintaining agreed
definitions of "the organization's purpose."

Perhaps we should turn back to "moral leadership" as a possible
remaining ground. And perhaps we might examine authoritative
ecclesiastical pronouncement to see how this secular question might
appear in a sacred light.

As Pope John XXIII says in *Pacem in Terris:*
The order which prevails in society is by nature moral. . . .
*Human reason is the norm of the human will, according to
which its goodness is measured* [quoting Aquinas]. . . . Human
society can be neither well-ordered nor prosperous unless it
has some people invested with legitimate authority to preserve
its institutions . . . authority . . . is the power to command
according to right reason, authority must derive its obligatory
force from the moral order. . . .

Enough? More explicitly:
Where the civil authority uses as its only, or its chief, means
either threats and fear of punishment or promises of rewards,
it cannot effectively move men. . . . Even if it did, this would
be altogether opposed to their dignity. . . . Since authority
is chiefly concerned with moral force, it follows that civil
authority must appeal primarily to the conscience. . . .

And finally (my italics):
Since the right to command is required by the moral order . . .
it follows that if civil authorities legislate for, or allow, *anything that is contrary to that order . . . neither the laws made
nor the authorizations* granted *can be binding on the con-
sciences of the citizens.* . . .

Is the university government perhaps not a "civil authority?" Are students perhaps not "men"—in the plain sense required by the context? Indeed, if proof were required, are they not showing themselves to be men in the very question they ask, their manner of asking it, their willingness to suffer prison, weariness, cold and contumely to get an answer? Does the moral order demand the drawing of some arbitrary age-line at twenty-one? Is moral weight outweighed by biological age? Are three years or less morally disabling—as female sex used to be?

If not, we have a challenge to the legitimacy of an order and an authority, and perhaps neither the ground of the challenge nor the source should unduly surprise us.

The idea of a "government of laws not of men" is deep in the American grain. And it has never meant what Sheriff Jim Clark or Bull Connor in the South or those at and around Berkeley who call the students lawbreakers would like it to mean: a system where "under color of law," substantial rights like voting can be defeated in the name of minor ones like orderly traffic flow. It has meant by common consent and open recognition a principle of appeal from lower law to higher, in the course of which, on desperate occasions, minor law has sometimes been violated with impunity.

As to the source of this new questioning, it is perhaps only because we have been given so much nonsense about students over the last few years that we are at all surprised. There has not in fact been a time in living memory, as far as I have known students and their teachers, when the students were not directing their inquiries with passion upon just such problems: the rights of governors to govern or to govern as they did. The left-right political agitation of my day was undergirded by a passionate concern for peace-freedom-and-justice. The so-called period of apathy of the forties was an interlude in which the passion for right met a welter of conflicting issues none of which readily picked itself out as a possible channel for effective action. As for the brief spell of "playing it cool," even this represented the protest of an exquisite moral sensitivity in a world where morality seemed to have no place or, at least, no relation to the relentless march of events. There is a straight line from Holden Caulfield through all these seeming twists and turns to the latest questioning of the phoney and the unfounded.

And the movement is not limited to university students: in one after another of our high schools, particularly the supposedly "spoiled" suburban ones, the same questions are being asked. And no less among those who are not students—returned Peace Corps volunteers and the like.

I think the questions are to be welcomed, though the university as we have known it may not survive.

I say "as we have known it." How? As a despotism. As a "creature of the state." As a place where neither faculty nor students—who alone constitute the organization *into* a university— have control over its most general policy. As a place where administrative practices that would no longer be countenanced in business are enshrined and elaborated. As a place where PR in the worse sense is practised to the limit: where, under the canopy of the highest high-flown statements, commencement oratory and effusion of lofty sentiments, clothed in the semi-sacerdotal, semi-medieval cloak of monastic tradition, gowns, "degrees," scepters of office, hierarchies of honorable titles freedom is fettered and honor suborned. It is not just the badness of these practices, but their badness in the context of the virtues celebrated and claimed, that gives the protest, like Luther's, its burning quality, its fire and force.

And it is precisely this threat—the threat of deep, far-reaching and long-needed change—that makes the current "administrators" pursue so immorally and justify so feebly their "morality of fear" —the morality that justifies their present deviousness in terms of "preserving a valuable institution"—which they are by their deviousness destroying while it stands.

The students may save it yet. But only if they can find other and older responsible academics, equally bold, equally honest, equally dedicated to education—and prepared to educate each other by remaking the law together.

II

A
CAMPUS DIVIDED

In September, 1964, the Berkeley administration suddenly hurled a ban on politicking at the students who manned fund-raising and membership-recruiting tables in the open area in front of the campus traditionally reserved for these activities. Rather than cooling the student political spirit, this arbitrary ruling raised it to the boiling point; the campus was thrown into a state of virtual civil war with students entrenched against an unyielding administration. The faculty, caught in the middle, at first assumed Clark Kerr's much-heralded guise of mediator and tried to reconcile the opposed camps. However, the professors could not long remain neutral. Some supported the administration, but the great majority went over to the students, as expressed by the Academic Senate's 8 to 1 vote of confidence on December 8.

Berkeley is probably the only campus in America where a revolution of this size could occur. In his article, "The Student State of Mind," Michael V. Miller describes the distinctive student culture and political atmosphere that provided the context for a full-scale student movement. The students' view of their opposition, which Miller also describes, is exemplified in detail by socialist writer and editor Hal Draper in "The Mind of Clark Kerr." Draper chooses the trappings of scholarly analysis in examining Kerr's published works in order to deliver a fiery polemic against the Kerr style of administration. Originally circulated in Berkeley as a pamphlet, Draper's piece quickly became a central document in support of the student cause.

51

From a more distant perspective than Draper's, A. H. Raskin, noted labor writer and assistant editor of The New York Times, *examines the attitudes of the two parties in conflict—Clark Kerr and the student activists—and presents an account sympathetic to both. Raskin places the blame on the bigness and impersonality that exists at all levels of contemporary American society.*

John Searle, professor of philosophy at the University of California, focuses on the attitude of the Berkeley faculty and traces the evolution of its sympathies toward the support for the students that culminated in the faculty resolution of December 8.

MICHAEL V. MILLER

The Student State of Mind*

I. Nearly everyone who has tried to account for the recent uprising on the Berkeley campus has drawn a picture of students struggling for identity in a vast, impersonal educational and research factory run by IBM cards, remote professors subsidized by federal funds, and administrators with the temperaments of corporation executives. This analysis has the curious effect of making University of California President Clark Kerr the prophet of the student revolution against his administration. Kerr's description of the bureaucratized "multiversity," set forth in his Godkin lectures at Harvard in 1963, has even been converted into an ideology of justification for the revolt by its leadership.

There is more than a grain of truth in this account. The students were waging war against absurdities and hypocrisies that seem endemic to modern bureaucracy. And no doubt some form of pervasive alienation drove numerous students into the fray. But however plausible it may be, the multiversity analysis portrays the landscape of the Berkeley rebellion without sufficient color or contour. The student assault upon the attempt of Berkeley deans to control their tiny strip of land at Bancroft and Telegraph Avenues marshalled support from students and faculty on a scale unprecedented at American universities. Freshmen whose minds had never been violated by a political thought, as well as hardened politicoes, became caught up in direct action in-fighting with the authorities. But all shades of motivation were functioning here, and alienation is only part of the story. Perhaps student supporters of the revolt could be lumped under three rough categories:

* From *Dissent,* Spring 1965.

Some students derive gratification and a sense of meaning from their involvement in politics. They are the ones who have fought in the student movement on several fronts—against HUAC and capital punishment, for peace and civil rights. Rather than feeling that school has nothing to give them, they get good educations because they have found a way of making knowledge relevant, by immersing it in the social present. By and large, these seem to me among the least alienated students on campus, at least from themselves. But they did feel that alienation threatened when they saw the administration attempt to sever the connection between school and society.

Another segment of the student body constitutes, more or less, a community of self-pity. It is made up mostly of older undergrads and a few beginning graduate students who have sulked through their years at Berkeley in a pose of militant sensitivity. These students tend to be bright and talented, yet feel themselves edging ever closer to a failure of self-realization. They like to see themselves as misunderstood and unable to communicate—and not only with professors; they have bittersweet histories of brief and tragic love affairs to relate. Now and then, they may leave school for New York or Europe on the hunt for significance, but they usually wend their way back to Berkeley.

Perhaps such students are a little too quick to blame their stifled creativity on the system, or their inability to find love on the structure of modern society. Their politics border on melodrama. They are the specialists in alienation.

My impression is that the revolt drew its leaders and its most vocal and committed supporters mainly from these two groups. With the final group, the vast mass of sympathizers who signed petitions, swelled the ranks of sit-ins, or went on strike, alienation is not so much the issue, although many are undoubtedly uneasy about the University's size and red-tape procedures. What enraged them was the realization that the administration was being overbearing and unfair by suddenly trying to chop the guts out of student politics, which are as much a part of Berkeley as its tradition of Nobel prize winners in science. And they feared that apparently arbitrary restriction on freedom in one area might quickly lead to similar infringements in others.

II. Many features of the impersonal machine exist at other large universities like Harvard, Columbia, or U.C.L.A., which is itself part of the West Coast multiversity. Yet Berkeley is probably the only campus in the country where students could transform a general mood of restlessness and resentment into an effective political weapon against their administration. One of the most striking characteristics of the revolt was its interplay of spontaneity and efficient organization. When negotiations between students and deans over the original administration ban on political activity broke down, a few student organizations set up booths in protest. The administration threatened disciplinary action and subsequently suspended eight student leaders. Almost instantaneously a full-scale student movement was afoot with its organizers, orators, heroes ready to commit themselves to action, even martyrs.

Clearly a movement of such magnitude and sophistication could not have been born overnight—as the Free Speech Movement virtually was—without experienced tacticians to create it, in addition to widespread unrest to nourish it.

Students interested in tactics and ideology hang out on the Terrace, an elevated outdoor cafeteria in the student-union complex with a touch of Left Bank atmosphere. The Terrace was already humming with discussion of the recent ban on politics last September 30, when five students who had manned political tables in defiance of the administration ruling were summoned to appear at a dean's office that afternoon. A couple of hours before this eventful appointment, a leading opponent of the ban stood near the Sather Gate entrance to campus and shouted at students coming off the Terrace, "All right, all you Terrace intellectuals, here's your chance finally to *do* something!" In this manner, he recruited many of the several hundred students who appeared later at the dean's office along with the five to protest the impending suspensions.

Those students who paused on their way to class from the Terrace are part of an important—by now even traditional—subculture of the Berkeley student body. A melting pot of campus intellectuals, aesthetes, and politicoes, it includes a lot of the "non-students" who have unjustly been used as a scapegoat by opponents of the FSM (most non-students involved in FSM activities are temporarily out of school, very recent graduates, university employees, or students' wives). Any afternoon in the week this crowd is found lounging between classes on the Terrace or in Telegraph Avenue's two coffee-houses arrayed in styles from classic beat to classic Harris tweed. Admittedly, its ranks contain a quota of the hipsters and revolutionary zealots concerned with little but the right names and phrases, the devotees of the latest chemical highs, the lunatic fringe of the avant garde. But here also are a surprisingly large proportion of the most intellectually serious and morally alert students on campus, fellowship holders as well as veterans of the Mississippi wars. And sometimes the lines are extremely difficult to draw.

The bright and serious students in this group are the ones' who demand the most from the University. They get good grades, although they often feel cynical about the system. Many of them are genuinely more concerned with putting knowledge of the past to work in the present than regurgitating it on a final. In a sense they are always putting administrators on the spot, because they believe that the educational process should provide a continuum between ideas and social and political action. For instance, when these students sit in for Negro rights in San Francisco or go off to register Negro voters in Mississippi, they are convinced that they are only carrying out a literal application of the democratic ideals they are supposed to memorize in the classroom. Such behavior unnerves the administration, which has to soothe the ruffled feelings of tax-payers and their representatives who grow anxious about the threats their sons and daughters are posing to the Established order.

III. The overall cast of Berkeley campus politics is distinctly to the left of center, despite a sprinkling of moderate Republicans and Goldwaterites. In general, the student political framework is flexible, communal, non-ideological. Of course there is plenty of organizational room for left-wing ideological temperaments in YSA, YPSL, the DuBois Club, and other groups. But Slate, the unaffiliated Berkeley political organization, has always been an issue-oriented and action-oriented group, a collectivity of political independents and various shades of socialists who came together to work on specific issues.

Political enthusiasm with an emphasis on action pervades the cultural habits of Berkeley student intellectuals to an extraordinary degree. This shows up even in their choice of entertainment. For instance, Bogart's films are among the most popular attractions at movie theaters around Berkeley just as they are in Cambridge, Massachusetts. At Harvard, the Bogart rage is mainly a cult of style. I have even heard of Harvard students parading through the Yard in early 1940s trench coats and snap-brim hats picked up in second-hand clothing stores. But the Berkeley film audience, though it digs the Bogie style, also tends to regard his films as ideological morality plays, in which Bogart, the lone-wolf private eye or soldier of fortune, risks his neck for his principles and eventually wins out over the fumbling, insensitive bureaucratic cops or military officers.

To understand the explosive nature of the administration's restriction on campus politics, one must bear in mind that political activities have become in the last few years a primary means of personal expression and social contact for numerous students. Because of its size and setup, the University of California does, after all, have some of the impersonal features of a modern metropolis. Students have had to build their own sense of community, and bonds formed in fighting for causes supply a powerful way of filling this need. When the administration suddenly barred all meaningful political activity from campus—recruiting members, soliciting funds, advocating action—it created a situation that threatened partially to rupture these bonds.

IV. Two features peculiar to the Berkeley campus have played an essential part in determining the recent drift of student politics. In the first place, there is a running controversy among students, faculty, and administration about the nature of the University. Everything is forever being revised, from methods of registration and length of terms (about to be changed from semesters to quarters) to styles of architecture and, of course, rules governing student political behavior. Like the state itself, the University of California still feels new, a little rootless, unsure of the boundaries between itself and outside social forces. It is not surprising that Cal students feel they should have a say in shaping the University's image, their own role, even the society around them.

Secondly, the University is constantly buffeted by currents of animosity from the surrounding world. This puts students on the defensive and the administration under pressure. The campus atmosphere is modern and cosmopolitan; for several years now Berkeley has attracted urban youngsters who in previous times might have gone to the University of Chicago or CCNY. But the campus is enclosed by a typical conservative California town— and the two tend to grate on each other. Elderly Berkeley land-ladies often seem to loathe and fear the emancipated habits of students from whom they earn their bread and butter. Certain city councilmen cry out about once a week for investigations into student activities, both moral and political. Furthermore, Cal is a public school in a state the government of which contains a powerful minority on the right. A number of conservative state legislators make a habit of tossing bills in the hopper that promise to chop off large amounts of University budget unless the administration undertake purges of controversial students and faculty members.

Part of the local press is only too happy to abet the friction between the University and California taxpayers. For this purpose, red-baiting and beatnik-baiting are favorite devices, Every now and then, the Berkeley *Gazette* prints a column of "campus news" written by ladies with three names who express profound shock over rumours of female students walking around campus in their bare feet. San Francisco *Chronicle* columnist Lucius Beebe, a self-styled connoisseur of expensive restaurants and rugged individualism, frequently launches attacks in atrocious polysyllabic rhetoric on the unwashed hordes of "Red Square in Berkeley" or "Kremlin West," as he alternately terms the school. One can imagine the attitude of William Knowland's paper, the Oakland *Tribune*.

V. During the height of the campus struggle, some newspaper reports, national magazine articles (including the liberal press on occasion), and statements by university administrators accused the FSM of being dupes for Castroite and Maoist agitators. Of course this is so much garbage; neither Peking- nor Havana-brand Communism had anything to do with FSM methods or goals. However, a few student activists do like to praise the revolutionary deeds of Castro and Mao Tse-tung. There are several aspects to this admiration, and one should put them in perspective and not simply write off these students.

Though most student offspring of thirties' radicals are wary of Communism, a few gravitate toward a doctrinaire left position, and for them Mao and Castro are the ideological replacements for Lenin and Stalin. Some do not love Castro and Mao as much as they detest Batista and Chiang Kai-shek. Behind their praise lies a critique of American society; an intuition that perhaps America has played an underhanded game in its treatment of the Cuban and Chinese Revolutions; that democratic ideals too often do not seem to extend beyond the borders of the U.S. if that far.

Another factor is that extolling of Castro and Mao, in the minds of a few, confers special avant-garde status that goes along with being tuned into the most far-out, especially if banned, films and the newest and most unconventional poetry. Castro's bearded revolutionary swagger with its touch of the *bandito,* Mao's militant anti-bourgeois posture and championing of underdog countries make these figures into culture heroes that conjure up a sense of the forbidden, the experimental, the provocative.

Finally, nearly all radicals are fascinated to some degree with two men who—whether for better or worse—have so completely transformed their societies.

VI. Nothing is gained from regarding the Berkeley uprising as a Freudian clash of sons against the fathers, as some commentators (fathers) have suggested. There is, of course, a sense in which the events at Berkeley involve a battle between generations. Students against administrators obviously means youth against its elders. Generational conflict, however, is so ancient and archetypal a social mechanism—certainly it functions in almost every revolution, political or artistic—that it affords little insight into the campus turmoil. It is far more important to realize that the revolt was the latest and most explicit confrontation at Berkeley between two antagonistic political styles.

Let us look at the Berkeley administrator's style as viewed by the students. From the time they began trying to negotiate the administration ban on politics, students came up against constant buck-passing of responsibility for decisions. They were shuttled back and forth between a battery of deans and obscure committees. What the students found behind all this were not corrupt villains who wished them ill, but rather nervous modern liberals dressed out as bureaucrats.

To many students, there is something ineffectual and a little slippery about the new liberal-bureaucrat with his tools of mediation and compromise. He reminds them too closely of Peter Sellers playing the U.S. President in *Dr. Strangelove,* who tries unsuccessfully to juggle forces in a society gone mad; or of Major Major Major, the squadron commander in *Catch-22,* who signs his daily allotment of papers but leaps out his office window whenever anyone shows up with a problem.

Furthermore, the more militant students regard modern liberalism as a whole with something less than pleasure. They feel it is somehow implicated, if only by default, in the heritage of nightmares that compose recent history: Auschwitz, Hiroshima, the Cold War, McCarthy. They consider liberalism far too cumbersome an instrument for altering evils like the nuclear stalemate, U.S. support for tyrannical rule in foreign lands, the exclusion of the Negro from his fair share of society's rewards.

The Berkeley student activist has fashioned a style of political action out of materials borrowed from the South in order to make himself a gadfly in the hide of the local liberal Establishment. When all else fails, he resorts to impoliteness. He refuses to go through proper channels when they lead nowhere and turns his back on the decorum of committees when all the real issues have already been quietly tabled. Impoliteness, politicized, is civil disobedience.

The experience of these students is that it takes radical action on their part to get the liberals in motion. Last spring a huge number of Berkeley and other northern California college students helped stage sit-ins in a fight for equal employment opportunities for Negroes at a major hotel and several automobile dealers in San Francisco. Eventually agreements were hammered out between the Hotel Owners' Association, the auto dealers, a commission appointed by San Francisco's liberal Mayor John Shelley, and NAACP and CORE. Meanwhile, several hundred students had been arrested; many ended up paying fines and being put on probation. But they considered the outcome their victory. Similarly,

814 FSM supporters were carted off to jail before Berkeley's mostly liberal faculty came out in force to affirm the movement's goals.

VII. Students at Berkeley say that incredible changes have occurred on campus as a result of the struggle, which the FSM for the moment appears to have won. Everyone speaks of an authentic, campus-wide feeling of community in the air; of professors and students greeting each other by first names; of innumerable plans cropping up to give students more control over course content and professors over student discipline; of traditional divisions between campus cliques—bohemians, "dormies," even fraternity and sorority types—having been bridged. Will this state of affairs endure? Or are the victors only basking in the warm afterglow of revolutionary solidarity?

HAL DRAPER

The Mind of Clark Kerr

With his book *The Uses of the University* (Harvard, 1963), Clark Kerr, president of the University of California, became the outstanding theoretician and proponent of a particular view of the university. It is true that his foreword claims that the views put forward do not constitute "approval" or "defense" but only "analysis" and "description." He is only "describing" the Wave of the Future (he uses this term), and all realistic people must bow and accept it, like it or not.

Kerr, like many others, has perhaps forgotten that the very phrase comes from the 1940 book by Anne Lindbergh, *The Wave of the Future,* which presented the thesis that fascism or some type of totalitarianism was inevitably coming. She did not argue that this fascism be approved but only that it must be accepted. This was the identical approach also of Burnham's *Managerial Revolution.*

The new type of "multiversity," Kerr writes later, "is an imperative rather than a reasoned choice." You cannot argue with an imperative. It is not Kerr's methodology to say, "This is what I think should be done." He represents himself simply as the interpreter of inexorable "reality." He is, so to speak, the administrator of history, merely informing us how to act in conformity with its rules.

What is beyond question is that Kerr does present a "vision of the end," and that he tells us it *must* be accepted, just like any other ruling of the administration. What is his vision?

In the first place, Kerr presents the university as an institution which is, and will be, increasingly indistinguishable from any other business enterprise in our industrial society. The reader is likely to think, at first, that this is only a metaphor: "the university's invisible product, knowledge," or "the university is being called upon to produce knowledge as never before." But Kerr means it literally:

> The production, distribution, and consumption of "knowledge" in all its forms is said to account for twenty-nine per cent of gross national product . . . and "knowledge production" is growing at about twice the rate of the rest of the economy. . . . What the railroads did for the second half of the last century and the automobile for the first half of this century may be done for the second half of this century by the knowledge industry: that is, to serve as the focal point for national growth.

Naturally, there is a kernel of truth in this language; but can Kerr mean literally that his "multiversity" must become increasingly like a factory and its professors reshaped as businessmen? Consider this:

> The university and segments of industry are becoming more alike. As the university becomes tied into the world of work, the professor—at least in the natural and some of the social sciences—takes on the characteristics of an entrepreneur. . . . The two worlds are merging physically and psychologically.

One might think that the writer of these lines would hardly have patience with a university president who sternly forbade members of this university community to "mount" activity on campus which eventuated in political and social action off-campus —that is, a university president who issued a decree against the "merger." We shall resolve this contradiction later; but we must note that the book is chock-full of statements about the infeasibility of enforcing a boundary line between the university and the society with which it must merge.

The university, Kerr quotes, is "inside a general social fabric of a given era." He rejects with justified contempt the cloister and ivory tower approach. He points out that American universities are more "intertwined with their surrounding societies" than the European:

> When "the borders of the campus are the boundaries of our state," the lines dividing what is internal from what is external

become quite blurred; taking the campus to the state brings the state to the campus.

But do not think that Kerr is here thinking of (say) CORE picketing the Bank of America, on the ground that if Finance takes its problems to the campus, then the campus will be moved (by inexorable History) to take up certain problems of Finance.

Indeed, Kerr even writes the following in this connection: "Today the campus is being drawn to the city hall and the state capitol as never before." This was true in the Bay area especially in 1960: the campus was drawn to the San Francisco City Hall, and a platoon of police tried to liquidate History by washing them down the steps. But it is not likely that Kerr was thinking of *this* brilliant confirmation of his thesis, for his next sentences are these:

> The politicians need new ideas to meet the new problems; the agencies need expert advice on how to handle the old. The professor can supply both.

He is thinking, of course, of the role of the university in providing intellectual servicemen for the ruling powers—not students but professors, who are not barred from "mounting" *their* interventions into the political and social action of society.

> The campus and society are undergoing a somewhat reluctant and cautious merger, already well advanced. MIT is at least as much related to industry and government as Iowa State ever was to agriculture.

It is a *good* thing to be related to the industrial and grower interests and to the state in the notorious fashion of Iowa State and MIT, and Kerr reiterates and insists on the term "merger":

> The university is being called upon . . . to respond to the expanding claims of national service; to merge its activity with industry as never before; to adapt to and rechannel new intellectual currents.

To become a "truly American university," what are the "new intellectual currents" which we must adapt to? It turns out, at bottom, to involve a large amount of currency, indeed, but less intellectuality. The new current, the "vast transformation," the wave of the future to which the university must adapt is the impact of the new mass of government money (federal grants) pouring out of Washington "beginning with World War II," under the stimulation of the Cold War, the space race, Sputnik, the concurrently stimulated concern with health programs, etc. And: "The multiversity has demonstrated how adaptive it can be to new opportunities for creativity; how responsive to money . . ."

Not just money: Big Money. Kerr has a very useful section, highly recommended for reading, on the essence of this "vast transformation." "The major universities were enlisted in national defense . . . as never before . . . 'the government contract became a new type of federalism.' " He is illuminating on what we should call the *statification* of the university in the Cold War. "Currently, federal support has become a major factor in the total performance of many universities . . ." There has been "a hundred-fold increase in twenty years" in higher education's revenue from government; and the two-thirds of this sum devoted to research projects in or affiliated to universities went to "relatively few" universities, accounting for seventy-five per cent of all university expenditures on research and fifteen per cent of total university budgets.

These are stupendous figures, truly. This is what we get; what do we give away for it? Kerr draws the consequences—which, remember, we must all accept as inevitable:

> The federal agencies will exercise increasingly specific controls and the universities dependent on this new standard of living will accept these controls. The universities themselves will have to exercise more stringent controls by centralizing authority, particularly through the audit process. In a few situations, self restraint has not been enough restraint; as one result, greater external restraint will be imposed in most situations.

Writing these lines took moral courage, for, as is obvious, this is precisely the charge which the Goldwaterites have thrown at federal money in education, against the indignant denial of the liberals. Kerr is saying that it is true and must be accepted, because, he says, the nation and the universities are "stronger" as a result. It is at this point that, to the distinguished audience listening to these lectures at Harvard, he made the following cogent point about the consequences of taking certain kinds of money, in the form of a limerick:

> There was a young lady from Kent
> Who said that she knew what it meant
> When men took her to dine,

Gave her cocktails and wine;
She knew what it meant—but she went.

And he follows with this comment: "I am not so sure that the universities and their presidents always knew what it meant; but one thing is certain—they went."

Now in turn I am not sure whether I can plainly state, in a book intended as reading for the whole family, just what Kerr seems to be calling his fellow presidents; but at least one thing is clear. In all this Kerr himself is *not* striking the pose of the innocent maiden who is in danger of being bowled over by a fast line and losing virtue unawares.

In fact, we had better drop this Kerr line of metaphor altogether, because the image which he does try to project is a different one. It is that of the tough-minded bureaucrat.

Please do not think this term is a cussword or a brickbat; you will be selling Kerr short. He likes it.

Discussing the role of the university president today, as distinct from the old days of the campus autocrat, he writes:

Instead of the not always so agreeable autocracy, there is now the usually benevolent bureaucracy, as in so much of the rest of the world. Instead of the Captain of Erudition or even David Riesman's "staff sergeant," there is the Captain of the Bureaucracy who is sometimes a galley slave on his own ship . . .

And he is gratified that the "multiversity" has emerged from the phase of "intuitive imbalance" into that of "bureaucratic balance." Mainly he is intent on emphasizing that the Coming Men in the new university-factory are *not* the scholars (either humanist or scientist), *not* the teachers, *not* the faculty, but that its "practitioners" are "chiefly the administrators, who now number many of the faculty among them, and the leadership groups in society at large."

Administrators—and "leadership groups in society at large": it may be somewhat clearer now what Kerr means by "merging" the university with "society," i.e., with what part of "society." The multiversity, writes Kerr, is no longer to be thought of as an "organism," as Flexner did:

It is more a mechanism—a series of processes producing a series of results—a mechanism held together by administrative rules and powered by money.

Now another difference between an organism and a mechanism is that a mechanism is always controlled by a superior power outside. This points up the inaccuracy of Kerr's constant use of the term "merger": a mechanism does not "merge" with its controller. The kind of "merger" that Kerr is celebrating is the "merger" of a horse and rider.

He quotes Nevins: the main strain for the growing multiversity is "not in finding the teachers, but expert administrators," and he propounds the theorem that the multiversity president is now "mostly a mediator." This brings us to Kerr's vision of himself, not as an individual but as the multiversity president; and it is a poignant one. Especially if we read it right after the events of the Battle of Berkeley of October 1–2, 1964:

> The mediator, whether in government or industry or labor relations or domestic quarrels, is always subject to some abuse. He wins few clear-cut victories; must aim more at avoiding the worst than seizing the best. He must find satisfaction in being *equally* distasteful to each of his constituencies. . . .

And so should the student constituency be harsh on him if it finds him distasteful in chopping a piece here and there off student rights? After all, they must think of how distasteful he is to some of the Regents who believe it is the will of inexorable History that all dissenters be thrown in the clink immediately; they must think of the abuse he invites when he explains (in effect): *No, we can't do it that way; we have to be liberal*—and proceeds to chip (not chop) off a liberal piece. Isn't it realistic to understand that the difference between the "liberal" bureaucrat and the reactionary is the difference between chip or chop?

Does this make him seem two-faced? Kerr goes one better:

> It is sometimes said that the American multiversity president is a two-faced character. This is not so. . . . He is a many-faced character, in the sense that he must face in many directions at once while contriving to turn his back on no important group.

It will be readily agreed that this is a good trick if you can do it. It might even seem to explain the tricky course of the Berkeley campus administration in the days preceding the October 1 explosion, when it appeared to be adopting a different line every twenty-four hours to explain why student political activity had to be restricted. The deceptively easy conclusion is to equate Kerr's aspiration toward many-facedness with what old-fashioned people called simple hypocrisy. But this is misleading because it finds the locus of the trouble in Kerr, and this is not the point.

The locus is elsewhere. It is in a contradiction which Kerr refuses to face in his writings and perhaps in his head.

We have pointed out that there seemed to be a wide gap between Kerr's published theory about the "merger" of the university and "society," and his moves toward restricting student involvement in political and social action off-campus. On the one hand he tells us we must accept the integration of the university with the state and industry in this Cold War (in fact, with what has been called the military-industrial complex) and must erase the boundary lines; on the other hand, he tries to muzzle and rein student activity on campus which tends to step beyond the boundary line—which, as his administration puts it, "mounts" political and social action off-campus—while at the same time other "constituencies" in the university community are lauded for doing just that.

This contradiction is not due to muddleheadedness. Behind it is a clear consistency, which appears as soon as we make explicit the assumption which permeates Kerr's book.

This is: the use of the university, or the role of the multiversity, is to have a relationship to the present power structure, in this businessman's society of ours, which is similar to that of any other industrial enterprise. There are railroads and steel mills and supermarkets and sausage factories—and there are also the knowledge factories, whose function is to service all the others and the state.

We are here to serve the powers that rule society: this is the meaning of Kerr's reiterations that the university is merging with society. But now, suppose you have "nonconformists" and "extremists" who *also* want to move outside the obsolete boundary line, *but as dissident or radical critics and adversaries, not as intellectual flunkies?*

Obviously, this is not the same thing. The contradiction disappears. It is not "society" that the multiversity must merge with: it is the *"leadership groups in society,"* which, to the mind of the

captain of the bureaucracy, are identical with "society." Kerr
virtually says as much, in a revealing sneer at "nonconformists":

A few of the "nonconformists" have another kind of revolt
[than one against the faculty] in mind. They seek, instead, to
turn the university, on the Latin American or Japanese models,
into a fortress from which they can sally forth with impunity
to make their attacks on society.

A whole thesis on the bureaucratic mind could be derived from
a dissection of this last sentence alone, but here we are interested
only in one facet of the gem. As we know, it is honorific for the
good professors of the University of California's Giannini Foundation and the Division of Agricultural Sciences to sally forth with
their apologias for the growers' bracero program. And similar respectable activities are "mounted" not only with impunity but even
with appropriate raises in salary and perquisites. But when CORE
students sally forth to picket the Bank of America or, perhaps
worse, Knowland's *Oakland Tribune,* this is an attack on—

The Giannini financial empire of the Bank of America? Or
Knowland?

No: they are "attacks on *society.*"

This gives "society" a local habitation and a name. Now non-
Latin-Americans and non-Japanese can understand how repre-
hensible are the students who wish to attack *society!* We can also
understand the worth of Kerr's claim, in his foreword, that he is
not "defending" any view but merely handing down the rules of
history.

There is more to Kerr's theory of "society." It is given in a
passage in which he deprecates the "guild view" of the university
which is held by some faculty members, because it "stands for
self-determination and for resistance against the administration and
the trustees." In opposition to this deplorable resistance view, he
advances (*fasten your seat belts*) nothing less than—

the socialist view, for service to society which the administration and the trustees represent.

"We are all socialists now," said a Tory long ago. "We are
socialists," say the Russian despots now, the Nasser bureaucrats,
the Indian nationalists, and some other demagogues. It is interesting to see these varied characters reach for the word "socialist"
when they need a good-looking label for their wares. But don't buy

it. What Kerr is selling under the label is the old mildewed article: that "society" is represented by the capitalist Establishment, its bureaucrats, agents and braintrusters.

It is true we have been told that the multiversity president must be many-faced, but at this point we must ask whether there isn't a limit. A man who conscientiously tries to face in *this* "many directions at once" faces an occupational hazard: the risk of eventually forgetting where the boundary line is between a soft-soaping mediator and an academic confidence-man. It is only a risk, to be sure, like silicosis for coal miners, but it is well to be forewarned.

The Independent Socialist view is that students must not accept Kerr's vision of the university-factory, run by a captain of the bureaucracy as a parts-supply shop to the profit system and the Cold War complex. We do not think they will.

Behind Kerr's vision of the university-factory is a broad-gauged world-view, a view of a Brave New World (his term) or Orwellian *1984* toward which all this is headed. What we have discussed so far is, according to him, only the "managerial revolution" of society at large as applied to the campus world. There is a larger picture, of which we have examined only one corner.

Kerr described the coming New Order in 1960 in *Industrialism and Industrial Man.**

It is a remarkable work, which failed to get the attention it deserves.

The methodology we have already seen: Kerr is presenting the Wave of the Future, which must be accepted as the imperative of history. It is roughly a variant of Burnhamism, with "bureaucrats" and "managers" interchangable. We have space here for only a summary of its leading ideas. While no element is new, the whole is presented with frankness unusual nowadays:

(1) The New Order will result (is resulting) from the presently ongoing *convergence* of the two dominant systems: a capitalism which is becoming more and more authoritarian and bureaucratic,

* Kerr is the chief author of this work, listed first, with joint authors J. T. Dunlop, Frederick Harbison and C. A. Myers (Harvard University Press). An Oxford paperback edition has appeared this year, with some parts shortened or condensed; a cursory examination indicates that some of the frank passages, but not all, have been left out. This discussion is based on the original work.

along the road *toward* Russian totalitarianism; and a Russian Communist system which has softened up and become somewhat milder; the two merging somewhere in-between into an undifferentiated "Industrialism." The imperative is the force of industrialization; it is the road of progress.

(2) It is refreshing to note that Kerr wastes no space on ritualistic obeisances to democracy. There is no pretense, no lip-service. It simply is not in the picture. The reader must remember that this does not mean Kerr dislikes democracy, any more than Anne Lindbergh approved of fascism, or Von Papen of Hitler. In the shadow of the New Order, you do not approve, you merely have to *accept*.

(3) *Statism:* the leviathan state has taken over; it has expanded everywhere. It is "omnipresent." (There is no mention of TV eyes in the glades, but "Big Brother" is in the book.) The state will never "wither away" as Marx utopianly predicted, Kerr assures us.

(4) *Full-blown bureaucratic (or managerial) élitism:* The progressive and socially decisive elements are only "the managers, private and public," with their technicians and professionals. "Turning Marx on his head, they are the 'vanguard' of the future." Kerr bluntly defines the elements he is addressing: "In particular, we hope to speak to the intellectuals, the managers, the government officials and labor leaders [another species of bureaucrats, to Kerr] who today and tomorrow will run their countries . . ." There is no pretense of a role for "the people" other than as the working cattle who are to be herded by the manager-bureaucrats.

With this theoretical equipment, Kerr comes to the last chapter, "The Road Ahead," in which his perspective of "a new slavery" is sketched: here is a quick run-down:

There is a convergence toward one-party-ism in form or fact. "The age of ideology fades." "Industrial society must be administered . . . The benevolent political bureaucracy and the benevolent economic oligarchy are matched with the tolerant mass." "Parliamentary life may appear increasingly decadent and political parties merely additional bureaucracies . . . Not only all dictatorships but also all democracies are 'guided' [a term for authoritarian]." "The élites become less differentiated . . . all wear grey flannel suits." Professional managers run the economy: "Eco-

nomic enterprise is always basically authoritarian under the necessity
of getting things done . . . Authority must be concentrated . . ."
The managers "will be bureaucratic managers, if private, and managerial bureaucrats, if public." "Class warfare will be forgotten and
in its place will be the bureaucratic contest . . . memos will flow
instead of blood." An individual will identify as "the member of a
guild," not of a class or plant community. The individual will be
neither an independent man nor a human ant, but something between. As a worker, "he will be subjected to great conformity,"
regimented by the productive process, and will accept this "as an
immutable fact. The state, the manager, the occupational association
are all disciplinary agents."

There will be a certain "freedom" in a certain sense (if not
democracy). "Politically he can be given some influence. Society
has achieved consensus and it is perhaps less necessary for Big
Brother to exercise political control. Nor in this brave new world
need genetic and chemical means be employed to avoid revolt.
There will not be any revolt, anyway, except little bureaucratic
revolts that can be handled piecemeal." [Has anyone before actually written down such an orgiastic dream of the Bureaucrat's
Paradise?]

Where will the freedom lie? Maybe, muses Kerr, "in the leisure
of individuals." "Along with the bureaucratic conservatism of economic and political life may well go a new bohemianism in the
other aspects of life and partly as a reaction to the confining nature
of the productive side of society . . . The economic system may
be highly ordered and the political system barren ideologically; but
the social and recreational and cultural aspects of life diverse and
changing . . . The new slavery to technology may bring a new
dedication to diversity and individuality."

Hence his comforting conclusion, offering a glimmer of cheer:
"The new slavery and the new freedom go hand in hand."

In this Kerrian future, the alienation of man is raised to
clinical heights: if this society "can be said to have a split personality, then the individual in this society will lead a split life
too . . ." (Since ideology has faded, the only "ism" will be
schizoidism.)

There is a good deal more, but this sample will have to do.
Now a natural question arises: won't people fight *against* the com-

ing of this monster-bureaucratic state, no matter how cogently it is alleged to be inevitable? Won't there be protest, opposition, struggle—from people who take seriously exhortations to stand up for democracy, given (say) at commencement exercises? What about all the people who are now supposed to be eager to defend the American way of life by sternly sacrificing to pay for H-bombs, polaris missiles, and Livermore research programs?

Will there not be troublemakers who will say: *"Is it for this that we have to sacrifice? Is this why we have to fortify even the moon? Is this why we have to spend more for an Atlas missile than for all cancer research? Is it the right to this future that we are asked to defend by our statesmen, pundits, editors, and (on most occasions) even university presidents?"*

Nonsense, says Kerr. There will be no protest. That's *out*. (Can you now understand the *full* depths of the "disappointment" which he publicly professed to feel on October 2, after so many students ignored this rule of the administrator of history?)

There will be no protest, Kerr wrote. From whom could it come? The intellectuals? Here is how he deals with them:

> The intellectuals (including the university students) are a particularly volatile element . . . capable of extreme reactions to objective situations—more extreme than any group in society. They are by nature irresponsible, in the sense that they have no continuing commitment to any single institution or philosophical outlook and they are not fully answerable for consequences. They are, as a result, never fully trusted by anybody, including themselves.

In all likelihood, dear reader, you did not read this carefully enough. Did you notice that the entire tradition of humanistic and democratic educational philosophy has been contemptuously tossed into the famous garbage can of history? It teaches "irresponsibility"; you cannot trust people brought up that way. . . .

How does the bureaucratic manager or the managerial bureaucrat deal with these untrustworthy irresponsibles? Kerr is concerned about this problem because today we have a war of ideas, and ideas are spun by intellectuals:

> Consequently, it is important who best attracts or captures the intellectuals and who uses [sic] them most effectively, for they may be a tool as well as a source of danger.

There are the alternative roles of the intellectual in the Kerrian world: *tool* or *danger*. It is a notorious dichotomy, celebrated in the literature of totalitarianism. But we need not go abroad to translate it. If we apply the Kerr method of extrapolation, we get this: everybody must be either on the FBI informer rolls or on the subversive list. . . . Remember that you do not have to approve this; you are expected only to accept it.

Will there be protest from the ranks of the workers' movements? No, says Kerr: *vieux jeu*. In the new order, labor is controlled in institutions hierarchically set up. "One of the central traits is the inevitable and eternal separation of industrial men into managers and the managed." Not only inevitable: *eternal!* There are few men since St. Peter who have thrust their vision so far. . . .

But Kerr's confidence in his no-protest prediction derives from undeniable models:

Today men know more about how to control protest, as well as
how to suppress it in its more organized forms—the Soviet
Union has industrialized and China is industrializing without
organized strikes. A controlled labor movement has become
more common.

It is no part of our present task to pause on the scandalous puerility of this view of the history of protest in Russia and China, where literal millions of human beings had to be destroyed in the process of "controlling protest." We wish only to remind that on October 2, 1964, there was an army of almost one thousand police called onto campus—to "control protest" by students—by the man who wrote these lines in cold blood.

Obviously we are, in these few pages, able only to exhibit Kerr's views, not refute them; we do not pretend otherwise. Many of the elements therein are rife in academic élitist circles in more or less attenuated form, more or less "underground," or else formulated in "minced" and allusive terms, instead of with Kerr's candor, which is the main contribution of his work.

But Kerr's candor is partly due to the device which we have already mentioned several times, and to which we must now return in a different way. This is his posture as the detached, uninvolved historian of the future, registering his vision of eternity, and as far above approval-or-disapproval as the recording angel.

This posture is an intellectual imposture.

There is an extraordinarily serious question here of intellectual responsibility. *By adding a single sentence, Kerr's book would become the work of a proto-fascist ideologue.* But, of course, this he is not; he is a sort of liberal; he really does *not* approve, and so the single sentence is not there.

Yet he is not detached and uninvolved. There is another basis for judgment than approval-or-disapproval.

By 1932 the pressure of (what we now know to be) the impending assumption of power by Hitler in Germany was enormous. The Nazis and their conscious tools were, as is well known, yelling at full cry that their victory was in the cards, that heads would roll, and that all realistic people must jump on their bandwagon. What now should we think of a professor, *not* a Nazi tool, who at this juncture announced that, in his utterly scientific opinion, the triumph of the Nazis was indeed written in the scrolls of history and must be accepted (not approved)?

This is itself a political act. It is also, of course, a self-fulfilling prophecy. It is a blow struck to bring the event predicted. But is it not also a scientific opinion? No, it is not, because there is no historical "science" so reliable as to make an opinion on this subject more than an estimate of probability and tendency. We have a right to make a value-judgment on political acts, even when they result from self-delusion (like most evil political acts, including those of the Nazis). There is no academic right to grease the road to fascism in the name of "scientific" detachment.

Whenever the juggernaut of power starts rolling, there always are, and always will be, the servitors and retainers who will run before, crying: *It cometh! Bow down, bow down, before the God!* The men who perform this function have done more than made a choice of what to believe; they also have made a choice on how to act. We have the right to make a moral, as well as a social, judgment of the *act,* even apart from the accuracy of the announcement.

But there is a bit more involved in Kerr's book.

We present our views, says the introduction, to aid understanding of this moment in history—

and possibly, as an assistance to some of those who would guide
this moment to its next stage . . .

With this statement the author strikes a different note. It is not
detached and uninvolved; he is seeking to *assist* the transformation
toward the new slavery. Is it because he really does approve after
all? No. Is it because he is simply in the intellectual habit of
servicing whatever is in the works anyway, because he has no
other mode of being than that of the bureaucratic assistant of whatever power is rolling? It may be a slip, but only in the sense that
underneath the cap and gown peers out the retainer's livery.

There is another passage that gives pause. It is not merely the
repeated statements, in the introduction, that he has changed his
former views: "We unlearned many things . . ." "We changed
our program . . ." "Many of our original convictions turned into
nothing but once-held prejudices." The last remark is followed by
this meditation on the critical question of state control of labor:

> "Free trade unions" under some conditions become no more
> than Communist unions sabotaging efforts at economic develop-
> ment. Should they be that free? Completely free trade unions
> are sometimes not possible or desirable at certain stages in the
> industrialization drives. . . . The "free worker," in our sense,
> cannot exist in some social systems; in others he might exist, but
> to his detriment. . . . The "heavy hand of the state" over
> trade unions and enterprises may be the only substitute, at
> times, for the "invisible hand" of market competition which
> we have so long preferred. And some generals, in some situa-
> tions, may be by far the best leaders of an industrializing na-
> tion, all doctrine of civilian control of the military to the
> contrary.

Kerr is speaking here of changed views, not new cables from
the future on recent changes in the nature of eternity. His changed
views concern, in a word, *democracy*. He continues:

> Thus we came to be much more conscious of the significance
> of time and place in the evaluation of some judgments, and of
> all slogans. [Slogans like democracy?] The whole world cannot
> be like the United States or the Soviet Union, or India, and
> one should not be morally indignant about it.

But may one be politically indignant about despotism at any
time and place? or just indignant? Is this advice offered only to

well-fed political scientists, or is it also relevant to the human beings who are starving and suffering under the despotisms which are declared inevitable? Or let us try this one on the platitude-machine: Since not everybody can be like Clark Kerr, why should Clark Kerr get morally indignant at the rebellious students who did not behave according to his lights?

Now, perhaps this injunction against moral (or other) indignation at despotism and authoritarianism is also to be regarded as a detached and uninvolved report on eternal verities. We do not think so. The issuance of this injunction against moral indignation is itself a moral choice on Kerr's part. The compleat bureaucrat does not approve of moral indignation or of political protest and struggle, not because he is cruel and unfeeling, but simply because these phenomena do not file neatly; they cannot be efficiently punched onto IBM cards; they upset routine; they raise non-regulation questions; they cannot be budgeted for in advance; they are refractory to manipulation.

The compleat bureaucrat does not believe that protest and struggle really exist even when they explode under his nose: since all this has been ruled out by the historical imperative, he ascribes it to a "Maoist-Castroite" plot. He tries to meet it first by facing in many directions at once, and then, when this gyration naturally lands him on his face, by blowing the whistle for the cops.

Clark Kerr believes that the student's relationship to the Administration bureaucracy can be only that of a tool or a danger. This is also a self-fulfilling prophecy. A university president's very belief of this sort tends to *force* students into one or the other camp.

It is easy enough to become a tool. There are all kinds of tools, and they can come without head, teeth, or point. On the other hand, there is danger in becoming a danger. Which will it be?

Everyone must choose, and it is a matter of life or death: life as an independent human being, or death as a man.

A. H. RASKIN

The Berkeley Affair:
Mr. Kerr vs. Mr. Savio & Co.*

What turned the University of California's world-renowned campus
into a snake pit of unrepressed animosities? As my helicopter rat-
tled across the moon-dappled water of San Francisco Bay on its
way toward this strangely riven academic center, it seemed to me
two men were probably best equipped to supply the answer. In the
process, they could go far toward explaining a simmering unrest
on other campuses across the nation, and in every corner of our
corporate society.

One man was Dr. Clark Kerr, fifty-three, the quiet-spoken
Quaker whose duties as president of the University make him Big
Daddy to 72,000 students on nine California campuses. The other
was Mario Savio, the charismatic twenty-two-year-old undergraduate who had emerged as the archangel of student revolt at Berkeley.

My effort to get the answer from Savio got off to a rocky start.
We had arranged to meet at the headquarters of the Graduate
Coordinating Committee. This is a key unit in the Free Speech
Movement (FSM), the coalition of undergraduates, graduate students and teaching assistants that grew out of an ill-timed, worse-
explained and now-rescinded administration order that barred all
on-campus solicitation for political or civil-rights demonstrations
mounted off the campus.

The committee office is a garret over the university's drama
workshop, not far from the main gate to the huge, hillside campus.
The visitor climbs a flight of wooden outside stairs and finds him-

* From *The New York Times Magazine,* February 14, 1965.

self in a barren room that is dark despite the dazzling sunlight out-side. The nearest thing to a real piece of furniture is a battered green sofa, with sags where the springs should be. A square table with a telephone fills one corner, and there are a half-dozen camp chairs. Under the table is a mound of picket signs. The mood is *Waiting for Lefty* done off-Broadway.

Savio, a slim six-footer with frizzy pale hair, peeled off the short, fleece-lined coat that has become a sort of personal trade-mark. His first words were a flat refusal to participate in any inter-view if I intended to focus on him as *the* communicator for the FSM. "Anything like that will just perpetuate a misrepresentation that the press has already done too much to build up," he said. "This is not a cult of one personality or of two personalities; it is a broadly based movement and I will not say anything unless it is made clear that the FSM is not any single individual."

A way around that roadblock was ready at hand—a joint dis-cussion with the six other members of the collective leadership who had accompanied Savio to the conference. It started with everybody sounding off against Sidney Hook's view in *The New York Times Magazine* that academic freedom was primarily for teachers and that the only imperative right for students was freedom to learn. Savio said they wanted equal space to reply; also they wanted to sue. I told them to go ahead if they thought they had a case. Finally, we got to what I wanted to talk about—namely, what they thought the issue at Berkeley had been and whether there was still any real issue left.

It was a somewhat formless encounter, a blend of a graduate seminar in political science and *Catch-22*. People wandered out and others filled their chairs; getting in questions was harder than get-ting back answers. Yet, it was an engaging group—lucid in exposi-tion, quick in rebuttal, manifesting no unease at differences of interpretation or emphasis within their own circle.

The Berkeley mutineers did not seem political in the sense of those student rebels in the turbulent thirties; they are too suspicious of all adult institutions to embrace wholeheartedly even those ide-ologies with a stake in smashing the system. An anarchist or I.W.W. strain seems as pronounced as any Marxist doctrine. "Theirs is a sort of political existentialism," says Paul Jacobs, a research asso-ciate at the University's Center for the Study of Law and Society, who is one of the FSM's applauders. "All the old labels are out; if there were any orthodox Communists here, they would be a moderating influence."

The proudly immoderate zealots of the FSM pursue an activist creed—that only commitment can strip life of its emptiness, its absence of meaning in a great "knowledge factory" like Berkeley. That is the explanation for their conviction that the methods of civil disobedience, in violation of law, are as appropriate in the civilized atmosphere of the campus as they are in the primordial jungle of Mississippi. It was an imaginative strategy that led to an unimaginable chain of events.

Trouble began on September 14, a week before the opening of classes, when the dean of students suddenly shut off the only area on campus where students had been free to collect funds and enlist adherents for off-campus political or social action. This island for activists was a twenty-six-by-sixty-foot patch of bricked-over ground, called the Bancroft Strip, just outside the principal pedestrian entrance.

The decision to embargo the Strip, made in the climactic days of an election campaign that would settle both the Presidency and the fate of California's controversial fair housing law, forged a united front of protest extending from campus Goldwaterites to Maoist members of the Progressive Labor party.

With the memory of the mutiny thick in the gloomy garret, the collective leadership of the FSM spent the next three hours telling me what they thought the rebellion was *really* about.

They are convinced that the abrupt decision to close the Bancroft Strip represented a University capitulation to right-wing forces angered by student picketing and sit-ins to compel the hiring of more Negroes in Bay area businesses. Specifically, they blame former Senator William F. Knowland, editor of *The Oakland Tribune,* whose paper was a special target. (Knowland says he didn't do it.)

The cutoff in political recruitment confirmed a conviction already held by some of the students that bankers, industrialists, publishers and other leaders of the establishment in the board of regents were making a concentration camp out of the "multiversity" —a term coined by Kerr in a series of lectures at Harvard nearly two years ago to describe the transformation of a modern university, like Cal, into a vast techno-educational complex.

This conviction was not diminished by the extreme freedom the university has long allowed students to express their own political views, however unorthodox, at "Hyde Park" areas inside the campus. Even during the ban on the use of campus property for organizing off-campus political action, students retained their liberty to invite Communists, Nazis or Black Muslims to address meetings at the university. They also could—and often did—agitate for the right to smoke marijuana, to be able to buy contraceptives at the University Bookstore or for other far-out objectives.

All this has been going on for years in an atmosphere particularly congenial to the flowering of undergraduate rebellion. The whole Bay area has a long Left Bank tradition of hospitality to radical movements and off-beat behavior. Czeslav Milosz, a Polish poet and defector, who served on the faculty, left convinced that Berkeley and Greenwich Village were "the only two places in America you can be free." The mild year-round climate also helps. "There is no place in the world where uncomfortable people can feel so comfortable," said a visiting British professor.

Taken aback by the vehement student reaction to the recruitment taboo, the regents in November restored the right to mount political action—not only in the Bancroft Strip but in several areas where it had never been allowed before. However, the FSM is still unhappy because the new ruling specifies that only "lawful" off-campus activities can be planned on campus.

The rebels argue that students should have the same right as other citizens to participate in the political and social affairs of the outside community. What is "unlawful" ought to be determined solely by civil and criminal courts, not by a university administration or faculty. The university's only area of proper regulation over political activity should be the establishment of minimal time-place-manner rules to guarantee that anything the students do on campus does not interfere with classes or the orderly conduct of university business. Such is the current focus of what is left of the "free speech" issue.

Remembering centuries of "town vs. gown" controversies all over the world, in which universities had always fought to keep their campuses from coming under police rule, I asked the FSM leaders whether their insistence on leaving disciplinary authority to the municipal law-enforcement agencies might not destroy the whole concept of academic sanctuary and expose them to much harsher treatment.

.Savio, a philosophy major who graduated at the top of his class from New York City's Martin Van Buren High School, had a blunt answer: "That is a specious argument. The campus is already crawling with cops of the most insidious kind from the 'red squad' and every other kind of undercover agency." Myra Jehlen, a comely, solemn Phi Beta Kappa from CCNY and a Woodrow Wilson graduate scholar in English, added a postscript: "Immunity from police prosecution only applies to panty raids and fraternity guys. We're not interested in that."

She was the only coed in the group. Across the room was her husband, Carl Riskin, who had gone to Cambridge in England on a fellowship after graduating *magna cum laude* from Harvard and was now completing his Ph.D. thesis at Berkeley. He spoke seldom, but with force and precision.

Next to him sat Martin Roysher, a sophomore from Arcadia, Calif., whose casually correct clothes reflected the freshman year he spent at Princeton. He looked so young it was hard to believe he was out of high school, yet he, too, spoke crisply about everything from alienation to the importance of erasing any differentiation between the freedom of students and citizens to act upon their political beliefs.

Here, too, was Jack Weinberg, a former graduate student in math and now a civil-rights activist in CORE, who gained fame overnight as "the man in the police car" in the first of the mass upheavals last October 1. Stephan Weissman, the red-bearded chairman of the Graduate Coordinating Committee, pulled a few picket signs from under the table and squatted on the floor. Robert Starobin, a Cornell B.A., who has been a teaching assistant in history at Berkeley for three years, is writing his Ph.D. dissertation on industrial slavery before the Civil War. Stocky and assertive, his talk bristled with complaints about the "power structure" and its determination to stifle civil-rights activity at Berkeley.

The one whose views evoked least challenge was the youth group's senior citizen, Hal Draper, a part-time librarian at the University who graduated from Brooklyn College in the Great Depression and is now fiftyish. A leader of the old American Student Union, he drifted through various wings of the Trotskyite movement and is currently an editor of *New Politics,* a journal intended to offer an outlet for all shades of socialist thought. A Draper pamphlet called "The Mind of Clark Kerr" has become the FSM's bible in its fight against "the university factory." Dedicated to the students who immobilized the police car, the leaflet depicts Kerr as the preacher of docile submission to a technocratic juggernaut that will stamp out all individuality and all liberty.

The longer my conversation with the students went on, the clearer it became that the political battle was only a symptom of a larger revolt against the bigness and impersonality of the "multiversity" itself. If Clark Kerr is the high priest of the multiversity, social critic Paul Goodman is its Antichrist and thus beloved of the FSM. The opening theme of an FSM pamphlet is a declaration by Goodman that in the United States today, "students—middle-class youth—are the major exploited class. . . . They have no choice but to go to college." Rejecting their role as factory workers on an academic assembly line, the FSM demands a humanized campus, a "loving community" based on comradeship and purpose.

"We must now begin the demand of the right to know; to know the realities of the present world-in-revolution, and to have an opportunity to think clearly in an extended manner about the world," says the FSM credo. "It is ours to demand meaning; we must insist upon meaning!"

What is behind this manifestese? Does it betoken a desire to dismantle the University of California, or to establish a student soviet that would make all educational policy? The FSM leaders disclaim such grandiose ideas.

"This is not a matter of rolling back the multiversity," says Myra Jehlen. "But it is our view that this university does neglect its students. We have no contact with the community of scholars, except to see a professor across 500 feet of lecture hall. Teaching assistants have to serve as parents for the students."

Savio deplores the extent to which the University's professors and facilities are involved in research for the government and giant corporations. "It is a distortion, and too bad, that the university does not stand apart from the society as it is. It would be good to return to an almost totally autonomous body of scholars and students. But what we have now is that the Pentagon, the oil and aircraft companies, the farm interests and their representatives in the regents consider the university as a public utility, one of the resources they can look on as part of their business."

And who should run things? Says Starobin: "Our idea is that the university is composed of faculty, students, books and ideas. In a literal sense, the administration is merely there to make sure the sidewalks are kept clean. It should be the servant of the faculty and the students. We want a redemocratizing of the university. Courses are clearly up to the faculty, but students should be able to convey their ideas. Dormitory regulations should be up to the students who live in the dorms. A bipartite or tripartite committee should have the final say in promulgating minimal rules on the time, place and manner of political activity."

There was much, much more before I asked whether they felt that the turmoil had accomplished anything. Myra Jehlen answered first: "Of course, you never win finally. New problems will always arise. But there has been a great strengthening of democratic institutions on the campus. The kind of actions we've taken, the important function of students in society—these have been vindicated. Yes, we have won, though how much is not clear."

Savio was more succinct: "We committed the unpardonable sin of being moral and being successful."

The setting was very different that evening when I visited Kerr at his home in El Cerrito, five miles from the campus. It is a glass-walled ranch house on a lofty bluff overlooking the Bay. Velvety lawns roll down to an old quarry in the canyon far below. There is a swimming pool, and flowers, shrubs and vines grow in jungle-like profusion in a great glass-roofed patio.

But Kerr is not a man for rich living, even though his salary of $45,000 a year puts him $900 ahead of Governor Edmund Brown as the state's highest-paid official. He is frugal even of time. If Kerr gets to an airport and discovers the plane will be fifteen minutes late, he is furious at the lost time. But if it will be an hour late, he is contented; he will sit quietly in a corner of the airport, begin writing memos, speeches, articles or even a chapter for a book.

Kerr works with the same intensity at home. Each afternoon a squad of eight secretaries at his office in University Hall pack a great sheaf of papers into a cardboard box. A driver returns them before noon the next day. Each carries a notation in green ink written in an incredibly pinched, yet distinct, hand—the marching orders by which the biggest of big universities is run.

The commander's invariable uniform is a navy blue suit and white shirt. His mind has extraordinary range and a rare capacity for turning discord into consensus. Kerr ranks among the country's half-dozen most effective peacemakers in the volatile realm of labor-management warfare—a skill that has prompted every President since Harry S. Truman to enlist his help. In the middle of the disturbances at Berkeley, President Johnson asked him to accept appointment as Secretary of Health, Education and Welfare. All Kerr will say about that or any other post is that he still expects to be president of Cal on its centenary in 1968.

Among the many ironies of the Berkeley explosions is that Kerr now finds himself under savage attack from the left after more than a decade of demands for his ouster by right-wing critics. Leading the fight against a loyalty oath, he became so popular with the rest of the Berkeley faculty that in 1952, when the regents decided to restore the goodwill they had lost in two bitter years, they named Kerr as chancellor. In 1959, a year after the regents moved him up to president, Kerr again aroused right-wing ire by granting an honorary degree to Professor Edward C. Tolman, who had been forced to resign for refusing to sign the oath. A year later he induced the Regents to name a new building in Tolman's honor.

When Berkeley students were arrested in 1960 for disrupting a hearing of the House Un-American Activities Committee in San Francisco, Kerr resisted demands to suspend or expel the demonstrators. He ignored similar conservative outcries last summer when undergraduates were arrested for a civil-rights sit-in at the Sheraton-Palace Hotel.

The liberalization of faculty and student rights during the Kerr administration earned for him and the Regents the American Association of University Professors' 1964 Alexander Meiklejohn award for conspicuous contributions to academic freedom. Less than six months later he was being denounced as an enemy of free expression by many on his own campus.

Kerr was not consulted on the fateful order shutting the Bancroft Strip. He was in Tokyo on his way home from a seven-week economic mission to the Iron Curtain countries on the day it was issued.

"It was perfectly apparent," Kerr says, "that the decision was a mistake, both in the action itself and in the way it was done. There was no advance consultation with the students, the over-all University administration or anyone else. When a privilege had been extended as long as that had been, there should have been consultation—and especially against the background of an impending national election and intense student involvement in civil rights."

(A Dostoevskian bit of background, still unknown to the students: Kerr foresaw in September, 1959, that the Strip would eventually be a source of trouble because there was no logical basis for exempting it from the no-politics rule that applied everywhere else on campus. He got the regents to agree that it ought to be turned over to the ciy for use as a public plaza. But, for reasons still unexplained, the University's treasurer never carried out the instructions to deed over the Strip. If he had, the whole melancholy chain of events might never have begun.)

Kerr agrees with the FSM thesis that students should have as much political freedom as anyone else in the community. The only difference is that he thinks they already have it. In his judgment, the rules governing political expression on campus, including the right to invite heretics of all political persuasions to speak at student meetings, give Berkeley undergraduates more freedom than bank clerks, factory workers or ninety-nine per cent of the general citizenry.

He ridicules the notion that the University has been succumbing to the "power structure" in the dispute over civil-rights activity. "I had to fight some extremely tough battles against some very powerful legislators who felt we should kick out students who were arrested for sit-ins in the Bay area, but we never yielded an inch," Kerr says. "It just would not have been in character for us to say that the only place the students could fight for Negro rights was in Mississippi."

As for the Bancroft Strip, Kerr says that "whatever pressure preceded the order involved the loading of the galleries at the Republican convention with Berkeley students whooping it up for Scranton against Goldwater."

The FSM indictment of the "multiversity" brings a special

twinge to Kerr because every charge the insurgents now raise he foresaw with greater incisiveness as long ago as April 1963, when he gave the Godkin lectures at Harvard.

Those talks described, with apparent fatalism but decided unenthusiasm, the evolution of a "mechanism held together by administrative rules and powered by money." Kerr predicted that undergraduates would feel so neglected and depersonalized that the revolt they once engaged in against the faculty *in loco parentis* would turn into an even more destructive uprising against the faculty *in absentia*. Everything Kerr warned of then is embodied now in the FSM lament that the student is being downgraded to the status of an IBM punch card in a computerized multiversity.

Kerr concedes that the multiversity is a disturbing place for many students, but he disputes that it is devoid of meaning. "One of the advantages of a big city or a big university—as against a smaller and more monolithic closed community—is that people can find those things which may mean something to them," he says. "They are given a choice.

"It would be terribly stultifying to find yourself in a place which has a single meaning, and that meaning is the same for everyone. The only kind of society that has only a single meaning is an authoritarian one. It seems to me that is a place where you would really expect rebellion. Essentially, what the FSM are saying is that they are rebelling against freedom of choice."

When I noted that the students objected not to too many meanings, but to the absence of any, Kerr replied:

"In fact, there is a lot of opportunity to participate, only it takes a little longer and requires more initiative to find it. Many tend to be overwhelmed by their opportunities; there are so many lectures to choose from, so many things to do, that they tend to become lost. They are torn too many ways and wind up condemning the whole structure."

The notion that the university, for all the magnitude of its federal and industrial involvement (it is receiving $246 million this year for operating three giant atomic installations, plus $175 million in research grants and contracts), has become an arm of the Pentagon or big business also draws a rebuttal from Kerr. "The university," he says, "is intertwined with all society. And if it is overbalanced in any direction as compared with the surrounding

society, it is in the fact that it is a source of dissent and social criticism. You could say it is a tool of the critics, and that is one of
the things that makes it so dynamic."

All this brought us back to the students' overriding complaint
—the enormous size of Berkeley, with 27,500 students on a single
campus, and the obliteration of the individual's relationship to faculty and administration. Kerr's answer dwelt more on society's
inescapable needs than confidence that alienation could be overcome.

"Every day makes it clearer that the university's invisible product, knowledge, is likely to be the most powerful single element in
our culture," he says. "With so many young people pounding at our
gates, we're up against a tremendous assignment. To take the position that we won't grow would be a terribly irresponsible thing."

Kerr is a philosopher-pragmatist of the technocratic society,
probably the ablest and most creative in the educational field. His
guiding principle is individual disengagement. He preaches the idea
that each person can best protect his own happiness in a society of
bigness by developing pluralistic attachments. "If you invest all of
yourself in an institution," he says, "you become a slave. It becomes
a prison, not an agency of liberation." This road to the independent
spirit is just the opposite of that traveled by the FSM and its
leaders. Their goal is commitment, but there is a good deal of
confusion about precisely what it is they are committed to.

And who is listening, now that the clear-cut issue created by the
closing of the Bancroft Strip and the blackout of political recruiting
has been resolved? The signs are that the overwhelming support for
FSM aims among students of all political hues and of no hues has
evaporated along with the issue.

Moreover, there are strong indications of strain inside the FSM
steering committee, now a much more ingrown group than in the
initial days of across-the-board coalition. Many would like to disband the movement. Hal Draper said frankly that it might go into
"an inactive phase." Ed Rosenfeld, the FSM's press officer, says
that one thought under consideration is to establish a cooperative
coffee house, on a nonprofit basis, near the campus. "It would be
a civilized gathering place in the best European manner," he savs,
"a suitable forum for debates and discussion."

Back at the heliport for the return flight, I tried to evaluate the

Berkeley uprising against the memories of my own days of rebellion as president of the CCNY class of '31. It was a time when one worker in four was jobless and the misery of the Great Depression was beginning to grip the land. We had been ready to picket our own commencement in cap and gown, but we chickened out at the last minute for fear of losing our degrees.

These students, for all their talk of setting up an espresso joint as a monument to their mutiny, were a tougher, smarter breed, more ready to go for broke.

But what did they accomplish, besides effecting the cancellation of an order the University admits never should have been issued?

They have done one important thing that may prove of considerable help to Berkeley and all other big universities. They have cut through the multifarious concerns of an administration that must deal with every agency of government, including those in fifty countries abroad, and forced it to recognize that it is sitting on a volcano of neglected, seething students.

Kerr, who has always recognized the need for diversity in multiversity, already is hard at work on measures to improve the quality and the immediacy of instruction. He aims to break down the idea that research, not teaching, is the mission of the good professor. Both roles are vital, Kerr believes, and so does the man he has brought in as acting chancellor, Dean Martin Meyerson of the College of Environmental Design.

Last fall's earthquake also has shaken the administration and faculty into a heightened awareness of the need for teamwork ·to lessen the students' belief that no one cares whether they go or stay, that undergraduate needs are passed over in favor of lucrative research contracts, book-writing projects and traveling lectureships all over the world. Professor Arthur M. Ross, the enterprising chairman of an emergency executive committee elected by the faculty in the blackest period last December, expresses confidence that a genuine educational overhaul is in prospect. Most of his colleagues agree.

What goes into the curriculum and who teaches what courses will be a matter for the faculty to determine, but both Kerr and Ross feel students can have a useful advisory role. A larger area of authority for students in disciplinary committees and in other forms of self-government also is in prospect. All these developments should help still the discord at Berkeley, but—much more important—they will help make it a better institution of learning.

One of the imponderables in trying to guess whether peace has really come to the campus is that some FSM activists obviously have developed a vested interest in finding things to fight about. They seem to operate on the theory that, in a system they believe is basically corrupt, the worse things get, the easier it will be to generate mass resistance.

This is not a novel theory in radical movements, but it is not one that makes for stability. When the police dragged Savio and the 800 others out of Sproul Hall, he exulted, "This is wonderful —wonderful. We'll bring the University to our terms." When Paul Jacobs told an FSM leader that he had advised Kerr to enter Sproul on the night of the sit-in and talk to the students (advice Kerr did not take), the insurgent asked sourly, "What side are you on?"

The reckless prodigality with which the FSM uses the weapon of civil disobedience raises problems no university can deal with adequately. Mass discipline carries the danger of martyrdom and a spread of sympathetic disorders to other campuses.

Garrisoning the grounds with police runs so counter to the essential concept of the university as a redoubt of tolerance and reason that it is perhaps the worst solution of all. At Berkeley it brought the faculty into open alliance with the students against the administration. Yet, the alternative of giving students total immunity could engender a situation akin to that in the University of Caracas, where student revolutionaries use the campus as a fortress from which to sally forth to attack the general society.

"We fumbled, we floundered, and the worst thing is I still don't know how we should have handled it," Kerr acknowledges. "At any other university the administrators wouldn't have known how to handle it any better."

Menacing as is this new disruptive device, one even graver danger sign outranks all others raised by the mess at Berkeley. That is the degree to which it evidences a sense of lost identity, a revulsion against bigness, that is affecting all of our society. On the campus it takes the form of antagonism against the multiversity. In the mass production unions this same feeling of impending obliteration recently spurred rank-and-file strikes against General Motors and Ford, and may erupt again in the basic steel industry this spring. The longshoremen, fearing the shiny face of automation, voted down contracts that gave them lifetime job security and a generous wage guarantee—principally because they felt the machine was grinding them and their jobs into nothingness.

A similar mood of irrationality, of vaporous but paralyzing apprehension, stalks all our institutions in a time of unmatched material prosperity and individual well-being. Young people, in particular, study the unemployment statistics and decide that society is in a conspiracy to provide security for the older generation at the expense of the youngsters outside waiting to get in. Education is the magic carpet over the hurdles that make the dropout the shut-out in our society. But, even at this most distinguished of universities, bigness robs many students of individual dignity or purpose. This feeling helps explain the spread of drug addiction and senseless crime among many well-to-do youngsters. All are part of an alienation that turns even affluence and security into worthless prizes.

This may prove to be the nation's critical challenge, potentially more damaging than the international crises that monopolize so much of our concern and our budget. If Berkeley cannot imbue life with a sense of fulfillment and content, where will we find it? Kerr, the mediator-innovator, must become a gladiator—pioneering new paths in intergroup relations and giving new vitality to democratic standards that rest on knowledge.

JOHN SEARLE

The Faculty Resolution

On December 8, the Academic Senate passed by a vote of 824–115 a resolution dealing with the Free Speech controversy and thus brought a solution to the crisis at Berkeley. The resolution had four substantial provisions: (1) that the University should not place any restrictions on the content of speech or advocacy; (2) that the rules concerning political activity on campus should regulate only the questions of time, place, and manner; (3) that the faculty should have the responsibility for discipline of violations of political rules; (4) that the University would not take punitive measures against students for previous actions in the Free Speech controversy. To anyone with even a modest commitment to the ideal of the university as an institution dedicated to free speech, such a motion must seem pretty harmless stuff. Certainly at the universities where I was educated—Wisconsin and Oxford—its underlying principles were taken for granted. Yet on our campus it was no less than a revolution. Its passage brought to an end a series of protests—demonstrations, sit-ins, and a strike—that had wracked the campus throughout the autumn and by December 3 had brought the normal university activities to a halt. Its passage has been represented in much of the press and by its opponents within the campus as a faculty revolt, a capitulation to the students, and even as an invitation to disaster. I want now to explain something of how those 824 professors came together in that room and voted the way they did. For make no mistake about it, they—and not the students nor the administration nor the regents solved the crisis and brought the present atmosphere of normal peace and freedom to the Berkeley campus.

I shall assume the reader is familiar with the bare chronology of events and shall try to convey something of the flavor and moral character of those extraordinary days, at least as they appeared to many faculty members. The theme of my remarks will be very simple. As events progressed it became more and more obvious that as far as the Free Speech issues were concerned, the students were right and the administration was wrong. Lots of qualifications need to be added to that statement—about the illegal actions taken by the students, the progressive decline of the administration's moral authority, and the frequent state of total confusion in most people's minds about what exactly was going on. But in the end the students succeeded in arousing the conscience of the faculty to an awareness of the fact that the university was restricting their political freedoms, and that the only decent and effective solution to the crisis lay in granting those freedoms. It is important to realize at the outset that the 824 professors were not converted to the cause of civil liberties on December 8. They believed in civil liberties all along, as is indicated by the passage of a senate resolution in the early days favoring maximum political freedom. Rather, they became converted to the view that the situation on the campus required them to do something about their convictions.

I. The Background and the Beginning. Although there have been some important liberalizations of late, the University of California has had a long tradition of political restrictions. The famous loyalty oath is its most spectacular efflorescence, but the more humdrum workaday civil liberties incident has set the campus atmosphere in recent years. An assistant professor is fired on political grounds over the protests of the Academic Senate Committees, a student gets a punitive F in ROTC for picketing while in uniform, a student group is refused permission to show a controversial film ("inconsistent with the educational objectives of the University"), a faculty group is reprimanded for asking an exam question not suitably respectful of the FBI, a speech by an assistant professor critical of the film *Operation Abolition* is canceled by the administration at the last minute, a Black Muslim leader is refused permission to speak on the campus. And so on.

Such events, even when infrequent, set an atmosphere and a tone to a campus. Another part of the atmosphere, more important to the students, was created by the famous rules concerning political activity. To a person of traditional American political convictions, reading our old political rules is embarrassing to the point of discomfort. While on the campus students and faculty are forbidden to advocate, organize, or plan any "off-campus" activity; they cannot collect money or recruit members, they cannot even urge people to vote for political candidates or ballot propositions. Students cannot chair a meeting with off-campus speakers, they have to get a faculty chairman (and he has to have tenure—I especially like that touch). Clearance has to be obtained from the police department and policemen may have to be present, paid for by the students. (One student group was told their meeting would require three policemen, at fifteen dollars an officer, and of course the rules forbid them to collect money, hence no meeting.) And finally there was the catchall provision—the chancellor may cancel any meeting he "deems to be inconsistent with the educational objective of the University."

All of this set the stage for the events of last semester and it is well to bear these things in mind when one reads statements by the opponents of the 824 that "there was no Free Speech issue" or that there has always been free speech on the campus. Now that the crisis is over the administration has admitted that the old rules were of doubtful constitutionality. These rules provided the battleground for a semester-long war between the students and the administration. The war began, like many wars, over a boundary dispute. An escape hatch from our rules existed at an entrance to the campus at the corner of Bancroft Way and Telegraph Avenue on a strip of land some twenty-seven feet wide; there student organizations could set up their card tables, and collect money for this or that cause, sell bumper strips, distribute leaflets, etc. In the official mythology of that now distant era the land did not belong to the University but to the city of Berkeley and so a citizen could there exercise at least certain of his rights. On the 14th of September the chancellor officially put an end to this narrow libertarian island by announcing that the land belonged to the University and that henceforth the University's "historic policies" would be enforced there as elsewhere. It is generally believed, but hard to prove, that this decision came after pressure by ex-Senator Knowland's right wing newspaper in Oakland. The official reason given at the time was that the tables created a traffic problem. This statement was obviously false, and its falsehood set the tone of much that was to come from the administration, and served only to increase the exasperation of the students. Another falsehood immediately followed to the effect that collecting money on campus for partisan political activity was against state law.

The students ignored the new ban and set up tables at the old stands. A dean took the names of five of them and ordered them to report to the dean of students office. Some 400 appeared in the corridor outside the office asking to be held responsible for the same offense, but ignoring the 400 the administration suspended the five along with three others believed to be leaders. All were given an "indefinite suspension"—a punishment that does not appear in the list of possible University disciplinary measures. The students called a demontration for the next day.

The character of the struggle to come was already foreshadowed in those very early days. The strategy of the administration was to sit tight on its "non-negotiable" rules and to try to make an example of the student leaders by suspending them from the University. The strategy of the student movement was the classical civil rights strategy: by massive civil disobedience to make enforcement of the rules impossible and to arouse the conscience of the public, in this case the faculty, to the merits of their cause. Already the administration was drawing heavily on its moral credit and already the rank and file of the students were moving toward the most militant and intransigent of their leaders as their only hope of victory.

II. October 2–November 20. The attention of most faculty members was first focused on the controversy at the time of the police car incident of October 1–2. Indeed it was because of the efforts of a group of faculty members, together with a phone call from Governor Brown to President Kerr, that the authorities agreed to negotiate matters they had previously declared non-negotiable. After the agreement most faculty members adopted a wait-and-see attitude. There were of course faculty members involved in the negotiating committee set up by that agreement, and some of us were active as individuals. The senate passed two rather vaguely worded resolutions, one favoring maximum political freedom and another stating that force and violence had no place on the campus.

And after the failure of the official negotiations several informal groups were formed attempting to produce a solution. One of these, composed mostly of members of the department of history, produced a compromise agreement. It involved only such University restrictions on free speech as were constitutionally allowable, and it provided for due process and the possibility of University co-operation in test cases before the courts. The FSM leaders informally agreed to this and there were many informal talks about it with the administration. In the end the administration did not accept it. This incident deserves to be better known, for it demonstrated that the FSM leaders were willing to compromise, at least in mid-November.

Changes in faculty opinion in this period can be described as a growing awareness of and agreement with the students' civil libertarian objectives, hostility to many of the tactics employed to achieve those objectives, and slowly accumulating irritation with the administration.

This irritation was in part due to the simple failure of the administration to solve the crisis, but also was partly the result of the near constant stream of false official statements. It was suggested by the authorities that the students were communists, in particular "Maoists and Castroites," that there was no Free Speech issue, that very few students were involved anyway, and that there were large numbers of off-campus agitators. Anyone on campus at the time could see that all this was false. Later, at the time of the strike, this sort of image protection reached new proportions when the authorities tried to pretend that the strike was a failure. At one point it was claimed that only thirty-nine classes were canceled on the entire campus (I know of several individual departments where more than thirty-nine classes were canceled) and that attendance always drops off slightly on Friday and was no worse than usual (this was said at a time when thousands of students were milling around the campus and there were picket lines at every major building).

In short, in a community dedicated to the search for truth, the official lie does not sit well, and in its efforts to preserve its image with the larger public the administration was slowly undermining its moral authority with the faculty.

Another important factor in the steady shift of faculty opinion

was that more and more of the best students, particularly the graduate students, were backing the FSM.

III. November 20 and After. The regents' meeting of November 20
produced major liberalizations in the campus political rules. Indeed,
assuming they meant what they seemed to mean, and ignoring the
status of the then existing rules there was only one major area of
disagreement left. The regents said that the students could have
freedom of speech in designated areas of the campus, except that
they could not advocate any illegal acts. Now that might sound
reasonable enough (though of course it is unconstitutional, since
the first amendment makes the act of advocacy legal even in many
cases where the act advocated is illegal) but for the fact that, as is
generally recognized, only one sort of student group is at present
likely to advocate any illegal acts: the civil rights movement. CORE,
SNCC, etc., are the only student groups to which the rule would
seem to apply, so the students, quite naturally, took the regents
policy as equivalent to an attempt to destroy the campus civil rights
movement. Still, organizations like the FSM exist only by polarizing
the issues and after November 20 the issues were not nearly as
polarized as they had been. I, for one, was convinced that the FSM
was dead and that the war was over, with the students winning a
partial and ambiguous, but still substantial, victory. A proposed
Sproul Hall sit-in on November 23, against which several of us on
the faculty had argued with the students, was a failure, as only
about 300 students sat in. The size of rallies was declining, and
there was a distinct feeling of impending peace all round. A more
or less pro-student motion failed narrowly in the Academic Senate
on November 24—partly because after much amending its wording was so confused nobody knew quite what it meant any more.

However, on Thanksgiving weekend as happened several times
before and since, the administration gave the FSM a huge shot of
adrenalin: it began expulsion proceedings against four of the student leaders for alleged actions of the students two months earlier
at the time of the police car incident. In view of the fact that the
reforms of November 20 seemed to grant, implicitly, the justice of
much of the students' cause, this action seemed to contain an element of the vindictive.

It was a watershed in the development of faculty opinion. For the first time a large number of professors were in a state of really serious indignation against the administration, and there was a growing feeling that a solution to the crisis would have to come from the Academic Senate.

When classes resumed on November 30 the war was once again in full swing. FSM rallies were as big and as militant as they had ever been, and the students' mimeograph machines were turning out thousands of copies of shrilly worded "demands" and "ultimata," with a deadline set for Wednesday. The Graduate Coordinating Committee met and issued a strike call for Friday.

At Wednesday noon the great Sproul Hall sit-in began. Mario Savio made a passionate speech calling for a "grinding halt" to the University, and with Joan Baez leading them in the song "We Shall Overcome," 1,500 students marched into the building, carrying the American flag at the head of the procession, and sat down in the hallways. The grinding halt speech was fairly typical FSM rhetoric; the extraordinary thing was that the administration apparently took it literally. The students sat peaceably in the hallways, taking care not to interfere with traffic or to block any doorways or offices; the monitors divided the hallways into zones, quiet areas for study, a folk song area, lecture and discussion areas where some classes were given, and some Jewish students held a Hanukkah service. However annoying such scenes may be they are unlikely to seriously impair, much less halt, the operations of a vast university. But such was the state of unreason in those days that someone must really have believed that Mario Savio was going to huff and puff and blow the house down.

By late that night there had been no arrests and several hundred students had gone home to bed, the rest having bedded down in their sleeping bags on the floor. It appeared to me that at last the administration was getting clever. I thought they would let the students sit there harmlessly while the faculty came up with a solution. They could thus capitalize on the faculty's annoyance with the sit-in as a tactic, and also demonstrate once and for all that no sit-in could bring the University to a halt. But at about 3:00 AM, after consultation between the administration and the governor, six hundred policemen assembled on the campus and began removing the demonstrators one by one, a process that lasted over twelve hours.

This really did bring the University to a grinding halt, for the next day the students joined in a massive strike and hundreds of professors canceled their classes in sympathy with the students and in disgust at the use of the police. The arrests made the strike a success.

An unofficial emergency meeting of the faculty was hastily convened at 1:00 PM, and more faculty members showed up at that meeting than ever before at an official senate meeting. Those of us who had felt all along that the students had genuine free speech and disciplinary grievances suddenly found that we had hundreds of allies. Proposals to eliminate all restrictions on advocacy and to place discipline in the hands of the faculty passed by huge majorities, and a call for the resignation of the chancellor was received with loud applause. The dam of faculty reticence and reluctance to express their convictions had at last been broken, and the chances were now strongly in favor of a liberal solution to the crisis.

But the battle was not yet won.

IV. The Committee of Two Hundred. On Friday, December 4, while the strike was still in full swing—with thousands of students milling around the campus, picket lines at all the buildings, and empty classrooms everywhere—a group of faculty members met to try to formulate a solution to the crisis. After several sessions and in an atmosphere of considerable tension two motions for the Academic Senate meeting of the following Tuesday were formulated. Motion A dealt with the substantive issues, and eventually became the famous 824–115 resolution. Motion B called for the creation and election of an emergency executive committee to carry out motion A and do whatever else was necessary to solve the crisis. On Saturday afternoon when they were finally satisfied with the wording (always a difficult task with academics), the group decided to hold a larger meeting to publicize and get support for the motions. Someone reserved a room big enough to hold about two hundred people.

It is difficult to convey the atmosphere of that weekend. After the disorder of Thursday and Friday, the campus itself was quiet. But many of the faculty and literally hundreds of the students were in a state of frenetic activity. Worst of all were the rumors. It was said that the administration was determined to stop the strike at all cost, that they would call in the national guard, that the regents would expel a couple thousand students, that they would fire a few hundred professors, that possibly the University would be closed down. Hard news trickled out slowly: the chancellor was hospitalized Sunday afternoon, all the department chairmen were meeting with the president and some of the regents. They would present their agreement to a university meeting Monday morning in the Greek theater. All university activities were to be canceled for the occasion.

In such an atmosphere two hundred professors gathered Sunday night to consider Motions A and B. After several hours of intense discussion and some rewording of the resolutions, they were both accepted unanimously. It is important to emphasize about this meeting that there was nothing panicky or frightened in the proceedings in spite of the seriousness of the situation. Like the subsequent senate meeting at which the motions were passed, the discussion concerned the issues involved and in spite of—or perhaps because of—the urgency of the situation, it was conducted at a level of rationality and intelligence seldom attained at this or any other university. But the meeting did not conclude on an optimistic note, for at its end one of the chairmen announced that they had reached an agreement with the authorities, and the terms of the agreement, when presented, were seen to be out of touch with the realities of our situation.

V. The Greek Theater. Monday after individual meetings of the departments, about 15,000 people filed into the Greek theater for the presentation of the chairmen's agreement. Many of us had deep forebodings for it appeared that the agreement had little chance of bringing peace to the campus. Its only constructive provision, an important one, was a pledge that there be no University disciplinary proceeding against students for previous actions. But it made no mention of the substantive free speech issues involved, it was arrived at without any consultation with the students or faculty other than the department chairmen, and it contained rather unconstructive criticisms of the students: "The sit-ins," it announced "were unwarranted." Well, one asked oneself, what about thirty years of unconstitutional rules, were they "warranted"? And what about the use of the police as the University's means of coping with the moral indignation of its students?

In the eyes of many in the Greek theater, it was inappropriate for those who bore some of the responsibility for our troubles to invoke the entire panoply of University authority and academic solemnity to convey accusations. The students resented what they perceived as the paternalistic, almost authoritarian, character of the meeting. Many of the faculty on the other hand resented their being identified with an "agreement" they found unsatisfactory and which was being presented to them as a *fait accompli.* An inadequate covenant, secretly arrived at. I was convinced that little good could come from such a meeting, but I feared its powers for mischief.

In the end it was not a success. The speakers were booed by several thousand of those present, and not all of their efforts served to enhance their moral stature. At one point President Kerr's speech contained the line, "It [the Greek theater] has seen many great operatic and theatrical performances." On paper it must have looked fine but at the expression "theatrical performances" the somewhat theatrical aspects of the present performance came home to the audience and people began to laugh. The speaker stepped forward, and took his eyes from the text—a single self-deprecating remark might have turned the tide—and said, "I agree with you that this may seem to be a rather theatrical performance today —thanks to the audience, not to those of us up here."

When the meeting was over the chairman, Professor Robert Scalapino said "The meeting is adjourned," and swiftly moved away from the microphone. And there at the side of the stage, where he had been waiting in full view of all and was now walking toward the center, was Savio. He reached the microphone, placed both hands on it as if to collect his thoughts before speaking and then they struck. I don't suppose that there can have been more than two or three policemen who grabbed him but it seemed that all one saw was Savio being dragged and knocked down in a flurry of uniforms and in an instant he was off the stage. The effect on the audience was quite striking. It was as if certain new aspects of the meeting and of the nature of the University's present authority over its students were being made public. The contrast between the high moralizing of the speeches and the brute force of the campus police symbolized a certain illusion-reality contrast present in the entire proceeding.

The students began to chant: *We want Mario.* Professor Scalapino, with the help of Professor Tussman, got the police to release Savio and he was led to the microphone where he quietly announced that the FSM would hold a rally immediately thereafter on Sproul Hall steps and invited everyone to attend.

The failure of the chairmen's agreement involved a fairly subtle point that its makers apparently failed to grasp. The disciplinary proceedings against the leaders had indeed reopened the struggle, but once reopened it could not be stopped simply by suspending the discipline, for once reopened it focused everyone's attention on the principles left unsettled by the regents' compromise of November 20. Now, any attempt to solve the crises without meeting those issues was bound to fail, and the chairmen were giving the students University amnesty at a time when that was no longer enough. Having ignited the fuel, one can't stop the fire by blowing on the match.

The administration made a similar mistake throughout in confusing the objectives of the FSM with the general disaffection of undergraduates with the University. Correctly perceiving that much of the motive force behind the FSM came from student dissatisfaction with the bureaucratic conception of a university, they failed to take seriously the students' concern over free speech. They couldn't seem to grasp that it was both the case that the students fought so hard because they felt "alienated" and at the same time fought sincerely for free speech objectives. Thus in discussion with some members of the two hundred on the afternoon immediately after the Greek theater meeting, it became clear that a high official of the University simply did not understand the issue about advocacy. He had to go out in the hall to have the University lawyers explain it to him.

Another glaring example of this failure to understand the student movement occurred on the night of the arrests when the pretext given for calling the police was that the students had broken into President Emeritus Sproul's office and littered papers and files about. Anyone familiar with the ideals and aspirations of the students found such a story incredible, and of course the next day

Sproul's secretary pointed out that it was entirely false, saying, "We keep a messy office." Communication had so broken down that the authorities apparently failed to realize that the students were not simply rowdies.

To perceive the true character of the FSM, one must understand that its informing principles were those of the civil rights movement. Ten of the eleven steering committee members of the FSM are active in civil rights organizations, and two of the top leaders, Savio and Weinberg, are the heads of campus SNCC and CORE respectively. Efforts to construe the FSM on the model of the ideological student movements of the thirties and forties or the campus frivolities of the fifties are bound to lead—and have led—to serious misunderstandings.

Motion A. Late Sunday night after the meeting of the 200, the drafting committee of that group made what turned out to be a crucial decision. Several thousand copies of Motion A should be printed and distributed on the campus Monday morning. A departmental secretary was called out of bed and down to the campus and the mimeograph machines began to roll. This decision had the consequence that after the failure of the Greek theater an alternative solution was known to be available to fill the vacuum of power and authority left by that failure. By noon Monday hundreds of faculty members knew the contents of Motion A, and later Monday afternoon the Academic Freedom committee decided to reword it slightly and submit it as their report at Tuesday's meeting. The president discussed its contents with several members of the 200 and indicated a willingness to accept the substance, if not the letter, of its provisions, except for the one which placed disciplinary authority in the hands of the faculty. Many of the committee were reluctant to have the president's name associated with Motion A at all at that point, but there was no holding back the news of this discussion and it soon spread over the campus. The chairman held another meeting and agreed informally to back Motion A. The strike was halted Monday night out of respect for the senate meeting to be held Tuesday, and it looked as if Motion A was home.

Tuesday, shortly after noon, began one of the more curious conversations of the whole semester. Several members of the committee of 200 were called into the office of one of the department chairmen in order to aid in consultation with the president by phone. The president, it appeared, was having second thoughts about Motion A. He would not speak directly to any of the committee but only to the department chairman who conducted the conversation, relaying question and answer. Was not Motion A simply the FSM platform? Was it not a challenge to the authority of the regents? Had not the committee of 200 deliberately tried to gain support for it by spreading the rumor that the president agreed with it? The answer to all of these questions was no. In any case the president was seriously considering openly opposing Motion A at the senate meeting. This prospect raised grave questions concerning the already somewhat strained relations between the faculty and the administration; and the conversation continued, with various interruptions until nearly 3:00 PM. The meeting began at 3:15. In the end the president chose not to express opposition to Motion A.

Why did the faculty support Motion A? The answer is obvious: because it enunciated a principle which most of them accept. The principle is simply that students are entitled to the same rights of free speech on the campus that they have in the community at large. This implies, among other things, that there should be no double punishment in these matters, and that the University should leave to the courts ticklish questions of what is and what is not constitutionally protected speech. The march of events had made it clear by December 8, that such were the principles at issue and that the responsibility for making its convictions known and thus solving the crisis was squarely on the Academic Senate. Perhaps there were some who did not care much for principles but just voted for the motion as a way of ending the strike, and no doubt there were others who voted against the motion just out of resentment at the students' tactics. But the principles underlying the motion are so fundamental to the American political ideal that it is hard to comprehend those who fought it so tenaciously.

III

AFFIRMATIONS
AND ADMONITIONS

*Although the students named their revolution the Free Speech
Movement, the complex and controversial questions it raised went
far beyond the confines of the First Amendment. For several
months, the pages of liberal journals contained a spate of articles
and debates by prominent social and political commentators,
among them many Berkeley professors.*

*Foremost among the controversial issues was that of advo-
cacy: the students were fighting for the right to continue using
University property as a base from which to campaign for and
organize social and political action directed toward the surrounding community. Moreover, they demanded the freedom to engage
in such activities without fear of discipline by the administration
whether or not civil courts declared the results illegal. One reason
this legalistic principle became a storm center is that it was raised
against an immediate backdrop of local civil rights sit-ins and
demonstrations heavily populated by Berkeley students. Another
major point of discussion and debate was whether the situation at
Berkeley justified the civil disobedience tactics that the students
employed against the University itself.*

*In "Behind the Protests at Berkeley", John Boler, visiting pro-
fessor of philosophy at U.C. during the uprisings, emphasizes the
powerlessness of the students to negotiate the restrictions on their
political activities with a domineering administration. He suggests
that an absence of meaningful channels for the redress of their*

grievances left students with nowhere to go except to direct-action protest.

Although Sidney Hook, in "Second Thoughts on Berkeley," believes that the administration was wrong in its handling of the students, he criticizes not only the students' tactics on the grounds that they were harmful to the educational process, but their goals as well. Hook claims that the students were demanding unwarranted freedoms and that the Free Speech Movement's supporters as a whole, including many of its faculty sympathizers, were deceived by leaders with ulterior revolutionary motives.

If he does not altogether disapprove of the students' political ideals, U.C. sociologist Nathan Glazer in "What Happened at Berkeley" ultimately condemns their tactics as a threat to the order and stability of democratic procedures. However, in a specific reply to Glazer, his colleague in the Berkeley sociology department, Philip Selznick, feels that the ideals of the students regarding civil rights in the community and political advocacy on the campus were of sufficient moral urgency to warrant the techniques of direct action through which the students attempted to realize these ideals.

The lively exchange between Glazer and Paul Goodman grew out of Goodman's article "Thoughts on Berkeley," included in "Images of a University," the first section of this book.

JOHN F. BOLER

Behind the Protests
at Berkeley*

No public crisis ever seems to develop on the clear-cut issue its proponents or opponents would have chosen had they been able. But somehow amid platitudes from the administration, slogans from the students, and pomposity from the faculty, some altogether unnecessary violence, *not* from the demonstrators but from the police and a few disorganized bands of students hoping to break up the demonstration, and a good bit of comic relief that probably is funnier now than at the time, there has been a sincere and deep concern on the Berkeley campus for some very important problems.

There is a popular belief that the whole thing need never have occurred: "If the administration had been reasonable," "If the students had been patient." And with that, the quick solution: "Fire the administration," "Expel the students"; or even more distressing, the attitude a recent newspaper account ascribes to University President Clark Kerr: that the machine should be adjusted here and there, as if the whole matter resulted from a temporary failure in administrative technique. Unfortunately—or fortunately, for that is the positive value of a crisis—the problems exposed cannot be easily smoothed over. The issues clearly extend beyond the limits of the Berkeley campus.

A public university in California that is somewhat of a combined Harvard and City College can be an exciting place even on a quiet day. The university community, as its life overlaps the campus boundaries, constitutes a kind of social oasis. Besides the

* From *Commonweal*, February 1965.

107

usual service businesses and the families of faculty, staff and students, there is a whole coterie of more or less temporary drop-outs, "professional students," and the usual variety of hangers-on. The undergraduate body has always had a paradoxical reputation for Greek-row society, intellectuals, and activists. Concentrated in a relatively small area are more than 27,000 students (over a third of them graduate students) and 1,800 faculty members, with an administration and staff that, as in any large institution, are legion. The atmosphere of confidence that this is the world's leading university strikes outsiders—including the other campuses of the scattered thing that is the University of California—as simply overweening pride. But even an often hostile public and legislature can still be appealed to on the basis of Berkeley's intellectual prominence.

The current academic year began with student activities at a high pitch. With national and state elections of unusual ideological import underway, with students back from civil rights work in the South and many projects for local demonstrations being planned, anyone even mildly in touch with student sentiment could anticipate that the administrative rules controlling "off-campus" student organization (i.e., non-academic student groups), however "liberalized" they might seem in comparison with the past, were going to cause trouble. The Bancroft and Telegraph Avenue entrance to the campus, a wide spot in the sidewalk erroneously assumed to be city property—the City of Berkeley issued permits for student political groups to set up tables there—was an inadequate but much used safety valve. The plaza behind it, originally a part of Telegraph Avenue and traditionally a place for "off-campus" activity, is now an area about the size of a football field, with Sproul Hall, the main administrative building, on one side and the Associated Student Union of California (ASUC) building on the other. At the far end of the plaza, a bit of ornamental iron work, called Sather Gate, was the spot selected for testing the "illegality" of collecting funds, distributing literature and general "politics."

The Bancroft and Telegraph plaza is one of those happy scenes of chaos that mean so much to everyone except the most order-conscious minds, and the original justification for a clamp-down on activities to expedite the flow of traffic was an obvious fraud. At this point, student and faculty opinion overwhelmingly supported the off-campus organizations, but the carnival atmosphere (typical of the opening of school), while it contributed to the vocal expression of discontent, seems to have obscured the seriousness of the issues at stake. Throughout the controversy, one group of faculty, administration, and students was unable to shake the idea that the whole mess was simply a rowdy extension of the "boys-will-be-boys" problem beyond the limits of good taste. Another smaller but more serious group followed the knee-jerk reaction of the local press, persisting in the conspiracy theory of more or less organized agitation directed at some kind of "take-over" of the university by dissident elements.

The immediate occasion for the present dispute came about when someone informed the administration that the entrance way at Telegraph and Bancroft was, except for the normal stretch of sidewalk, indeed university property. The dean's office notified all "off-campus" groups that their normal activity would not be permitted there. While a number of concessions were made subsequently, it was not until the December 18 meeting of the regents that the (probably unconstitutional) effort to control the "advocacy" of social and political issues on campus was abandoned. Early statements from the administration objecting to "action mounted against the outside community," coupled with its insistence to the last that "advocacy of illegal off-campus action" be prohibited, seem to substantiate the general assumption that the action of the dean's office was the result of pressures to prevent the organization on the campus of sit-ins and other civil rights demonstrations directed against local businesses. At any rate, the issue was a real one, and not simply an excuse for rebelling against authority.

Despite the practical difficulties encountered by those faculty and students who made the effort, the matter might eventually have been resolved by negotiation had not the administration tried to pick off the student leadership. Before both of the student demonstrations (the surrounding of a police car on October 1 and the sit-in at Sproul Hall on December 2–3), there were attempted reprisals against selected students and organizations within the large group that had publicly expressed its opposition to the rules. It was this, and the needless massing of the police on both occasions—the demonstrators were always orderly—that gained the support of both faculty and students for the extreme measures the students undertook.

The nineteen off-campus organizations affected by the original ruling included such diverse groups as the University Society for Individualists, the DuBois Club, the Young Republicans, The Young Socialist Alliance, SNCC, CORE, and the Inter-Faith Council. They originally formed a loose coalition, the United Front, and after the first demonstration established themselves as the Free Speech Movement (FSM). While liberal elements have generally prevailed, conservative representation was never absent; despite internal conflicts, the FSM has made many serious efforts to achieve and maintain a broad representation in its various committees.

The vocabulary and style of a few of the more vocal student leaders is evidence of probably more than one brand of Marxism (and not of the highest quality); but the charge of "outside" organization is untrue. According to a survey of arrested demonstrators, there were more from religious organizations (seven per cent) than from the "radical" groups (five per cent).

During the controversy an important but unpublicized organization of graduate students was formed, the Graduate Coordinating Council. Besides providing a stabilizing element and valuable counsel to the FSM, they were particularly influential in raising faculty interest in the crisis. It was the GCC which, after serious deliberation, organized the strike of December 4. (The fascination of TV cameramen with beards, sandals and long-haired young ladies in dark stockings made it difficult to believe that there was any participation by even recognizably moderate elements.)

The actual strength of the student movement comes through most clearly in terms of the lack of opposition. Hard-core opposition opinion (student and faculty) probably never exceeded five per cent of the total university community. The ASUC Senate and the student newspaper posed as "responsible" voices of dissent, but found themselves, as a result, even further isolated from student opinion—and, even more important, confirmed the fact that they are not and never were viable channels for the airing of student grievances. "Students for Cal," an organization to show support to the administration, was still-born. The fact is that from the beginning, the FSM had the support of a high percentage of students interested in social and political affairs from all parts of the political spectrum.

At the moment, the campus is relatively quiet. The danger of the immediate crisis has passed, and the less obvious but essential work of reconstruction is going on at a surprisingly swift pace. The major stabilizing factor was clearly the concern of the faculty shown by their overwhelming vote (seven to one) on December 8 and especially the open and reasonable way they went about it—the result, by the way, of tremendous labors on the part of individual faculty members. The regents' reaction was not all that could be desired, but the issue of advocacy was settled in favor of the students. The senate proposal to place the "political" area under a faculty appointed committee, which was rejected (*de jure*) by the regents, has been established (*de facto*) by the acting chancellor. During the enforced moratorium of Christmas vacation, extensive work by faculty committees made an encouraging start toward opening up channels to allow for the airing of grievances without recourse to "civil disobedience." It remains to be seen—for there is some anxious watching—how far and how quickly the faculty and administration will go towards a more permanent policy.

There are also two investigating committees made up of regents who apparently are not as yet satisfied about either the past or the future of the matter at hand. According to the rumors, at least, the regents were rather strongly divided themselves about the significance of the disturbance and how to handle it. Probably the most immediate source of further irritation, however, lies with the cases of the arrested sit-ins which are now pending before the courts. But since the university is not itself a party to the charges against them, it seems that only Governor Brown is in a position to stop the proceedings before they come to trial.

The issues now facing the Berkeley campus—and other American universities—concern the internal structure of the university community and the relevance of politics to the campus. But both these issues must be situated within the context, realistically understood, of the movement of contemporary society. Dissatisfaction with the forms of the immediate past and the demand for dialogue and renewal are not limited to the religious consciousness.

Although disappointing, it is no surprise that the breakdown of communication across generations and between fragments of our society should also be evident in the universities. "The administration," hero of a generation ago when salvation seemed to lie in organization, is an obvious target; but the growth of administrative power, in any institution, is not a simple phenomenon. The students' complaint about being manipulated by a group of conspirators to serve the economic needs of business, or whatever, is naïve. On the other hand, their sense of alienation is painfully real and justifiable. The proxy-parent—the administration rather than the faculty seems everywhere to play this role—is more powerful and more impersonal than any mother and father, and less inclined than many parents to treat the students with the dignity and respect accorded adults. The reasonable-sounding suggestion that the students had avenues of appeal open to them is simply not true in practice. In this context, it should be clear, I think, that until the students are really given responsibility, they should not be charged with being irresponsible.

A common misconception is that the students are negotiating from a position of power. But the whole point of the form and manner of their protest is that they had to operate from a position of weakness. Cooling off periods, going through normal channels, or waiting to see are fatal moves when there is no effective hearing outside demonstrations. Moderate leadership in the FSM was constantly being embarrassed and eventually defeated not by the radicals but by the repressive actions of the administration.

Faculty members made a number of efforts at mediation throughout the controversy and developed the same frustrations as the students. (Even the recommendations of one faculty committee were simply by-passed.) Actually, the channels of communication were long since closed, but they had been so infrequently resorted to as to go unnoticed. The faculty is not without blame in this. Their own relations with the students were far from ideal; the recognition of this may be one of the most satisfying results of the crisis. The faculty at Berkeley (as elsewhere) had voluntarily given up its prerogatives, not only on the nagging issues of "beer and sex," but in vital areas of student and faculty concern. (A guilty conscience about their failure to take a stand during the loyalty oath controversy of 1949–50 was surely a factor in solidifying action in the present case.) While the local press has pictured the regents as backed into a corner by unruly faculty and students— thus placing them and the governor, especially, in an uncomfortable political position—a reorganization was clearly overdue. Nor is it altogether an exception in our present cultural scheme that it should be the students who *acted* to make this clear.

The administration in most American universities is a curious hybrid of big business, a grade-school attitude towards education, and the myth of exalted authority of "the professor." The last may be a surprise to many, but administrations have nearly always been able to bring the faculty to their side with a simple suggestion that "the next thing the students want will be to tell you how to teach your classes." The current bogeyman is student control of the South American universities. Passing over the insult to the evident democratic sense of our students and their sincere desire to learn something—which suggests, by the way, that the blame for a breakdown in respect for authority be located elsewhere—the obvious answer to such a frightening suggestion is that we need more and not less democracy in our educational institutions: not a more effective police force but open lines of communication and effective channels for appeal and redress, including the equivalent of a "separation of powers." As we should all be aware now, this cannot be achieved simply by added committees or organizational technique, but only by the hard work and honest shouldering of responsibility which any community of free men requires.

As for the political issue, I would like to make one point clear. The problem is not one of bringing politics onto the campus (e.g., the so-called "open-speaker policy"). That question has its own difficulties, but it clearly falls within the scope of educational matters—the effort of students and faculty to inform themselves— and while not every university has been able to establish acceptable procedures, the general precedent has been well established. The University of California may be a bit behind but the gap can be easily closed. The problem raised by the Berkeley controversy goes much deeper: it has to do with bringing the university into politics (i.e., the life of the *polis*).

The idea that the university is isolated from the rest of the community rests upon various historical factors. In its earliest days, and in some places in Europe yet, the universities have actually been political sanctuaries: independent, self-governing states within the state. In this country, the situation of such a community within a community is not so clearly defined. The present conditions are probably reinforced, on the one hand by an alienation of the intellectual with a resulting sense of withdrawal on both sides, and, on the other by the treating of students as non-adults, as if they were not full members of the community at large. (Neither of these attitudes is either simply irrational or simply wrong.) More directly, however, the present situation seems to rest on a mutual but unwritten contract to "buy" sanctuary with isolation.

State institutions, such as the University of California, are obviously prohibited from making official pronouncements expressing religious or political preference: from throwing their weight behind, or becoming subject to, religious and political institutions. But this should not be allowed to obscure the fact that the university is now, to varying degrees always has been, and to an increasing extent will be a vital part of the community and an influential force within it. (Although one must draw some distinction between the local community and the society at large.)

The notion of the university as an isolated world is partly myth. And the real importance of the Berkeley disturbance, I think, is that it is an important event in the process of exploding that myth. The reason why the myth must be removed is simply that it obscures the actual structure of campus and community relations which, under the "emperor's new clothes," has not been honestly acknowledged. In the present instance, the students have called attention to some of the inconsistencies that have been generated in these circumstances. But, aside from certain immediate grievances about which their complaint was perfectly justified, they have provided plenty of heat and little light. Despite the quantities of local debate and the spate of articles in national periodicals, the basic issues are nowhere near settled and probably have not even been adequately delineated.

Like any myth, the myth of university sanctuary protects some important values: peace and quiet, academic freedom, self-determination of policies, etc., on the side of the university; but just as important, the ability of the local community to live with an "alien" and—let us admit it—artificial community within it. With the protective myth removed, these values must now be re-established on a realistic basis; this will not be easy. The present student attitude demands (not always consistently) that the isolation of the two communities be abolished; I personally would think that it must at least be drastically reworked. But saying it will not make it so.

A little dialogue with the rest of the community would not be as fruitless as seems to be assumed by many on both sides. Once they get over the initial fright of open confrontation, it may just be that the university and the rest of the community have some very important things to say to one another. On the face of it, however, the first move lies with the university community: to work out in a clear fashion just what it wants to say.

SIDNEY HOOK

Second Thoughts on Berkeley

Hardly anything I have written in more than forty years of an active career as an educator has provoked so widespread a reaction as my article on "Academic Freedom and the Rights of Students" in *The New York Times Magazine* of January 3. This was partly a result of the title under which the article appeared: "Freedom to Learn but not Freedom to Riot," and the accompanying illustrations of the Berkeley student sit-ins. (I have never been able to understand the claim made by editors that titles and subheadings belong to *them,* and that they are free to dramatize the contents of what they print as they see fit.) In consequence, many readers assumed that I was writing primarily about the events at the University of California although my interest was to develop a set of principles to guide faculty-student relations in liberal arts colleges throughout the country. My references to the situation at Berkeley were peripheral and illustrative, and some of the principles I developed had no more specific relation to Berkeley than to other institutions.

In addition, some careless readers excitedly jumped to the conclusion that I had condemned the students at Berkeley for rioting although there was not a word in my article warranting such an inference. This led some of the leaders of the so-called Free Speech Movement (FSM) to denounce me in terms that brought back warm memories of the thirties when the Young Communist League in the name of "free speech" would attempt to break up the meetings of socialist students I addressed to prevent them from being hypnotized and misled by "a counterrevolutionary reptile."

I shall have more to say about "rioting" at Berkeley in a moment but I should like to declare at once that, in principle, I have no objection to democratic students rioting to protest racial, religious and grave political persecution, *if no other means are available to them.* And not only behind the Iron Curtain but in Mississippi and some other southern states in which Negro students are denied their elementary rights to study on the same terms as others. The form resistance should take, once the principled justification has been established, whether passive or active, is a matter of strategy and prudence. Now since the leader of the FSM, Mario Savio, has explicitly declared that the struggle in Mississippi and at Berkeley is "the same struggle," one wonders about his show of indignation at the attribution to the FSM of willingness to riot. After all what could be clearer than his own words:

> The two battlefields [Mississippi and Berkeley] may seem quite different to some observers, but this is not the case. The same rights are at stake in both places. . . .

If, in the absence of any viable alternatives, rioting were permissible in Mississippi, but not at Berkeley, this would mean that the battlefields were *not* the same. Since this is denied by Mr. Savio, he should be as prepared to riot in one place or another in defence of human rights. And how far he is prepared to go is apparent from his caustic criticism of Dr. Martin Luther King's leadership at Selma, Alabama. Attacking Dr. King for not continuing the march at Selma, after the federal injunction had been issued, Savio said "What is the march for? To make martyrs? Then you've got to march or else you hold a press conference."

The thing that troubled me at the outset in reflecting about Berkeley, even before I began investigating the facts in detail, was the appropriateness of the means adopted by the FSM leaders to protest obviously unwise administrative educational policies. In consequence I resolved to make an intensive study of the facts at Berkeley, the issues at stake, and how they were settled. I was all the more determined to do this because of the widespread ignorance I encountered among college groups about what actually occurred at Berkeley. In particular I wanted to examine more carefully the role of the faculty. In my original article, I had stated as a basic principle of academic freedom the right of the faculty to determine not only educational policy but, with the participation of officially elected representatives of the student body, the rules governing disciplinary action where students are concerned. Since I had been critical of the action of the faculty, several colleagues had sardonically inquired about the validity of my faith in entrusting the determination of educational policy to the faculty.

In what follows, I shall state some of the relevant facts not known by most individuals with whom I have discussed the situation at Berkeley. I shall then analyze the issues, and assess the role of the administration, the leaders of the FSM, and the faculty. The larger questions concerning the nature and function of the university which I have discussed elsewhere * I omit here since they do not bear directly on the events. Much that has been written about the nature of the university has no more specific relevance to what happened at Berkeley, and not elsewhere, than a general discussion about the sociology of crime has on the question of who killed whom, when, where, and why.

Some Relevant Facts. There was not *one* civil disobedience sit-in demonstration at Berkeley but *four!* The first was on September 30 and followed the announcement by the administrative authorities of disciplinary hearings for five students who had manned tables for purposes declared illegal by sudden administrative edict on September 14. Three leaders of this demonstration were "indefinitely suspended."

The second sit-in occurred on October 1. This date is very important for the understanding of subsequent proceedings. Demonstrators surrounded the police car which contained Jack Weinberg, a former student, the arrested violator of the new University ruling, and threatened violence if the police attempted to remove the prisoner. Additional protestors stormed into Sproul Hall for another sit-in. When the campus police sought to close the Sproul Hall doors, a physical clash occurred.

The third sit-in took place on November 22. It was a dismal failure, for it followed the reversal by the regents of previous University policy on November 20 which granted the legitimate demands of the FSM:

> The regents adopt the policy effective immediately that certain
> campus facilities, carefully selected and properly regulated,

* *Education for Modern Man,* Sidney Hook, New York, 1963.

may be used by students and staff for planning, implementing, raising funds or recruiting participants for lawful off-campus action, not for unlawful off-campus action.

The fourth and final sit-in of the year occurred December 2–3. This led to removal and arrest of students on the orders of Governor Brown *without* the approval of President Kerr.

There is reason to believe that if the last sit-in had not taken place, in the light of the regents' ruling of November 20, matters at the University of Berkeley would have composed themselves despite the plans of the leaders of the FSM. What sparked the final flare-up?

Here several misconceptions prevail among those who have not carefully studied the record. The popular view is that on November 28, Mario Savio and the Goldbergs suddenly received word that disciplinary action was being taken against them for their peaceful actions of civil-disobedience of September 30 and for setting up illegal tables prior to that; and that this action "reneged" on the agreement that President Kerr had made with students on October 2.

This is false. The agreement President Kerr had made with the students called, among other things, for the dropping of University charges against the ex-student Weinberg, the arrested man in the immobilized police car, and for turning over the cases of the eight suspended students to a Committee of the Academic Senate of the Faculty. These provisions were carried out. The Faculty Committee was formed (the Heyman Committee) and after elaborate hearings, it made its report on November 12.

In its report it pointed out that with the assent of all parties, it "has considered only those events occurring up to the night of September 30, 1964, when the students here involved were indefinitely suspended by the chancellor." The Heyman report is couched in very mild and gentle, almost apologetic, language. Nonetheless it is quite critical of some aspects of administrative policy. At the same time it concludes that the students did violate University regulations. The penalty for each of six students was "censure" to take the place of the penalty of "indefinite suspension" which was to be expunged from their record. The suspension of Messrs. Goldberg and Savio, however, was *upheld* but limited to six weeks.

One key paragraph of the Report of this Ad Hoc Faculty Committee on Student Conduct reads with reference to events on September 30:

> While we are not prepared to condemn on moral grounds the device of demonstration by peaceful and orderly sit-in, we recognize that those who organize and participate in a sit-in which is judged to violate valid regulations must be prepared to pay the price for such conduct. In this instance (September 30), we believe that the price must be higher than [for] the manning of card tables, another form of civil disobedience, not because of any discernible difference in motivation, or moral position, but because of *the potentially more serious consequences of the action* (my italics).

This closed the matter, for all practical purposes, of the September 30 demonstration. What then sparked the fateful sit-ins of December 2 and 3? It was a resolution adopted by the regents on November 20, the very day it liberalized the rules for Political Action on Campus. This second resolution on Disciplinary Action read in part:

> New disciplinary proceedings before the Faculty Committee on Student Conduct will be instituted immediately against certain students and organizations for violations subsequent to September 30, 1964.

The actions subsequent to September 30 covered the incident of the entrapment of the police car on October 1 and the fracas in Sproul Hall on the occasion of the second sit-in. The regents' resolution was a directive to Chancellor Strong who, on this matter at any rate, cannot be regarded as responsible for the action. His letter to Savio and Goldberg did not announce any punishment. It merely requested them to attend a hearing before the Faculty Committee on Student Conduct. It did not charge them with *peaceful* sit-in demonstration, even of the kind the Heyman Committee had condemned. It charged them with acts of violence—forcefully resisting the efforts of police officers who attempted to close the main doors of Sproul Hall, assault (specifically Savio) for biting a police officer in the thigh, entrapment of the police car and threats of violence. In addition, they were charged with organizing the invasion of Sproul Hall on October 1 and by deliberately blocking the exits compelling personnel from the Dean of Students' office to flee through a window and across a roof.

Obviously the leaders of the FSM were *prepared* to riot, did riot in Sproul Hall, and technically were guilty of riot in preventing an arrest of an individual charged with breaking the law. Even staunch faculty friends of the FSM admit that if the administration had not yielded October 2 and withdrawn the police, there is every likelihood that bloodshed would have occurred. For had the police attempted to move the car or remove the demonstrators, the latter would have resisted them. Under the circumstances, the indignation of the FSM leaders over the title the editors of *The New York Times* placed on my article is synthetic.

The Issues Examined: When one examines the actual *issues* in dispute at Berkeley one must conclude that to the extent that the students in the FSM were primarily concerned with organizing *civil rights* demonstrations, legal or illegal, *off-campus,* their request that they be free of administrative or faculty disciplinary jurisdiction was morally and educationally justified. What they failed to see, and the great majority of the faculty with them, was that, in the nature of the case, one cannot formulate a *rule* to the effect that *all* illegal off-campus activity, whether political or not, falls within the *exclusive* province of the civil authorities. The action of the faculty, for reasons I shall try to make clear, can only be *ad hoc* depending upon the nature, the place, and the attendant circumstances of the activity of the students.

The administration itself had recognized that there were certain permissible off-campus demonstrations in which students had participated in which they had been arrested for flagrantly violating the law, e.g., the sit-ins at the Sheraton-Palace Hotel, and before that, the disruptions of the San Francisco hearings of the House Committee on Unamerican Activities. Although President Kerr took the position that they had been organized off-campus, and hence were altogether a citizen's activity, actually both demonstrations were at least partially mounted on the campus. Yet the administration had courageously refused to add educational punishment to the civil punishment. For obviously, whether ill- or well-advised, there had been no educational interest of the University affected. Nor could one sensibly say that the organization and support of student activity in behalf of the extension of the democratic process in southern states or in behalf of the unorganized migrant workers, even if they were illegal under a local or federal statute, in any way was prejudicial to the ethos of the educational community. During the thirties we helped students go to Harlan County, Kentucky, and arranged for them to accompany Norman Thomas when he went to Jersey City to violate the decree against freedom of speech by "I-am-the-Law" Mayor Hague. There was no demand even from reactionary elements that these activities be subject to University restriction.

Nonetheless one can easily imagine situations in which student off-campus activity, legal or illegal, might very well have a definite bearing on values and standards regarded as precious to the educational community. That the students involved are more likely to be reactionary than radical does not affect the principle. And I have seen radical students sometimes act toward other students (usually other radical students) in the same way as they are sometimes treated by the reactionaries. Suppose a group of students in order to prevent the policy of desegregation at a college or university waylay and violently haze the Negro students, being careful to carry out their attacks off the campus. Would it be wrong for the university community to be concerned about such activity and take action against those who by their illegal (or legal) off-campus activities were destroying its educational ideals? American universities have not yet become as politicalized as universities in India and Japan although some members of the University of California have expressed the fear that they are well on their way. I have been at universities abroad where students, dissatisfied with their grades or disagreeing with the *political* views of their professors, have mobbed them off-campus. Suppose some students of the FSM, instead of jeering at Professors R. and L. or calling them "Fink," were to mob them (making sure they were not on university ground) because they disagreed with their political or educational views. Would this be of no concern to the university community, would it be morally or legally wrong for the university to take disciplinary notice of this off-campus behavior? A day may come in this country when those who presently fawn on the students who share their views, may face another and more hostile generation of students. Those who have any memories of the First World War opposition in this country, or have read about it, will know what I mean.

But if students were ever to be punished by a faculty for an action that had already been punished by the sanctions of the civil authorities, would that not be placing them in "double jeopardy"? This is another thought-stopping phrase when introduced in an educational context. It is curious that so many able minds in the academy in a crisis fail to reflect on their own experience. Almost anyone exposed for some years to reports of faculty discipline committees can match the following cases. A student steals examination papers, usually an off-campus job, sells them, is arrested, and punished. His case comes before the faculty. I have never known anyone who, whatever his recommendation for action, even protested that this placed the student in double jeopardy. Or a student is arrested for rifling lockers or stealing books from the library or dipping into the till of the college bookstore and the law takes its course. Is the faculty guilty of violating the constitutional rights of the student if it concludes that in the educational interest of the community some disciplinary action is justified? Actually, there are many actions that strictly speaking are not illegal and yet are a legitimate concern of the academic community, e.g., plagiarism, especially of something in the public domain, and other forms of cheating that are not illegal. Indeed, students have a *constitutional* right to join any fraternities they please. Yet who would deny the right of faculties to declare on educational grounds that fraternities would not be tolerated on the campus? When a university faculty disciplines a student, it does so or should do so on *educational* grounds, irrespective of the legal aspects of the student action. When a court punishes a student it is *not* primarily on grounds of educational policy. If off-campus fraternity hazing or other off-campus student activity seriously imperils the educational goals and ideals of the academic community, the freedom of students to learn and of the faculty to teach, it falls within the area of academic concern.

One further objection. The off-campus student activities which are legitimately subject to regulation, it may be retorted, are not political. Both the Regents' rule forbidding unlawful off-campus action and Point 3 of the Faculty Resolution of December 8, denying the right of the University to forbid or regulate such action, are aimed only at political and social action. Even if true, this is irrelevant. People can get hurt just as much in political and/or social action as in any other. What is political and/or social action anyhow? Is a lynch mob a form of social action? Is a non-political off-campus raid of a rival campus, in which property is destroyed and students hurt, a legitimate concern of the faculty of the raiders but not if the raid is against a Socialist Club on the raided campus? Who is to determine what falls within the purview of privileged political and social off-campus action?

On March 5, 1965 after the hubbub at Berkeley had subsided somewhat, Stephan Weissman, one of the leaders of the FSM, declared at a Plaza rally that obscene speech was an integral part of the civil rights movement, and demanded immunity from university regulation in terms of the faculty's own resolutions. It is obvious that the faculty must decide issues of this kind from case to case. The term "political" designates a rubber-band concept.

If my analysis is sound, then *both* the Regents' rule of November 20 and the flat faculty statement "Off-campus student political activities shall not be subject to University regulation" are equally objectionable from the point of view of enlightened educational policy and common sense, a resource, alas! which seems to have been in short supply at Berkeley during this period.

More extraordinary is the very first sentence of Point 3 of the faculty statement. "The content of speech or advocacy should not be restricted by the University." What makes this sentence extraordinary is the word "content." It is *not* synonymous with "advocacy." It goes far beyond anything referred to by "advocacy." It makes sense to contrast "advocacy" and "incitement." But it makes no sense to contrast "content" with "incitement." The content of speech may have nothing to do with either advocacy or incitement. In actual fact, the content of most of our speech has no bearing on either advocacy or incitement. What the faculty at Berkeley voted is that the content of any speech should be free, not merely of prior restraint, but of *any* kind of restriction.

Let us test this by a few examples. Here are a few statements that have been circulated on the campuses of some American institutions of higher learning. I use letters for names.

"X is an anti-Semite and notorious politician whose change of religion facilitated his advance in the school system, and who is now under surveillance of the Commissioner of Accounts' office for possible fraud . . . (He once sent a circular notice to his department chairmen asking them not to hire Jewish workers if they could help it)."

"Y is a New Prexy stooge. Apparently Professor Y has decided to take the cue from his colleague Professor W, who by dint of loyalty to his President has risen to a professorship despite his limitations as a scholar in Mathematics . . . A certain W.S., a stooge of Y, who as an alumnus illegally participated in Student Council activities, has already reaped the harvest of his pro-administration stand. He has been appointed as a personnel director."

"Z is a charlatan, a ruthless exploiter. He also stands indicted on many other charges. He has appropriated Prof. M's Personality Rating Scale, changed the name of the Scale to Index, and "neglected" to mention in his publication of the scale that the Index was Prof. M's Personality Rating Scale with Prof. M's name omitted. He has had mimeographed, on college supplies by college employees at the expense of the college, a great deal of material which he has been using, for his private practice . . . A perusal of some of Dr. Z's contributions to the pseudo-psychological magazines such as *Modern Psychology* justifies the nomination of him by prominent scientific psychologists as Public Charlatan No. 1. . . ."

There are other statements that have been circulated which are even more rank, broadly insinuating that certain faculty members have been guilty of seduction, trafficking in grades, and defalcation of University funds.

What would the Berkeley faculty of the University of California think of the "content" of these remarks, were they printed and widely distributed on and off the campus? This is no fanciful assumption since they actually appeared in leaflets and publications on an eastern campus in a campaign to discredit X, Y, and, Z politically. Would similar content of speech be privileged? I am informed that some Berkeley students have paraded with signs "Kerr is a cur!" Some of them apparently regard this as a contribution to free speech. "Content" takes in a lot of ground. It covers anything that may be said. But how long would the educational processes of a university remain unaffected if students could with impunity slander and libel whomever they pleased? What remedy has a teacher falsely charged with plagiarism or with having passed a failing student for a bribe? A public disavowal? Some slanders are spread by the very acts of disavowal. Should a faculty woman taxed with having slept with the chairman of the department to get a promotion write to the student newspaper denying that she slept with him—for that reason?

What is presupposed here is that a faculty has no right to require of students (or for that matter its own members) a standard of conduct in speech or behavior higher than what will enable students to stay out of jail. This is preposterous on its very face. For a university is fundamentally a community of scholars dedicated to the discovery and teaching of the truth. No one is compelled to seek entry to it. It has not only a legal and moral right but an educational obligation to raise its standards *above* that of the community whose law often expresses no more than the lowest common denominator of what is necessary to prevent men from breaking the social peace. It can therefore require both of its students and faculty conformity with a code of manners, speech and conduct, provided it is not unreasonable or unjust, *higher* than what obtains in the market place.

In any event it is impossible for any intelligent faculty to *act* on the principle explicitly affirmed by the overwhelming majority of the Berkeley faculty that the *content* of speech should be beyond any restriction by the University. There need be no prior disciplinary impunity for any kind of utterance.

The obvious truth of the matter is that after the Resolution of the Regents on November 20, a false issue bedeviled the situation. The students were granted everything that had been taken away from them when the strip of sidewalk outside the campus had been yanked from under their feet in September. It is simply not credible that if *after* November 20, the students had, say, collected funds for anti-segregation sit-ins in the South or even in California or enrolled volunteers for such actions, that the administration would have taken any action against them. And as a matter of fact the FSM set up its tables once more on November 24 without let or hindrance by the administration. Even the adherents of the FSM realized this. In effect the *status quo ante* September had been restored and liberalized by the elimination of some ambiguities in the administrative rulings. This explains why the third student sit-in on November 23 fizzed. Only the hard core of the FSM kept up a half-hearted ranting, and even it was split. It was at this point, when the FSM agitation would have petered out, that the notices to appear for hearings before the Faculty Committee on Student Conduct were received by Savio and the Goldbergs.

The issue then shifted radically from one of *policy* to one of discipline and the justice of the proposed disciplinary action. Who would have imagined that a proposed disciplinary action involving four individuals would have convulsed the largest university in the country? The outcry of the FSM leaders was that this was a betrayal of the agreement with President Kerr reached October 2 and which prevented bloodshed on Sproul Plaza. Could they have been really ignorant of the regents' specific directive of November 20 to bring this disciplinary action? Assume that the student leaders were persons of good faith, indignant at the betrayal of what they sincerely believed to have been the signed understanding of October 2. What would be their normal reaction to a notice to appear for a hearing before a *Faculty* Committee? They would jump at the opportunity to demonstrate the injustice of the charges and to denounce the administration for double dealing. They could have called as witnesses in their behalf the members of the faculty who had negotiated the agreement with the president and who would gladly have testified for them. They could have even pleaded that since they were under suspension after September 30, they were not bound by University rules. At the very least, they could have waited to see whether the Faculty Committee on Student Conduct would dismiss the charges against them *before* resorting to direct action which, even when it is justified, is always an instrument of last resort. But the student leaders did nothing of the sort. They weren't interested in exoneration from the charges. They issued an ultimatum, carefully couched in language certain to provoke the administration, demanding on pain of "bringing the University machine to a grinding halt," to use the words of Savio, that all charges be dropped by noon December 2. This was a clear threat of a student strike! And as Stephan Weissman, another FSM leader, relates in his article in *The New Leader,* the decision and vote to call the student strike was taken even *before* the final sit-down was called which led to subsequent police action. He has admitted even more. Had the administration not sent out the notices to four FSM leaders to appear for a hearing, Weissman and his group were prepared to provoke the administration into bringing the police on campus by a public showing of obscene films against the walls of Sproul Hall. The importance of this can hardly be exaggerated because it shows how far the student leaders were prepared to go independently of the manner in which the sit-in terminated. It shows they were out to bring about the very state of affairs which they pretended subsequently to deplore—a state of affairs which they cleverly exploited to enlist both student and faculty sentiment on their side.

And the administration played right into their hands—as it had done all along!

Administrative Blunder and Ineptitude: Everyone seems convinced, with reason, that the administration made errors in handling the situation at Berkeley. But I have found no analysis of what the errors consisted in. Even Dr. Kerr who frankly avows that the administration fumbled and floundered is still puzzled about the situation. "The worst thing is," he acknowledges, "that I still don't know how we should have handled it." There is no space to go into the matter in depth. But his first great mistake, on his arrival at the campus from his trip abroad, was his failure to rescind the order barring the use of the Bancroft Strip, since he realized that the decision was wrong "both in the action itself and the way it was done." A man of his intellectual candor and moral courage should not have hesitated out of fear of losing administrative face. He endured much greater humiliation later, and everyone knew that the order did not emanate from him. To be sure, the situation was complicated by the division of authority, by the fact of campus autonomy, and the primary role of the chancellor in administering the rules of discipline. I am not minimizing the difficulties but in a crisis educational statesmanship must find ways of coping with the rules and, by the proper use of psychology and authority, of inducing the persons involved to undertake the proper action.

His second great mistake was in not drawing the proper lessons from the first sit-ins and the narrowly averted mass violence and bloodshed on Sproul Plaza at the time of entrapment of the police car. Dr. Kerr has been criticized in some quarters for capitulating to the student leaders. Instead of criticisms he deserves the highest credit for yielding at this time, instead of insisting on law enforcement and thus giving the student leaders the martyrs they so obviously wanted. His error lay in not grasping the enormity of what he was now up against, the intransigeance of a skilled group of organizers of dissent prepared to go to almost any length to get their way. He underestimated his opponents, and the effectiveness of the combination of intense fanaticism about goals and maximum flexibility in the means of fighting for them. When he did identify them, he overestimated the willingness of the moderates among the faculty to dissociate themselves from the radical student leadership.

It is at this point that he should have brought the Faculty Senate into the picture focally, entrusting to them the negotiation and implementation of the rules governing student behavior. This could have been achieved by a series of special meetings with the faculty acting as a committee of the whole. Had faculty committees taken over discussions with all student groups, the duly elected, like the ASUC, as well as the FSM, their reports would have given the faculty a better idea of what the leadership of the FSM was really after. Even if matters had developed to a showdown, the faculty, except for a small group sympathetic with the ideals of the student leaders, instead of condoning the final mass illegal sit-in would have strongly condemned it, and imposed appropriate disciplinary penalties on all who engaged in it. Although strictly speaking this was a problem for the chancellor working with the Berkeley faculty. Dr. Kerr could have inspired these activities without taking a more conspicuous public role than he was later forced to assume.

Dr. Kerr must have done yeoman work in restraining the regents from taking further disciplinary action against the suspended students, inducing them to approve their reinstatement, and to authorize opening up the campus to all student political activities except organization for illegal off-campus activity. (This last phrase, as we have seen, is a mistake. But it need not have been enforced unless and until the off-campus illegal activity affected an educational interest of the University.) With respect to the second resolution in which the regents *instructed* the administration to bring disciplinary actions for rowdy and violent behavior connected with the events of October 1–2, Dr. Kerr's position is not clear. If the agreement with the students promised them immunity for *all* actions through October 2 and not September 30, he should have pointed that out to the regents. If he had done so, it is not likely that they would have repudiated him. Since apparently he did not protest, he must have been honestly convinced that the agreement exempted actions only through September 30. Even so, it is hard to believe that Dr. Kerr was so unimaginative as to fail to calculate the effect of this directive, however mild and morally justified it appeared to him, on the extremist leaders and their followers, now in disarray. So far as I have been able to discover some of the faculty members who drafted the agreement, Professors Feuer and Glazer, were under the impression that its provisions in all likelihood promised immunity for the students through October 2. This was not written into the agreement, and they can recall only the verbal assurance of the likelihood. This, however, is not confirmed by other participants in the negotiations. Almost no one knew at the time that the charges against the students involved acts and threats of violence by them. They thought that the offense charged was solely a violation of University regulations. Under the circumstances the students, it seems to me, were justified in believing that the immunity extended through October 2, and if they had pleaded their cause to the Faculty Committee, I have no doubt that the charges against them would have been dropped despite the regents' resolution.

The next great error was committed, not as I originally thought, by Dr. Kerr but by Governor Brown, who has long suffered from a constitutional ailment known as foot-in-the-mouth disease. As a rule the best way to handle a student sit-down is to let it run its course except where destruction of life and property are imminent. The longer the sit-downs, the greater the hardships imposed on the other students. Sooner or later the students who had seized Sproul Hall would have been driven out by their own stink. Instead of dragging them out, the building should have been cordoned off, preventing for the sake of safety any further ingress after the students were in. Just as soon as the students marched on Sproul Hall, the president should have called an emergency meeting of the Faculty Senate and the students put on notice by appropriate resolution of the faculty to vacate the premises on pain of expulsion. Perhaps this would have induced the governor to hold off bringing in the police.

Two further errors, if avoided, even after the students had been removed might have prevented the rout of reason and the triumph of fear at the final faculty meeting. Instead of addressing the huge outdoor gathering at the Greek theater, Dr. Kerr should have called an emergency meeting of the faculty and presented the proposals of University chairmen headed by Professor Scalapino for faculty action. Negotiations with student organizations could have followed. As Dr. Kerr knows from his labor experience, *details* cannot be worked out at a mass asembly of 15,000 people. Finally, Dr. Kerr should have attended the final faculty meeting and actively participated in the critical discussion of a set of proposals which a considerable section of the faculty voted for on the strength of false but artfully disseminated rumors that the proposals—which were in effect a stinging rebuke to him and an endorsement of the student action!—had his approval. He should not have been deterred by the fear that some members of the faculty might have regarded his presence as supererogative or been discouraged by the evidence that in reaction to the police intervention a sizable portion of the faculty, by far not a majority, had turned against him. For he was defending the common cause—the integrity of the educational process, the relative autonomy of the University, and its independence from threats of coercion.

Whatever the mistakes of President Kerr and Chancellor Strong they have suffered punishment far in excess of anything warranted —and at the hands of a faculty whom they have served better than previous administrations. President Kerr's activities have been sufficiently notable in the defense of academic freedom to earn him an award from the AAUP, an organization so jealous of the prerogatives of faculty members that, according to one of its founders, Arthur Lovejoy, it has neglected to uphold proper *professional* standards of conduct. Chancellor Edward Strong obviously made errors of judgment in September but like President Kerr, far from being the snorting bureaucratic ogre lampooned by student leaders, he can be classified with more justice as a person with strong liberal convictions. Neither one waited until the civil rights movement became popular to support movements for extending democracy in the fields of labor, education, and public housing. That they should become the target of envenomed attack as illiberal and reactionary seems strange until we examine the position of the leading attackers.

The Strategy and Triumph of the FSM Leadership: There has been a great deal written about the generational conflict, about the sense of alienation, the absence of meaning and the meaning of its absence in an attempt to explain what happened at Berkeley. Much of it seems to me to be sheer mythology, written with a breezy dogmatism about matters of dubious relevance to the actual events and the responsibility for their occurrence. Ideas and friendships are sufficient to sustain most students as they mature into persons. The college can supply only the first by effective teaching, students must find their own friendships. Neither one nor the other is a function merely of size. Students can be bored at a small college, and inspired at a large one, and conversely. It is the caliber of members of the faculty, their interest in teaching, and in the students as human beings which is decisive.

What happened at Berkeley, of course, did not occur in a vacuum. But those who played the greatest role in making things happen were the leaders of the FSM. They made no bones about the fact that their aim was to bring about a situation on the Berkeley campus very much like the one that resulted in consequences of the sit-ins and strike. They consistently refused to use available opportunities to bring about "a peaceful and orderly change" in existing regulations deemed either unnecessary or unjust. They could have petitioned the Faculty Academic Senate to hear and act on their appeals. Instead they resorted to organized illegal action, to threats of violence and some actual violence, to boycott and mass picketing that threw the University into turmoil for almost the entire fall semester and made normal educational activity impossible.

It was clear that the leaders of the FSM had hoped to get their martyrs at the time their followers put up mass resistance to the police arrest of Weinberg. They were jubilant when the police were finally called in to clear Sproul Hall. Savio declared at the FSM rally of December 1, "We will march into Sproul Hall tomorrow and stay there until they take us off to jail." The sit-in was to have no limited duration. In addition, a strike was proclaimed to bring "the University machine to a grinding halt" barring capitulation by the University, which Savio himself had declared would be naïve to expect.

Once the police action had been taken, Savio astutely used this fact to rally additional student support. In FSM leaflets, distributed December 3, calling for "Strike!" students who opposed the sit-ins were told: "IT DOES NOT MATTER WHETHER YOU SUPPORT A PARTICULAR TACTIC—THE MATTER IS THAT THE POLICE ARE ON OUR CAMPUS . . . THERE ARE ONLY TWO SIDES . . . YOU MUST CHOOSE YOURS . . . SUPPORT YOUR FELLOW STUDENTS. JOIN THEM IN A MASSIVE UNIVERSITY WIDE STRIKE." The leaflets did not say, of course, that Savio's tactic was designed to bring the police on campus. This was his real hope. For it alone could bolster up the sagging morale of the FSM. No wonder he cried: "This is wonderful!" when the police began to clear Sproul Hall.

The strategy of the FSM leaders was obvious to anyone who is informed about the psychology and practice of some irresponsible factional radical groups in the United States. In broad outline, it runs something like this: Organize a Committee for Free Milk for Babies of Indigent Mothers. Couple this demand for free milk (already available through welfare agencies) with a series of *political* demands not related to free milk, like Hands Off Cuba! or Unilateral Nuclear Disarmament! or Withdraw from Vietnam! Organize a noisy sit-in on the busy premises of some office building, and arrange for maximum publicity. Refuse repeated requests to leave the seized premises. When police finally arrive to remove the demonstrators make a great outcry that those who ordered the police in, or approved their action, are monsters opposed to free milk for babies, and to indigent mothers, too! Sometimes the slogan employed as a decoy is Peace! or Free Speech! to the embarrassment of those groups that genuinely believe in peace and free speech.

Judging by what could publicly be heard on campus, there was no basic issue of free speech at Berkeley. Speech was so free that some members of the FSM, having exhausted the vocabulary of political extremism, felt they could only enjoy their freedom by publicly reveling in the obscenities of filthy speech. And certainly after November 20, there was no doubt that all the constitutional freedoms recognized by the highest court in the land obtained.

The organization and agitation for illegal off-campus activities in the nature of the case can have no constitutional protection. The issue here is mainly who exercises the regulation. This has nothing to do with free speech.

As has been pointed out by Professor Lewis Feuer and others, the main problem of the leaders of the FSM was to find issues which would enable them to keep the situation embroiled even after the administration and regents had made concessions retrieving their original errors. What the leaders of the FSM were obviously after was to bring the University to a halt not in the interests of free speech but for other reasons.

What are those reasons? The answer to this question is not simple. Listening to Savio denounce "the military-industrial complex" which allegedly dominates the university, and repeated outcries against the educational establishment, it is obvious that neither free speech nor civil rights was the basic issue in the eyes of the leaders of the FSM. We are indebted to one of them, Stephan Weissman, for spelling this out in an article, entitled "What the Students Want" (*New Leader*, January 4, 1964). The FSM, we are told, is making a "very complex political demand." This demand goes beyond the power to use University facilities "to organize illegal acts in the community at large." It is related to a whole series of other demands to reform and reconstruct the University of California, whose educational process has been perverted by the "contradictions" (objective, of course!) of capitalism, and of capitalism in the era of the cold war. "Big business buys researched knowledge as well as the two batches a year of technicians and intellectual servicemen needed to manage and operate the economic establishment." That is why "training replaces education" and threatens the intellectual and academic freedom of the teachers and students as well as civil rights. Kerr is the ideologist of this system—a system whose contradictions must be "related to the more pervasive contradictions in the society at large." The faculty and students must join forces to change this system. At the very least they must "participate in making those decisions which affect them." As for the students, "they will be reluctant to advise when they have the power to bargain." Since the regents have refused to accept the faculty stand endorsing the FSM position, "further demonstrations are a distinct possibility," and "if this obstacle is hurdled, there is still the problem of weakening the structural ties between university and industry." (The word, "industry," is a slip. It should read "capitalism." After all, the young comrade has forgotten that "industry" will exist under socialism, too.)

Mr. Weissman concludes: "In place of a board of regents selected from and responsive to the economic establishment, the university community should be governed by persons selected by and responsible to the faculty, and where appropriate, to the student body. Only with structural changes of this type can the multiversity be resisted."

For the moment let us not assess the validity of these ideas—it would be less cruel to ignore some of them than to take them seriously—but appraise their significance for the FSM as a movement. Mr. Weissman is the Chairman of the Berkeley Graduate Co-ordinating Committee—the largest single group in the FSM. This is an official leader's view of what the FSM is after! I doubt whether more than a handful of students and faculty members are aware of these goals of the FSM—goals which in the eyes of the FSM leaders are furthered by any actions that bring the educational "establishment" into chaos. But in their sectarian zeal they forget that one can still oppose capitalism and war—after all, the only valid reason for supporting the cold war is to prevent a hot one!—without destroying the hard won ideals of academic freedom.

Anyone who understands the meaning of a university and the meaning of an ideology, either in the Marxist or the more popular sense, knows that the American university has no ideology. It has mostly problems—and deficits. The greatest of its problems is to win, sometimes to preserve, its educational autonomy from all sorts of pressure groups in religion, politics, agriculture and business—happily, not yet from politicalized student bodies. Clark Kerr is not the ideologist of the American university or even of the University of California.

The FSM, on the other hand, definitely has an ideology both in the Marxist, and in the popular, sense. In the Marxist sense, it imagines it is fighting a great battle for free speech, and deceives itself and others in the belief that any restrictions on act or utterance except those imposed by a court constitutes a denial of the

sacred rights of a citizen. As well say that compulsory chapel or
ROTC or Gym I violate the Bill of Rights! The leaders of the
FSM also have an ideology in the popular not the Marxist sense,
since they are not deceiving themselves but only their followers
with their talk about free speech. This ideology is expressed in the
article referred to by Stephan Weissman and in Mario Savio's
speeches. But the fount of its soap-box puerilities is the fifty-year
old youth, Hal Draper, the gray Eminence of the Steering Committee of the FSM.

It would not be necessary to mention Mr. Draper except for
the fact that the student leaders take so much of their line from
him. His pamphlet, *The Mind of Clark Kerr,* is distributed by the
FSM and has been called the source book of its diatribes. It is as
faithful an account of Kerr's educational ideals as Julius Streicher's
caricatures of the Jews. Draper was a Trotskyist who left the
Socialist Party when the Trotskyists were exposed as a faction
conspiring to take over the Party in flagrant violation of the
pledged word of their leaders to refrain from factionalism—the
condition of their acceptance. I do not know what his current
political views are except that he is not an orthodox Trotskyist
and no longer regards Russia as a workers' state. I recall that, like
the Trotskyists, he opposed the war against Hitler. The Trotskyists offered several grounds, one of them that Roosevelt was as
great if not a greater enemy of the American working class than
Hitler. Whatever the grounds for Draper's position, it would have
led to the enslavement of the free world including the American
working class; and whatever his political views are today, his
polemical manners and style of thinking are like those of the
Trotskyists. The student leaders of the FSM are indifferent or
confused about doctrines but they obviously have been influenced
by Draper's polemical manners and style of thinking.

The phenomenology of the Trotskyist mind reveals two compulsive tendencies. One is a desire to prove to Stalinists that despite the denunciation of Trotskyists as counterrevolutionary
traitors, they are the purest and most revolutionary of all. In consequence, in every concrete situation the Trotskyists will take the
extremest position possible, always the leftest of the left. The
Stalinists can always be relied on for a certain degree of responsibility—to the interests of the Soviet Union; but the Trotskyists

are proudly irresponsible since all they need do is trump the Stalinists with a more daring proposal.

The second compulsive tendency of the Trotskyist mind is to concentrate most of their attacks, whenever they are part of a radical coalition, on liberals and democratic socialists in order to prove that the latter are preparing the ground for fascists, or proto-fascists, or almost-fascists despite their "subjective intentions." Normally this makes for hilarious reading. This second tendency is apparent in Draper's pamphlet. According to Draper, the world view behind Kerr's book *The Uses of the University* is Orwellian 1984. Kerr professes that he is just a historian describing the tendencies that make for 1984. But this candor, says Draper, is a fake. It is "an intellectual imposture." Indeed, "*by adding a single sentence, Kerr's book would become the work of a proto-fascist ideologue.*" (Italics in original.)

Draper does not tell us what the sentence is and how long it would have to be but since the sentence is not there he admits that Kerr is not a proto-fascist ideologue—*but,* insists Draper, any man who accepts the future on the basis of a "scientific" prediction (even if he *doesn't* approve it) is taking a political stand. He is helping to bring that future about. Kerr in the introduction to a book on an altogether different subject, *Industrialism and Industrial Man* in 1960 wrote that he was presenting his views to aid understanding of this moment in history and possibly "as a guide to the next stage." This proves, says Draper in a typical abuse of context, that Kerr "is seeking to *assist* the transformation toward the New Slavery." (Italics in original.)

It turns out that even though Kerr doesn't approve, his very "mode of being" makes him a proto-fascist after all, consciously *assisting* to bring about the New Slavery. Draper gravely declares: "There is no academic right to grease the road to fascism in the name of 'scientific' detachment." No academic right means that Kerr cannot even claim academic freedom to peddle these dangerous intellectual wares in a university. Communists, of course, even members of the Communist Party which gives instructions to its teacher members to abuse their educational trust, have a right to teach in the University. Clark Kerr, greasing the road to Fascism, has not! Mr. Draper is a librarian in a university in which Clark Kerr as president protects him from those who have the same conception of academic freedom as Mr. Draper. How lucky for Clark Kerr that he is not a librarian in a university in which Mr. Draper is president!

This is the mind which nourishes the leaders of the FSM movement. I do not wish to imply that Draper is the only influence that has played on them even if he is the most important. Other extremist tendencies have also been present. But it is not the minds or ideas of the FSM leaders that are dangerous. They need only be exposed to critical discussion. It is their *actions* which deserve the strongest condemnation, and on two grounds.

The first is their systematic attempt to bypass the duly constituted and democratically elected heads of the student body, the ASUC who, although sympathetic to the specific demands of the FSM, disapproved of their tactics and wished to negotiate with the administration and faculty. The student leaders of the FSM, who talked about democracy but did not practice it, in response to this criticism denigrated the ASUC, as a company union. When this response failed of its effect, they claimed that the ASUC was not representative, that the graduate students had been "disfranchised from the Student Government in 1959." ("Disfranchised" is the word also used on page 13 of the Preliminary Report, "The Berkeley Free Speech Controversy," prepared by a self-styled Fact-Finding Committee of Graduate Political Scientists which contains no facts prejudicial to the FSM.) The actual facts turn out to be that, far from being disfranchised, in April 1959 the graduate students were allowed to withdraw after 1,300 of them had petitioned for "disassociation" from the ASUC and for relief from paying the fees involved. The move was upheld in a poll of graduate students. Finally, when the student body, misled by the leaders of the FSM and angered by the mistakes of the governor and administration, was aroused, the leaders of the FSM set out to contest the posts of the ASUC in the student elections in order to capture what they had labeled a company union.

The second and morally the gravest dereliction was the abuse of the principle of civil disobedience in a democracy, the needless risk of mass violence and bloodshed, thus opening the door to a politicalization of the University which may weaken and compromise the degree of University autonomy achieved in the past. Whatever the gains of the FSM, and the situation is now back to where it was in September before the first ruling, they could have been achieved without the sit-downs and sit-ins.

Civil disobedience, since it violates the democratic rule that abuses in a democracy must be remedied by legal means, should be employed only in extreme situations, and in behalf of a great and noble cause like national freedom in India or civic freedom in the United States. The doctrine which inspired Dr. Martin Luther King, Jr. was drawn from the teachings of Gandhi and Tolstoy. "I am here," said Gandhi before the British Court in Ahmedabad, "to invite and cheerfully submit to the highest penalty that can be inflicted upon me for what in law is a deliberate crime and what appears to me to be the highest duty of a citizen." And later to his own countrymen: "Rivers of blood may have to flow before we gain our freedom, but it must be our blood." In summarizing the rationale of non-violent resistance to evil, Dr. King said at Oslo:

> We will not obey unjust laws. We will do this peacefully, openly, cheerfully, because our aim is to persuade. We adopt the means of non-violence because our end is a community at peace with itself. We will try to persuade with words, but if our words fail, we will try to persuade with our acts of civil disobedience. We will always be willing to talk and seek a fair compromise, but we are ready to suffer when necessary and even risk our lives to become witnesses to the truth as we see it.*

Both Gandhi and Dr. King stress the fact that while they would not submit to unjust laws, they were prepared to submit to the penalties provided by those unjust laws.

These doctrines and practices are not to be lightly invoked and trivialized by being irresponsibly injected into situations to settle complex questions on which reasonable men of good will can legitimately differ. Whether a rule should be formulated to forbid or command university authorities to restrict on-campus organization for off-campus illegal activities is such a question. It is a question, I have argued, on which both sides are wrong. To throw a university into turmoil, to risk violence and bloodshed, over issues of this sort is the height of irresponsibility.

* I am indebted to the writings of Dr. Milton Konvitz for these quotations on civil disobedience.

To make matters worse, the leaders of the FSM fail to understand that the techniques of civil disobedience and the site of its action, according to Gandhi and Dr. King, must be related to the specific evil being opposed. If it is wrong to discriminate against Negroes or untouchables at lunch counters or temples, it is at those places that the law must be disobeyed. If a board of education refuses to desegregate its schools, the sit-in may be justified on its premises but not on a bridge or highway miles away used by out-of-town motorists. If a university refuses to register Negro students, a sit-in may be justified in its administration building, not in its boiler or fire-control rooms. If students regard the setting up of tables on campus as a non-negotiable issue comparable to the great causes of civil freedom and independence, their civil disobedience would be expressed by setting-up tables, not by seizing the administration building or striking classes to close down the University.

And once the FSM leaders bravely defy the dreadful rules of the University and chase the administrators from their offices, the ethics of civil disobedience requires that they cheerfully accept the punishment they voluntarily invited instead of making loud lamentation or whining complaint about the enforcement of the law. When Thoreau refused to pay his tax, he didn't run for the hills or refuse to plead.

It is obvious that for the FSM leaders, the sit-in as a form of civil disobedience is just a tactical "gimmick." They are not pacifists; their mentor agrees with Lenin and Trotsky about the role of pacifism in the struggle against capitalism. Aware that the trivialization of the civil disobedience movement can only end in making them absurd, they strive with desperate rhetoric to identify their cause with the cause of the civil rights movement in Mississippi, their danger in California with the dangers of the Mississippi martyrs, and their opponents, Kerr, Strong and the faculty critics of the FSM, with the conscienceless Mississippi officials who have trampled the Bill of Rights into the dust.

What adds to the moral offensiveness of the behavior of the FSM leaders is their unexampled effrontery and arrogance. One reads with astonishment in the Heyman Report of their invasion and interference with a University function as early as September 28. I know of no other faculty which would tolerate behavior of this kind, a disruption of an official meeting carried out in open defiance of requests to leave. Whoever heard of negotiations with students prefaced by ultimata from them—"Yield within twenty-four hours or else—"? Where except at political meetings is a microphone grabbed in the way Savio grabbed the microphone at the ill-fated Greek theater meeting? "Horrendous!" he proclaims of the regents declaration of December 18 which even the Emergency Executive Committee of the Academic Senate, after the Senate had capitulated to the FSM at its meeting of December 8, professed to find quite encouraging on the whole. A "sell-out" and "a violation of the spirit of the December 8 resolution," declares Miss Myra Jehlem, a member of the FSM Executive Committee, of the Report of the Academic Freedom Committee on how to implement the surrender to the FSM. "We will sue *The New York Times*," threatened leaders of the FSM, these impassioned advocates of free speech, in their interview with Mr. Raskin of its editorial staff.

The Berkeley episode was not only unprecedented in the history of American education: unprecedented was the gall and tone of contemptuous arrogance the leaders of the FSM took toward the administration and faculty. "We made monkeys out of them!" crowed one of their supporters in an abusive but revealing letter to me. And actually the leaders of the FSM were acting on a maxim that can best be rendered in a Jewish idiom: "When dealing with *Yolden, Chutzpah becomes Chochmah!*" When dealing with the simple-minded, nerve becomes wisdom! Who were the simple-minded in the Berkeley situation? To answer this question we must examine the sad, sad role of the faculty at the University of California.

The Failures of the Berkeley Faculty: The role the faculty played is described by Mr. Draper in a speech (January 9) defending the leaders of the FSM, acting under his tutelage, against the charge that the FSM could have done as well or better by different methods, methods more "reasonable" and less "intransigeant."

> But it's not true. And the proof that it was not true came on December 8th, when the "intransigeants" were satisfied— weren't they, that day, when the Academic Senate's resolution was adopted, which adopted the position of the FSM.

Now remember, this is what it was all about. It was this—the question of "free speech" and the rights of social and political activity—which the Academic Senate adopted. That was it . . . And it was on this issue that, at this time, the FSM smashed the "non-negotiable" position of President Kerr and the administration, and won the faculty to support its position.

Now I tell you that this was a titanic achievement. It had never been achieved before by any student movement in this country. I say that as an expert on the subject . . . I was, in the 1930s, a member of the first national committee of the American Student Union . . . In 1934 and '35, I and another chap organized the very largest of the student anti-war strikes of these years. [At these strikes, students took the Oxford Oath never to bear arms in defense of their country. Hitler was already rearming!—*S.H.*]

And I tell you solemnly that no where, at no time in this country, has any student protest ever scored such a smashing achievement [as this one] over a hostile administration.

Mr. Draper is wrong in his dogmatic contention that no other method but the violation of law would have succeeded in modifying university policy. After all, community and legislative opposition to Communist Party speakers on campus was much more vehement than to illegal student picketing for civil rights for Negroes off campus. Yet Dr. Kerr had been able to reverse regents policy without benefit of student sit-ins. Had they occurred, the ban probably would never have been rescinded. And even before that, under President Sproul in 1956, faculty and students had been able to revise Rule 17, the regulation which barred political activity on campus, *without* any sit-ins.

Nonetheless, Draper is justified in claiming a smashing victory. It was a victory which, with the help of the overwhelming majority of the faculty, smashed the traditions of orderly educational process and opened the gates to the politicalization of the American university system. Although the leaders of the FSM may not press their luck further, their actions will probably inspire others.

How did all this come about? Certain relevant facts must be considered. The first is that the Faculty Senate was originally vested by the State Legislature with disciplinary authority in enforcement of University rules. It subsequently relinquished this power formally to the Regents who then entrusted it to the administration. The Faculty, however, could always express its position on matters that had a bearing on educational policy, which is still officially in its province. The issues of substance and discipline created by the conflict between the FSM and the administration were definitely within the purview of educational policy. There was nothing to prevent the Faculty from taking a stand on these issues or considering appeals made to it. And it did take a stand! On several occasions before the final FSM sitdown, it condemned the use of "force and violence" on the campus but without specific reference to the FSM. It also failed to repudiate the action of the administration, which it could have and should have done, at its October meeting. It referred the issue and problems to its Academic Freedom Committee. At its meeting of November 24, it *defeated* two resolutions. The first motion, defeated by a vote of 274 to 261, proposed to limit University regulation of student speech and activity only to the extent "necessary to prevent undue interference with other University affairs." The second resolution defeated sought to establish a new Faculty Committee to deal specifically with student political conduct.

Up to this point, the majority of the faculty, whatever its doubts about the administration, seemed opposed to the FSM primarily because of its resort to the disorderly and illegal tactics of campus sit-downs. After the students were removed by the police from Sproul Hall, an agreement was reached between the department chairmen and President Kerr to restore educational peace and order on the campus (the Scalapino proposals). These were presented at a convocation of Faculty and students at the Greek theater on December 7. The chairmen were unanimously behind the Scalapino proposals and discussed them with their respective departments before the convocation. Although there was some disagreement with these proposals expressed in some departments, there is little doubt that they were acceptable to most of the faculty.

Of the five proposals, the two which are most relevant in understanding the nature of the subsequent triumph of the FSM leaders were, first, the promise of complete disciplinary amnesty for the actions of all students involved in the events prior to and inclusive of December 3, and, second, the statement that *"the*

*Department Chairmen believe that the acts of civil disobedience
on December 2 and 3 were unwarranted and that they obstruct
rational and fair consideration of the grievances brought forward
by the students."*

What the mass meeting in the Greek theater was supposed to
accomplish has remained mystifying to me as well as to others
who have described its proceedings. And once Savio had reached
the microphone, he should have been permitted to talk and not
been dragged away and then given access to it again—an opportunity he cleverly exploited by substituting a brief announcement
for the intended harangue, thus giving the impression to some
naïve minds that all he had desired in the first place was to cooperate with the purposes of the meeting. He had made no request
to be permitted to broadcast an announcement.

At the final Academic Senate meeting the next day, not by
so much as a word did the adopted resolutions condemn the
tactics and behavior of the FSM. On the contrary. A motion to
amend these resolutions which was interpreted as a minimal rebuke for the FSM was overwhelmingly defeated. The faculty thus
explicitly refused to condemn "the lawlessness" of the FSM action.
Coupled with the demand for a complete amnesty for the arrested
students, this was tantamount to an *approval* of the sit-in actions.
What was condemned in effect were the policies of the regents,
President Kerr and his entire administration, the past policies of
the faculty itself, and the position of the hundred-odd members
of the faculty who opposed this capitulation to the demands of the
leaders of the FSM. Draper was justified in crowing over the
smashing victory he and his disciples had won.

The mechanics of the victory depended upon a hard core of
about two hundred members of the faculty who were in complete
sympathy with the FSM from the very beginning and whose
leaders were obviously in touch with the leaders of the FSM. This
group met the day before the meeting at the Greek theater to plan
the strategy to win the Academic Senate to endorse the FSM position. After the meeting of the Greek theater, "word is spread that
he [President Kerr] has endorsed the resolutions of the two hundred," says *The Report of the Fact-Finding Committee of Graduate Political Scientists* (page 9). The Report does not say that
the "word" about Kerr's approval was false, and that those who

spread it were leading members of "the 200." The teachers were learning factional political tactics from their students.

At any rate, the Academic Freedom Committee of the Senate accepts the resolutions. At the meeting of the Senate, the next day, one of the leading members of "the 200" gives his colleagues the definite and uncontradicted impression that the administration itself is behind these proposals! The department chairmen sit silent. President Kerr is not present to speak for himself or his administration. The vote rolls in to the cheers and jeers of a huge crowd of students and non-students massed outside the assembly hall of what must be regarded as the strangest faculty meeting in the history of American education.

It is this *approval* of student lawlessness on the part of the faculty, no matter what its alleged causes—ignorance of the facts, resentment against the administration, weariness with the whole business, conformism, desire to curry favor with students—which constitutes the most shocking aspect of the role of the faculty in the Berkeley episode. The misled students have the excuse of youth, and the administration that it didn't understand until too late the fundamental political orientation of the FSM leadership. But the faculty took its position on the only issue that was clearly defined in the situation, *viz.,* whether the complex of problems arising from the effects of speech and action, on-campus or off-campus, on the educational objectives of the university, should be resolved by educational means or by student resort to civil disobedience. Its vote can only serve to encourage further lawlessness.

Unfortunately there were even some individuals among the faculty who abused their position of academic authority to help the FSM. Some called off classes to make the student strike more effective. One assistant professor listed the term "civil disobedience" among the main topics to be discussed in his course on biochemistry and coolly defended its relevance to the subject matter on the grounds that he was concerned with the "social" organization of cells. Another professor of biochemistry included as one of five questions on his final examination: "In your opinion, what were the events, conditions, acts, and other factors which led to the campus turmoil of the last few months and, in particular, to the sit-in at Sproul Hall and the campus-wide strike?" The professor explained that he had included this question because some students had told him they were behind in their studies in consequence of the FSM activity. He defended himself against criticism on the ground that the question was optional. Those who could answer the other questions based on their knowledge of the course work were not compelled to answer it. It is difficult to tell which shows greater contempt for the standards of academic integrity—the actions themselves or the justifications offered for them.

In view of the foregoing, I have been asked on what grounds I can justify my educational philosophy that the faculty should have the ultimate authority to determine all basic policies of education and discipline in the university. I can only reply by paraphrasing a remark of Justice Frankfurter—the appeal from the decision of an unenlightened faculty must be made to the decision of an enlightened faculty. There is no need for administrative or political action which would further undermine the relative autonomy of the University. The need is for further reflection by the faculty.

In what follows I shall examine not the causes of the actions of the Berkeley faculty but the grounds offered in defense of them.

Some Faculty Rationalizations: A considerable mass of literature by members of the Berkeley faculty justifying their actions already exists. That they should have felt it necessary to explain and to defend their refusal to condemn student lawlessness is natural enough in view of the bewilderment of their colleagues elsewhere. But the character of the explanations only increases one's bewilderment.

I restrict myself to a series of statements published by some leading members of the faculty to explain matters to "the troubled friends of the university" and to the plea submitted to the justice of the municipal court by approximately 200 members of the Berkeley faculty urging that the legal action against the students— not university sanctions, which had all been lifted—be dismissed on simple grounds of *justice*.

A lengthy statement by Professor Charles Sellers flatly states that "the great majority of the faculty heartily disapproved the methods and tactics of the FSM." Why, then, didn't the great majority say so? Because "seeing faults on both sides, [it] nevertheless scrupulously sought to avoid praise or censure." But this is a complete nonsequitur. First, the faculty could have condemned *both* administration policy and the FSM behavior; second, its resolutions constituted a sharp repudiation of administrative and previous faculty policy, and a complete vindication of the FSM, whose cries of total victory could be heard as the vote was tallied (the very fact that Professor Sellers explains at such lengths is an indication of how the faculty vote was interpreted); and third, there was no evidence that the FSM leaders cared a farthing whether their tactics were condemned, provided they received their amnesty and their policy was approved (even after their victory, Draper, Savio and Weissman spoke with utter contempt of the faculty as frightened into agreement by the shock tactics of sit-in and strike).

Professor Sellers then adds that the policies expressed in the resolutions adopted by the faculty "do not condone and would not permit the kind of student demonstrations that have occurred on the Berkeley campus this semester." If this is true, it could and should have been said as part of the motion or in a preamble; it would be merely dotting the *i*'s and crossing the *t*'s of the motion. But it is not true. What his words suggest is the hope of a sizeable section of the faculty that if the University yielded to the FSM, their leaders would be surfeited with their success, and cease from further disorders.

The next statement is by Professor Henry Nash Smith. This one is entitled "Why Has the Berkeley Faculty Failed to Condemn Violations of the Law by Students?" I wish I could quote it entire. It is like the story of the man who maintains he has returned the same borrowed pot three times and then ends up denying he ever borrowed it. First, the faculty did not want to condemn the FSM sit-in at Sproul Hall because the country might think that Professor Smith and his colleagues were opposed to civil rights in the South! As if a clear statement of the distinction between a sit-in in behalf of sacred human rights and a sit-in to oppose a request to appear before a civilized faculty committee for a hearing were beyond the rhetorical powers of a distinguished faculty! Second, the idea of "law" has become in the eyes of many respectable citizens "problematical." One cannot answer the question: "Do you condemn all violations of law?" with a simple "yes" or "no"! But no one proposed that the faculty declare that it condemned *all* violations of law! The question was a *specific* violation of a *specific* law with respect to a *specific* issue, the consequences of which disrupted the entire University. Thirdly, "some men learned in the law believe that present University restrictions on advocacy are probably unconstitutional." Some men who are even more learned in the law emphatically deny it—but the whole issue of constitutionality is here irrelevant because the question Professor Smith started out to explain is not why the faculty voted to abandon the restrictions but why it failed to condemn what he himself calls violations of law! Is he suggesting that some men learned in the law believe that the seizure of a University building, in reply to a summons to a hearing from a faculty committee, is constitutional and that to condemn the seizure is not?

Finally, although admitting that a "judicious condemnation" of *both* administration policy and student illegal behavior is "perfectly comprehensible and has a certain moral grandeur," he believes the faculty is justified in begging off from doing this understandable thing because judicious condemnation, even when austerely phrased, can only be expressed in this situation as "invective." What extraordinary things can be heard in California! Why "invective"? After all, the policy of the administration was condemned by the faculty without "invective" or even explicit mention? Yet everybody knew who was meant. Why could not lawless behavior on campus also have been condemned, even without mention of the FSM? Everybody would have known who was meant. It did not require "moral grandeur" to condemn the FSM and the administration. It required only a little wisdom, a sense of fairness, and courage!

This brings us to a printed flyer, widely circulated, from eight faculty members of the University of California at Berkeley and addressed to colleagues and friends in the state-wide University, to members of other colleges and universities, and to fellow citizens. It lists the propositions adopted at the Academic Senate meeting, and tells what they mean. The collective statement is followed by eight individual statements. The collective statement is a gem of modesty—almost humility—designed to reassure everyone that nothing very important has happened. "Very little change" in the current regents rules governing political activity is involved. "It is meant to apply only to the Berkeley campus." No need to take alarm elsewhere. The faculty has merely "suggested one small but important procedural change—that disciplinary jurisdiction over breaches of regulation concerning the time, place and manner of student political activity be transferred to a committee of the Academic Senate." Just a big bang—over an important trifle!

I regret to observe that this simply does not correspond to the facts. There is no reference whatsoever in the collective statement to the meaning of the key proposition number 3, the first two sentences of which read: "That the content of speech or advocacy should not be restricted by the University. Off-campus student political activities shall not be subject to University regulation." Both are flatly contrary to the regents' statements of November 20 and December 18. The first regents' statement proscribes student advocacy of unlawful off-campus political activity —which illustrates a favorite maxim of F. H. Bradley that the opposite of an absurdity may be every whit as absurd. The second regents' statement, of December 18, asserts that no restrictions beyond the purview of the First and Fourteenth Amendment are envisaged, but there are plenty of restrictions *within* the purview of these amendments. Some of them were spelled out in Professor Lewis Feuer's amendment, which was defeated, to Proposition 3.

Professor Philip Selznick claims that the action of the Berkeley faculty upholds "the highest ideals of university education and educational life." He fails, unfortunately, to relate these ideals to the FSM sit-ins and student strike—which he elsewhere characterizes as "direct action, pressure and intimidation." (*Commentary,* March 1965.) "A great many rules and some state laws were broken," he admits. Regrettable, to be sure, but, he adds, we must "get at the root of the trouble." He leaves the matter there. *One* of the roots of the trouble is a mode of thinking which he himself illustrates and which seems to be shared by others. It is expressed in one of the most remarkable sentences to have come out of the situation at Berkeley. "He who insists on obedience to rules should be ready to justify the rules themselves." The context suggests that Selznick interprets this to mean that unless a rule or law seems justifiable to us we are under no obligation to obey it. This is the formula of anarchy. No ordered community life is possible on this basis, for it means that if a minority is outvoted on any proposed law, it is absolved from any obligation to obey it. This goes beyond the extremism of those who say that *unjust* laws should never be obeyed, for it implies that *foolish* laws, which we are not prepared to justify, should also be disobeyed. It was thinking of this kind which contributed to the self-righteous intransigence of the FSM leaders and their faculty supporters. From a moral point of view, one cannot take an unqualified position here. If we distinguish between a substantive law and a procedural rule, we may obey some substantive laws that are unjust or foolish or both because the violation of the procedural rule may lead to morally worse consequences. Sometimes the substantive law is so morally outrageous that we are prepared to accept the consequences to ourselves of violating the procedural rules. Selznick does not say which laws or rules he believes the FSM students were justified in breaking. Setting up the tables on campus in defiance of a foolish rule or seizing the administration building or resisting the police arrest of Weinberg? One could make a case for the first, for had Selznick and the faculty taken a firm stand in October, instead of December, against the first administrative order, events would have taken a different turn. That he is now compelled to justify disobedience to *any* unjust or foolish law indicates the desperate intellectual straits to which he is reduced in his attempt to gloss over the real contempt by the FSM leaders for the democratic process, concealed beneath their ritualistic invocations to principles of free speech.

Professor Carl Shorske must be applauded for the brave opening sentence of his *apologia*. "The primary task of the University of California has always been and must always be teaching, learning and research—*not* political activity." But alas!—with this effort he falls back exhausted. He, too, repeats mechanically that the University cannot regulate "the content" of expression, from which it would follow that, e.g., if a student falsely charges that his teacher demanded a bribe for passing him or her, "the content" of the statement presumably is no business of the University. His common sense reasserts itself in his final sentence:

"Offences against the University community should be punished by the University." Excellent! Now suppose these offences are committed off-campus! But he has just voted for a resolution that *forbids* the University to regulate any off-campus political activities. "Political" is an umbrella word under which almost any kind of activities can be brought, from hazing Jewish or Negro students, to destroying the books and papers of politically unpopular teachers, and all sorts of things one reads about in the press concerning the off-campus behavior of students in the politicalized universities of other countries. Professor Schorske surely cannot rule out the possibility of the occurrence of off-campus student activities, offensive to the University community, as impossible. Some of these offences may not even be technically illegal. Students may organize fraternities based on principles of segregation the faculty declares harmful to the common educational interest. These off-campus derelictions, according to the Resolutions for which he voted, are not subject to University regulation.

Professor Tussman's *apologia* is even more disappointing because as a political philosopher one expects a little more intellectual sophistication from him than from his colleagues concerning the key proposition 3. But he blandly says it is a "sensible" rule that "obviates most of the difficulties in this sensitive area." It is a pity he leaves the difficulties unmentioned. There are many ways of obviating difficulties. What is wanted is a rule that will help solve difficulties that cannot be properly obviated. What is not wanted is a rule that will create additional difficulties. And this rule does.

Tussman concludes by saying that this rule "expresses the conviction that ours is an institution whose *proper* mode of dealing with the mind is *educational,* not coercive." The conviction is commendable but unfortunately the rule does not express it, since it is obviously concerned with parceling out the sphere of disciplinary *coercion* over student *activities,* on-campus and off-campus. Tussman's conviction is much more appropriate with reference to his condemnation of "radically inappropriate means" of dealing with "problems of mind and spirit," means such as those used by the FSM—sit-downs and student strike, in answer to a request to appear for a *hearing.* I am confident that Tussman agrees because he supported the Scalapino proposals that declared the acts of civil disobedience of October 2 and 3 unwarranted in that they obstruct "rational and fair consideration" of the issues. He therefore owes his colleagues an explanation of why this proposal or some variant of it is absent from the list of propositions whose adoption he justifies.

Professor Miles gives the faculty three *A*'s for supporting three principles; Advocacy, Academic Responsibility, and Amnesty. Since the faculty made no mention of the students' "lawlessness," she could have added Amnesia. The principle of Advocacy is simple. It is "the citizen's constitutional right to *speak* and be heard without the limitations set upon *action*." Professor Miles undoubtedly is aware of what happened to the dean of women at Stanford who did no more than *speak* about the purported behavior of the young male English teachers toward their attractive coeds. And what the dean spoke about wasn't a capital offense either! And yet if she hadn't resigned, since her speech was deemed false, she would have suffered from some "limitation."

The joint declaration of Dean Maslach and Professor S. A. Schaaf make one wonder what the faculty voted for so overwhelmingly at their final meeting. Is it possible that the excitement inside and din outside was so confusing that a considerable number didn't understand what they were voting for or against? I realize that this is a startling suggestion to make about an assembly of distinguished minds. But my justification is the final paragraph of the joint statement of Messrs. Maslach and Schaaf:

> The Berkeley Senate's policy recommendation is the direct followup of the substance of the interim administrative agreement made between all Berkeley Department Chairmen and President Kerr, which was announced to the entire Berkeley campus community at the Greek theater meeting on Monday.

As far as the plain English of the texts of the two sets of propositions goes, it would be far more accurate to say that the second constituted a repudiation of the first.

We need not consider in detail the statement of Professor Henry Nash Smith because we have already analyzed a longer one by him. He gives three reasons for voting for the propositions: (1) *They are in conformity with the United States Constitution.*

But so were the Scalapino proposals. So are the regents' rules. Constitutionality is not relevant here. Only unconstitutionality. (2) *Alternative policies are unworkable.* This is false. The *de facto* policy in existence before Dean Towle's arbitrary administrative ruling was workable. It could have been reinstated without the proclamation of the silly and doctrinaire key proposition number 3. Finally, (3) *the civil rights movement expresses the moral idealism of a whole generation of young Americans.* True, but irrelevant. It was not the moral idealism of the FSM which was objectionable but what they *did* on October 1–2 and December 3–4. Surely even Smith cannot believe that moral idealism is a justification for any or all actions, although he sometimes gives that impression.

Professor Parkinson is another English scholar who also cuts difficult Gordian knots of constitutional law with simple, straightforward speech. "There is no such thing as more or less freedom; men either have freedom or they do not, and limitation of the content of speech destroys freedom." Since there is no legal system in the entire world which does not limit to some degree the content of speech, we must conclude that men are nowhere free. Fortunately for mankind, however, freedom is not like pregnancy. There *are* degrees of it.

Professor Parkinson's second point is that there should be an amnesty for everybody on the Berkeley campus—administration, faculty and students. Few would contest this. He should, therefore, have moved an amendment to Proposition 1 which amnestied *only* the students. Since this proposition provides for the remission of punishment for the students' lawlessness rather than for the extinction of their offense, the amendment could have contained an expression of disapproval of the offense without curdling the charity that inspired the original motion.

I have left to the last the statement of Professor Chamberlain, the eminent physicist and Nobel Laureate, because of a reluctance to criticize the words of so distinguished a scientist. They provide a paradigm case of the phenomenon of nontransference of training from one field to another. Constitutional law and politics are fields in which apparently everyone is an expert. There are so many independent variables involved that many worthy persons imagine that neither study nor thought is necessary to discuss problems in these fields intelligently. What adds to one's acute embarrassment is that Professor Chamberlain's nontransference of scientific training extends to a field in which most parents on the basis of experience acquire some expertise—*viz.,* child-psychology. Professor Chamberlain voted for the resolutions because, as he interprets what he heard the FSM students say, it went something like this:

> Show us you do not have to treat us always as children, but more as adults when we achieve adult skills and facility. Show us that you can, if we insist, treat us like men and women, each responsible for his actions. Show us that we do not have to be treated as children who now and then follow some "insidious" leader.

But surely Professor Chamberlain knows as a parent that the first principle in treating children who want to be regarded as adults is actually to hold them responsible for their conduct, not to apologize or extenuate what they do on the ground that they were children who really meant well; to apply the same rules to them as to other adults in the same relevant situations; to expect them to take the consequences of their deliberate conduct, not necessarily always to punish them but to make them understand when they violate laws that their acts are punishable, and that, even when amnestied, they cannot be continued with impunity. I agree with Professor Chamberlain that the leaders of the FSM were responsible according to their own lights, that some were prepared to accept the appropriate punishment for their actions in breaking the law. The question at issue is the responsibility of the faculty in letting them get away with it. To this Professor Chamberlain does not address himself.

On the question of responsibility, Professor J. ten Broek, and others, have taken up the gauntlet. In their statement to the court before whom the FSM students were brought for violating the law, they claim that all the charges against the students should be dismissed on grounds of *justice.* The "lawlessness" of the FSM is not denied but the responsibility for it is laid completely at the door of the administration. The FSM students are idealized in fulsome language that goes beyond the encomiums their leaders pay themselves. They are hailed as an expression of the highest idealism and promise of American life—as inheritors of the legacy of a martyred President, "answering in force but not in violence" his trumpet call for struggle against the enemies of mankind.

The rhetoric of the document is very strong but it is correspondingly weak in factual accuracy and in the analysis of the key issues. Its most original feature is its discussion of academic freedom and its conclusion that its rights and privileges extend to students as well as teachers. This is reached by an elementary but eloquently expressed confusion between what is desirable on educational grounds and what is entailed by academic freedom.

The factual inaccuracy of the report is manifested as much by what is omitted as by what is misstated. Omitted is the fact that the student leaders were summoned on authority of the regents to answer charges of *violent* lawlessness. Omitted is the record of the Academic Senate motions of November 24 which in effect voted down the demand of the FSM. Omitted is reference to the behavior of the FSM to the ASUC. Misstated is the truth about the policy of the administration, which for all its errors was not one of consistent "vindictiveness" but of compromise, concession and retreat from its foolish positions. Misstated is the implication that all the gains won by the FSM, gains that had almost restored the situation in September, were suddenly snatched from it by the summons of its leaders to a hearing. Misstated crudely is the position of the United States Supreme Court on the illegality of sit-ins in *defiance* of laws that are constitutional. Sit-ins in defiance of local laws that are unconstitutional is one thing: sit-ins in defiance of constitutional law quite another. Even the FSM leaders do not go so far as to say that the state laws that forbid the seizure of public buildings are unconstitutional. And misstated to the point of daring invention is the reference to the alleged action of the state legislature in amending the trespass provisions of the state law and which would make the FSM sit-ins legal!

These omissions and misstatements—and I have not listed them all—are extreme even for a partisan brief. They have one purpose, to indict the administration as totally blameworthy for the events at Berkeley, to exonerate the faculty from any blame, and to present the FSM as completely innocent of wrong-doing, as harassed into lawlessness against its will. The truth is that the administration's faults are very grave, the students' behavior out of all proportion to them, and the conduct of the faculty, in what it at first failed to do and in what it finally did, the most irresponsible of all.

What is odd to the point of being bizarre is the attempt of the signers of the brief to describe the behavior of the students as motivated by a concern for academic freedom.

> The recent events on the Berkeley campus were an expression of the deep concern of students for their rights of membership both in the university community and in the larger political society. It is a concern intimately connected to academic freedom. . . .

But academic freedom cannot exist if the teaching, research, discussion or dialogue is disrupted by pressures, demonstrations, and strikes. The faculty is on record as deploring actions threatening the integrity of the educational process. No one interfered with the students' freedom to learn. There was interference with the freedom to teach. There was no interference with the students' freedom to learn even by doing, after the regents' resolutions of November 20, unless the freedom to learn by doing means freedom to do as one pleases.

The writers of the brief not only falsely invoke the decisions of the Supreme Court and the memory of a martyred President to justify the lawlessness of the FSM, they cite some words from Justice Frankfurter, the great opponent of absolutism, for the same purpose.

> It is the special task of teachers to foster those habits of open-mindedness and critical inquiry which alone make for responsibility in citizens, who in turn make possible an enlightened and effective public opinion . . . The unwarranted inhibition upon the free spirit of teachers . . . has an unmistakable tendency to chill that free play of the spirit which all teachers ought especially to cultivate and practice; it makes for caution and timidity in their associations by potential teachers.

If one were to assess the events at Berkeley in the light of these sentiments—where, one asks, will one find the "open-mindedness" and "the critical inquiry" which make for "responsible citizens"? In the lawlessness of the students who refused to continue the process of negotiations? In their failure to appeal to the faculty? In their threats to close down the University? Do not such actions inhibit "the free spirit of teachers"?

Professor ten Broek and his colleagues escape from drawing the proper conclusions from the above passage by professing to believe that "the academic freedom" of the students has been violated. In order to make the notion of academic freedom applicable to students, they overlook the fact that the students' freedom to learn presupposes but is not presupposed by the teacher's freedom to teach. Where teachers have no freedom to teach students have no freedom to learn, but even where teachers have freedom to teach students may be deprived of freedom to learn by poverty or other social evils which as citizens we must abolish. But where students are deprived of freedom to learn because of poverty or discrimination of various kinds, it is an abuse of language to say that they are being deprived of their academic freedom. They are being deprived of their human rights. The faculty friends of the FSM seize upon the phrase, "potential teachers," and argue that since students are "potential teachers," they are also part of the academic community, "scholars-in-training." As "scholars-in-training," they are "apprentice or junior members of the scholarly community," and therefore are entitled to the rights and privileges of academic freedom, which must be enjoyed by the educational community as a whole.

Every step in the argument is a nonsequitur. And even if it were not contested on logical and factual grounds, all it would show is that students as "junior" members would be entitled not to "academic freedom" in its proper sense but, so to speak, to a "junior" kind of academic freedom.

The view that because students are *potential* teachers, they enjoy or should enjoy the academic freedom of teachers is absurd on its face. As well argue that because children are potentially parents, they already enjoy or should enjoy parental or conjugal rights of a sort. Proper parental guidance and education will someday, we hope, make it possible for children to live better lives as parents than if they are given bad education and bad examples, but it would be ridiculous to recognize their claim to parental authority now. More children will become parents than students professors, but in any case their functions, duties and privileges are distinct.

Academic freedom may not be appreciated by teachers; it may not even be properly used: it may sometimes be abused in order to teach objectionable things or not to teach true or useful things. Nonetheless it does not affect the validity of the ideals of academic freedom. Just as the best remedy for the abuses of a democracy is a better democracy, so the best remedy for the weaknesses of academic freedom is the strengthening of its safeguards. In the twentieth century, academic freedom at different times in different countries is endangered not only by capitalists, politicians and commissars but by students, too. In any University worthy of the name, students can have no academic freedom to violate the academic freedom of their teachers.

Another false cry is that the University wishes to isolate the students from the life of the community. Of course the university is part of the social order, and the broad struggle for civil rights, equality and human welfare will catch up students and teachers both, in its surge and sweep. On the other hand, the leaders of the FSM are highly critical of the University's existing relations to the rest of society—to business, to government, to labor, defense, medicine and other social groups. Is it not hypocrisy to assert that the FSM wishes to take the ideas and ideals it has acquired at the University to the community and yet, at one and the same time, to condemn the multiple ways in which the University now functions in serving and criticizing society? No, the apparent hypocrisy is resolved by the leaders of the FSM in the expectations that the universities will not merely get into the social struggle—they are already in it!—but that they can be made to get in on the right side of the class struggle on which they firmly believe social progress mainly depends.

The fact that the university today functions as the source of more criticism and dissent of the reigning orthodoxies and confusions than any other segment of society is ignored by the leaders of the FSM or interpreted as a carefully tolerated activity to channel off peacefully the discontent endemic to a capitalist society. They confuse the legitimate concern with political issues, their discussion and study, which should be an important part of the curriculum of the university with the politicalization of the university which would spell its ultimate death.

The views, arguments and positions of the leaders of the FSM would hardly be worth the effort involved in analyzing them, if they were alone in holding them. But, as the *amicus curiae* brief or statement presented to the municipal court of the Berkeley-Albany Judicial District indicates, they are also held by twenty-five per cent of the voting faculty of the University of California at Berkeley. A still larger number, although not wholly in agreement, probably supports the major beliefs and actions of the FSM. Having declared itself on December 8, the faculty is not likely to reverse itself and condemn the lawlessness of the FSM, thereby repeating the blunder of the administration in refusing to acknowledge error. On the contrary, the attitude will harden. Original doubts of the wisdom of the position among many members of the faculty will disappear as the necessity to justify their actions to their colleagues on other campuses arises. In time even the history of the events will be transformed. Already legends are springing up not only at Berkeley but elsewhere. It is not likely that there will be additional disturbances at Berkeley. In the next period, the faculty will shut its eyes and ears to almost anything the students will say or do. The leaders of the FSM know that they have milked the operaton for all it is worth politically. They, their friends and congeners will seek greener campuses to widen their sphere of activity. No matter what the cause of student discontent, whether justified or not, the memory of Berkeley will be invoked. It will also inspire fear among administrators who, if the faculty advocates its responsibilities, will swallow almost anything in order "to avoid another Berkeley." Whether it inspires hope or fear, the truth about what actually happened there should be made known.

More important than the events at Berkeley are the issues they pose. I am convinced that on the proper answers to them depend the future relations between faculties and student bodies of American universities. The primary purpose of the university is to pursue the truth and to teach it, subject only to the discipline of the rational methods of achieving the truth. It may have other purposes, too, but none incompatible with this basic ideal of liberal education from Socrates to John Dewey.

NATHAN GLAZER

What Happened at Berkeley*

As I write this, in late December, we in Berkeley are in the Christmas lull. The University's 18,000 undergraduates are for the most part at home, many of the faculty and even some of the graduate students are away. But despite the quiet, the campus is full. The American Physical Society is meeting, which probably explains why it is still difficult to find a parking space even with a faculty sticker ($72 a year). For the first time in weeks, the steps of Sproul Hall, the administration building, are bare of demonstrators and loud-speakers, the entries to the campus are empty of tables collecting money, students handing out literature, or posters announcing meetings. But faculty studies, teaching-assistant rooms, and libraries are busy and show no signs that this is a holiday.

The regents of the University of California met the day before the Christmas recess began, declared that they "do not contemplate that advocacy or content of speech [on the Berkeley campus] shall be restricted beyond the purview of the First and Fourteenth Amendments to the Constitution," and set up a committee to review University policies in consultation with faculty and students "with the intent of providing maximum freedom consistent with individual and group responsibility." (After an earlier meeting, on November 20, during which thousands of students were sitting outside being led by Joan Baez in singing, the regents had said that their policy was to make campus facilities available for "planning, implementing or raising funds or recruiting participants for lawful off-campus action, not for unlawful. . . .") The Emergency Executive Committee of the Berkeley Division of the Academic Senate

* From *Commentary*, March 1965.

(the faculty) issued an optimistic statement after the regents' meeting, asserting that substantial progress had been made.

Despite all this, I—and many other faculty members—are filled with foreboding. We see neither a clear nor a near end to the crisis. And I am afraid it will not be easy for our friends in other places to understand what is going on here; it is hardly possible for those of us closest to it to agree on an interpretation.

To begin with, we must dispose of the ingeniously simple slogan of "free speech" which has made it possible for so many who are far from the events at Berkeley to send in forthright statements in support of the Free Speech Movement or the position adopted by the Faculty on December 8 (that political advocacy or organization should be limited only by minimum regulations designed to permit the University to function normally). Those of us who watched the Free Speech Movement (FSM) daily set up its loud-speakers on the steps of the administration building to denounce the president, the chancellor, the newspapers, the regents, the faculty, and the structure and organization of society in general and universities in particular, could only admire the public relations skill exhibited in the choice of a name for the student movement. Life, however, is not so simple as to present us with a classic free speech issue on the shores of San Francisco Bay.

During 1963–64, my first year as a teacher at Berkeley, student political activity was vigorous beyond anything I had recently seen at any other American college. In front of the concrete posts that mark the main pedestrian entrance to the campus from the busy intersection of Telegraph Avenue and Bancroft Way, one could find, on an ordinary school day, students handing out leaflets advertising many different kinds of political meetings and actions, to be held on the campus itself and off it as well. Various student groups would set up tables stacked with literature, both free and for sale, and members of the group would be available at the tables for discussion, information, and argument. The chief groups represented were socialists—evolutionary, revolutionary, and ambiguous; civil rights organizations such as CORE, or Friends of SNCC; Young Democrats; Young Republicans; and Conservatives. One could expect to come upon supporters of Khrushchev or Mao, Castro or Ho Chi-Minh, marijuana or LSD, not to mention the more garden-variety political and social positions. (We smiled then at the backwardness of eastern campuses where straight sex was still an issue; only homosexuality or perversion, it seemed, could make an issue at Berkeley.) Outdoor meetings were also held at this same location, often as preludes to expeditions to San Francisco, Oakland, and downtown Berkeley to picket business establishments which had failed to negotiate or sign an agreement with CORE or some other civil-rights organization. On the campus itself, large posters were always in evidence announcing a great variety of events, many of them political. Berkeley was one of the few places in the country, I imagine, where in 1964 one could hear a public debate between the supporters of Khrushchev and Mao on the Sino-Soviet dispute —there were organized student groups behind both positions.

Of course regulations existed, administered by deans of students, which these groups had to observe in conducting their activities on campus. For example, the University required seventy-two hours' notice for visiting speakers. If a speaker was controversial, the University would demand that a tenured member of the faculty chair the meeting. On occasion, disputes broke out between the University and a student group over who should pay for putting out the chairs on Dwinelle Plaza (the open-air area in the center of campus where particularly large meetings are held), or whether a student group sponsoring a speaker who was expected to draw a large crowd (for example, Malcolm X) should be required to pay for police protection. These disputes were perhaps portents of what was to come, but the regulations did not seem to inhibit a degree of political activity that was perhaps unique on American campuses.

Nor did they inhibit a number of actions that can only be considered questionable political stunts. Thus, Slate, a student political party, decided that it would be a good idea to bring the West Coast leader of the American Nazi party to the University. He spoke in the largest enclosed space on campus, the men's gym. I do not recall any objections from the administration. The morning of his talk, young men and women wearing Nazi uniforms were posted at the chief entrances to the campus, handing out leaflets announcing the meeting. Later I heard an intense argument between two students at one of the entrances; it transpired that the young Nazi-clad figures were not really Nazis, but adherents of the liberal-progressive Slate, who had hit upon this as a clever way to publicize the meeting.

On another occasion, Slate invited the chief western organizer for the John Birch Society—I chaired that meeting. One could only conclude that inviting Communits to the Berkeley campus had become pretty tame, and an aspiring progressive organization had to invite John Birchers and Nazis to get an audience or to assert its absolute belief in free speech. But whatever one thought of this particular tack adopted by Slate, it was clear that free speech prevailed on the Berkeley campus.

It turned out, at the beginning of the fall semester of 1964, that this grand chaos—as it appeared—of oratory, advocacy, and action, was based on a tangle of distinctions that only the administrative staff that dealt with regulations affecting student organizations, and the leaders of the organizations they regulated, understood—and perhaps not even they. The regulations go back to a time when no political activity of any kind was allowed on campus. Under this earlier situation, even candidates for the Presidency were not allowed to speak at Berkeley: to have permitted such a thing would presumably have involved the University in "politics," and as a state university it was not supposed to be involved in politics. But gradually these rules were qualified and changed to the point where the Berkeley campus, like all other campuses that are proud of their devotion to the principle of free speech, was allowed to have Communist speakers. Largely as a result of such changes, last spring President Clark Kerr was given the Alexander Meiklejohn award by the American Association of University Professors for having made a major contribution to academic freedom.

But through all these modifications of earlier restrictions, a distinction was maintained. The campus was a place for "free speech." It was not, however, a place for advocacy,* for organization, or for collecting money. Thus an "off-campus" political organization (like CORE) could run a meeting "on-campus" but would have to explain to those present that certain kinds of discussion (for example, on implementing a demonstration) must be held off-campus. This was not as great a hardship as it might have

---

* "Advocacy" was used throughout the ensuing dispute to mean advocacy of *action*, not of ideas.

been in other colleges or universities, where the campus is separated physically from the town (as is Stanford) or where the community possesses few meeting places suitable for student groups. Further, just as Berkeley is required to be free of "politics," it is also required to be free of religion in all forms—proselytization, worship, or even the organizational activities of student religious groups. The city of Berkeley, however, surrounds the university. And across the street which marks off campus from city, there is a row of institutions—YMCA, Methodist, Jewish, Episcopalian, etc.— which have often been available for political meetings banned on campus.

To return to the distinction that underlay the regulations (or that some people in the administration believed underlay them) —that is, between "speech" on the one hand, and "advocacy and organization" on the other: traditionally, the chief area for advocacy was the sidewalk in front of the concrete posts which mark the boundary of the University. This was also the area where impromptu meetings would precede the march to the picket lines and the demonstration sites. But ahead, while students leaders were attempting to produce the degree of chaos in the surrounding community that they calculated was necessary to achieve fair treatment for Negroes.

When the chancellor's office passed on to the lesser members of the administrative hierarchy the decision that the strip of land on Bancroft Way outside the concrete posts was now to become subject *de facto* (as it had been *de jure*) to the University ban on advocacy, collection, and organization, the student leaders and their constituencies were already attuned to and experienced in the use of the new tactics. The first rank of the administrative hierarchy to deal with the new regulations, on the other hand, were deans who up till now, one assumes, had been concerned principally with such matters as lock-out rules in female dormitories. Initially the student groups protested the new regulations to these deans. They were immediately able to show that the distinction between "speech" and "advocacy" was difficult or impossible to maintain and ridiculous in an election year; they also showed that traffic could easily flow despite the tables. The administration withdrew somewhat; tables were permitted and advocacy was allowed, but collection and organization were still prohibited. This was unsatisfactory to the students, who resorted to a direct test of whether the administration would enforce the new regulations: they set up their tables and collected money. A number were then directed to appear before a dean on September 29 to discuss these violations. The official account of the chancellor to the faculty, presented a few weeks later, will suggest something of the quality of the ensuing confrontation:

At 3 o'clock that afternoon some 300–400 students moved into the second floor of Sproul Hall and Mario Savio announced that all of them acknowledged violating University regulations in the same manner as those students who had been instructed to make appointments with the dean of students, and they all wanted similar appointments. The dean of men declared that he was then concerned only with observed violations, and if students wanted appointments they could leave their names and he would determine if and when such could be made. He also asked [the students who had been observed in violations] to go in and see a dean because each was involved in a matter of personal discipline, and requested that the crowd disperse, since he had scheduled a meeting of the leaders of the student organizations and their advisers to discuss the problem at 4 o'clock. Savio responded that the group would not leave unless they were guaranteed that the same disciplinary action would be meted out to all there. Unable to make such guarantees, the dean of men again asked the group to leave, and later announced that since, in the opinion of the administration and some of the advisers of the student groups who had come to attend the 4 P.M. meeting, the environment was not conducive to reasonable discussion, the meeting was canceled. . . . The group remained in Sproul Hall until 2:40 in the morning.

In this way, what had originally been a protest by all the student political groups—from revolutionary socialist to extreme conservative—was transformed very early into a movement run by the civil rights leaders. For as soon as the tactics of the protest "escalated" into questionably legal activities (like sitting-in at Sproul Hall, which was done for the first time on September 29) the right-wingers could not go along. They were still part of the protest movement for a few more days. But they stood aside from further escalations—the surrounding of the campus police car containing an arrested prisoner on October 1, the loose and then the tight sit-in at Sproul Hall that day which prevented the deans from leaving or anyone from entering, the decision to maintain the sit-in around the police car throughout October 2. By that time, it was clear that the leadership of the movement was now coming exclusively from the civil rights and left-wing political groups. But there were too few students directly committed to the left-wing groups to provide the necessary "bodies"—to use the term popular with the civil rights leaders. Only the civil rights groups, and only with the good issues handed to them by administration action, could raise hundreds ready to sit-in.

On October 2, the movement won its first great victory—the withdrawal of the menacing array of police that had been concentrated on the campus, and a meeting with Clark Kerr in which a pact was signed calling for an administration-faculty-student committee to deal with the issue of political activity. At this meeting with President Kerr, the right-wing and religious student groups were still represented. Then the Free Spech Movement, at a marathon two-day meeting, organized itself officially, and from that meeting neither the right-wing nor the religious groups emerged with any positions of leadership. More than that, the Young Democrats and even the right-wing Socialists, who had played an important role in the demonstration around the police car, were excluded. In a pattern similar to other and grander revolutions, the student uprising had moved to the left—into the control of the civil rights leaders identified with direct action, and of the leaders of groups in a direct or indirect line of descent from the Communist and Trotskyist student political groups of the past. As for the followers, they mainly came from students involved in or touched by the civil rights movement.

If the leadership of the student movement was rapidly concentrated into a coherent and tightly knit cadre, sharing very much the same philosophy and outlook, the other elements of the University community were split and in disarray. Let us look first at the "administration." Where in the history of American higher education has the administration of a university loomed so large as at Berkeley? In the past, presidents, faculties, and boards of trustees have been important—but *administrations?* This is another sense in which Berkeley may be unique; and yet one fears that the future of American higher education may be foreshadowed here. Everyone—arriving faculty members, arriving deans, visiting authorities —is astonished by· the size of the administration at Berkeley, and in the statewide University of California. One large building near the campus is completely devoted to the statewide administration, another on the campus to the Berkeley administration. The title "dean," which at other universities carries dignity, is used at Berkeley to cover a wide variety of jobs, only some of them academic (where the traditional dignity still attaches to the title), but many deans have not come up through the faculty and have little to do with it. They deal with student affairs. For presumably 27,000 students provide a good number of non-academic problems which neither the faculty nor the academic deans would want to be bothered with.

Academic matters are handled by the academic deans and their assistants. The size of these staffs is impressive, and unfortunately —given certain conditions—necessary. Many students move to Berkeley from other campuses of the state university, from state colleges, from junior colleges, from other institutions outside the state. Each institution has its own requirements—for entrance, for graduation, for majors—and the work done elsewhere therefore has to be evaluated and harmonized to the Berkeley requirements. The evaluations are often argued and fought over, and the student is often frustrated in his fight. In the end a bureaucracy is probably the only system by which a vast number of cases can be managed equitably. Yet while the rules may be just, the sense of justice done is rarely communicated by a clerk or an assistant dean's determination. Could we operate with a smaller administration? Very likely. Yet one thinks of such matters as vast numbers of migrating undergraduates to be fitted into the university, and thousands of graduate students, a large proportion of whom are also employees receiving regular checks for research assistantships, teaching assistantships, fellowships. There are also hundreds of new faculty members every year, each of whom has had to be passed on by various committees. There are scores of research institutes, hundreds of research contracts, each involving separate budgets, all to be coordinated. It is difficult to communicate any sense of the scale of the administration at Berkeley. Let me give a personal report: when I arrived in Berkeley after working for the federal government, my feeling was that the quality of the two settings—organization piled upon organization, reaching to a mysterious empyrean height—was remarkably similar. I understood from other faculty members that this was rather new, that it was only in recent years that the administration had become so huge.

Ironically, President Kerr, in his Godkin lectures, has offered the best general text—perhaps the only existing one—on what is happening. The students have been among its most avid readers, and have not shared the admiration of some reviewers of the book who see in the University of California, as described by its president, the democratic university of the future, combining high standards and mass education. President Kerr describes the shift from the liberal arts college offering a humane education, to the early university which trained men in the traditional professions and for scholarship and college teaching, to the modern "federal grant" university, half of whose budget may come from federal research grants.

It would be an error to think of these grants as being devoted only to war-making and to statecraft. Vast sums flow for social and psychological and policy research, research as useful to a benign welfare state—or, for that matter, a modern authoritarian state—as to a Cold War America. Obviously, however, the federal grant university is not entirely dependent on federal grants. All undergraduate and graduate teaching is covered by state funds, and in many departments—languages, philosophy, history, English, art, and music—little if any part of faculty salaries comes from research grants. Nevertheless, the effect of the federal millions is larger than one would suspect from a direct accounting of where the money goes. The research funds strengthen the University's capacity to compete for faculty, for they allow members to be relieved from teaching and to supplement their regular nine-month salary from a research budget during the summer. These funds also permit the recruitment of greater numbers of graduate students, who normally expect to be supported out of research and teaching assistantships —and even if the latter are covered by state funds, the students are there because federal money will eventually support their own research.

It is easy to conclude that everyone benefits from this except the undergraduate, whose instruction is largely in the hands of teaching assistants. And yet a year ago, when I was spending my first term on the Berkeley campus, I could not find much restiveness or resentment among the undergraduates. Indeed, several told me they preferred Berkeley to the junior colleges and state colleges from which they had come, despite the fact that a layer of graduate students was interposed between them and the professional staff. And they said that the lectures at Berkeley were more stimulating despite the size of the classes. Of course, such undergraduates had moved to Berkeley from schools with smaller classes for other reasons besides the quality of the education, whatever that might be: the life of the campus and the college town around it was undoubtedly a great attraction.

But resentment ran higher, I would judge, among graduate students, many of whom discovered that their professors were just as busy when it came to bothering with them as they were where undergraduates were concerned. Once again the pleasurable environment of learning had escaped them; they were working hard as research assistants and teaching assistants, on other men's research and courses, but they were denied the satisfaction of an intellectual community which brought students and teachers together. Their relations with faculty were too often quite businesslike, the exchanges of services for money. And how could it be otherwise when the professors were burdened with so many governmental, teaching, administrative, and research duties?

Resentment also ran high among the faculty. Many remembered an easier life as junior faculty, on the Berkeley campus or elsewhere. They could not understand why they were always so busy, and found that scholarly labors could best proceed away from the campus. Thus many protected themselves from their students and their colleagues by working at home. But there was another source of resentment for them—the incorporation of Berkeley, which had previously enjoyed a good deal of independence, into the structure of the statewide university, with its eight or nine campuses and its statewide administration, trying to coordinate the varied institutions that had been brought together or were coming into existence as parts of the University of California. Berkeley's incorporation meant that in one matter after another which affected faculty—the shift from semesters to quarters, the setting of standards of admission, the distribution of students among campuses—decisions could be and were taken that were not the decisions the faculty, or individual members of it, wanted.

As a result of these changes, and as a result of the administration's insensitivity to the problems involved, a degree of distance developed between statewide and campus administration, between administration and faculty, between faculty and students, that may well have been unique in American education. The question we must ask, however, before distributing blame is this: given the need or the desire to create an enormous system of statewide university education, how could such a situation have been avoided?

Certainly the faculty, while complaining of the inaccessibility of the administration and its insensitivity to faculty needs, was not very responsive on its own part to student needs. A public meeting some of us ran on the problems of education at Berkeley last year was attended by only a handful of faculty (and not much more than a handful of undergraduates and graduate students). The faculty does not respond enthusiastically to occasional efforts by the administration to get it to consider ways of improving undergraduate education. But at the same time it must be said that faculty members generally censor their impulses to educational reform because they are aware of the many barriers that would have to be vaulted to get the change through. The new faculty member learns rapidly enough that if he devotes himself to his research, his courses, and his pro forma service on committees, he is doing all that is expected of him—and all that any reasonable man, in the prevailing system, would want to undertake.

The university administration, then, was both rigid—as we all knew from experience—and fragile—as we discovered in the crisis raised by its attempt to change the *de facto* rules governing student political activity. For in the situation created first by reasonable student demands and secondly by new and radical student tactics, the administration showed itself incapable of consistent, decisive, or effective action. Again and again it was forced to withdraw from positions either because they were poor ones, or poorly argued and defended, or because the higher levels (the president) moved in and changed the positions taken lower down (the chancellor).

The confusion above, a confusion veiled by silence and inaccessibility, could only increase by geometric progression down below. Asked to enforce policies about whose rationale and stability they were uncertain, the deans could only put up a very poor show, and in the course of the crisis the student leaders—having discovered very early how to break through to the top—treated them with greater and greater insolence and arrogance. Rapidly becoming more expert in the techniques of organization and publicity, these leaders soon added a powerful wing to their original movement—the graduate students. They soon discovered too that there was little to fear in breaking the rules, for the faculty was so unsympathetic to the administration and its rigid and mechanical handling of the problem that, while it would not at first directly support the students and their tactics, it was always ready to attack the administration.

The next casualties were the chancellor and the vice-chancellors. As early as October 2 the president, ignoring the advice and actions of the chancellor's office, had intervened to make a direct pact with the students—which the chancellor was expected to carry out. More important than the structure of authority which permitted the chancellor to be overridden was the fact that neither he nor his staff could come up with a leader to handle a political crisis for which a close study of the French and Russian revolutions might well have provided the only suitable training. Certainly there was no one at this level who could influence the students or deal effectively with them. Nor, as it turned out, was there anyone at this level who could deal effectively with the faculty and convince them that the matter was being handled intelligently or morally. On at least two important occasions faculty members—including myself —who did not support the tactics of the students felt that the administration had acted against the spirit or the letter of an agreement in trying to discipline student leaders. In both cases it was unclear whether it was the chancellor, the president, or the board of regents—the highest authority—who had ordered the action. But whatever the facts, the chancellor's authority was weakened by these incidents.

We must now speak in more detail about the role of the faculty. At the start, the faculty for the most part looked upon the conflict between the administration and the students as detached and neutral outsiders. From the beginning, however, groups of faculty members thrust themselves into the situation as mediators. They (or some of them) were distinguished from the great majority of their colleagues by the fact that they had been involved in student politics in the past and remained interested in them in the present. The first such group of mediators (of which I was one) helped to draw up the pact of October 2. But we eventually joined the administration as casualties of the developing crisis. We became casualties, I believe, owing to the critical change in the issues of the conflict that occurred around the beginning of November. This change became apparent in the discussions of the faculty-student-administration committee that had been set up by the October 2 pact. For the first month there had been two fairly straightforward issues: the attempt of the administration to change the status quo, which all the student political groups, left and right, and all interested faculty opposed; and secondly, the student tactics, which some of the student groups and most of the interested faculty opposed, but which everyone agreed should not lead to disciplinary action (on the ground that the original issue which had occasioned the tactics had been a just one). To my mind, these two problems were settled when the administration's representatives on the committee provisionally accepted a much wider range of political advocacy and organization on campus than had been permitted before, and when a second committee (faculty) set up under the October 2 pact called for the lifting of the suspensions that had been pronounced against the students who had violated the old regulations.

Until this point, the interested faculty members and the student FSM leaders had stood together. But now the student leaders and the administration raised a new issue, created by the prospective liberalization of the rules. If the campus was to be opened up for advocacy and organization, what of advocacy and organization that led to illegal actions or was designed to produce illegal actions? This was no abstract question. The administration's insistence on a line between the legal and illegal—a line it had not drawn when no advocacy or organization was permitted on campus —seriously strained the court system of San Francisco. The fact that the State of California has a law banning discrimination in employment and a commission devoted to ending discrimination in employment seemed to leave the demonstrators unmoved. Indeed, they often insisted that they themselves rather than the state agency should police the agreements they had won from the employers.

The civil rights movement created a situation among the student political groups on campus quite different from the one which had prevailed when such groups were fighting for the loosening of the strict regulations which once governed their political activity. Besides introducing new tactics, the civil rights movement developed a large body of students committed to these tactics, and a substantial body of public opinion—in the faculty and among the liberal population of the area—sympathetic to them. Admittedly, Berkeley was ideally suited to serve the expansion of the radical civil rights movement in the North. It had never been affected to the extent other colleges were by the mood of the "silent generation" of the fifties. (In 1960, remember, when the House Unamerican Activities Committee met in San Francisco City Hall, hundreds of Berkeley students were willing to attempt to disrupt its hearings.) Indeed, in 1957, when I visited Berkeley for the first time, a number of socialist youth leaders from the East had just migrated here, because they found the political climate peculiarly congenial to their work. (In addition, it was my impression that Communism too retained more life and relevance in the Bay area than in the East.) Some of these socialist youth leaders became students; some worked at the University; others worked in the community, becoming part of the penumbra of campus life which at Berkeley involves many people who are neither students, faculty, nor staff, but who may have been part of the University at one time in the past and who possibly will again be part of it in the future.

The strains produced by the application of the new tactics in the mild racial climate of San Francisco had already been intense. Was the Bay area Mississippi, it was asked, that actions had to be taken which destroyed private businesses when there was legal redress for the wrongs that the students believed existed? Few people in public life thought so. Even many liberals were troubled, and during 1963–64, some state legislators and others demanded that the University move against the students who had been arrested in civil rights actions. President Kerr refused, asserting that what students did off-campus was their business, so long as they did not use campus facilities for it. Here again was the distinction between speech on the one hand and advocacy and organization on the other. On this distinction the president, the regents, and chancellor Strong of the Berkeley campus apparently hoped to ride out the hard year at the beginning of the fall semester of 1964, the University administration decided to enforce the distinction between "speech" and "advocacy and organization" on the strip of sidewalk in front of the posts (which is also the property of the regents of the University of California).

Various reasons for this decision have been given. The administration at first asserted that the number of tables and meetings had become so great as to interfere with traffic. The students argued that there were more forceful reasons. During the preceding summer, while the Republican Convention met at the Cow Palace, students were recruited here not only for the usual civil rights activities (which included in this case blocking the entrances to the Cow Palace for a while) but to pack the galleries for Scranton. During that summer, in addition, civil rights demonstrators decided to move against the *Oakland Tribune,* owned by the family of former Senator Knowland, and the students charged that it was his complaint that led the administration to ban "advocacy and organization" on the strip of sidewalk in question.

There now began a conflict between two very unevenly matched opponents: the student political organizations and the administration of the Berkeley campus of the University of California. Berkeley has a long history of student agitation for the widening of freedom of political action on campus. This history has involved petition, picketing, demonstrating, research and argument, and the like. Many alumni of these efforts are still on and around the campus. A number of lawyers, in and outside the law school, have been involved in such past disputes and know them in detail. But the present student constellation differs markedly from that of only a few years ago, and thus a radically new style was adopted for this newest conflict with the administration over political activity.

The great new factor has, of course, been the civil rights movement, and particularly the development of the new techniques of civil disobedience, which opened up the lunch counters of the South and then spread to the North. Nowhere have these techniques been adopted with more enthusiasm and success than in the Bay area. Last year hundreds of Berkeley students—along with students from San Francisco State College and elsewhere, and non-students as well—"sat-in" at a chain of lunch counters, "shopped-in" at a chain of supermarkets (they would fill a cart with groceries, let the clerk reckon the total on his machine, and then leave the mess of groceries on the counter, insouciantly declaring they did not have the money to pay for them), "slept-in" at the Sheraton Palace Hotel, lay down in the automobile showrooms of Van Ness Avenue. This activity led in each case to an agreement to hire a certain number of Negro workers. It also led in some cases to mass arrests and mass trials, which were immediately seen by the students as a threat to actions they were already planning (against the *Oakland Tribune,* various local merchants, etc.) and which in their minds were being held up by the involvement of their forces in the campus dispute. (They were, of course, aware of the large number of potential recruits they had attracted on the basis of the free-speech issue.) The student leaders fully expected further mass arrests as a result of these actions, and they hoped to protect their rear against University discipline.

On this issue of illegal action the faculty-student-administration committee split in November. The student representatives insisted on a specific guarantee that nothing they advocated or organized on campus would lead to any measures by the University against them or their organizations. The administration members insisted on the right to discipline individuals or organizations who advocated or organized illegal action. The faculty group proposed a formula which neither gave the students a specific guarantee of immunity nor the administration a specific ban against illegal action on campus. Under this formula the students would have conducted their demonstrations and sit-ins in all likelihood safe from University interference, for the University's policy of the year before had been not to discipline those arrested for civil rights activities and it seemed improbable that this policy would be changed. If, however, the University decided on a change, the students could have tested in the courts its right to punish them for illegal action advocated or organized on campus—a contingency which, they asserted, would be "against the First and Fourteenth amendments" and would constitute "double jeopardy."

This course, which would have permitted the students to turn their attention to what they felt to be such critical substantial problems as discrimination on the *Oakland Tribune,* they rejected. Their movement would not give up the issue provided them by the split on the question of illegal action. Those faculty members like myself who had been sympathetic until this time, but now withdrew their support, were denounced orally and in print as "finks" and stooges of President Kerr (who had become the *bête noir* of the students, his hand seen in every move).

On this issue the students decided to abrogate the pact of October 2 (in which they had agreed to stick to legal action), pronounced (on their own authority) new rules to govern political activity on campus, and began to operate under them. The students now hoped that the regents would give them what the committee set up under the pact of October 2 had not, but on November 20, the regents insisted on maintaining the distinction between lawful and unlawful actions. At this point the student leaders split, some arguing for further drastic measures, others urging *de facto* acceptance of the new rules under which they had full freedom of action, but were threatened by the possibility of University punishment for illegal action. A new sit-in was staged at Sproul Hall, which involved only 300 students; the administration did not act against it, and it was called off after a few hours.

Then, on November 30, it was learned that the administration (Strong? Kerr? the regents?) had summoned four student leaders to appear before the Faculty Committee on Student Conduct (advisory to the chancellor) to hear charges against them stemming from their tussles with the police on October 1 and 2. As a result of this blunder, an issue that was capable of arousing the students —the disciplining of their leaders—was fortuitously tied to one that could not—immunity for advocacy or organization of illegal action. The rest of the story has been coverd by the national news media. Once again, on December 2, Joan Baez—no other figure in the United States could better symbolize the tangle of protests, amorphous and specific, that moved the students—sang with them as they occupied Sproul Hall. In the early morning of December 3, a small army of police began carrying out students—about 800 of them. That afternoon, yet another impromptu group of mediating faculty, the department chairmen, met to formulate a compromise which offered full amnesty to the students for the actions of the past two months; they hoped to sell this to the president and the regents. On December 4, a long threatened strike of teaching assistants was launched, and on Sunday, December 6, the president and the regents accepted the department chairmen's compromise.

By this time, however, the student leaders had glimpsed the possibility of complete success. For some days a substantial number of liberal faculty members had been preparing a resolution which asserted that political activity on campus should be regulated only as to "time, place, and manner" in order not to interfere with the functioning of the University, and they were rounding up support for its adoption. The great majority of this group had little sympathy for FSM tactics, but they believed its position on the rules was right. In any case, the larger part of the faculty had now become involved, because they had been forced to confront and take a stand on the strike of their teaching assistants. Many were also shocked by the December 3 police action. The FSM hoped that the faculty resolution supporting their position would pass and they joined its drafters in campaigning for it.

On December 7 the compromise negotiated by the department chairmen was presented by Professor Robert Scalapino and President Kerr to the student body and faculty at a large open-air meeting at the Greek theater. The radicalization of the students—thousands of whom had now participated in sit-ins, strikes, and picketing—had proceeded at a frightening pace over the weekend; full victory was now seen as possible, and the compromise was denounced by the student leaders as a "sell-out." It was at this meeting that Mario Savio, head of the FSM, attempted to seize the microphone, and the campus police dragged him away.

Because of their desperate desire to settle things, because of their experience of one administration failure after another, I believe most of the faculty was by now ready to accept any agreement that might lead to peace. The administration—President Kerr and Chancellor Strong—was absent and silent when a thousand members of the academic senate met on December 8 and by a huge vote endorsed the resolution of the liberal faculty members mentioned above. This resolution—in addition to backing the view that political activity should be unrestricted except for time, place, and manner—demanded that responsibility for disciplinary measures in the area of political activity should be placed in the hands of the faculty. Having lived through months of non-existent or ineffective leadership and increasing disruption and disorder, the faculty also voted for the election of a strong Emergency Executive Committee to represent it. A few days later, however, as if in recoil from the resolution, the faculty elected a moderate executive committee, the majority of whom had not been identified with the preparation and propagation of the resolution that had been adopted so overwhelmingly.

But what of the issue of illegal political activity itself? Did the seven-to-one vote of the faculty resolve that? I do not believe so. At the December 8 meeting Professor Lewis Feuer proposed an amendment to the main resolution which would have excepted speech or advocacy "directed to immediate acts of force and violence" from the general immunity. In support of this amendment, he spoke not of the civil rights movement, which was uppermost in the minds of all the protagonists, but of Mississippi, where such a resolution as had been endorsed by the faculty would deny a university administration the right to move against a chapter of the Ku Klux Klan, and of pre-Nazi Germany, where a similar position in effect prevented university administrations from moving against Nazi students engaged in the destruction of the ground-rules of democratic society. The discussion was intense. Many of those who opposed Feuer were convinced that his amendment raised serious constitutional issues. On the whole it was obvious to those of us who supported his amendment—and had other amendments in mind as well—that the temper of the faculty did not favor any extended consideration of the issues at that time. The students were barred from the meeting, but thousands were outside, and we could hear their roars of approval or disapproval as the debate went on. It was scarcely necessary to be reminded of the terrible power of the student movement, though two professors, both of whom supported the majority resolution, did remind us that chaos was at the door. I think there was a good deal of hysteria mixed in with the action of the Berkeley division of the academic senate that day. Afterward men who had been friends for years but had taken opposite sides approached each other with hesitation, and felt it necessary to reaffirm their friendship, so deeply had their emotions become involved.

I hope it is now clear why the issue on the Berkeley campus is not simply one of "free speech." The immediate issue is the student demand that the University allow them facilities for full political action and give up its right to discipline them for what it considers improper use of these facilities. If the University is to be equated with the administration, the students have a point. For the administration has the least claim to the power to determine the standards which govern the University. But what of the regents, who represent the people of the state? What of the faculty? What of the students? Are all incapable of determining what is proper on a university campus? The constitution of the University—the distribution of powers among its various elements—may well be out of joint. At one time the faculty exercised student discipline at Berkeley; on some campuses it is the faculty and students together. Constitutions can be changed. But should the constitution of a university include a grant of immunity to any and all forms of action that go by the name of politics? If it did, the university would abdicate its responsibility to set standards for its students, its faculty, and its staff in one critical area of their life on the campus. We are now in the following ridiculously inconsistent posture at Berkeley: no religious activity of any kind is allowed on the campus and no one challenges that; students can be penalized for infractions of rules involving the consumption of liquor and the like, and no one challenges that; but it is asserted that any political action whatever should be permitted without any step being taken by the University against any person or organization as a result.

It is possible that this huge and on the whole practically-oriented University has no basis on which to set any standards. I am not sure we have come to this yet. The students—now backed by most of the faculty—view any assertions of power by the University as designed only to reduce the scope of their self-evidently good and just activity. They do not see that the power to regulate on the basis of standards appropriate to a university also increases the potential scope of their activity and protects them from the civil arm. It is easier to run meetings on the Berkeley campus than on the city streets—even the streets of enlightened cities. The students and their faculty supporters do not agree that this higher degree of freedom, established under the protection of the University's authority, may be organically connected to the University's power to regulate this freedom and prevent its abuse.

How then is the dispute to be finally resolved? One can envisage circumstances that would give us a temporary peace, but it would be a very fragile one. Many of the FSM leaders are also deeply concerned with the academic conduct of the University, the curriculum, the courses, the character of the faculty, the nature of student-faculty relations. It is a concern which many faculty members applaud. But if strikes and sit-ins should be held on the campus to impose student views of how the University should be run academically—and nothing in FSM ideology prevents this—there would be an end to peace once again.

Secondly, one must see these events in the context of the students' desire to protect their University status and privileges while conducting their operations in the community. Will the community in turn, however, respect these rights and privileges if the actions of the Berkeley students maintain their intensity of 1963–64, or if, as the students hope, they increase in intensity? A number of supermarkets against which they directed some of their most powerful efforts, I notice, have closed down. Will the community, which votes hundreds of millions of dollars for the University through the state legislature, remain docile in the face of what they may consider a one-sided bargain?

At a press conference called by a group of faculty members after the mass arrests on December 3, Professor Henry May, chairman of the history department, was asked by newsmen what lay at the bottom of the crisis. He answered thoughtfully that he saw two major issues. One was the inevitable strains and pressure stemming from the attempt to create at Berkeley a mass university that would at the same time be great; the second was the rise of new forms of political action which aroused deep emotions and whose legal status was in doubt. I believe these are the two chief underlying causes of what is happening at Berkeley. We have the answer to neither problem; this is why we must be concerned and disturbed, and why what is happening at Berkeley is more than a local story.

Epilogue, January 6. On January 1, the regents suddenly appointed a new acting chancellor for the Berkeley campus, Martin Meyerson.

He took office at a time when the emergency executive committee of the academic senate was performing prodigies in negotiating with and mollifying all parties. With the advice of the emergency executive committee, the new chancellor issued temporary and minimal "fail-safe" rules (the language of nuclear warfare is common in the controversy) with which to greet the students returning from vacation, and FSM is abiding by them. Meyerson has brought a new atmosphere to the campus, and every day we congratulate each other on an unaccustomed peace.

PHILIP SELZNICK
and
NATHAN GLAZER

Berkeley:
Two Comments*

Philip Selznick: Professor Nathan Glazer's account of the student protest at Berkeley, published last month, is distressing to many who have been close to the events. This is hardly surprising, for Glazer is associated with a policy overwhelmingly rejected by the Berkeley faculty. He has, I am sorry to say, obscured the basic issues, faltered in his assessment of the moral quality of the students' actions, and misread the role of the faculty. I am grateful for the opportunity to present a different interpretation.

Professor Glazer says that he is "filled with foreboding." There is indeed much to worry about, and the ultimate effects of the protest cannot now be fully assessed. Nevertheless, I am not inclined to wring my hands. Something basically good has happened here. If we still have something to teach our students about the relation of means to ends (and I believe we have), it is also true they have had much to teach us. Their mode of instruction has been passionate and in part irresponsible, but it has not been such as to justify a shrinking back in horror. Much of what the students did was clearly necessary, if we were to be made to *really listen.* Moreover for the immediate future, the student actions have helped to create a significant reservoir of support within the faculty for a new look at what we are about.

* From *Commentary,* April 1965.

In the early days of the crisis President Kerr denied that there was a "freedom of speech issue" at Berkeley. This point of view is adopted by Professor Glazer. Observing the heady activity around him, he concludes that "free speech prevailed on the Berkeley campus." This approach shows a peculiar insensitivity to the fact that issues of free speech in a democracy often arise out of marginal cases. We do not decide whether an issue has been raised by pointing to all the free speech that abounds. The hard case and the forlorn sect may give us trouble beyond their due, but they also summon us to reaffirm our fundamental commitments.

The basic policy was phrased as follows in a handbook for student organizations published by the dean of students: "University facilities may not be used to support or advocate off-campus political or social action." Action included supporting or opposing particular candidates or propositions in local, state, or national elections. One may decide that such activities are improper for a university campus, but it is strange indeed to be told that they do not represent restrictions on political speech. The whole point was: should partisan advocacy—surely a form of speech—directed to influencing specific decisions in the community be allowed on campus? Whatever the merits, that is a free speech issue.

The ban on speech directed to action was sustained by a combination of wishful fantasy and timid opportunism—both arising out of a sincere responsiveness to the needs of the University as perceived by the administration. The fantasy consisted in an attempt to distinguish "discussion" and "advocacy." President Kerr hoped to fulfill his own ideals, and satisfy long-standing demands for a more open campus, by enunciating an "open forum" policy. This policy provided enlarged opportunities for the hearing of all viewpoints, but the line was to be drawn against direct involvement in politics. However defensible on abstract grounds, this distinction runs so contrary to the normal continuities of political expression, and is so little supported in the political experience of the larger community, that it had little chance of surviving a determined assault. And indeed it did crumble, almost at the first challenge.

Professor Glazer has recounted the successive retreats of the administration on the issue of advocacy during the two weeks following the first student protest. It is interesting that the "realist" defense of the original policy, as necessary to the protection of the University from conservative criticism, was given small weight by the administration when the need to abandon untenable distinctions became apparent. This suggests that the basic policy never had any good reason for being, even as a defensive tactic, and was a needless affront to the sensibilities of the students.

Although the general ban on advocacy was swiftly eroded, a sticky problem remained. On November 20, the regents officially accepted the idea that political activity, including recruitment and fund-raising, could be conducted on campus. However, they included the proviso that such activity must be "for lawful off-campus action, not for unlawful off-campus action." Thus free speech was still at issue, for the University apparently reserved the right to regulate speech or organization that in its judgment was directed to illegal off-campus action. Under ordinary circumstances, this might not have been a fighting issue. But civil rights-conscious students saw a direct threat to the possibility of organizing on the campus "direct action" in the community. At the same time, the energy and commitment that had already won large gains against the policy of September were still available for the achievement of unabridged freedom of speech.

That is how things stood in late November. On the 22nd, a brief sit-in was staged in Sproul Hall. On the 30th, it was announced that four leaders of the Free Speech Movement (FSM) faced charges for actions connected with the demonstration of early October. There followed the massive sit-in of December 2–3, the removal and arrest of some 800 demonstrators, the student strike, the fiasco in the Greek theater on December 7, and the critical meeting of the Academic Senate on December 8.

By the overwhelming vote of 824–115, the senate adopted a resolution whose chief provisions were:

(1) "The time, place, and manner of conducting political activity on the campus shall be subject to reasonable regulation to prevent interference with the normal functions of the University."

(2) "The content of speech or advocacy should not be restricted by the University. Off-campus student political activities shall not be subject to University regulation. On-campus advocacy or organization of such activities shall be subject only to such

limitations as may be imposed under [the regulation of time, place, and manner]."

Professor Glazer's interpretation of this resolution is very odd. He speaks of "the student demand that the university allow them facilities for full political action and give up its right to discipline them for what it considers improper use of these facilities," and he asks, should the university constitution "include a grant of immunity to any and all forms of action that go by the name of politics?" We are now, he laments, "in the ridiculously inconsistent posture" that "students can be penalized for infractions of rules involving the consumption of liquor and the like . . . but it is asserted that any political action whatever should be permitted without any step being taken by the University against any person or organization as a result."

Now compare these statements with the faculty position that the "time, place, and manner of conducting political activity shall be subject to reasonable regulation to prevent interference with the normal functions of the University." In fact, of course, we did not grant immunity to all forms of action; nor did we forsake all discipline for improper use of University facilities. We proclaimed freedom of speech—not without rules, but with only such rules as are truly necessary to preserve the normal tenor of university life. This would exclude rules imposed arbitrarily, or to quiet outside criticism, or to serve administrative convenience.

No one is against regulating "time, place, and manner," although the word "manner" may produce some future controversy. The heart of the faculty resolution is the provision that *the university should not regulate the content of public expression on campus*. If a member or guest of the University community wants to advocate the seizure of private property by Negro tenants in Harlem or Oakland, or the forcible and illegal expulsion of Negroes from Mississippi, the University is to grit its teeth and restrain its punitive hand.

It is easy to list political abominations, easy to understand the desire to restrain them. But the regulation of what people say has its own problems, not least of which is the difficulty of finding a formula that will reach the contemplated evil and no other. The Constitution contains no general language defining the limits of free speech. There are such limits, but they are contained in a judicial gloss and in laws limiting activities like conspiracy, incitement to crime, defamation, and obscenity. The tangled byways of constitutional interpretation in this field are notorious, and our faculty decided that there was no need for the University, in its governance of student affairs, to go down that troubled road.

For the university's purposes, at least in this phase of American history, it is enough to regulate time, place, and manner. If in *what* they say students go beyond the pall of legal speech, then resort may be had to civil authorities who must act within the evolving framework of constitutional law. In any case, if many students are affected by offensive ideas communicated on campus, it is our job to intensify their education. Restrictive rules will avail us little and cost us much.

Professor Glazer is understandably concerned lest a free society and a free university be unable to move against a terrorist or totalitarian movement. But the impotence of democracy, where that has been displayed, has had little to do with a Hitler's freedom to publish or to harangue a crowd. Political palsy, not constitutional freedom, toleration of abominable acts, not of abominable speech, have contributed most to the political cankers of our time.

It is instructive that the formulas offered by President Kerr (no advocacy of illegal off-campus action) or by Feuer and Glazer (no advocacy "directed to immediate acts of force or violence") have little precision as defenses against grave evils. On the contrary, they cast a wide net and would catch first of all proponents of civil rights resorting to "direct action" tactics and convicted of minor infractions. This is an instance of the classic dilemma faced by every would-be legislator against speech.

The complexities and dangers of regulating speech are compelling, but they are not the whole foundation of the faculty's policy. Even more important is the contribution we seek to make to an atmosphere of freedom. The university is not the whole polity. We have our own nature and commitments, and these include a special concern that students *feel free*. There may be something to the argument that participation in political action is a valuable adjunct to the curriculum. I do not give it great weight. Somewhat more persuasive is the view that free speech on campus permits and encourages students to hear all points of view. But to me the decisive point is that students should have a sense of belonging to a community that is completely open to the free play of persuasion and argument.

At this writing, there is apparently very close agreement between the faculty resolution and the position adopted by the regents on December 18 that "the policies of the regents do not contemplate that advocacy or content of speech shall be restricted beyond the purview of the First and Fourtenth Amendments to the Constitution." This still leaves some ambiguity, especially as to who shall interpret what lies beyond that purview, but most people here are confident that the basic issue is settled. The students seem content with the protections of the First Amendment.

Reference to the United States Constitution can be misleading, however. Some have argued that the university should not abridge freedom of political expression because it is a state agency and therefore subject to constitutional constraints on government. The preferable view, in my opinion, is that the university may well draw upon the experience and wisdom of the larger community in matters of speech, but its policy should be its own. It follows that the university should be free to change that policy if fresh thought and new circumstances require it. A university may wish to allow considerably greater freedom of expression, so far as its own rules are concerned, than may be protected under a current constitutional doctrine.

Having stated my view of the faculty position on the main issue, I should like to turn to Professor Glazer's assessment of the role of the faculty in this controversy. Referring to the meeting of December 8, he writes: "I think there was a good deal of hysteria mixed in with the action of the Berkeley Division of the Academic Senate that day." Earlier he says: "Because of their desperate desire to settle things, because of their experience of one administration failure after another, I believe most of the faculty was by now ready to accept any agreement that might lead to peace." These assessments color Professor Glazer's entire treatment of the faculty's role. I think the facts show that he taxes his colleagues unduly, and wrongfully casts doubt upon the integrity of their decision.

Until the crisis broke in late September, the faculty played no large part in the determination of policy regarding speech and political activity. Over the years a number of faculty members were actively interested in liberalized rules and, in cooperation with student leaders and President Kerr, helped to bring them about. Still others protested when, for example, a restrictive distinction was made between "on-campus" and "off-campus" student organizations. But passivity was more common, and the faculty dangerously allowed the president to elaborate, without dissent, his own perspectives on freedom and the university. These perspectives were very strongly influenced by his experience with trade unions. In Kerr's view, the university is an organization like other large-scale organizations in our society. Individual freedom and institutional well-being are best served if there are limited commitments on both sides. He lacked a vital theory of the university community and of the conditions under which its greatest potentialities might be realized. Perhaps the worst thing that can be said about the role of the faculty in recent years is that it failed to enter into a dialogue with the president concerning basic educational philosophy.

The disorders of early October were profoundly disturbing to many faculty members. There was considerable feeling that the administration was behaving very badly, but there was also widespread uneasiness about the students' conduct. Nevertheless, there was a quick response on the main issue, coupled with a determination to avoid open condemnation of either the administration or the students. On October 13 the academic senate passed by a large majority a motion favoring "maximum freedom for student political activity," and calling upon its committee on academic freedom to formulate an appropriate policy. It was already clear where many of the faculty stood.

While various committees studied the matter, the agitation continued during October and November. There was of course an enormous amount of discussion within the faculty, including active work on petitions and resolutions. By late November, the impasse seemed so great that sentiment for determined faculty action grew rapidly, and various groups began to look to the meeting scheduled for December 8 as a time of decision. Immediately following the police action of December 3, an unofficial meeting of 800 faculty, chaired by Professor Nathan Glazer, passed a series of resolutions foreshadowing the actions of December 8. On December 6, an informal meeting of about two hundred faculty members discussed, amended, and then unanimously approved a series of resolutions that had been prepared by a group of faculty liberals. These resolutions were substantially the same as those adopted on December 8. In the meantime, the committee on academic freedom decided to present its own version of the same policy.

On December 7 classes were canceled in the morning and department meetings were scheduled for the purpose of discussing a compromise agreement reached among the department chairmen, President Kerr, and some of the regents. This was to be presented to an 11:00 AM convocation of the entire university community in the Greek theater. At the same time, the resolutions of "the 200" were being widely circulated and discussed. There was much resentment of the compromise agreement, which did not speak to the basic policy issue, and even more antagonism toward the idea of a full-dress convocation called to announce and celebrate non-existent consensus and settlement. The show was a historic failure, and all eyes turned to the senate meeting scheduled for the following day.

Thus the meeting of December 8 was preceded by an unusual amount of discussion and preparation. To be sure, the atmosphere was tense and there was a crisis to be met. However, the whole pattern of faculty actions since October was consistent with the outcome. Almost everyone disliked the administration's policy, and most were now determined to say so.

If the faculty policy had been adopted by a slim majority, Professor Glazer might have had a point. Surely not everyone was equally convinced, and there must have been some who responded mainly to the desire for an end to the affair. On the other hand, there were members who agreed with the majority's policy but voted against the resolution, or abstained, because they felt under pressure. But almost the entire faculty voted, and the majority was over seven to one. Moreover, there has been no sign of weakening. Two days later, at a comparably large meeting, a resolution was introduced which, while reaffirming the action of December 8, could have been interpreted as a concession to the administration. Some well-known members of the "200" group supported the motion. Nevertheless it was tabled—in the context a clear indication of the majority's determination to stand fast by what it had done. The emergency executive committee, though billed as "moderate," has taken the December 8 policy as its charter. In sum, the senate's decision was deliberate and firm. Nor is there any real reason to doubt that most members voted their convictions.

I agree with Professor Glazer that the issues at Berkeley have gone beyond free speech. Many have been troubled by the tactics of "direct action" applied in a university setting. Certainly the students resorted to pressure and intimidation. They relied on the model of the labor or civil rights dispute rather than on that of intellectual controversy or even normal political action. The excitement produced some excesses, both of invective and of conduct. All this is sobering, worthy of attention, in need of remedy.

Yet I feel that Professor Glazer's disapproval of the student tactics—especially after they had won what *he* thought was enough —has obscured his vision and blunted his sensibility. He has not adequately perceived the moral character of the students themselves—their claim to our respect, support, forgiveness, and sympathy. Professor Glazer tellingly documents the administration's rigid and inept handling of the dispute. But he does not grasp the significance of the fact that arbitrary administrative action lay at the base of the controversy, and was fuel to its flames at every stage. These matters bear closely on the charge that somehow "law and order" went down the drain at Berkeley.

The obligation to obey the law is among the more subtle and variable of human commitments. In assessing that obligation, we take account of the nature of the setting, the character of the rules and of their enforcement, and the legitimate interests of the offender. Unquestioning obedience to lawful orders has more apparent point in a military organization than in business, and in both it weakens as we ascend the echelons or move from line to staff. While we cannot do without it altogether, a very strong emphasis on administrative authority is out of place in higher education. Here, if anywhere, the spirit of consultation should prevail. So, too, arbitrary rule-making or administration saps its own authority and provides the offender with a defense. And if the offense carries forward a legitimate purpose, such as freedom of expression, or self-defense, it has some chance of vindication.

This approach was clearly manifest in a report of the Ad Hoc

Committee on Student Conduct established to hear the cases of eight suspended students. The chairman of the committee was Professor Ira M. Heyman of the Law School. The Heyman committee made many discriminations and took account of much beyond the simple fact of rule-breaking. Two points are especially pertinent. First, the committee gave due weight to the context—namely, that a controversy over rules was raging and that the chancellor had made it clear "that the president and the regents had rejected in final form the request of the ASUC [the Associated Students of the University of California] for changes in the rules. . . . The door was thus seemingly closed to any negotiation on these central points." Second, the committee took account of what the students were up to, viewing it "as a symbolic act of protest and not as an act of private delinquency."

Legality is a two-way street. He who insists on obedience to rules should be ready to justify the rules themselves. At Berkeley the administration adopted a posture of intransigence and as much as said that it would yield only to pressure. There was little concept of true consultation with students on matters affecting their interests. In this setting, a loss of confidence and respect was inevitable. To many of the students, it seemed to justify direct action.

There has been much talk of "riots" at Berkeley. In fact there were no riots at all. One very serious incident—the surrounding and immobilization of a police car for thirty-two hours—could have come to that and should not be minimized. But most of the action consisted of orderly mass rallies, not less orderly sit-ins, and a brief student strike. A great many rules and some state laws were broken in the process. That is certainly regrettable, but we lose our bearings if we respond to such activities as if they were political or even academic outrages. A more appropriate response, learned long ago in other contexts, is to get at the root of the trouble.

A final word about the students and their leadership. The Free Speech Movement has been led by student radicals. In that sense, it is certainly unrepresentative of the student body as a whole. But the struggle these young radicals mounted struck a deeply responsive chord. Most of the students approved the goals of the FSM. At least a substantial minority, especially in the social sciences and humanities, approved of the demonstrative tactics as well. One survey, conducted by a class in social research methods under the direction of Professor Robert H. Somers, showed that in November, thirty-four per cent of all students supported the direct-action tactics of the FSM. This amounts to perhaps 9000 student sympathizers, not counting the larger group who also supported the goals of the movement and whose sympathies could presumably be activated if the administration behaved especially badly. This was borne out by the size of some of the rallies.

On the other hand, student support was clearly tied to the issues at hand. It was not mindless or mechanical, and many had reservations about the more extreme actions, such as the use of a police car as a podium or indulgence in unrestrained invective. The FSM sympathizers did not respond to *any* appeal. They responded above all to concrete deprivations, like the withdrawal of earlier *de facto* rights and, especially, the indefensible reinstitution of charges against the FSM leaders on November 30. (Professor Glazer speaks of this as a "blunder," but the students more rightly perceived it as a sickness of soul.) On more abstract issues, the FSM could get large crowds for rallies but not for illegal action.

For my own part, I was offended by the posturing and scorn of a few of the FSM leaders, but I was deeply impressed by the earnestness, dedication, and basic moral enlightenment of most of the student supporters I encountered. These are among our very best students. They are not thugs or scoundrels, neither are they caught up in any impenetrable ideology. They are acting out what they have learned, without the patience and restraint of maturity. The students had a just cause and they yearned for affirmation of it. If there was an excess of zeal, it did not forfeit their claim to our sense of fellowship. In a community of scholars, that is something we should reject, not in fearful recoil from the first signs of stirring and change, but only at a last extremity. Happily, there is no prospect of that at Berkeley.

Nathan Glazer: There is no disagreement between Professor Selznick and myself as to what happened at Berkeley; there is little disagreement even over the interpretation of many of the facts. We both ascribe the origins of the dispute and its continuance and revival to the ineptitude of the administration (though I would not go so far as to characterize this ineptitude as "a sickness of soul"—these men, after all, are our colleagues and it is hard to see that they suffer from such radical defects). We both agree that the FSM was led by students whose political views were not representative of the student body but who, on the basis of the issues created by the administration, were able to mobilize large numbers of students, in particular those moved by the civil rights revolution. We do, however, disagree on three central points: the extent to which this was a fight over free speech; the wisdom of the faculty action; and the moral quality of the students' acts.

When the representatives of the University administration in the committee on student political activity agreed early in November to the opening of the campus to the planning and preparation of political action as well as speech, then to my mind the free speech issue, to the extent that it had existed, disappeared. This committee was composed of student, faculty, and administration representatives. It decided that all the actions originally banned by the administration (collection of funds, organizing, advocacy of action) would now be permitted on campus. These were the original issues, and they were settled. The new issue that now arose —whether advocacy and organization of *illegal* action was also legitimate—was referred to a subcommittee of this committee, consisting of a representative of the statewide University administration, a law-school professor (one of the faculty group), and a lawyer representing the FSM. The subcommittee agreed on language which satisfied the administration and which, in the judgment of the faculty representative and the students' lawyer, fully protected student civil and political rights. FSM adherents on the full committee, however, rejected the compromise. Professor Selznick accepts the view of the FSM leaders that the University's insistence that the campus must not be used for the launching of illegal action involved a restriction of free speech: "The University apparently reserved the right to regulate speech or organization that in its judgment was directed to illegal off-campus action." I did not interpret the regents' position in this way; nor did the faculty members of the committee on student political action so interpret it; nor did Chancellor Strong's new regulations for student political activity, issued to implement the regents' position, give support to such an interpretation.

There was never a hint of prior censorship; nor was there any suggestion that the administration would ever move against any kind of speech. The issue was specifically illegal action and the launching of action from the campus by groups using its facilities. The problems arising from this issue (e.g., who decides what is illegal?) could have been ironed out in the committee on student political action, which was designed for the precise purpose of dealing with such details. I attended one of their meetings, and it was clear to me that discussion in any real sense was made almost impossible by the legalistic quibbling that the FSM students reveled in. They acted as if they were preparing themselves for service on the UN Security Council or the Korean Truce Commission, when they might have acted as members of an academic community trying to work out reasonable rules.

But what speaks most forcefully against Professor Selznick's restrictive interpretation of the regents' position is that this position still holds, and that nothing has fundamentally changed in the administration's stand of the first week of November as ratified by the regents on November 20, two weeks before the sit-ins and arrests of December 2 and 3. The Berkeley campus will have to abide by these rules; and as far as I can see, both the faculty and the students are now ready to live with the condition that the campus is not to be used for the launching of illegal political action. If free speech exists on the campus (and I think everyone agrees that it does), then it is clear that this position does not restrict free speech.

The regents' ruling strictly interpreted can be used to penalize students and student groups who organize actions which are declared illegal by the courts. But a general declaration of principle by the University does not require it to act in an area as uncertain, as rapidly changing, as ambiguous as present-day civil rights demonstrations. Everything will depend on the temper of the administration, on the development of public opinion, the direction of legal decisions, the evolving character of the civil rights movement. But whatever happens, it is inconceivable to me—as it is, I am sure, to Professor Selznick—that a general University ruling against the use of its facilities for the launching of illegal political action can be withdrawn.

Now as to the role of the faculty: Professor Selznick suggests that we still have something to teach our students about the relation of means to ends. I agree. I also believe that the resolution of December 8—presented at the time it was, and so overwhelmingly adopted—made the task of such teaching infinitely more difficult. The previous day we had seen the collapse of an effort to reach a compromise. This collapse, we must realize, was engineered in large measure by the leaders of the FSM, through the use of the kind of disruptive tactics that extremists everywhere have made familiar to us, most recently in the unsuccessful campaign of Patrick Gordon Walker. (One of the most brilliant analyses of such tactics—whose purpose is to deny any dignity to an opponent and to prevent him from conducting a meeting with the agenda and speakers he sees fit—is, of course, to be found in Professor Selznick's *The Organizational Weapon.*) In this case the opponent was the president of the university and the department chairmen who had worked out the compromise. On December 7 and 8 the university was on strike. One group of graduate history students taking an examination was interrupted by an FSM activist who called upon them to go out on strike. One striking teaching-assistant was prepared to put up a sign on the door of another teaching-assistant who was conducting a class; the sign read, "This class is taught by scab labor." Such was the atmosphere when the academic senate met on December 8.

Here was a moment that required teaching as to the relations of means to ends. But it was impossible at this time to get the academic senate to adopt any position which could be interpreted as critical of FSM actions. What the student leaders learned from the academic senate meeting of December 8 was that extreme tactics could be used without censure from the faculty. (Many individual faculty members—including, of course, those in the great majority that adopted the resolution of December 8—did, in smaller meetings with students, criticize their actions.)

The size of the faculty vote for the resolution of December 8 was, I believe, unnaturally swelled by a number of special factors, including the confusion of many faculty members who had been told that the main resolution was supported by the president and the administration, and that it was in fact a peace settlement reached to end the strike. Nothing was done to dispel this confusion. The faculty knew that if the resolution were turned down, the strike would continue. Our teaching-assistants had been protected against reprisal for two days; could they be protected if the strike went on, and would 800 graduate students dismissed from teaching and research positions be added to 800 arrested students? I do not doubt that the resolution would have passed in any case; the vote, however, would have been much less one-sided in the absence of this confusion and pressure.

The most difficult question is how one assesses the moral quality of the students' actions. The students are committed to the expansion of freedom; many of their leaders and members have risked the dangers of fighting for justice in Mississippi. I admire and respect the students who have committed themselves to the civil rights struggle, and who have transformed the temper of our universities. Unquestionably the knowledge that many of the students in the FSM were also involved in the larger fight for justice and equality for Negroes made many faculty members hesitant in judging their actions, in a different place and for a different cause.

But no movement in this world is immune from the threat of distortion and corruption, even a movement working for the good and the just. Power may corrupt, even when it is power mobilized for a good cause, and committed to the philosophy of non-violence. These are possibilities; and at times they have come close to realization on the Berkeley campus.

A new period has opened at Berkeley, one of wide communication among administration, faculty, and students, one of great concern with the nature of the University and the process of education within it.

A great wave of energy has been released here, particularly among the students, by the crisis of the past few months, and it has been wonderful to see what prodigies of work—in organization, in research, in writing—have been evoked from them by the struggle. Certainly many professors have been given quite a start to discover that stores of energy are locked in our students and untouched by the normal educational routine. This is a moment that should be seized, for there are only a few chances in the history of an institution when large changes become possible. It is also clear that the new chancellor welcomes proposals for change. This can be a valuable and fruitful time for us. But this time of potential change can be perverted and aborted if the student leaders do not recognize how such a wide-ranging discussion concerning the character and future of the University should be conducted. Certainly the tactics of force and disruption can play no part in it. I know the faculty shares this view; I hope the radical student leaders do too. But it is just this point that has not been settled in the recent crisis.

NATHAN GLAZER
and
PAUL GOODMAN

Berkeley:
An Exchange

To the Editors:

I understand Paul Goodman's difficulty in writing about Berkeley from a distance, but there are things in his brief article that are really odd, when read on the scene:

". . . when administration becomes the dominant force . . . it is a sign that extra-mural powers are in control—State, Church, or Economy . . ." State was in control at the state university long before administration became dominant. Church, in any form, is banned. Administration's dominance is not explained by the extra-mural power of the economy, unless Goodman means that the University requires a good deal of money to run, and the faculty prefers to cede the management of the budget to others, so long as their salaries are sufficient. The dominance of the administration is based on the facts of 18,000 undergraduates, 10,000 graduate students, 1500 faculty members, 200,000 grades per year, etc., etc. It is not the administration that imposes a system of education involving innumerable courses and examinations—it is the faculty. Nor is it the administration alone that hampers reform. It is the indifference to educational reform of both faculty and students.

"The faculty, energized by the students, wants to resume prerogatives that it had given up to the administration, e.g., discipline."

* From *The New York Review of Books,* February 11, 1965.

Quite untrue. Read: "The faculty, disturbed and frightened by administration ineptitude and mass student protest, was stampeded into demanding this right as the student price for peace." The faculty is not interested in exercising student discipline over liquor, sex, cheating, and other things that they are happy to leave in the hands of the administration. Nor do they relish devoting endless time to hearings in which students and administration are represented by lawyers, and in which any normal lay intelligence finds itself overwhelmed by legal technicalities and political in-fighting. Mr. Goodman should come to one of these. Faculty discipline will become the pro forma activity of faculty members dragooned into it, or willing to waste their time at it. It will become another cog in the committee system that uses up faculty time and helps prevent student-faculty contact.

"At present in the United States, students—middle-class youth—are the major exploited class . . . they have no choice but to go to college." Nonsense. Intelligent youth may accept the minimal income for freedom Mr. Goodman has so effectively argued for, and which the society provides. The non-student representative in the FSM executive committee estimated there are 3,000 non-students around the campus at Berkeley, who have done just this. Their families or the unemployment insurance system, or the many odd jobs around the University, or their friends support them. They may be unhappy, but not because they are being exploited. Mr. Goodman is making hash out of a useful and respectable word.

"The administration cannot agree to the faculty resumption of prerogatives, because . . . this could unmake the academic-factory . . . the faculty might hire or teach in disregard of Image, Endowments, or Research Grants." More nonsense. The issue is politics, not education. The administration holds on to its prerogatives because it thinks the faculty is politically irresponsible and will get the University into trouble with the legislature. But not through anyone it hires or anything it teaches. It can and does teach Marx, Goodman, Genet, Mao Tse-tung, or what you will. And it hires anybody it wants. The point is, these are guilds of scholars and researchers. To make them act differently from the way they do does not require taking power away from the administration; it requires administrations strong enough and coherent enough to break up the conservative patterns of teaching and hiring that develop within the guilds. This makes a much less arcadian picture than Mr. Goodman, I am afraid, would care to deal with.

The student uprising at Berkeley is indeed for very mature ends: the end of a powerful student political movement with impact on the community. The educational aims are less clear, but their clearest part is that the educational process should serve the political ends. This should not be so unfamiliar to us.

". . . freedom of students to ask for what they need to be taught and if necessary to invite teachers." A grand idea, and I am sure it would work wonderfully at Bennington or Black Mountain. The student movement here may turn into that. If it does it will find that the problem is the faculty, not the administration. And Mr. Goodman, in his fine book *The Community of Scholars,* agreed that one reasonable alternative approach to setting up a university was to have the faculty teach what it felt had to be taught, and the students could come, or not, as they wished. Perhaps we will have something new on the academic scene, a faculty transformed not by an administration à la Hutchins, but by a student body. But if it is to happen at this University, with this student body and this faculty, it will be quite a fight.

NATHAN GLAZER

PAUL GOODMAN *replies:*

If Nat Glazer believes his ending, that the Berkeley movement "may" turn toward fighting for an authentic community of scholars and that "perhaps" a faculty may be transformed by a student body, I am puzzled by the zeal with which he refutes me and calls my remarks nonsense! rather than saying sadly and firmly, "Alas, not yet true; we must yet make it true." In my article I was not sanguine: "The question will be whether there are enough professors who are concerned for the academic community" and "Given the supine history of American faculties and the present careerism of the important professors, the students must lead." But there is a conflict in the students themselves between the causes that have made them more mature and their prior and present educational exploitation that tends to make them insecure and immature.

Nevertheless, the faculty voted seven to one for the students, and it seems to me presumptuous of Nat to call this being "frightened and stampeded." I have been told, rather, that it was a faculty reaction of *nausea* at the administration lies, spineless subservience to outside pressures, infantile tantrums, avoidance of confrontation and calling the cops. I believe it, for it is this kind of nausea that indeed recalls decent but self-centered people to their plain duty. Besides, what about the 200 faculty members who supported the students from very early in the game? They were not stampeded. And most important, what about the almost unanimous support of the section-men and research-assistants, who took the greatest risks by striking?

I deeply trust that faculty is not interested in exercising discipline over "liquor, sex, cheating, and other things." For they are none of its damned business, nor administration's either. Surely Nat knows this; what is he up to? e.g., would he himself bother with grading if it were not administratively demanded?

And what are we to make of his denial that State and Economy have increased administrative dominance? Clark Kerr himself has said, "The University is being called on to respond to the *expanding* claims of national service, and to merge its activity with industry *as never before* [my italics] . . . It is a mechanism held together by administrative rules and powered by money." This is true and Kerr likes it; the students don't like it; and I call it exploitation of the young. By extramural power of the economy I do not mean that it costs a lot of money to run a school, but simply such bashful items as seventeen billions annually for research and development, of which two billions direct from government to University and other billions through private contracted research in the universities; lots of money from the National Defense Education Act; the piratical raiding of name-professors in order to get contracts and foundation grants; the National Science Foundation's Ph.D.—processing curriculum reforms in the lower schools; state and economy underwriting, in the few dozen most prestigious schools, of from forty per cent to eighty per cent of the total budget; the tuition-hikes and rent-gouges of the neglected undergraduates; the frontier testing for apprentice skills, and hot campus-recruiting by the corporations . . . Need I go on?

I am unimpressed by the theory that it is sheer numbers that have made administration dominant. Have administrations hastened to decentralize in order to lessen their burdens? Have they tried to

discourage the popular superstition of school-going? Have they tried
to shift the contracted research to non-academic institutes? No.
They have acted as crude imperialists.

By "exploited class" I mean simply that the students' powers
and time of life are used for other people's purposes; I am *not*
making a hash of the word. Let us remember that one hundred
years ago, the young were exploited from ten to twenty-five years
of age in other kinds of factories. (Needless to say, middle-class
youth are also pampered, but this merely confuses them in their
exploitation.) The demand for *Lernfreiheit* is the student claim
to learn intrinsically, when they are ready and what they are ready
for, like free men. Surely Nat is not serious when he speaks of the
freedom of middle-class youth to "accept the minimal income"
instead of getting degrees, and he mentions the 3000 non-students
in Berkeley. How oddly he puts it!—the "intelligent," who have
quit school, he says, are *not* exploited; he seems to be saying that
those who are pressured into remaining in school *are* exploited,
which is my point. But then why does *he* continue teaching there,
among the stupid?

Finally, however, there is one profoundly important statement
in Nat's letter; and I am thankful for the chance to comment on it,
which I failed to do in my original piece. He speaks of "the indifference to educational reform of both faculty and students." This,
it seems to me, is the crux for the future of the Berkeley movement
as a mass-movement.

There is a dilemma. As I have repeatedly written, the majority
of these youth ought not to be in a serious scholastic setting at all,
for that is a very specialized way of growing up and does not suit
most, including most of the bright. In the usual present-day university, my guess is that about fifty per cent are there only incidentally,
with their attention mainly on (serious or frivolous) extra-curric-
ular activities but they need the diploma; another thirty per cent are
there like sheep because they have always gone to school and done
lessons, and they are clinging to the routine for another four to six
years; about fifteen per cent are set on some diplomated career and
want to get competitive grades and "master the subject"; and perhaps five per cent would like to learn something academically (and
are hampered by the others). This does not provide a mass-base
for academic reform! although there evidently has been a mass-base

for civil liberties (especially when energized by civil rights for Negroes), and for being treated as human beings and not manipulated.

But now that the chancellor is gone and Senator Knowland no longer needs to have fits about the election and Proposition 14, how can the Free Speech Movement live on? For the majority, the struggle against bureaucracy and exploitation cannot be posed as a claim to better teaching; it must be a claim to a more decent physical and social community of young people, less harried by petty mechanical tasks, and perhaps with more contact with the professors not as teachers but as likable friends and guides. That is, they ought to demand the B.A. at birth if it is economically necessary; or demand to be paid for doing onerous lessons; or attempt to destroy the illusion that a paper degree is good for anything, and quit the University and educate themselves in various other environments; or fight for the guaranteed decent income for everybody, with or without diploma, and meantime use the multiversity to practice cultured leisure and mount political actions. On the other hand, those who want to learn something ought frankly to conspire with favorable professors to teach them in freedom, and simply disregard the administration as otiose. This is really quite easy, for in the essential, administration *is* otiose. E.g., the professor can say at the opening class, "Everybody gets A; those who are not interested, need not attend; I'm not a constable and I don't hand in names." If the administration attempts sanctions, the student community as a whole can proudly come to the defense of its proper scholars; and, it seems to me, the professors would have an academic freedom case. Lead the way, Nat! do you have Tenure?

IV

THE
STUDENT SPOKESMEN

Like all political movements, the growing student movement has been developing its own intellectual spokesmen to articulate its goals and provide apologia for its methods. Most of these writers are highly skilled in the latest techniques of historical, political, and sociological analysis so characteristic of the society they oppose; and with these tools they criticize the social structure and institutions of modern America in order to demonstrate the need for radical change.

The young writers who have been espousing and analyzing the student cause at Berkeley are mostly graduate students in the humanities and social sciences or bright drop-outs who have left the University to escape the "system" and devote themselves fully to active political and social reform. James F. Petras and Michael Shute in "Berkeley '65" show the flaws and contradictions in a brand of liberalism whose distinguished proponents—Nathan Glazer, Seymour Martin Lipset, and Lewis Feuer—attacked the Free Speech Movement as a danger to democracy. Petras and Shute claim that these liberals manqués are really a breed of "new conservatives" more committed to the framework of law and order than to even traditional liberal reform in the direction of civil liberties. Sol Stern's "A Deeper Disenchantment" extends this same kind of attack against Clark Kerr.

For the more ideological temperaments among the spokesmen of the new left, the works of C. Wright Mills have become the gospel canon. Larry Spence's article, "Berkeley: What It Demon-

strates," is characteristic of this style of radical student thinking. Spence employs Mills's book, The Power Elite, *as a point of departure for a highly generalized analysis of the Berkeley crisis in relation to the over-all tendencies of contemporary American society.*

Like Spence, Mario Savio, the leader of the Free Speech Movement, suggests in his short piece "An End to History" that the struggle at Berkeley is only one symptom of a national dilemma. The mechanisms of power throughout much of American society, he feels, are so plagued by bureaucratic rigidity that they are unable to adapt to the changing needs of the people they govern. In Savio's view, the Berkeley administration is analogous to the government of Mississippi in that each serves to help a controlling elite preserve the status quo.

We have included "The Naked Emperor" by Paul Krassner, editor of The Realist, *for although Krassner is not a student, he is most assuredly a spokesman for a large number of students.*

JAMES F. PETRAS
and
MICHAEL SHUTE*

Berkeley '65

For the past four months students at the University of California have been engaged in a struggle with the administration. Regardless of the motives of the students or the means they have employed, one fact is evident: the declared goals of the student Free Speech Movement are shared by the entire American liberal community. The main issue in the dispute at Berkeley was the ban by the administration on on-campus advocacy of, and organization for, activities like civil rights sit-ins, which had been declared illegal by the courts. Students argued that they be accorded the rights of citizens, that their civil offenses be judged only by civil courts and not by academic deans as well. Above all, they claimed the constitutional right of freedom of advocacy, a right which applies even to the advocacy of activities which are later ruled by the courts to have been illegal. This kind of issue has been inscribed on the banners of innumerable liberal struggles, from protests by the ADA against the encroachments of Congressional committees and the defense of persecuted faculty by the ACLU, to the efforts of unions to defend the free speech of their members within a plant.

The similarity of the FSM's aims, as distinguished from its means, to the aims of other democratic movements, was recognized not only by the overwhelming majority of students, but by the vast

* The authors wish to thank Michael Rogin, Assistant Professor of Political Science at the University of California, for substantial contributions to this article.
From *Partisan Review,* Spring, 1965.

majority of the faculty, which voted seven to one for a resolution incorporating student demands. Campus chaplains also supported the FSM program; as did unions like the Building Service Workers and the United Automobile Workers of California; and James Farmer, Bayard Rustin, Norman Thomas, Michael Harrington, and Paul Jacobs.

In view of this broad base of liberal support, it came as a shock to the FSM that the analysis of the Berkeley events in liberal magazines was overwhelmingly hostile. Lead articles in *The New Leader,* the *Reporter* and *Commentary* denounced the FSM as a threat to law and order, and many students were stunned to find that these articles were written by four prominent Cal faculty members— Lewis Feuer (*The New Leader*), Seymour Martin Lipset and Paul Seabury (*Reporter*) and Nathan Glazer (*Commentary*). Since these men are respected as sophisticated spokesmen of the liberal community, their articles have a wider political significance—in their political values, and in their style.

American liberalism has traditionally been committed to social reform and civil liberties, through orderly means and legal institutions. Liberals have argued that democracy and freedom can be extended through the accepted channels of American political structure. They regard the use of disruption as a means of democratization as unnecessary and dangerous.

Yet there are times when events make liberal goals incompatible with liberal means of orderly process. What are liberals to do when those in power are so resistant to pressure that "normal" channels are closed to any who seek to broaden freedom? What happens when victimized citizens must choose either to submit abjectly or to use disruptive tactics? The Negro movement in Mississippi, for example, must resort to civil disobedience. And this was the alternative the University of California students took in their conflict with a bureaucratic administration which made important decisions without consulting even the faculty.

But Feuer, Lipset, Seabury and Glazer object to the students' recourse to civil disobedience. They do not argue that there were other ways of attaining the students' ends. Their main point is that no matter what the exigencies were, the students committed some terrible kind of crime in bypassing normal processes of change. Unlike the majority of the faculty, these writers feel that the students who resorted to civil disobedience are to be condemned more than the administration that repressed them.

These writers' loyalty to "order," then, supersedes their commitment to democratic goals, and their bias stands out in all the articles. But almost as significant as their bias is their method of argument. Feuer, Lipset and Seabury (Glazer to a lesser degree) attack the Free Speech Movement in a manner that is flagrantly abusive. The polemical style we expect, but not the shrillness. Professor Lipset, in a University address, compared the FSM to the Ku Klux Klan and the White Citizens Council: both, after all, promote disorder. Professor Feuer, disregarding the almost unanimous support of a statement by prominent faculty members that the FSM was made up of the most intelligent, intellectually serious students, characterizes the situation at Berkeley in these terms:

> The conglomeration of students acts as a magnet for the morally corrupt; intellectual lumpen-proletarians, lumpen beatniks and lumpen agitators wend their ways to the university campus to advocate a melange of narcotics, sexual perversion, collegiate Castroism and campus Maoism.

And even their fellow faculty members are characterized by their association with extremes. Lipset and Seabury would have us believe that the Academic Senate's stand on civil liberties reflected the influence of "a few extremists."

When men like Feuer, Lipset, Seabury and Glazer abandon the defense of civil liberties in their rush to defend administrative order, then they must be classified as spokesmen of a new conservatism rather than of liberalism. In fact, the New Conservative ideology is not so new. While many were shocked to find these scholars and political figures hostile to the democratic ethic of the student movement, it was no surprise to those familiar with the trend toward "pluralism."

The modern "pluralists," or New Conservatives, as we shall call them, have written extensively in recent years about the phenomenon of democratic mass politics.* Basically, the New Conserva-

* One of the most prominent studies is Lipset's *Political Man*. Other scholars of the same persuasion, who have not been involved in the Berkeley controversy, are Daniel Bell (*The End of Ideology*), Richard Hofstadter (*The Age of Reform*), and Edward Shils (*The Torment of Secrecy*).

tives argue that democratic mass movements, like American Pop-
ulism, which liberals had always felt to be connected with their own
tradition of social reform, are dangerous. The Populist Party, of
course, did not engage in civil disobedience, but it did operate outside the two-party system and threatened to disrupt it. It did involve
masses of people in rallies, agitation and political action against
established social and political institutions.

Since it has become evident that totalitarian groups, like the
Fascists and Communists, can rally large numbers of people in a
crisis, the New Conservatives, concerned about this problem, as are
all democrats, argue that the direct intervention of the masses in
politics is in itself dangerous. Generalizing from the Fascist and
Communist experience, they regard every mass movement, whatever its avowed aim, as a potential carrier of totalitarianism. The
popular mind, they assert, is uninformed and prone to prejudiced
and undemocratic attitudes. The masses do not understand how a
large and complicated society is run and how much compromise
and bargaining go into an orderly democratic life. Experienced
leaders, on the other hand, are less provincial, more appreciative of
the subtleties of compromise and, most important, are more committed to democratic values.

The New Conservatives' emphasis on stability should not be
taken to mean that they are opposed to political conflict. But
conflict, they argue, should take place between contending leaders
and political élites, as Lipset calls them. Conflict is healthy when
it is between groups with different interests, so long as they do not
seek to transform the political structure, and, so long as the
demands of these groups are limited, the more conflicting groups
the better. Furthermore, the masses may enter into politics by
choosing between contending leaders and groups at the polls. So
conflict need not be disruptive, because there are few modern
problems that cannot be resolved in negotiations or bargaining
between political leaderships.

In the New Conservatives' vision of society, where liberal
objectives can be attained through the political establishment,
there is no need for direct mass intervention. While they do
recognize that the South is an exception (in Mississippi civil
disobedience is legitimate, for the racist power structure denies
even the most restrained forms of political participation to

Negroes), in the North such mass action is both unnecessary and dangerous. Constitutional stability is seriously threatened, Lipset argues, when "popular passions wreak their aggression against the structure of the polity" (*First New Nation*).

"Equilibrium" is the metaphor commonly used by the New Conservatives to describe their social ideal. Equilibrium means balancing: the pairing-off of opposing forces and attitudes that negate each other and thus preserve the existing institutional structure, with only marginal changes. In his book *Industrialism and Industrial Man,* Clark Kerr, president of the University of California, remarks: "Industrial society is such a complicated mechanism . . . that keeping it going without major disruption becomes an over-riding concern." Solutions to crises, Kerr adds, "are negotiated among representatives of the leading interest groups rather than being fought out on the level of principle." This kind of balancing means limited popular participation in politics, limited commitment of individuals or groups to principles and a "polity" which gives the widest latitude in decision-making to those already in decision-making positions.

Many of the New Conservatives teach at the University of California, and when the crisis began they had to apply their theories to their own back yard. With the rest of the academic community, they were forced to enter the controversy as both analysts and participants. The situation provided an unusual opportunity to test New Conservative theory, since the university, in size and diversity, is a prototype of modern society. Many groups —faculty, students, administrators, politicians, the government— take an interest in University affairs. Furthermore, the University is administered by men who not only have practical experience but who also are aware of the intellectual implications of their position. They are "rational" leaders.

In practice, however, the New Conservative recipe for resolving the conflict did not work. The crisis arose at the beginning of the fall semester, when the administration informed student groups that they could no longer collect money or recruit members on a narrow strip of sidewalk on Bancroft Way, which had been the only site permitted for such activities. When students protested, through normal administrative channels and by legal picketing, the administration declared that the issue was "not negotiable." It was then, *when the administration refused to negotiate,* that the students decided on civil disobedience. And when, as a concession to the aroused students (they had surrounded a police car in protest against the suspension of eight students and the arrest of a non-student), the administration agreed to negotiate, the students called off their violations of the new political regulations. In effect, what the students demanded were the kind of procedures for settling legitimate conflict generally advocated by the New Conservatives.

Subsequent events followed the pattern of October. Prominent faculty members and respected figures like the chaplains have testified that the administration repeatedly broke its faith with the students, provoking them to further acts of civil disobedience. The climax came on November 30, when the dean's office startled the campus by bringing disciplinary charges against four FSM leaders for acts committed during the original protests, two months earlier. Aroused by this demonstration of the administration's refusal to bargain sincerely or respect the legitimacy of student aims, the Free Speech Movement resorted to a massive sit-in in the administration building. It was this that led to the intervention of the state police, on order of Governor Brown, and the forcible, largely secretive, and brutal eviction of the sit-inners described in the national press. A three-day strike of students and teaching assistants began the next morning, effectively closing down the campus.

The New Conservative reaction to these events must be seen in the light of the breakdown of the "equilibrium" at Berkeley. "Leaders" were not more disposed to bargain democratically and rationally than "masses" (i.e., the students). In this instance it would seem that an exception must be made to the New Conservative admonition against mass action to insure democratic goals. The test of democracy at a university is not whether students "democratically decide" university policy: curriculum, for example, is outside the realm of student control. But in a university freedom of advocacy is analogous to the right of citizens in a civil democracy to vote and organize politically. If New Conservative theory is to have any meaning, students must be able to achieve such rights through existing avenues of change. If, however, the authorities are so committed to the repression of those rights that they cannot bargain in good faith, then they must be challenged in more unconventional ways, unless we abandon our democratic ideals. But even when the "leadership" does not live up to its part of the bargain, the New Conservatives denounce any attempt to confront it. In such a crisis, the student right of political advocacy becomes to Lipset no more than a "privilege." The New Conservatives' analysis of the situation at Berkeley suggests that the logic of their antipathy to mass politics stems from, and leads to, an unquestioning allegiance to established legal and bureaucratic institutions rather than a concern for democratic values.

The New Conservative apologia for administrative repression was a curious blend of pseudo-liberal rhetoric with overtones reminiscent of Edmund Burke. Lipset seems to regard the students' assertion of constitutional rights as some kind of danger: "The indifference to legality shown by serious and dedicated students threatens the foundations of democratic order." But that "legality" to which Lipset refers is precisely the set of bureaucratic regulations preventing the exercise of rights traditionally considered fundamental to a democratic order.

There *was* disruption at Berkeley, yet it would be difficult to find anyone who favored disorder for its own sake. Disruption, however, is at times necessary to remedy injustice. The term "order" cannot in and of itself define a society, for order may be based upon authoritarianism or upon democracy. The values Lipset expressed are the foundations of the former, of a bureaucratic society which he chooses to call "democratic."

One of the things revealed by the events at Berkeley is the extent to which certain social scientists have altered the operational meaning of the word "democracy." Their adherence to the "liberal" liturgy obscures the real values on which their politics is based. At Berkeley, where issues like free speech were live, the conflict between the FSM and the administration exposed the values which inform action. But while the administration had consistently used force—in form of suspensions, for example—to repress constitutionally guaranteed liberties, Professor Feuer singles out the students as initiators of "force," that is, civil disobedience. The chancellor of the university, who was partly responsible for the police action taken against the 800 students, is characterized by Feuer as "a man of saintly character and an eminent scholar." The students become his persecutors.

This projection of violence onto the victims is typical of authoritarianism, as is the admiration of "firmness" and power in the establishment. Lipset laments the weakening of "authority" on the Berkeley campus. Pinning his hopes for the restoration of authority on a new acting chancellor, he writes in the language of modern authoritarianism: "Myerson already has shown strength and sophistication in dealing with the crisis and he commands wide support. . . ." Student political activity is regarded as abnormal; the use of civil disobedience to obtain constitutional rights is condemned for violating bureaucratic prerogatives. But police brutality and administrative action against students are glossed over or dismissed as minor "mistakes," and the New Conservatives find democracy in the reign of "saintly," omnipotent bureaucrats.

The New Conservatives do not defend all élites, of course. They do not defend authoritarianism behind the Iron Curtain or in Franco's Spain. But they are defenders of the more subtle antidemocratic tendencies in American political life, and, in particular, support the bureaucratic establishment on the university campus.* Their political ideas constitute an ideology.

The New Conservatives' ideological commitment to a defense of bureaucracy and legality (no matter how inadequate or perverse a form these institutions of law and order may sometimes take) leads to intellectual blindness and paranoia. These writers are in the process of becoming oblivious to the undemocratic and illiberal tendencies which bureaucratic institutions engender. According to the New Conservatives, argument or protest against the administrative hierarchy can never be legitimate, for it always stems from conspiracy, psychosis, and other antisocial forces. Thus they find it necessary to attribute the cause of antiauthoritarian protest to pathology (Feuer); to the naïveté of liberals and the cunning of "extremists" (Lipset-Seabury); and to "radicals" (Glazer).

* Although Professor Feuer defends the political prerogatives of the administration, he must be given credit for a cogent criticism of the university's educational policies.

Many of the New Conservatives received their earliest schooling from totalitarian parties and hard-bitten, isolated· political sects, and many of them seem to have become so disillusioned with their impulsive youth that they are now obsessed with the menace of "extremist" phantoms. Their personal histories, however, are hardly the central issue. More to the point is the methodological relationship between the Communist Party's preconceived and unalterable defense of an authoritarian power (the Kremlin) and the identification of many New Conservatives with a home-bred bureaucratic institution, regardless of its actions. Committed to certain institutions and fearful of their destruction, New Conservatives cannot accept challenges to these institutions calmly and dispassionately. Hence the readiness of New Conservatives, like Communists, to vilify their opponents.

The New Conservatives have frequently attacked "ideologists," those radical critics who advocate social change. The sickness of ideology, however, comes not from theories of social change but from blind acceptance of institutional authority. The New Conservative ideology and method presents a genuine threat to the intellectual health of American liberalism. Its inflexibility threatens to constrict and deaden thinking and remove intellectual dialogue from the realm of reason and objectivity to the world of fantasy and dogma.

Furthermore, their defense of élitist politics lacks the paternal charity of secure, tradition-bound, Burkean conservatism. Their ideology threatens to abort those moral values which underlie political involvement and to convert liberal thought into an appendage of a bureaucratic machine. For example, in his *Commentary* article, Professor Glazer attacks Negro sit-ins in the Berkeley area. This is, in effect, a criticism of the movement which has given new moral inspiration to the nation.

Finally, New Conservative ideology threatens the liberal vision of the open society. These writers accept a confrontation of views and a conflict of groups only so long as this is contained within preconceived institutional limits. The New Conservatives are not really writing about liberal politics. They are theorizing about the means of maintaining bureaucratic order.

Gearing themselves to the needs of a highly centralized and interdependent society, writers such as Lipset and Feuer mistakenly identify the political man with the functionary: citizen is replaced by system; administrative petition is substituted for popular activity. The role of advising the bureaucracy becomes the ersatz politics of sociologists and political philosophers. Ironically, this is hailed as moderate, while the democratic view of the open society is rejected as "extreme."

LARRY D. SPENCE

Berkeley:
What It Demonstrates*

Beginning in the early morning hours of December 3, 1964, more than 700 students of the University of California at Berkeley were arrested and dragged from the central administration building of the campus. During and following this mass arrest, picket lines were set up at major campus entrances and classroom facilities. By Friday, December 4, university operations were effectively brought to a standstill and more than 8,000 students rotated picket-line duty.

This was the first successful student strike at a major university in the United States. But more important, this was the first significant white-collar rebellion in our time. These sons and daughters of the middle class demonstrated and walked the picket lines, not behind the moral banner of the repressed Negro, but on the basis of their own grievances against a system that had deprived them of their rights of responsiblity and self-expression. More than sixty per cent of those arrested had never engaged in an act of civil disobedience before and fifty-seven per cent were political newcomers.

University President Clark Kerr recently admitted that the original ban, taking away the use of a small area in front of the University entrance for political activities, was a mistake. But he added, "It had just been taken away—we could hardly turn around and hand it right back." This attitude illustrates the

* From *Studies on the Left,* Winter, 1965.

administration's fatal error. Administration blunders consistently revealed that policy was decided on irrational and incompetent ground and thus regulations and practices that had formerly been irritating became intolerable.

In one sense the student revolt was only another symptom of the crisis of America's post-industrial society. But in another sense the revolt may be an initial step in the political process required to rebuild the structure of that society. This was the first sign of trouble within the organized sector of society that culminates in the triple apexes of C. Wright Mills' power élite. Recent insurgent groups such as the Negroes of the civil rights movement and the rear-guard entrepreneurs of the ultra-right, have come from areas outside the system of government, corporation and military organizations. These groups have aimed at effecting policy changes. In contrast, the students' demands are structural, calling for changes in the hierarchical relationships of organized power.

The university has become a key component of the organizational system. The University of California at Berkeley operates on the multimillion dollar budget, of which more than half is supplied by the federal government. The bulk of these federal grants (forty per cent) goes for defense research and another twenty per cent goes for basic research in science and technology. But this dependency on federal aid does not begin to demonstrate the scope of the University's service to corporations, government, and the military. Clark Kerr writes:

> Knowledge has certainly never in history been so central to the conduct of an entire society. What the railroads did for the second half of the last century, and the automobile for the first half of this century, may be done for the second half of this century by the knowledge industry . . .

The new "multiversity" is a factory that turns out scientists, technicians, and managers to meet the demands of an increasingly cybernated production system. At the same time it conducts basic research for industry and the military, supplies consultants and experts to federal and state agencies, and is often the training ground for future cabinet members and federal commission chairmen. It must also supply a steady stream of trained teachers and professors to meet the requirements of a "knowledge industry" that accounts for twenty-nine per cent of the gross national product. The "multiversity" is the anteroom of the power structure of monopoly capitalism, where managerial cadres are recruited and young men on the make are made.

Kerr has candidly described the University's change from an ivy-covered academic community to the aluminum and glass "knowledge .factory" in his book, *The Uses of the University*. Kerr's book is dominated by metaphors of prostitution as he describes the services the "multiversity" renders what he euphemistically calls "society." The influx of research funds, he admits, has corrupted the leading faculty members, transforming them into members of what Robert M. Hutchins has called the "academic jet set." They are the idea men of the organizational system, and the University is their resting place between dizzying conferences with the power élite. Beneath this "jet set" are the researchers in the sciences and the famous scholars who seldom teach. And yet below them are the lowly faculty members who are forced to come in contact with undergraduates.

What about the product of the new knowledge factory? Ideally, the graduate of the "multiversity" is a startling combination of a technological genius and a thumb-sucking fool. This ideal is reflected in the hierarchy of affluence among University departments. The physical and biological sciences are plush with new buildings, concentrated courses, and corporation-style salaries. The social sciences come next with excessive specialization, larger classes and their own "administrative" ideology. Last come the liberal arts departments, long-haired and rebellious like their students. The ideal also is reflected in the scholarly productions of the University. Nobel Laureates abound in the sciences, end-of-ideology books and monographs pour out of the social sciences, and esoteric criticism and scholastic squabbles leak from the liberal arts.

The "multiversity" is an institute of ignorance as well as intellect. It faces the contradictory task of producing technical knowledge while preserving unquestioned loyalty to the organizational system. Here the promises of the rational progress of cybernation meet the irrational reality of the modern power structure. The scientific knowledge of the university is not employed to improve society but to decrease production costs, increase profits, improve doomsday weapons, increase the efficiency and scope of control systems and decrease meaningful employment.

The paradox of this situation is that with the material means at hand to put into practice many of the most ideal theories of human existence, these theories have fallen into disrepute as impractical and utopian. This suppression of theory has left men without a map of their goals, and without such a map men not only wander in confusion but easily succumb to conformist demands. Bureaucracies become ends instead of means. Nearing the end of industrial slavery, men become, instead, slaves of their own organizational creations. In the recent past this "new slavery" has brought protest, but a particularly isolated and ineffectual protest of romantic rebellion against the supposed tyranny of science and machines. "Inevitability" has become a popular word among social critics.

The student revolt at the University of California represents a dramatic break with this milieu of inevitability. The tensions inherent in the idiot-genius man have exploded in the process of his production. Needed, and needed badly by an organizational system that seeks to stifle initiative and dissent, these students in revolt have exposed some basic flaws behind the smooth façades of bureaucratic power. Even more important, they have demonstrated faith in a radical course of political action.

There is a great discrepency between the size and power of today's giant organizations and their effectiveness. The military and governmental bureaucracies of the world's most powerful nation cannot find the means to conquer an over-sized rice paddy called Vietnam. The bureaucracy of the largest university in the world cannot admit simple mistakes or negotiate with dissident students without calling in the state police. There are two main factors operating in these organizational failures: (1) organizations have become too large to be effectively managed by individuals or élites and (2) the tasks attempted by these organizations, while technically feasible, are not possible without the suppression of all remaining human qualities in their members. The first factor indicates an overestimation of the efficacy of managerial techniques. The second indicates an underestimation of the part played in organizational success by the subjective elements of belief, morale, and individual judgment. Despite the contemporary emphasis on machines and management, these factors suggest that the central problem of the modern organization is human. It was not machines or programming techniques that failed the French in Algeria or are failing the United States in Vietnam. Victorious armies as well as successful organizations require men capable of rational and forceful actions based on reality, not automatons steeped in mythology.

The men and women in bureaucratic slots have been regarded as just such automatons by both enemies of, and apologists for, the organizational system. They have theorized that human loyalty can be bought with affluence and pension plans. But man's psychology is not so simple. Men must have some belief in the meaning of their work or retreat from reality. A widespread retreat from reality among organization members means a decrease in technical efficiency. On the other hand, men educated to perform the new complicated organizational tasks must be rigorously trained in scientific techniques of thought and judgment. Such training leads to an increased awareness about the implications of isolated work-acts and the need to synthesize meanings beyond the organization.

For half a decade, the students who are to make up the next generation of management have demonstrated that they do not think much of the work and tasks that await them. They have tried to find ways out of the grind by entering the Peace Corps, doing social work in metropolitan slums, and registering voters in Mississippi. Those technicians who have entered the organizational world have found their lives torn by the contradiction between the social and economic progress they know to be possible and the desperate gadgetry that absorbs their efforts. Such disenchantment is the forerunner of a social explosion. The revolt at Berkeley was only the first bang.

The more University functions were disabled by student demonstrations, the more other students recognized a means of translating their individual frustrations into effective protest. Beginning with rallies of from 500 to 1,000 students, the Free Speech Movement subsequently drew from 5,000 to 8,000 students. The students' consciousness became increasingly radical and critical of the organizational machinery grinding their lives into atomic fragments of cringing work and electronic leisure. This attitude was summed up brilliantly by student leader Mario Savio:

> There is a time when the operation of the machine becomes so odious, makes you so sick at heart that you can't take part; you can't even tacitly take part, and you've got to put your bodies on the gears and upon the wheels, upon the levers, upon all the apparatus and you've got to make it stop. And you've got to indicate to the people who run it, to the people who own it, that unless you're free, the machines will be prevented from working at all.

These events in Berkeley should be an impetus to American radicals to finally "kick the labor metaphysic" and drop the vulgar-Marxist belief (shared by administrative liberals) that men must be hungry or unemployed or discriminated against to participate in radical political action. A survey of successful revolutions and radical action leads to the conclusion that men must be *conscious,* not hungry, to attempt the reconstruction of society. The Berkeley revolt has demonstrated that such a radical consciousness can be created by means of successful acts of social dislocation. Civil disobedience and mass non-violent demonstrations can bring bureaucratic processes to a screeching halt. Such shocks to organizational routines are often enough to jolt many from their conformist slumbers. These shocks dramatically demonstrate that organizations exist on the basis of men's faith and allegiance. They force the individual to recognize his own power and the tacit commitment he has made to an organizational system that works against his own interests and aspirations.

All of this suggests that the radical potentials of the white-collar classes must be re-evaluated. Since Mills, this large segment of society has been written off as apathetic and organizational-minded. But a majority of these men and women are performing tasks far below their abilities, not to mention their human dignity. They are close enough to élites to recognize their blunders and far enough from the apex to recognize their trained incapacity. Their protestant work ethic is all but dead and their aspirations for advancement only too cruelly contradicted by fact. Significantly, the vacuous suburban ranch house is halfway through its second decade. For many the mortgaged home, the gadgeted housewife, and the communal martinis have lost their magazine-ad appeal.

A new radical program is needed to meet the conditions of cybernated abundance and organizational ascendance. Old definitions, goals, and tactics must be reappraised. Too often, facile definitions of socialism that concentrate on planning, centralization, and increased production sound like the managerial plans of monopoly corporations. Existing examples of supposedly socialist institutions in the Soviet Bloc exhibit many of the structural deficiencies of capitalist bureaucracy. Organized in the same hierachical form, socialist enterprises often reproduce the same apathy at the bottom and a similar trained incapacity and bureaucratic egotism at the top.

Private property and selfish interest do not fully explain the clogged political and economic system of the United States. When economic conditions outstrip organizational forms, élites can be expected to act stupidly and selfishly to preserve power. What often appears on the surface to be a conspiracy is merely a collective reaction of fear and failure. There is no doubt that private property and the profit motive are anachronisms under conditions of abundance. But they may operate differently than in the days of classical capitalist accumulation. It may be that organizational power is the new driving force of our society and that profits are mainly used as a statistical rationale for excess capacity and systematized waste. These questions require research and debate.

In considering such questions I would suggest that form of organization be considered as an important element in the analysis of modern social and economic institutions. Despite its claims to rationality the hierarchical form of organization is prehistoric in origin and based more on psychological patterns than technological demands. This form of organization originally centered around the charisma of chieftains and kings. Industrialization forced its rationalization into bureaucratic patterns. But the world has become too small, populations too large, and the means of production too vast to be run by élites of frightened men. These men must make daily decisions that outstrip even their latest computerized information. The anxiety induced by the superhuman demands of such decision-making, forces a recourse to magical formulas and mythologies. These myths and formulas are too often archaic, containing ideological equivalents of demons and fairies.

Industrialization and its latest phase, cybernation, have not only led to an increase in the size of organizations, but also have required the raising of educational levels and technical skills. Where once the mistakes and failures of leaders appeared to be acts of fate they are now seen by large numbers of men as intolerable blunders. The explosive contradiction of the modern organization is this discrepancy between the structural ignorance of élites and the increased insight of the masses. The attempted production of a new idiot-genius man is a frightened response to this conflict. But the students of the University of California have taken the first step in repudiating this solution. Faced with the ignorance of little minds operating from an ant hill of power, they demanded democracy. They said that universities are for teachers and students and that teachers and students should rightfully run them while administrators administrate IBM machines and empty the trash. That doesn't seem like a bad program of reform for many of the ponderous economic, social, and political institutions of this society.

SOL STERN

A Deeper Disenchantment*

The University of California is probably the most impressive and prestigious state university in the country. It boasts a world-famous faculty that includes a half dozen Nobel Prize winners and its many departments are all considered "first rate." It is the "compleat" university. There is something there for everyone: a sprawling, pleasant campus, top-notch recreational facilities (including an outdoor country-club and swimming pool nestled in the Berkeley hills), a huge library, and excellent medical facilities. A constant flow of illustrious and exciting speakers and performers appear on the campus: everyone from U Thant to the Budapest String Quartet to Joan Baez. The resident student gets all this, plus his education, for approximately one hundred dollars a semester.

The city of Berkeley itself is *the* pleasant place to live. With its coffee houses and art movies, its almost perfect climate, its proximity to such places as San Francisco, Big Sur and Yosemite, Berkeley would appear to be the "compleat" college town.

Despite all the academic glitter and the bountiful social life Berkeley offers, there is deep and bitter resentment among many students about their life at the University. It is a resentment that starts from the contradiction between the public image and reputation of the University and their actual day-to-day experiences as students. For these students recognize that all that is exciting and stimulating about Berkeley comes from the frills and extras of university life; the formal university-learning experience is generally a deadening one.

The new undergraduate learns quickly that of all the functions

* From *Liberation*, February 1965.

of the Great University his own education is perhaps the least important. He has almost no contact with the famous professors he has heard about. They, for their part, seek ways to escape the "burden" of teaching to be able to devote full time to the pursuit of their professions (which are not defined to include teaching). Graduate teaching assistants do most of whatever face-to-face teaching the undergraduate encounters. For the most part, however, the undergraduate learns that his success at school depends on his ability to master a four-year system of lectures, reading lists and examinations that have little to do with genuine learning. A student organization, Slate, publishes a *Supplement to the General Catalogue,* every semester, which advises the undergraduate on ways to beat the "system" and get a reasonable education in spite of it. Whether the undergraduate is morally revolted by the system, or whether he shrugs it off as merely another facet of the lifesmanship he must master, it is as a "system" that his education is commonly perceived and becomes a central part of the undergraduate folklore.

Many graduate students share a more special malaise. They have already made something of a commitment to academic and university life, but it is a commitment beclouded with ambiguities and doubts. The graduate students, in their closer proximity to the professors and the specialized disciplines, have also become privy to the intellectual dishonesties and political scheming that go on at the upper levels of academia. There is a widespread sense that they are prisoners in a system of professional rewards and penalties, determined by those very professors whose manipulations they observe at first hand. It is a system they have no power to change and leaves them only the option of playing the academic game according to the rules or getting out.

This alienation in the midst of the apparent good life finds symbolic expression at a campus gathering place known as "The Terrace"—an outdoor pavilion of the student union cafeteria, where one can bask in sunshine most of the year and enjoy a majestic view of San Francisco Bay. Many of the more active and concerned students gather here for the usual rounds of student gossip and political banter. Their range of political opinion and affiliation is extremely wide; they include every variety of revolutionary and reformist socialist, radicals and liberal democrats, civil rights activists, anarchists, pacifists and even an occasional Gold-waterite. When the talk is of national and international politics the arguments are heated, but when the talk turns to what can only be described as "University politics" there is a sudden change of perspective. A common note of cynicism enters the dialogue. Common enemies are easily identifiable: they are the University bureaucracy, the graduate school system, the political schemers among the faculty. Most often and most pointedly the enemy is the president of the university, Clark Kerr.

It tells us much about the mood of these students that the man who is most clearly viewed as the enemy carries all the traditional credentials of the modern political liberal. In his speeches and writings, Clark Kerr is indeed always on the side of the angels: for academic freedom, for free speech, for freedom of inquiry. He has received the highest award of the American Association of University Professors for his efforts on behalf of academic freedom. Yet if Kerr is a bona-fide card-carrying liberal he also typifies much of what the students consider the failure of American liberalism during the Cold War era. Official establishment liberalism offers nothing to these students because it has lost its passion and crusading spirit. It has become manipulative, crafty and cautious. In domestic and international politics it has become identified with *realpolitik* and opportunism.

Kerr, for all his liberal rhetoric and reputation, represents only the cold bureaucrat who could never command these students' confidence. His style and physical bearing do not help him in this respect. He looks ever so much like the officious bank president. His public appearances are carefully managed and he seems never to allow himself any spontaneous gesture or show of emotion. Even on those occasions when he is working for a liberal reform, as he did recently in getting the board of regents to lift its ban on Communist speakers on campus, his style tends to infuriate the students. For he does not act by moral persuasion nor out of great principle but as the behind-the-scenes manipulator, the committee man, the politician.

I recall a conversation with a young graduate student last September in which he mused that he could not imagine Kerr ever resigning his position over some matter of principle. It is this, he said, that symbolizes the difference between the new bureaucratic liberals and educators such as Robert Hutchins or Harold Taylor who are becoming a vanishing breed.

But more than matters of personality and style mark Kerr as an appropriate symbol for the bureaucratic "system." Kerr has also become the foremost spokesman and ideologist for the new bureaucratic style in American higher education. In his Godkin Lectures, at Harvard in 1963, he first coined the term "multiversity" to describe the model American university of the future. This "multiversity" is no longer primarily a citadel for learning. It becomes a service center for society. The "multiversity" will increasingly service the established institutions of business, government, labor and the national defense effort. In Kerr's own words, "the university is being called upon . . . to respond to the expanding claims of national service; to merge its activity with industry as never before."

Now all of this is not so terribly new or provocative. Many educators have commented upon and lamented this trend. But it is different with Kerr: he cheerfully accepts the trend as the inexorable path of development and draws the appropriate conclusions. For if the "multiversity" is to become more and more attuned to the needs of industry and national defense, then the requirements of tough-minded bureaucracy and management must have first claims on those who lead the "multiversity." The "Managerial Revolution" has come to the campus; now the most important stratum of the university is not the faculty, nor the students, nor any single educational Idea, but rather the manager and administrator. The "multiversity" is a "mechanism held together by administrative rules and powered by money." To guide this mechanism through its many complex functions, the university president must be guided primarily by the tools and arts of manipulation and mediation.

At the University of California Clark Kerr has indeed appeared as that model administrator-manager. As both the author of this scenario of the future and the leading player in it, Kerr has made himself the perfect target for all the resentment that the development of the "multiversity" arouses. That is why the students regard Kerr's liberalism as irrelevant. It is also why "multiversity" takes on, in conversations on the terrace, all of the emotional connotations of the term "1984."

Perhaps what has been most infuriating to the students on the terrace is the fact that all the physical evidence about them seemed to point inescapably to the power of Clark Kerr's vision of the future. The University of California was becoming more and more like the model "multiversity." Moreover, the average student, despite his private anxieties and resentments, did not appear to be in the mood for any rebellion against the role assigned to him by the "multiversity." Nor did the faculty appear terribly upset about the consequences of the "multiversity"; they seemed rather to be enjoying the increased emoluments it was bringing them in the form of grants, consultation fees, and most important of all, freedom from teaching.

During the course of the free-speech struggle last fall, the students at the terrace learned that they did have resources available to fight back against the "multiversity." They were not yet reduced altogether to private and impotent grumblings. They learned how they could stake out an area of autonomy and take some of the initiative out of the hands of the administrators and managers.

When the issue of free speech was first raised, it did not seem that all the above sentiments would be brought to bear. It was after all a move not uncharacteristic of the old-fashioned university that precipitated the free-speech struggle. At the beginning of the fall semester the administration enforced an old but never used rule which had the effect of prohibiting the use of the campus by students for soliciting of funds and recruiting for political activities. Representatives of nineteen student political organizations then formed themselves as an *ad-hoc* group to press for a removal of these restrictions. So far there was nothing in this that suggested the beginning of a student rebellion. Student protest is accounted for by the theorist of the "multiversity." Indeed it is one of the characteristic talents of the new administrator-manager of the "multiversity" that he is able to contain and divert student protests so that they do not interfere with the efficient functioning of the university machine.

What did give a clue that this was more than the ordinary student protest was the refusal of the students to play their roles entirely according to those "administrative rules" which keep the University bureaucracy functioning smoothly. From the beginning the students showed a unique and surprising determination to assert their autonomy. Whenever the University administration attempted to use the "normal" channels as a means of diverting them, the students were ready to take the dispute outside those channels for a more direct confrontation with the administration. A unique quality of audacity marked this protest. *Life* magazine was forced to recognize it, with a slight tinge of awe, as a "Tough Campus Revolt."

This toughness showed itself almost immediately. The students' first response to the new administrative regulations was direct and simple. They ignored them. Taking the position that the restrictions were a violation of their constitutional rights, they left it to the administration to try to enforce them. They set up their tables on the campus and continued to recruit and collect money. When the administration tried to bring disciplinary action against five of the students who had been manning the tables, 600 signed statements saying that they, too, had been guilty of violating the rules. When the dean summoned the five students to his office, 300 showed up and demanded to be seen too.

Finally the dean announced that eight students had been suspended for various activities in protesting the new rules. The students again had a ready response. They set up their tables directly in front of the administration building. The administration replied by having one of those manning a table arrested and placed in a campus police car (he had gone limp and a car had to be summoned to take him away). At this point a group of students spontaneously threw themselves in front of the car and blocked its path. Soon they were joined by hundreds of others and within an hour the police car was surrounded by a solid phalanx of one thousand bodies.

This spontaneous demonstration developed rapidly into a massive sit-in and rally around the police car that lasted thirty-two hours. As it grew and grew, student speakers mounted the embattled police car, using it as a podium from which to address the throng and state the demands the administration must meet to end the demonstration. At the end of the second day, five hundred helmeted police stood by with their night sticks, ready to wade in and disperse the students. Serious violence was averted only at the last minute as a settlement was reached between the student leaders and Clark Kerr. The crowd heard and approved the terms of the agreement and then dispersed voluntarily. Audacity had won the students a number of points. The suspensions of the eight leaders would be reviewed by a faculty committee, the University agreed not to press charges against the arrested student, and the rules on political activity would be submitted to a study committee on which students would be represented.

Much was learned during this first skirmish with the administration: the students realized that audacity and directness could move the bureaucracy where normal channels failed. Now the students turned to organizing themselves more effectively. The *ad-hoc* group of the political organizations was turned officially into the Free Speech Movement, and an executive committee of fifty and a steering committee of twelve were set up. Intensive organizing among the student body was conducted to gather more support, and new groups were urged to send representatives to the movement (or FSM, as it was now generally called). An FSM newsletter was published and leaflets by the score were put out to explain FSM's position and the latest developments to the student body. A massive and well-documented report was put together by graduate students, tracing the history of past administration attempts to limit student political rights.

After six weeks of student petitions, testimony at committees, and more rallies and demonstrations, the administration bent a little more. The eight suspended students were reinstated and the ban on soliciting and recruiting for political action was lifted. One major point remained at issue, however. The University now reserved the right to discipline individuals and organizations for advocacy on the campus of illegal acts off the campus (presumably such acts as civil rights sit-ins). This was an extremely important point, for the students were generally of the opinion that the original restrictions had been imposed as a result of pressures from local business interests, particularly William Knowland's *Oakland Tribune,* which were anxious to see the Berkeley campus cut off as a source for militant civil-rights activities.

At this point, however, the FSM was split on tactics for the first time. Many were for resuming the dramatic direct-action methods used earlier in the term. Others felt that the issues were not clear-cut enough to demand such a course. As the FSM floundered, the

administration gave it back its *raison d'être*. The administration
now decided that it was going to bring disciplinary action against
four of the student leaders for their actions during the demonstrations around the police car some two months before. This was seen
by the students as nothing less than an attempt to break the movement by cutting off its head.

Thus on December 2, over 1000 students marched into the
administration building, taking over all four of its floors. They
announced that they were prepared to sit there until the administration had called off its action against their leaders. In the meantime, the powerful organization of graduate students, which had
been formed during the free-speech struggle, announced its intention to call a university-wide strike in a few days in support of the
FSM demands.

It is significant that the next act in the steadily escalating crisis
came not from any campus official, but from the governor of the
state, Pat Brown. He ordered the arrests of the students. This was
done not because any clear breach of the peace had occurred (the
students were orderly and disciplined and were not blocking any
of the building's entrances or pathways), but essentially as a result
of the incessant pressures of the press and elements in the community who saw in the student rebellion a threat to their own well-
being. The next morning, with hundreds of state troopers surrounding the administration building and refusing even to allow any
faculty members inside to observe the arrests, Clark Kerr held a
press conference to support the governor's action for the maintenance of law and order. The "multiversity" as a service center for
society had now been confirmed in a rather ironic and twisted way
—the administrator had become spokesman and messenger for the
police power of the state.

On leading the students into the administration building the day
before, Mario Savio, the leader of FSM, had uttered the classic
words of the movement:

There is a time when the operation of the machine becomes so
odious, makes you so sick at heart that you can't take part;
you can't even tacitly take part, and you've got to put your
bodies upon the levers, upon all the apparatus and you've got
to make it stop. And you've got to indicate to the people who

run it, to the people who own it, that unless you're free the machine will be prevented from working at all.

This was a sentiment that now seemed to be shared by a majority of the student body, to whom the operation of the machine was now revealed as extremely odious. No longer was it merely a question of certain administrative rules that were at issue, but the whole stumbling and faceless bureaucracy that had stood by as political pressures forced a virtual police occupation of the campus.

So the students did indeed bring the machine to a grinding halt. A strike plan went into effect immediately and scores of picket lines were thrown around the classroom buildings. Many faculty members now supported the strike. A philosophy professor announced to the students gathered at a rally that he was calling off all his classes, as he could not in conscience conduct classes while the campus was under police occupation.

Most of the education that took place in the next few days came outside the classrooms, in the innumerable knots and crowds of students and faculty that sprang up everywhere on the campus. They argued and discussed the nature of democracy, the rule of law, and civil disobedience. The FSM organized classes off the campus at their "Free University of California." It was truly an amazing scene. Nothing less than a revolution, though a gentle one, seemed to be taking place.

In the meantime, the administration was acting characteristically. President Kerr announced that he was going off to Chicago on business—but then stayed on the campus to negotiate and mediate quietly behind the scenes. Sensing the enormity of the crisis, Kerr decided to go before the students on the third day of the strike; it was the first time he had addressed the students directly during the whole dispute.

A special University convocation was called to hear Kerr present a compromise proposal for ending the dispute, which had been drawn up by the department chairmen. The convocation was held at the University's outdoor Greek theater; it was an appropriate setting for a drama that was farce and tragedy all at the same time. Eighteen thousand members of the University community filed into the theater as in some feudal assembly, each to his appointed place: first the students in the rear, then the faculty up closer to the stage, then the department chairmen seated up on both sides of the stage;

finally the president himself made his appearance and took a seat in the center of the stage. It was a processional that had been followed before and is common practice on most university campuses. But coming at a time when the students had brought the University machinery to a halt, it must have seemed like the final absurdity of the administrative ethos.

The students whose action had forced the calling of the convocation were not to be allowed representation. Both the leaders of the FSM and the president of the student government had asked to be allowed to speak and were denied. President Kerr read his "peace plan" without even mentioning the existence of the FSM. It was as if to dramatize the missing factor that Mario Savio walked up on the stage and toward the microphone as the chairman was announcing that the meeting was adjourned. Before Savio could speak, two campus policemen rushed up from behind and dragged him bodily from the stage. To the thousands of students who witnessed this incident and roared their disapproval, it was another outrageous example of the crudities that the processes of the "multiversity" lead to.

Clark Kerr's peace plan only alienated the students further. He had learned nothing from the experiences of the past few months and seemed incapable of leading or teaching in such a situation. The strike went on, and was ended only the next day when the academic senate voted overwhelmingly to support almost all the demands of the students and pledged to work for their adoption by the board of regents. The students now put away their picket signs, stirred and exhilarated by the support they had received from the faculty and the prospect of total victory.

The issue of political expression at the campus is, at the time of writing, not yet settled. The regents of the State of California are a collection of all the practicality that the leaders of the state's political and economic system have to offer. Perhaps it ought not to have been expected that they would deal with a set of requests formulated under the pressures of a student rebellion, as a question of principle. At their first meeting on the subject they tried to fob-off all the parties concerned. To the citizens of the state, they pledged their determination to preserve Law and Order on the campus; to the students, they pledged their devotion to the First and Fourteenth Amendments to the Constitution. Finally there were more committees set up to study the problems of political advocacy on the campus.

Whatever the final outcome, it is clear that the meaning of these events lies deeper than the use of the Berkeley campus for political activity. The students themselves, slightly amazed at the proportions of the movement they had touched off, also looked about for meanings.

It was widely understood that some deeper disenchantment lay behind the free-speech fight. A campus minister had written to the school newspaper that he saw behind the student rebillion a reaction to "the modern isolation and alienation of the spirit" and that the students were trying to restore a lost sense of "community." "Alienation" and "community"; these words were much heard from the students during their rallies and demonstrations. The computer, too, somehow became a symbol of the "system" that the students were objecting to. "Are you a student or an IBM card?" Thus read one of the FSM leaflets urging students to support the strike.

Yet this revolt was not just a blind lashing out at the machine —a modern Luddite rebellion. The IBM card and "the bureaucracy" were symbols, but behind the symbols stood men. And among the students there was a widespread feeling that the men who ran the system here at Berkeley, those who rationalized it and those who spoke for it, had betrayed them. That these men spoke with the rhetoric of sophisticated liberalism was only more appalling. Here on the campus, Clark Kerr and others like him were bowing to and abetting all the forces of mindless bureaucracy and alienation. One must admit that even Clark Kerr had known and spoken of the alienation of students. In his Godkin Lectures he had recognized that the student was often confused and lonely and without purpose, in the "Knowledge Factory." But for Kerr, the source of this alienation lay not with any policies of men, nor with any institution. Like the "multiversity" itself, alienation was an immutable, inevitable consequence of the growing complexity of modern society.

Thus Kerr and many other observers could not fully understand the nature of this revolt against the University administration and against Kerr himself. Were not all the rallies and demonstrations and sit-ins irrational, like tilting against history itself? Sometimes, to Kerr and others, these events, being irrational and inexplicable, had to have some sinister force behind them. Thus Kerr at one point spoke of outside agitators, Maoists, Castroites and other such devils stirring up the students. A professor at the University, Lewis Feuer, in an article * which otherwise showed understanding of the terrible effects of the "multiversity," also had to explain much of the student revolt as being instigated by a collection of Maoist-beatnik-sexual libertine pseudo-students who were all looking for some synthetic revolution to make up for the emptiness which they felt in their lives. Finally, everyone spoke of the unreasonableness of the students. They were rejecting all the "normal channels" for settling disputes; they showed a contempt for law and order. They were, according to Clark Kerr, attempting to disrupt the orderly processes of the University and impose anarchy on the campus.

To the students however all the talk about "reasonableness," "orderly processes" and "normal channels" seemed but a façade behind which a "higher irrationality" was being practiced by the administrators, the bureaucrats and the politicians. These men defined "orderly processes" and "reasonableness" as all that was consistent with the on-going system. To Clark Kerr, for example, it was presumably "reasonable" that the University engage in contracted research for the Defense Department, "reasonable" for the University to allow its facilities to be used by the Marine Corps to recruit students, but it was "unreasonable" for the students to recruit civil rights workers to disrupt the flow of commerce in the outside community.

Behind all the talk of "orderly processes" was a demand that the students accommodate themselves to a style of protest that would have frozen them to the very administrative apparatus that they were trying to change. It was this administrative style that was as much a source of the students' alienation as "the complexity of modern society." Correspondingly, it was the style of the student protest that most upset so many of the important people of the state and the University. The students had set up their own countercommunity, independent of the University system. Their own

* "Rebellion at Berkeley," *The New Leader*, December 21, 1964.

standards of justification prevailed and they kept their own counsel, not paying too much attention to the pleas for "realistic" approaches that came from their elders, many of whom were jaded ex-radicals.

In acting as they did the students achieved some unique results. They took the first genuine steps toward that sense of community everybody was always vainly searching for. It was widely remarked that there was more face-to-face communication among the faculty and between faculty and students during the days of the strike than there had ever been before. The classroom had been replaced by the open and unstructured forum. In those innumerable spontaneous sessions between professors and students, important educational experiences unfolded. There was a give and take and an openness that could not have occurred in the classroom. The professors faced the students without their academic regalia, without their grade books, without the prospects of giving or withholding a recommendation. There was much talk during those days of a "Free University of California." Unlike Clark Kerr's "multiversity" it was an idea and a model of a future university that *the students* would have liked to create and participate in—one that would more often act in opposition to the powers-that-be in the society outside.

In all this a new mood seemed to grip the students. The "multiversity," with all its horrendous consequences, was not historically inevitable as the technological determinists were continuously announcing, but would come because men with power abetted it. The new technology should have brought with it greater opportunities for community and more meaningful purpose in life. The problem was how to make those in power and in the entrenched bureaucracy use those opportunities for decent purposes. To bring such pressure, it became necessary to shake up the bureaucrats and dramatize the gap between them and the students by creating new and audacious styles of protest.

One does not wish to exaggerate or romanticize what the students at Berkeley did. The "multiversity" is still omnipresent and students must go back and play by its rules. Yet it must not be forgotten that behind the façade of orderly and pleasant campuses there are deep currents of unrest and dissatisfaction. White, middle-class students in the North also need a liberation movement, for they have no community in which they exercise citizenship. They feel imprisoned and oppressed by a smiling and genial bureaucracy.

The issues at Berkeley are deeper than civil rights and civil liberties. These issues merely provided the form of this first serious revolt against modern liberal bureaucracy. When and if the "pocket" problems of civil rights and poverty are solved, this society will still have to deal with a crisis that is more basic to the lives of most of its citizens. It is this that concerns the students at Berkeley, and in response to that crisis they created an important little wedge against the creeping totalitarianism that threatens all of us.

MARIO SAVIO

An End to History*

Last summer I went to Mississippi to join the struggle there for civil rights. This fall I am engaged in another phase of the same struggle, this time in Berkeley. The two battlefields may seem quite different to some observers, but this is not the case. The same rights are at stake in both places—the right to participate as citizens in democratic society and the right to due process of law. Further, it is a struggle against the same enemy. In Mississippi an autocratic and powerful minority rules, through organized violence, to suppress the vast, virtually powerless, majority. In California, the privileged minority manipulates the University bureaucracy to suppress the students' political expression. That "respectable" bureaucracy masks the financial plutocrats; that impersonal bureaucracy is the efficient enemy in a "Brave New World."

In our free speech fight at the University of California, we have come up against what may emerge as the greatest problem of our nation—depersonalized, unresponsive bureaucracy. We have encountered the organized status quo in Mississippi, but it is the same in Berkeley. Here we find it impossible usually to meet with anyone but secretaries. Beyond that, we find functionaries who cannot make policy but can only hide behind the rules. We have discovered total lack of response on the part of the policy makers. To grasp a situation which is truly Kafkesque, it is necessary to understand the bureaucratic mentality. And we have learned quite a bit about it this fall, more outside the classroom than in.

As bureaucrat, an administrator believes that nothing new

* From *Humanity*, December, 1964.

happens. He occupies an ahistorical point of view. In September, to get the attention of this bureaucracy which had issued arbitrary edicts suppressing student political expression and refused to discuss its action, we held a sit-in on the campus. We sat around a police car and kept it immobilized for over thirty-two hours. At last, the administrative bureaucracy agreed to negotiate. But instead, on the following Monday, we discovered that a committee had been appointed, in accordance with usual regulations, to resolve the dispute. Our attempt to convince any of the administrators that an event had occurred, that something new had happened, failed. They saw this simply as something to be handled by normal University procedures.

The same is true of all bureaucracies. They begin as tools, means to certain legitimate goals, and they end up feeding their own existence. The conception that bureaucrats have is that history has in fact come to an end. No events can occur now that the Second World War is over which can change American society substantially. We proceed by standard procedures as we are.

The most crucial problems facing the United States today are the problem of automation and the problem of racial injustice. Most people who will be put out of jobs by machines will not accept an end to events, this historical plateau, as the point beyond which no change occurs. Negroes will not accept an end to history here. All of us must refuse to accept history's final judgment that in America there is no place in society for people whose skins are dark. On campus students are not about to accept it as fact that the university has ceased evolving and is in its final state of perfection, that students and faculty are respectively raw material and employees, or that the university is to be autocratically run by unresponsive bureaucrats.

Here is the real contradiction: the bureaucrats hold history as ended. As a result significant parts of the population both on campus and off are dispossessed, and these dispossessed are not about to accept this ahistorical point of view. It is out of this that the conflict has occurred with the university bureaucracy and will continue to occur until that bureaucracy becomes responsive or until it is clear the university can not function.

The things we are asking for in our civil rights protests have a deceptively quaint ring. We are asking for the due process of law. We are asking for our actions to be judged by committees of our peers. We are asking that regulations ought to be considered as arrived at legitimately only from the consensus of the governed. These phrases are all pretty old, but they are not being taken seriously in America today, nor are they being taken seriously on the Berkeley campus.

I have just come from a meeting with the dean of students. She notified us that she was aware of certain violations of University regulations by certain organizations. University friends of SNCC, which I represent, was one of these. We tried to draw from her some statement on these great principles, consent of the governed, jury of one's peers, due process. The best she could do was to evade or to present the administration party line. It is very hard to make any contact with the human being who is behind these organizations.

The university is the place where people begin seriously to question the conditions of their existence and raise the issue of whether they can be committed to the society they have been born into. After a long period of apathy during the fifties, students have begun not only to question but, having arrived at answers, to act on those answers. This is part of a growing understanding among many people in America that history has not ended, that a better society is possible, and that it is worth dying for.

This free speech fight points up a fascinating aspect of contemporary campus life. Students are permitted to talk all they want so long as their speech has no consequences.

One conception of the university, suggested by a classical Christian formulation, is that it be in the world but not of the world. The conception of Clark Kerr, by contrast, is that the university is part and parcel of this particular stage in the history of American society; it stands to serve the need of American industry; it is a factory that turns out a certain product needed by industry or government. Because speech does often have consequences which might alter this perversion of higher education, the university must put itself in a position of censorship. It can permit two kinds of speech, speech which encourages continuation of the status quo, and speech which advocates changes in it so radical as to be irrelevant in the foreseeable future. Someone may advocate radical change in all aspects of American society, and this I am sure he can do with impunity. But if someone advocates sit-ins to bring about changes in discriminatory hiring practices, this cannot be permitted because it goes against the status quo of which the university is a part. And that is how the fight began here.

The administration of the Berkeley campus has admitted that external, extra-legal groups have pressured the University not to permit students on campus to organize picket lines, not to permit on campus any speech with consequences. And the bureaucracy went along. Speech with consequences, speech in the area of civil rights, speech which some might regard as illegal, must stop.

Many students here at the University, many people in society, are wandering aimlessly about. Strangers in their own lives, there is no place for them. They are people who have not learned to compromise, who for example have come to the University to learn to question, to grow, to learn—all the standard things that sound like clichés because no one takes them seriously. And they find at one point or other that for them to become part of society, to become lawyers, ministers, businessmen, people in government, that very often they must compromise those principles which were most dear to them. They must suppress the most creative impulses that they have; this is a prior condition for being part of the system. The University is well structured, well tooled, to turn out people with all the sharp edges worn off, the well-rounded person. The University is well equipped to produce that sort of person, and this means that the best among the people who enter must for four years wander aimlessly much of the time questioning why they are on campus at all, doubting whether there is any point in what they are doing, and looking toward a very bleak existence afterward in a game in which all of the rules have been made up, which one cannot really amend.

It is a bleak scene, but it is all a lot of us have to look forward to. Society provides no challenge. American society in the standard conception it has of itself is simply no longer exciting. The most exciting things going on in America today are movements to change America. America is becoming ever more the Utopia of sterilized, automated contentment. The "futures" and "careers" for which American students now prepare are for the most part intellectual and moral wastelands. This chrome-plated consumers paradise would have us grow up to be well-behaved children. But an important minority of men and women coming to the front today have shown that they will die rather than be standardized, replaceable and irrelevant.

PAUL KRASSNER

The Naked Emperor*

Recently I was invited to speak at the University of Connecticut, which is located in the theoretically dry town of Storrs in that theoretically birth controlless state. Therefore I began may talk, "The Truth Is Silly Putty," with a special (false) announcement that the county government had just passed a bill which would at last permit the sale of liquor . . . but that the label on every bottle would be required to bear the legend: SOLD FOR THE PREVENTION OF DISEASE ONLY.

I then compounded this legalistic combination of hypocritical ingredients with a brief discussion of the university's position on a specific campus controversy, and it was interesting to observe the students' reaction when I quoted (*not* falsely) "fulfillment of the total education experience" as one of the administration's reasons for being *opposed* to undergraduate off-campus living.

The reaction was strong laughter, obviously indicative of cynicism regarding the administration's rationale.

Ironically, it is this concept of the total education experience *on* campus which I believe to be the basic significance of the much-misunderstood free-speech imbroglio at the University of California in Berkeley.

For example, two University of Miami students criticized a columnist in *The Hurricane,* official undergraduate newspaper, for describing the events in Berkeley as "rioting." They called the reference "one of the grossest misjudgments of a student demonstration. . . ."

* From *Cavalier,* April, 1965.

Their letter continued: "Here at UM, the only thing that seemed to arouse student ire was coed curfews, and that only led to an ill-fated, typically immature, panty raid. Would these same students protest as loud as Berkeley if their free-speech right were infringed upon?"

There was, of course, one Berkeley adminstrative official who mustered up his oversimplification gland and labeled the protest there as not much more than a "civil-rights panty raid."

How had it all started?

On September 14, Dean Towle banned posters, easels and tables at the Bancroft-Telegraph Street entrance to the Berkeley campus "because of interference with flow of traffic." She also reminded student groups of "rules prohibiting the collection of funds and the use of University facilities for the planning and implementing of off-campus political and social action."

Previously, according to Chancellor Strong, University officials had "considered no action to be necessary" to enforce these rules. The *San Francisco Chronicle* stated on December 4 that, although the rules were called "historic policy" by Strong, "the fact was, however, that it was a policy frequently winked at by University officials—until the convention controversy."

The reference was this: During the Republican National Convention last summer, Goldwater supporters complained that Scranton supporters were illegally recruiting student volunteers on campus.

The nineteen organizations affected by the ban registered a protest with Dean Towle.

On September 21, she modified her ruling: Informational activity, but not advocacy or organization of political and social action, would be permitted.

Now, boys and girls, what do you suppose could have happened that made her change her mind about the "traffic problem" just like that?

During the first week of classes last semester, a student had attended the chancellor's reception for holders of the Regents' Scholarship at University House. He overheard someone question Chancellor Strong about the reason for the University's new policy. He replied that the *Oakland Tribune* had called him and asked if he was aware that the picketing activity (protesting alleged racial discrimination in the *Tribune's* hiring practices) was being organized on University property. Strong said he didn't know it *was* University property, but that he would investigate.

And so, by the grace of Outside Pressure, the ban was on.

To the tune of "The Battle Hymn of the Republic," students sang:

Now academic freedom is among the finest goals,
But our administrators fear it taxes students' souls.
And the Tribune spreads the word to all the taxpayers at the polls—
Public Relations marches on.

These weren't students at the University of California in 1964 singing about the *Oakland Tribune,* though. These were students at the University of Illinois in 1960 singing about the *Chicago Tribune,* Dr. Leo Koch had been dismissed from the biology department when he wrote a letter to the *Daily Illini* condoning premarital intercourse.

But the lyrics, along with the principle, certainly applied to Berkeley. Several organizations decided to make a test case of the ban by manning tables to organize political and social action. Five individuals were cited for violating University rules and were asked to appear at 3 PM for a meeting with the deans.

Four hundred students signed statements that they, too, had manned illegal tables, and the challengers entered Sproul Hall and sat-in, please—demanding disciplinary hearings. At 11:45 PM the five students plus three others were indefinitely suspended—a punishment which does not appear in the regulations of this University whose administration had obviously gone anarchistic.

Time magazine described the individuals as "eight ringleaders of the demonstration." Dean Williams had testified that the suspended students were singled out from among many who had been observed violating the rules; this was done in order to discourage students from protesting the regulations.

The sit-in lasted till 3 AM. Next day, October 1, ten tables were manned again, a campus policeman approached one of the tables (manned by the Congress of Racial Equality) where a dozen persons were seated. One was singled out and placed under arrest. But before you could say nonviolent demonstration, the police car was surrounded, its captors numbering as many as 3,000 students. During the late evening, bored fraternity men gathered and tossed lighted cigarettes and eggs on those sitting in the plaza. The demonstrators responded with silence.

Next day 450 police assembled on campus to remove the police car and its arrested inhabitant, but an agreement to negotiate was reached and the demonstrators dispersed. One of the folk songs to come out of the Free Speech Movement, incidentally, was "If I Negotiate with You," to the tune of the Beatles' "If I Fell in Love with You."

Over the next couple of months there was a series of sit-ins and attempted negotiations, and then, on December 2, the infamous Sproul Hall sit-in. It took twelve hours for 800 students to be arrested by some 600 instructors of a new course called Introductory Police Brutality. These are from the lab notes students took:

"We should do like they do in them foreign countries—beat 'em senseless first, then throw them in the bus."

"Hey, don't drag 'em down [the 90 steps] so fast—they ride on their heels. Take 'em down a little slower—they bounce more that way."

District Attorney J. Frank Coakley, prosecutor of the arrested students, went on record as detecting the "usual Communist propaganda" in charges of police brutality.

There is an Establishment (translate: in-power) point of view about events such as these—usually predictable but nevertheless in a state of limited flux—and the mass media serve as vehicles for, and reflections of, the Establishment point of view. For a long time the television program, *The Defenders,* had a script dealing with the right to travel—based on the case of reporter William Worthy, whose passport was taken away when he defied a State Department ruling and went to Red China—but the show didn't get on the air because the Establishment was, in effect, against this particular freedom. And the script wasn't. But then Henry Steele Commager, an accepted Establishment critic, wrote an article in *The New York Times* Sunday magazine, an Establishment-oriented publication, in *defense* of the right to travel. And suddenly it was okay; *The Defenders* decided to televise that script after all.

That's the way it happens, baby.

Well, in January of this year, the *New York Times* Sunday magazine featured an article on the Berkeley Free Speech Movement, and it was headlined: FREEDOM TO LEARN BUT NOT TO RIOT.

Wrote Sidney Hook, another Establishment critic: "There is no direct connection between the student's freedom to learn and his freedom of speech."

The Establishment was denying the very meaning of education.

Hook also stated that "if outside groups send professional organizers onto the campuses of large metropolitan universities to recruit students . . . they should be barred from access." One wonders if that ought not apply to the armed forces.

In fact, at Berkeley, a group of students worried that, when the U.S. Marines set up a recruitment table in the Student Union Plaza, it was a direct violation of the University regulations barring on-campus recruitment for off-campus political or social action. They picketed the illegal Marines' table with signs reading:

MARINES, BEWARE THE DEANS

PLEASE DON'T ARREST THEM

FIGHT UNIVERSITY REGULATIONS,
JOIN THE MARINES!

THANK YOU MARINES,
FOR JOINING OUR PROTEST

IF THEY ARREST YOU, GO LIMP

The Marines weren't arrested. They are, needless to say, an arm of the Establishment. One picketer's sign commented:

BEHOLD THE CONSISTENCY
OF THE ADMINISTRATION!

While the Free Speech Movement was burgeoning in Berkeley, there was an unpublicized controversy at Long Island University in New York. Two columnists for the undergraduate newspaper, *Seawanhaka,* had written pieces that offended students and faculty alike. One was about the anniversary of President Kennedy's assassination; the other was about the Ecumenical Council's acquittal of the Jews in the death of Christ.

A member of the English Department, Ed Pomerantz, reacted to the furor by calling for a couple of voluntary sessions to discuss the columns. The room was crowded both times. It would be difficult to communicate here the beautiful spark—a passion for truth, really—that shot back and forth between Pomerantz and pupils. Suffice to say that one student asked another, "Does he teach his *classes* that way?"

And that's what the Free Speech Movement involves: It is the absolute crux of education as an ideal. And all the other phrases —from "multiversity" to "the right of advocacy"—are merely, depending on your own particular value-system, negative or positive subdivisions of the learning process.

What I'm saying, finally, is this: There is a freshman coed at the University of California in Berkeley who—long after she has forgotten what some professor spouted during an official lecture about Dostoevsky's *Crime and Punishment*—will remember, with perhaps a twinge of frightened pride, learning from a fellow demonstrator that if she planned to go limp when the police arrested her, it would be an act of practical feminine foresight to remove the earrings from her pierced lobes in advance.

V

THE NEW
RADICAL SPIRIT

Commentators who once accused the students of the fifties of silence and apathy now find themselves attempting to puzzle out the signs of a new political fervor among the students of the sixties. Within the last few years, a spirit like that of the thirties has reappeared on college campuses throughout the country; students who have become restive about American society seem increasingly willing to respond to its failings with action that aims for radical change.

The problems of the American Negro have been the special province of this new and growing radical movement, but now the grievances of Berkeley students have proved the movement more extensive than anyone had yet imagined. Previously only the more committed activists—the cadres of civil rights workers and peace demonstrators—undertook the often perilous course of civil disobedience. The semester of crisis at Berkeley, however, involved multitudes of students in direct action sit-ins and strikes against established authority. Moreover, the political discontents, which originally drove students off campus—even as far as Mississippi and Alabama—now brought them full circle back to the university. They applied the techniques of protest developed in the South to what they felt were violations of freedom in the institution closest to them.

This new radicalism is more a feeling than a program, more a moral style than a class conflict. Like all radicals, the student activists tend to be highly self-conscious, but the vocabulary with which they try to analyze their motives and concerns is impressionistic rather than ideological. They have come a long way from the doctrines of Marx; as both Paul Goodman and New Yorker *staff writer Calvin Trillin discuss at length, they are closer on the whole to the mood and values of existentialism.*

CALVIN TRILLIN

Letter From Berkeley*

One afternoon just after the spring semester began at the University of California, I paused on my way to the Berkeley campus to make a tour of the card tables that had been set up that day by student political organizations on the Bancroft Strip—a wide brick sidewalk, outside the main entrance to the campus, that had been the original battlefield of a free-speech controversy that embroiled and threatened the University for the entire fall semester. There were half a dozen tables, lined up, as usual, along the campus edge of the sidewalk, and hundreds of students were streaming past them onto the campus. By the time I had crossed the sidewalk to the tables, standup hawkers had presented me with a flyer announcing the picketing of Oakland restaurants by the Congress of Racial Equality, a flyer asking for contributions to raise bail for some earlier demonstrators from the Ad Hoc Committee to End Discrimination, and a homemade pamphlet called "Some Organizing Ideas: Excerpts from Idea Essay by Lee Felsenstein." The table at one end of the line was sponsored by the Young Socialist Alliance, an organization that is ordinarily referred to as Trotskyist, though few people seem to know just what the implications of that position are in Berkeley, California, in 1965. The YSA table was being watched over rather casually by a collegiate-looking young man in a blue blazer; he was reading a book, but would glance up occasionally at students who stopped to look at his display, which included leaflets in support of a local City Council candidate, pamphlets introducing the YSA, and a number of booklets on the

* From *The New Yorker*, March 3, 1965.

order of "Fidel Castro Denounces Bureaucracy and Sectarianism, Speech of March 26."

The YSA table was separated from the table of Slate, a campus political party of left-wing but non-sectarian views, by a cardboard sign announcing that placards for the CORE picketing of Oakland restaurants would be made on the steps of Sproul Hall, the administration building, the following afternoon. A young man wearing a lapel button reading "Free Oakland Now" was sitting behind the Slate table and calling out at intervals that he was selling the "Slate Supplement," a student critique of the University's courses. His table held not only a pile of "Slate Supplements" but also leaflets protesting discrimination in Oakland, a mailing list to be added to by those interested in receiving Slate literature, a stack of pamphlets about Mississippi put out by the Student Nonviolent Coordinating Committee, and a pile of buttons that included two varieties of the "One Man, One Vote" buttons produced by SNCC along with several of the "Free Speech" buttons worn by supporters of Berkeley's Free Speech Movement, a few "Free Oakland Now" buttons, and one button that said "Slate." A student stopped at the Slate table and, indicating a sign that asked for contributions to the bail fund for the Ad Hoc Committee demonstrators, asked the Slate representative, "Did you hear about the DuBois Club pulling out of the Ad Hoc Committee?"

"That's not what happened at all," the Slate representative replied. "The Ad Hoc Committee broke up. They're having a press conference at one o'clock, and Mike Myerson's going to explain it."

"Do you expect me to believe anything in the press?" the student asked.

"It's *their* press conference," said the Slate man. "Mike Myerson is the president of the Ad Hoc Committee."

"That doesn't make any difference," said the student, and wandered off.

The DuBois Club had the table on the other side of Slate's. A couple of students were looking over the literature available there —mostly pamphlets describing the DuBois Club, plus the various magazines of the American Communist Party—while the young man in charge discussed the relative merits of two sociology courses with a friend. At the table next to his, a representative of the California College Republican Club was explaining to a passing student that that club was the only moderate Republican club on campus, and, at the table beyond, the Independent Socialist Club was selling "The Mind of Clark Kerr," a pamphlet criticizing the president of the university, by the Independent Socialist Club's leader, Hal Draper, which had been one of the popular pamphlets of the free-speech controversy. At the end of the row, a girl wearing a button that said "I Care" was sitting behind a table sponsored by the Student Committee for Agricultural Labor arguing patiently with a young man who had stopped by to offer his suggestions. "I think we have to concentrate on organization at this stage," the girl was saying.

"No, no, no!" the young man exclaimed. "The thing to do now is to picket the grocery stores. Then we sit in at the factories."

In addition to stacks of literature and a paper to be signed by those interested in becoming members of the organization or receiving its mail, nearly every one of the tables set up on the Bancroft Strip has a pile of political buttons, the sale of buttons having become a popular way to raise money for student organizations at Berkeley. Students who want to protest against the House Unamerican Activities Committee—and that seems to include most of the students who stop at the Bancroft Strip—can usually buy a "Sack HUAC" button from the University Society of Libertarians or a "HUAC Eccch!" button from the Bay Area Council for Democracy; some of them already have a button that says "I Am Not Now Nor Have I Ever Been a Member of the House Unamerican Activities Committee." Another popular button says "A Free University in a Free Society," and is sold by Students for a Democratic Society, an organization affiliated with but often to the left of the League for Industrial Democracy, and someone has attempted the succinct approach with a button that says simply "I am an Enemy of the State." The Cal Conservatives for Political Action, who are sufficiently outnumbered to find humor their most effective weapon, wear buttons that say "I Am a Right Wing Extremist." During my stay in Berkeley, one of the most popular new buttons has been one saying "Abolish the Regents." It is being sold by Ed Rosenfeld, a young man with a shaggy beard who has been an active worker in the Free Speech Movement. Rosenfeld ordinarily mans a table of his own, holding up a sign decorated with covers of "The Regents"—a pamphlet that the FSM published during

the controversy in an attempt to show that the University board
of regents represented corporate wealth in the state rather than the
people—and shouting, 'Abolish the Regents,' twenty-five cents!"

"Does this money go for political activity?" a prospective customer asked while I was standing at Rosenfeld's table.

"Clearly," said Rosenfeld, who was himself wearing a "Get
Out of Vietnam" button on one lapel and, on the other, the pin of
the National Liberation Front, which is also known as the Viet-
cong, though rarely in Berkeley. "In this case, it will go to send a
student to the Youth Festival in Algeria next summer."

"Who is the student?" asked the customer.

"I am the student," Rosenfeld said. "Naturally."

The customer bought a button, and Rosenfeld continued his
chant. " 'Abolish the Regents,' twenty-five cents!" he called out.
"Send your favorite regent to Vietnam!"

With the start of the spring semester, the leaders of the Free
Speech Movement find themselves in a perhaps unexpected position—that of revolutionaries whose revolution has succeeded. The
FSM headquarters—a casually furnished store-front office where
business-like girls carefully compile logs of phone calls and cover
the wall with messages written in marker pencil—bears a startling
resemblance to the headquarters of the Council of Federated Organizations in Jackson, Mississippi. But, unlike COFO workers,
who still can't be sure that their civil rights campaign has made any
significant change in conditions in Mississippi, FSM workers need
only walk a block or two to witness unrestricted campus political
activity of the kind that was the goal of their movement, and, to
anyone who has spent some time listening to their reminiscences,
the FSM headquarters, which is a relatively recent acquisition,
seems to be a make-work echo of the days when the FSM had a
series of command posts, with names like Strike Central and
Press Central—a system of walkie-talkies for communication
among its scouts on the campus—and an emergency telephone
number, called Nexus, to be used when the regular number was
busy. During the fall semester, the free-speech controversy demanded the attention, and often the full-time participation, of a
large number of Berkeley students, administrators, and faculty
members; it involved an unprecedented use of mass action by stu-

dents and two potentially disastrous confrontations between hundreds of students and hundreds of policemen; and it eventually produced a situation in which a distinguished university of twenty-seven thousand students nearly came to a halt—a situation that the chairman of the Emergency Executive Committee of the Academic Senate called, with little disagreement from anybody who spent the fall in Berkeley, "one of the critical episodes in American higher education." Those events are in the past, however, and unless another issue involving free speech arises on the campus—or, as many FSM adherents would put it, "unless the administration commits another atrocity"—quite a few of the leaders of the Free Speech Movement are, in the words of one participant, "between movements."

According to the best-known FSM leader, an intensense, intellectully aggressive young man named Mario Savio, who was studying philosophy before he became involved in the controversy, "All that's left is the trial—legal and political defense—and making sure that the final rules on political activity are acceptable. Then, as far as the FSM goes, that's it; we disband." The trial he referred to is that of some eight hundred students who were arrested, on the orders of the governor of California, when they refused to leave Sproul Hall during the protest sit-in that is generally considered to have been the climactic event of the controversy. Political defense can be carried out through activities familiar to participants in mass movements (during the first week of the new semester, the FSM held a rally on "The Berkeley Trials: Justice or Vengeance"), but legal defense is another matter. The same students who, wearing blue jeans and singing hymns, had to be carried out of Sproul Hall by the police have conscientiously presented themselves, in quiet, well-dressed groups of fifty, in a makeshift courtroom in the auditorium of the Berkeley Veterans Building to enter their pleas. (For making a comment to the judge about "shameless hypocrisy" that would have been only a warmup for stronger language on the steps of Sproul Hall, Savio was given a two-day jail sentence for contempt.) The defendants have had to elect a Council of Twenty to deal with their staff of attorneys, who number at least twenty themselves, and FSM leaders have acknowledged, with some embarrassment, that their movement, which once attacked the computer as the symbolic agent of its followers' alienation and which adopted "Do Not Fold, Spindle, or Mutilate" as one of its war cries, has lately been borrowing the University's IBM machine to keep track of all the people involved in its legal affairs.

Officially, the issues that divided the Free Speech Movement and the University administration have not yet been completely settled. The board of regents, which has final authority over Berkeley and the eight other campuses of the University of California, still has a committee working to determine what its final policy on political activity should be; the Berkeley chancellor's office has yet to announce permanent campus regulations governing the precise times and places for holding the demonstrations that are now allowed, and ways of holding them that will not interfere wtih education; and the final point at issue between the administration and the FSM—whether the University would discipline those who advocate or organize illegal actions on its campuses—is settled mainly by the willingness of both sides to interpret each other's ambiguous statements with a minimum of conflict. However, there is so little disagreement left about the basic changes made in University policy during the controversy that President Kerr, who became the chief adversary of the FSM, has lately acknowledged in several speeches that the rules in effect before this fall—rules that prohibited students from planning, soliciting for, or advocating off-campus causes on University property—were of "doubtful legality." The dispute actually arose over the sudden application of these rules to the Bancroft Strip—where until last September they had been unenforced, in the belief (or pretense) that the property belonged to the city—but before it ended the regents had officially removed such restrictions entirely. The Bancroft Strip, where thousands of students enter the busiest plaza of the campus every day, has remained the area of greatest political activity, but now there is also a line of tables near the fountain in front of the Student Union, a group of three buildings that stand on one side of the plaza, and on the other side of the plaza political rallies are held on the steps of Sproul Hall itself. Martin Meyerson, a social scientist who was formerly dean of the College of Environmental Design and in January was appointed acting chancellor, has gained wide confidence among students and faculty—around the University the belief is widespread that his appointment was one of the chief benefits to come out of the dispute—and he is considered quite unlikely to commit an atrocity. Under the regents' new policy, the Berkeley campus is now operating peacefully, and, all in all, most people look upon the free-speech controversy as settled.

Any revolution that takes place in a uinversity community is observed by a particularly large number of people with a natural tendency to analyze such things, argue about their causes, and discuss their implications. The free-speech controversy has dominated Berkeley conversation for so long that its major events can be conjured up by phrases no more detailed than "The Police Car" (the car was held immobile on the plaza and used as a speakers' platform for some thirty hours on October 1 and 2 by students protesting the attempt of campus police to use it to remove Jack Weinberg, a former mathematics student who had been arrested while soliciting for CORE in defiance of the regulations), "The Big Sit-In" (this was held two months later to protest the university's belatedly announced intention of disciplining four FSM leaders for their roles in the episode of The Police Car, and resulted in the Sproul Hall arrests), "The Strike" (it crippled the University for the two days following The Big Sit-In), "The Greek Theater" (this was where the University held a meeting that was meant to end the dispute but aggravated it instead when Savio went to the microphone after the last speech and was dragged away by campus police), and "The Faculty Resolution" (a resolution in which, by a vote of eight hundred and twenty-four to a hundred and fifteen, the Academic Senate supported the FSM position that there should be virtually no University restriction on speech, and which—psychologically, if not officially—concluded the controversy in a victory for the FSM). Berkeley residents talk casually of documents with names like "The Pact of October 2nd" (signed by Kerr and the FSM leaders to end the episode of The Police Car at a time when several hundred policemen were standing ready to disperse the crowd). It is only when it comes to discussing committees that this kind of shorthand breaks down; there were so many committees during the controversy—committees trying to mediate, committees assigned to investigate, committees hoping to recommend—that even the most careful historian is likely to have difficulty keeping them straight.

Beyond mere discussion, a university community can apply its various disciplines to the situation at hand. While the controversy still raged, an undergraduate sociology student was surveying those who had participated in the surrounding of The Police Car, a group of graduate political-science students was collecting data on such matters as the effectiveness of The Strike and the political affiliations of the participants in The Big Sit-In, and the students in Sociology 105 (Introduction to Methods of Sociological Study) were taking a scientific sampling of student opinion on a variety of issues related to the dispute. As the spring semester begins, social scientists are still arguing about the nature of the FSM as a mass movement, historians are preparing studies of student protests and student radicalism, and essays on free speech and the nature of a university are continuing to emerge from faculty offices in blue ditto copies. A large foundation has been asked to support research for a scholarly history of the entire affair, and meanwhile a book is being compiled from the dozens of articles, studies, and documents already available; a study of the press coverage of the controversy has been prepared for the Center for the Study of Democratic Institutions, in Santa Barbara; FSM leaders are compiling a book of their own views, tentatively called "A Student Manifesto"; and a second committee appointed by the regents has retained a staff of investigators to draw up a report on the underlying causes of the disorder. In this atmosphere of earnest opinion-gathering, the FSM leaders, who in the past often emphasized the difficulty of communicating with authority, recurrently find themselves assembled in the chancellor's office and propounding their ideas on educational reform, or meeting with a polite, attentive education expert from the board of regents and explaining just how much they despise the entire system.

One afternoon, while I was sitting with some adherents of the FSM on The Terrace, the outdoor section of the cafeteria in the student union, we were joined by Mike Rossman, a member of the FSM Steering Committee, and Jerome Byrne, a Los Angeles lawyer who had been hired by the regents' committee to conduct its investigation into causes. Rossman, a graduate student in mathematics, has been at Berkeley for a number of years and has spent part of that time compiling a list of various infringements of student freedom by the administration—a list that was published during the fall as "Administrative Pressure and Student Political Activity at the University of California: A Preliminary Report" but is sometimes referred to as "Rossman's Litany of Atrocities."

After Rossman had mumbled some introductions and taken a seat, Byrne, an angular, conservatively dressed man with a straightforward manner, said, "I've just had a good talk with Mike, here, and I'd like to talk with all of you sometime."

"I'm very skeptical," said a graduate student in history named Steve Weissman, who is also a member of the Steering Committee, and is usually given credit for organizing The Strike.

"What I'm trying to get is an idea of what you think about the University," Byrne said. "I'm not interested in what happened during the fall. Well, I'm interested, but that's not really the purpose of the study."

"Well, maybe we can talk about my skepticism sometime," said Weissman.

"I was telling Mike that I have to go to an interview with the press—the *Daily Cal,*" Byrne said, smiling. "I'm going to put in a notice that I'll be in Pauley East at four tomorrow and that I'd be glad to hear from student leaders, representatives of interested student groups, and representatives of various shades of student opinion."

"That's the way not to have anybody there," said Weissman.

"Oh. Mike didn't say anything about that," Byrne said. "What should I say?"

"Maybe 'all interested students.' "

"I was afraid we might get several thousand that way."

"There isn't any right way to say it," Rossman said, scowling.

"Well, I hope you'll come anyway," said Byrne.

After Byrne had left, Weissman remarked to Rossman, "I really don't see the advantage of talking with somebody who's hired to make the report that the people who hire him want to see."

"What's the difference?" Rossman said.

"The difference is that if we talk with them, they can make the report saying they talked with Rossman and they talked with Weissman and this is what they came up with."

"You know, you're not as smart as you think you are," Rossman said. "You don't know anything about the way these people operate. They're obviously going to put that in whether they've talked with us or not."

Among Berkeley faculty members reflecting on the events of the fall, there is often disagreement even on precisely what happened, but two judgments seem almost universal. One is that the administration consistently mishandled the situation—first by its decision, apparently made under outside pressure, to enforce the regulations on the Bancroft Strip, then by its alternating positions of intransigence and concession, and particularly by its decision to discipline the four FSM leaders for their roles at The Police Car, an incident that everybody had considered closed. ("Student movements run on martyrs," Jack Weinberg said later, and it is true that the FSM got mass support for direct action only at those times when the administration was trying to pick off its leaders.) The other judgment is that the leaders of the Free Speech Movement were almost impossible to negotiate with—"rude" and "inflexible" are the two words most often applied to them—and were quick to use almost any tactics that they considerd "necessary." Those who supported The Faculty Resolution tend to look upon the behavior of the FSM leaders as understandable or irrelevant, and tend to believe that the students raised a legitimate issue of free speech, in which their view was essentially the correct one. Those in the minority that opposed it tend to argue that the issues were, to a large extent, concocted—or at least constantly inflated—by the FSM leaders, that their use of mass action was based more on a desire to foment trouble or keep the dispute going than on a sincere concern for free speech, and that the University was right in attempting to maintain some control over what was said on its campuses. Deep disagreements still exist among faculty members —and the leaders of the majority feel some mild resentment over the fact that virtually all articles on the situation by Berkeley professors have been the work of men identified with views held by a minority of one in nine—but lingering bitterness over the dispute does not appear to be widespread. Two months after the polarization of opinion that took place at the height of the dispute, most faculty members seem to have returned to the more or less neutral position they took early in the fall, and their differences now are often of tone rather than of substance. At its regular meeting on the first day of the spring semester, the Academic Senate seemed to be back to normal. In contrast with the nearly one thousand members who had been present in December to vote on The Faculty Resolution, only about a hundred people were scattered around the senate auditorium. President Kerr was on hand to answer questions, as he is from time to time, and the questions he was asked concerned such problems as salaries and summer sessions. Arthur Ross, a professor of industrial relations, who is the chairman of the Emergency Executive Committee, elected to act for the senate in matters growing out of the crisis, gave a relaxed report on committee activities, and, addressing an audience that had been warned a few weeks earlier that Berkeley was in danger of being transformed into a university of the Latin-American or Asian type, he drew considerable laughter by starting off his report with three headlines he had clipped from an English-language Japanese paper during a dispute at Keio University, in Tokyo, over a fee increase: "Keio U. Authorities May Rap Students," "All Keio Students Will Go on Strike from Tomorrow," and "Keio U. Trustees to Review Fee Hike."

Part of the talk about Berkeley's becoming an Asian-style university stemmed from the possibility that students might extend their demand to be considered equal bargaining partners to such matters as educational policy and even faculty appointments, and that they might apply direct-action tactics to this end. As the controversy continued through the fall, the FSM demands for unrestricted speech were mixed with criticism of the University as an impersonal factory, criticism of faculty members for "selling out" to governmental and industrial research projects instead of accepting their responsibility as teachers, and criticism of the backwardness of undergraduate education at Berkeley. Although practically nobody at Berkeley would deny that the University has fallen behind in undergraduate education, even the most sympathetic faculty allies of the FSM would hardly consider sit-ins or boycotts the logical agents of reform. Many professors believe, however, that the free-speech controversy demonstrated the limitations as well as the strengths of such tactics, since the mass support they required for success appeared to be present only when the opposition looked inflexible and when the complaint was not only considered justified but also was specific and dramatic. Complaints about undergraduate education are ordinarily not very exciting, and there is also some question that many students are aware of the fact that such complaints are justified. The Sociology 105 study—which was conducted by the class's instructor, Richard Somers, and is considered a fair sampling of student opinion—indicated that eighty-two per cent of Berkeley's undergraduates were either "satisfied" or "very satisfied" with "courses, examinations, professors, etc., at the University."

Whether or not the dispute reflected real dissatisfaction with courses, it is having some effect on educational thinking at Berkeley. Acting Chancellor Meyerson has been meeting with a group of FSM students who are interested in education, and they have occasionally been dismayed to find the chancellor's ideas on the subject more radical than their own. "They're actually a bit timid when it comes to education," Meyerson has told me. "I don't see why the size that everybody complains about can't be used to our advantage. I don't see why a university this size can't have a little St. John's, for people who think education is mastering a body of knowledge. I don't see why we can't have a little Antioch, for people who want to work part time, and perhaps even two kinds of engineering schools. People would have the advantage of the facilities, the library, and the type of scholars who, for better or worse, now seem to be attracted only to a large university, and they would be free to transfer from one college to another." Meyerson acknowledges that there is a considerable difference between proposing these ideas and having them adopted by the faculty and the regents —and also that at present any change is criticized by some people as a concession to FSM intimidation (an interpretation that the FSM is always happy to further)—but he feels that the uproar has already made the path easier for certain progressive plans that had been proposed before the controversy erupted. It has also meant that faculty members are now often engaged in conversations about how they can devote more time to their students, that several departments are hearing the ideas of students on the departmental programs, and that the Academic Senate is investigating, among other things, methods by which departments might rate teachers so that teaching would get more consideration, relative to research, than it does now in recommendations for promotion.

Among the students, the most definite educational idea to have emerged from the controversy—actually, it emerged from some makeshift classes held in Sproul Hall during the sit-in—is something called the Free University of California, which would operate parallel with the regular University and would use graduate teaching assistants as volunteer instructors. According to Weissman, one of its early proponents, the Free University "could teach classes that the University doesn't teach—the history of civil disobedience, for instance—or hold sections to hear a different point of view from the one given in the lecture—when lecturers set up a Marxist straw man to knock down and then say they're objective, for example—or do research projects in subjects like the power structure of Oakland, or the organization of the University itself." Some classes of this sort have already been held, but it is not yet certain whether the energy that launched the Free University and related projects during the controversy will last. Other expressions of that energy were a Teaching Assistants Union, a Graduate Coordinating Committee, and an Undergraduate Association; in the heat of controversy, the FSM even supported seven candidates (all successful) for the regular student government, the Senate of the Associated Students of the University of California, an organization that FSM leaders customarily speak of as "sandbox government." As FSM adherents might put it, "some of these structures may prove to be viable," while others probably will not, but unquestionably students all over the country have a better chance of being heard, through one channel or another, than they had last fall. Since the Berkeley controversy, many universities have been reviewing their administrative policies in respect to students, and the University of California is, of course, among them. Meyerson and his staff have been meeting with pastors of student religious clubs, for instance, who would like to see the regents' strict interpretation of the separation of Church and State eased enough to permit a Department of Religion, or at least the use of University facilities for special services.

President Kerr believes that no matter what good may come out of reappraisals undertaken at the University of California as a result of the controversy, it can never compensate for the damage the controversy did. It is now thought that the University has avoided investigation by the state legislature, partly because the regents have appointed their own investigating committee, and that the

House Unamerican Activities Committee will probably be dissuaded from visiting the Bay area this spring—a visit that would be very likely to bring on the largest demonstrations of recent times. Still, according to President Kerr, the damage done to the University in respect to fund-raising, appropriations, and the maintenance of good relations with the legislature and the alumni may continue for years. The position of many of the alumni was expressed by the editor of the alumni magazine, the *California Monthly,* when he wrote in last month's issue, "Frankly, I was very concerned about the future of our university." There is no doubt that strong disapproval of the FSM existed all through the state—ranging from condemnation of its activities as part of a Communist plot to mere headshaking over the use of civil-disobedience tactics against a University—and the gulf between the University's thinking and that of its constituency was certainly widened. At the same time that the Academic Senate was voting in favor of the FSM position and professors were expressing their alarm over the administration's use of police to end The Big Sit-In, polls in the state showed that three-quarters of the population held an unfavorable view of the FSM, and letters to the University supported the administration's disciplinary action twenty to one. Posted at the FSM office, where a policeman is almost automatically looked upon as brutal until he is proved otherwise, is a clipping from the Berkeley *Daily Gazette* announcing a police-appreciation campaign sponsored by the Berkeley Exchange Club and entitled "Mr. Policeman—We Love You."

Among the Berkeley faculty members, concern over the harm that the FSM victory might do the University has, naturally, been expressed with most force by those who supported the minority position in the Academic Senate, but even those who were strong supporters of The Faculty Resolution and continue to maintain that it was both right and necessary seem to have some lingering apprehension about the outcome of the free-speech controversy. Some of the faculty members are concerned about having condoned tactics that they ordinarily feel should not be encouraged anywhere —particularly in a university—and they worry about the effect not only on the student body but also on their own faith in the efficacy of proper procedures. "The trouble is, the FSM tactics work," says a professor who was an active supporter of the FSM. "It does make you wonder when time and time again you advise them against doing something outside the democratic processes we're used to and time and time again they do it and win their point that way." Faculty members often compare the free-speech controversy to their own fight with the regents a dozen years ago over the demand that teachers sign a loyalty oath—a fight that was carried on for a year but ended with all but a handful of the faculty's signing the oath. "During the oath fight, the faculty should have just said, 'No oath or we close the University,' " Savio has told me. "It's not very easy to hire strikebreakers to teach university courses. They either didn't know what power they had or weren't the kind of people who were disposed to use it."

There is also some concern over the possibility that the controversy increased the tendency of a large number of University of California students to emphasize the political at the expense of the academic, and over the undeniable fact that the position eventually supported by the faculty—one that would have the University leave it to the civil authorities to judge the legality of its students' political advocacy or political action—is a severe break with the tradition of the University as a sanctuary that should be left to take care of its own problems. Chancellor Meyerson, who voted with the majority, has said, "What we did in some ways rearranges the idea of what a university is for. It gives up the old idea of *in loco parentis,* and I think we realize that it's a two-way street. It used to be that a sheriff would call a dean to come down and pick up one of his undergraduates who was drunk and let him handle the punishment any way he thought best. But this kind of approach just isn't suitable for, say, a huge civil-rights demonstration. Of course, that means we can't ask to be a sanctuary from the local police, but, in practice, we were no longer a sanctuary anyway. I think academic people are apprehensive by nature. It is a big change, and the apprehension is certainly present. But I'm fairly optimistic."

Altogether, the faculty seems to share Meyerson's optimism. In fact, some of its members believe that the crisis itself, as well as what came out of it, was beneficial. According to Dr. Harvey Powelson, the head of the University psychiatric clinic—a facility that ordinarily treats between eight and ten per cent of the student population—the number of new admissions to the clinic, which had been steadily rising semester by semester, declined for the first

time in ten years. As the spring semester begins, Powelson is waiting for a rebound, and nobody expects the present burst of interest
in student-faculty relationships to be permanent, but most faculty
members, despite their concern over one point or another, feel that
the long-range results of the crisis may be helpful. "I don't go along
with the idea of trying to paste this over," Joseph Tussman, the
chairman of the philosophy department, says. "I think if we have
disaffected students we ought to be thankful we know about it, and
go about finding out why they're disaffected. I think if there's a
better way of organizing the University we ought to look for it.
I think it's possible to look at this as a symptomatic breakout that
may have prevented a real disaster."

Those who are concerned with the University's community relations are not looking forward to a peaceful spring. Two days after
students made CORE placards on the steps of Sproul Hall, they
were carrying them around the Sea Wolf restaurant, on Jack London Square—a posh restaurant in an expensive new entertainment
area on the Oakland waterfront. CORE was picketing the Sea Wolf
as the beginning of a drive to force the hiring of more Negroes by
restaurants in Oakland, and in its opening demonstration some
hundred and fifty people greeted the Sea Wolf's dinner patrons by
shaking their placards and responding "Must go!" to a cheerleader's
cries of "Jim Crow" or "Segregation" or—particularly as a customer was just about to enter—"White bigot."

Civil-rights groups were the ones most directly affected by last
fall's crackdown on political organizing—in the view of FSM
leaders, this was a matter of conscious design on the part of the
authorities—and are the ones likely to take most advantage of
the present freedom. Civil rights seems to be the one issue that has
a strong appeal for a great number of students, but it is not difficult
to organize demonstrations on other issues in Berkeley. As it happened, the opening day of the spring semester was the day after
the first American retaliatory bombing raid on North Vietnam, and
plans were quickly made for a protest rally that very noon on the
steps of Sproul Hall. In the morning, I had a talk with Bettina
Aptheker, a member of the FSM Steering Committee, who was
wearing a "Sack HUAC" button on one side of her collar and
a DuBois Club button on the other. As a representative of the

DuBois Club—whose members ordinarily acknowledge that it is Communist, though they prefer to use the word "Marxist," in order to avoid giving the impression that it is under Communist Party discipline—and as the daughter of Herbert Aptheker, a Communist historian, Miss Aptheker was occasionally cited by local newspapers during the dispute as proof that Communists were fanning the flames of revolt, but it is generally agreed on the campus that she was in fact a moderate influence on the Steering Committee. When I asked Miss Aptheker how the rally on Vietnam was being organized, she said, "We happened to be having a DuBois Club meeting last night, and I got a call from a member of the San Francisco Women for Peace that they and the S.F. DuBois Club were going to have a demonstration agianst the bombing at the Federal Building this afternoon. We thought we'd have a rally on Sproul steps at noon to try to get people, so I called Art Goldberg to see if the steps were available, since he's in Slate and usually knows about those things, and he said Slate had been planning a speech by David McReynolds, of the War Resisters League, on the steps today, so I asked him if we could combine meetings. Then we both got second calls—Art from the May 2nd Movement, which had invited Fred Jerome, of the Progressive Labor Movement, to town, and I from the Campus Women for Peace. It was okay with me for Jerome to speak, and Art asked if my father was in town, and the DuBois decided it would be a good idea to have him speak. We're going to meet at eleven o'clock at the fountain to make final arrangements."

By noon, when McReynolds was starting to speak into a microphone that had been set up on the steps of Sproul Hall and two young men were climbing up one of the pillars to tie on a sign saying "Withdraw Troops from Vietnam," hundreds of students had gathered in the plaza. The method of attracting a crowd to a Sproul Hall rally is to begin speaking and try to catch the attention of some of the thousands of students passing through the plaza in the middle of the day. The crowd in the plaza during the Vietnam rally was always in three parts—a group of enthusiastic supporters sitting on benches near the microphone, a much larger group of students standing silently in the plaza, apparently having stopped to find out what the speakers had to say, and passing waves of students who paid little attention to the noise from the steps. At the height of the rally, perhaps two thousand students were listening, but half a dozen more speakers had been added at the eleven o'clock meeting, and by the time the last of them came to the microphone, at about one o'clock, most of the students had drifted away. The loudest applause of the day greeted a declaration by McReynolds that all young men should refuse to register for the draft until the war in Vietnam had been ended. In general, however, there was little difference in the response to the various speakers, even though they ranged from a non-Communist pacifist (McReynolds) to a representative of the Progressive Labor Movement (Jerome), which ordinarily supports Peking's position, and the leader of the Berkeley chapter of the May 2nd Movement (Denis Mosgofian), a group that was named for a demonstration against the Vietnam war last May 2nd and that includes PLM members among its leaders. (According to a statement in its newspaper, the May 2nd Movement is open "to everyone interested and determined to actively participate in a peace movement that is conscious of the duplicity and guilt of the American government in its actions against peace throughout the world.")

The following day, the same microphone reappeared on Sproul Hall steps, and a few minutes before noon a blond girl stepped up to it and said, "End the war in Vietnam by winning it! End the war in Vietnam by winning it! Rally here at noon! Win the war in Vietnam!" The rally was sponsored by the Cal Conservatives for Political Action, which presented three speakers and attracted a crowd of two or three hundred, some of them hecklers. Some of the students who didn't stop to listen to the Vietnam speeches were on their way into the Student Union to hear Herbert Aptheker speak in one of its auditoriums on "The Civil Rights Movement in the United States and Socialism." Others gave their attention to the line of tables in front of the fountain, where a young man behind a sign that said "Students Against a Numbered Society" was selling "Legalize Marijuana" buttons for twenty-five cents ("mostly to pay the rent"), two members of Students Against Nazi Amnesty were collecting signatures for a petition protesting the statute of limitations on war crimes in Germany, the University Society of Libertarians was selling "Sack HUAC" buttons, and a representative of the May 2nd Movement was distributing a pamphlet entitled "A Message to the People of the United States from Ho Chi Minh."

Near the end of the first week of the new semester, Jerome Byrne held his meeting in Pauley East—one of the auditoriums in the Student Union—to introduce his staff, ask for questions and suggestions, and explain that his purpose was "to investigate the basic causes of unrest in the total university, with particular reference to the events this fall here, and to make recommendations of changes that might be advisable to the regents." The auditorium contained an audience of about fifty, including Savio and several other FSM leaders. One of the first questions came from Savio. Upon being recognized by Byrne, he said, "Yeah. Well, you're going to write some kind of report or reports, but with no final authority on whether they're published or not. Our experience with objective reports would indicate that the organization it's done for decides when to publish or if, and this calls into question the wisdom of doing the report in the first place."

Byrne admitted that the report would be the property of the regents, to be published only if they desired it to be, but he went on to state emphatically that neither he nor his staff had any interest in doing anything but a completely honest investigation.

"It seems to me there's a real problem," Savio said. "Let's say the people you interview want changes in the board of regents—maybe that they be chosen differently, or no political appointments, or composed of scholars or artists or musicians. Obviously, these objections won't be considered seriously."

Byrne again declared his intention of writing an impartial report, and then, in answer to a question from another student, said he would indeed feel morally obligated to object publicly if the regents published his report in edited form.

"What if part of what you did was released?" asked Savio. "What would you do then?"

"That's a problem I hadn't come to," Byrne admitted, smiling. "I knew you people were brilliant."

Many of the questions put to Byrne reflected a belief that "the University is never interested in what people are complaining about but just how to keep them from complaining"—a statement that Weissman is widely quoted as having made at the end of the dispute —and Byrne insisted several times that he was determined to investigate the basic problems of the University. For forty-five minutes, he accepted suggestions on how to avoid fulfilling Savio's

prediction that the investigation would be "a methodological disaster" and answered questions on such matters as how he chose his
staff, what his connection with the regents might have been to lead
to his selection, and why he would refuse to publish excerpts from
the investigation in the University paper every week as a way of
letting the public know what was being discovered.

"There's a limited time," Byrne said in response to the last
question. "If we want to do this in two and a half or three months,
I don't want to be in the position of having to put out press
releases."

A few questions later, one of the students asked, "If you put
out press releases and somebody edited them, would you feel morally obligated to object?"

"I certainly would," said Byrne.

The Free Speech Movement was originally formed in the early
fall by a decision to unite all the groups that had a stake in using the
Bancroft Strip for political activity, whether they were interested
in distributing pamphlets for the Young Socialist Alliance or in
recruiting students to ring doorbells for Barry Goldwater. It is now
agreed in Berkeley that the FSM eventually had the participation of
a large number of the University's outstanding students—not to
mention many of the ex-students, part-time students, and non-
students who make up what is sometimes called the Hidden Community in Berkeley—and that although it had the almost constant
opposition of the student newspaper and the student government,
it attracted wide support within the student population. The Sociology 105 poll indicates that two-thirds of the Berkeley students
approved of the FSM's goals and one-third of them approved of
both its goals and its methods. It is also agreed that despite the
presence of a representative of Students for Goldwater among the
twelve members of FSM's Steering Committee, the committee was
considerably more radical than most of its supporters. Although
radicalism during the controversy was more a matter of tactics than
of political beliefs, a good deal of attention was given to the left-
wing politics of those who led the FSM. There was wide circulation
of a statement, credited to President Kerr, that forty per cent of
the FSM's members were Maoists or Castroites—he later denied
having made such a statement—and wide discussion, some of it in

a humorous key, of the exotic political beliefs of some of those involved. "I'd considered my views rather far to the left until I went to an FSM meeting after Kerr's statement," I was told by an English girl doing graduate work. "Some speaker was saying that it was actually Kerr who was using Maoist tactics. The conservatives—the Young Democrats, for instance—were applauding, but then some people started booing. They were angry at what they considered a slur on Mao." In actuality, the only Steering Committee member who has been known, on occasion, to refer to himself as a Maoist is Art Goldberg, a large, amiable, sleepy-looking young man from Los Angeles, and his commitment to Peking is not taken very seriously, despite such gestures as carrying a sign at the CORE picketing which said "Racism Is a Paper Tiger."

Savio's usual reply to remarks about left-wing influence in the FSM was the statement that its Executive Committee, consisting of fifty members, included only four "revolutionary Socialists"—a figure he arrived at by adding the two representatives of the Young Socialist Alliance to the two from the DuBois Club. Savio now acknowledges that the figure was irrelevant, since membership in an organization with a revolutionary ideology was no measure of tactical radicalism within the FSM; moreover, it was so far from encompassing all those who considered themselves revolutionary Socialists that he was later approached by a number of people who wanted to know why they had been left out of the count. The Berkeley campus has organizations representing just about all forms of socialist ideology, and it is possible to hear references to people who are "rather fond of the Togliatti deviation" or are "hung up on democratic centralism." But student radicalism at Berkeley cannot be interpreted as if it were composed of the kind of disciplined ideological warring factions that dominated the radicalism of the thirties. It is believed in some quarters that the organizations themselves are less disciplined and less ideological than those of the past. What is far more important is that the tone of student radicalism at Berkeley is set not by the old ideological groups but by people whose approach is sufficiently different from that of the thirties that they have come to think of themselves as embracing a New Radicalism. New Radicals don't ordinarily use the term, but they constantly stress that they have a new approach to radical politics —and it was this approach that dominated the Steering Committee

of the Free Speech Movement. Most FSM leaders make no attempt
to disguise their deep alienation from American society, but they
regard allegiance to any specific alternative as utopian, divisive,
immobilizing, and—perhaps most significant—not their "style."
The word "style" is widely used among the New Radicals—most
of whom are indeed admirers of Fidel Castro, often because of *his*
style—and in giving reasons for their avoidance of the old radical
organizations they are as likely to cite distaste for the style of their
jargon and theoretical debate as disgust with the futility of what
Savio has called "spending hours trying to invent a motto that
makes you different from other sects." While part of this preference
for dissociation is undoubtedly a desire to avoid tarnished labels,
the New Radicals consciously avoid in their own actvities the auto-
matic condemnation of Communists—"pathological anti-Stalin-
ism," in their phrase—that has come to characterize the non-
Communist left in the United States during the Cold War, and they
count it as one of the accomplishments of the FSM that the DuBois
Club could be represented on the Steering Committee without any
more objection than was made.

In place of ideology, the New Radicals tend to rely on action.
"The word 'existential' is used a lot," Jack Weinberg told me.
Weinberg, who is twenty-four, is a full-time unpaid activist; he
wears a droopy mustache and work clothes, and in the pictures
taken during his imprisonment in The Police Car he somehow managed to resemble both Sacco *and* Vanzetti. "You could call it an
affirmation of self," he went on. "Just because we can't see what
the end might be doesn't mean we're going to sit here. It's a matter
of screaming. We have to justify everything in terms of the act
itself. The trouble with being ideologically oriented is that it's immobilizing; you have to justify all kinds of things in terms of the
ideology. We're really problem-oriented. Utopia is too far away to
worry about. FSM had a limited goal, but look what happened.
Look at the effect it could have on educational policy and student
activism across the country. Who could have planned that?"

Although Savio is considered the most moralistic of the New
Radicals, all of them explain their conclusion that America is
"sick" or "evil" at least partly in moral terms—emphasizing that
American society is not what it claims to be, that it engages in
sham and hypocrisy, that those in control are not concerned with

"telling it like it is" (a phrase borrowed from the SNCC workers in Mississippi). The New Radicals ordinarily share the views of the far left on foreign affairs, but more orthodox leftists are sometimes dismayed to find Savio and Weissman, for instance, apparently more concerned with the idea that the American government is being hypocritical about why it is fighting in Vietnam than with the idea that the United States is engaging in an "imperialistic colonial war." Suzanne Goldberg, a graduate student in philosophy from New York, who is a member of the FSM Steering Committee, has explained this moral tone by saying, "It's really a strange kind of naïveté. What we learned in grammar school about democracy and freedom nobody takes seriously, but we do. We really believe it. It's impossible to grapple with the problem of the structure of the whole world, but you try to do something about the immediate things you see that bother you and are within your reach."

Because of this approach, the New Radicals often engage in a kind of *ad-hoc* activism directed at specific problems whose solutions are no more than the stated goals of American democracy —free speech, the right to vote, the right to fair employment and housing. Obviously, it is in the field of civil rights that the most inconsistency is to be found between what the American structure says it is and what it is, and often the New Radicals work in Mississippi with SNCC, as Savio did last summer, or work with some of the more radical CORE chapters or with *ad-hoc* committees on such projects as rent strikes and sit-ins over hiring policy, or organizing ghetto communities. Since they take the position of demanding only what society claims to be giving in the first place, they tend to be contemptuous of gradualism or of compromise in negotiations. "We ask for what we should get, not for what we could get," Miss Goldberg says. Their techniques are often extra-legal, and they save their ultimate contempt for people who express agreement with their goals but not with their methods. " 'Liberal' is a dirty word here," Weinberg told me. "Liberalism is a trap. It's the impotence of having principles that make you opposed to something and other principles that keep you from doing anything about it." New Radicals ordinarily have little faith that anything can be accomplished by the "Liberal Establishment." Any mention of the American Communist Party is usually greeted with the scornful remark that the Party backed Lyndon Johnson in the last election, and the same kind of criticism is made of the DuBois Club—which, one of its members admitted to me half apologetically, "does believe in cooperation with non-Socialist groups." At Berkeley, where a number of the students are the children of Communists and other radicals of the thirties—they are often called "red-diaper babies" —a conversation about a member of the DuBois Club sometimes sounds like the sort of conversation that is held at other state universities about people who felt compelled to join Sigma Chi because of a family tradition. The one organization whose style seems to be almost universally respected among the New Radicals is SNCC; its project in Mississippi is admired for its moral tone, for its patient organizing of impoverished Negroes, for its activism, and for its frequent refusal to accept the advice of liberals.

One evening, I asked Savio for a description of the New Radicalism, and he said, "Certain words are more useful. Maybe they're a bit too theatrical. Words like 'moral protest,' 'existential revolt,' 'alienation'—as opposed to 'class conflict' or 'forces of proletarian revolution.' We're talking about the same objective reality, but it's a question of being more tentative. I don't know if all our problems would vanish if we had a state monopoly on production and distribution. I don't have a Utopia in mind. I know it has to be a good deal more egalitarian than it is now. Maybe the classic Marxist models and the classic Adam Smith models don't apply any more. There are a lot of people who have enough to eat who are incredibly resentful, because their lives are meaningless. They're psychologically dispossessed. There's a feeling that they have nothing to do; the bureaucracy runs itself. Why are we so alienated? I would say for three reasons: depersonalization, hypocrisy, and the unearned privilege that comes with great wealth. The country's forms aren't so bad, if we would take them seriously, if somebody were willing to say the emperor had no clothes. The worst thing about the society is that it lies to itself. Look at the last election. The two subjects that were not issues in the campaign were Vietnam and civil rights. What's the choice? What can you do in a situation like that? Oh, add to the good words 'anti-bureaucratic tendency.' American radicals are traditionally anarchistic, and that tendency is very strong here."

People here who try to define the New Radicalism in traditional terms usually say it resembles anarcho-syndicalism more than anything else, since it is characterized by a belief that laws and regulations have to be justified and by a dislike for centralized bureaucracy. The ideological radical who has been closest to the radical student leaders at Berkeley is Hal Draper, a long-time socialist editor, in his fifties, who now works in the University library. Draper's Independent Socialist Club, according to its statement of principles, stands for "a socialist policy which is completely independent of and opposed to both of the reactionary systems of exploitation of man by man which now divide the world: capitalism and Communism." In discussions with the New Radicals, Draper often argues that however much they insist on avoiding labels, their views amount to what in any other country would be called Left-Wing Socialism. But although Weinberg belonged for a time to Draper's Independent Socialist Club (it has many members in common with CORE, and although Weissman has said that Draper's ideas come closer to making sense to him than those of any other ideologist, the New Radicals insist that programs and theories cannot express their style, and they deny that this leaves them with nothing but negativism. "I think the student activist movement does offer new ideas," I was told by Martin Roysher, a polite, articulate, scholarly-looking sophomore from Southern California, who transferred to Berkeley from Princeton because he wanted more political activity. "When the structure is challenged, the response may not often be exactly what we want, but it's helpful. Take the wide range of student demonstrations—sit-ins, rent strikes, organizing the communities. They definitely bring about changes in the power structure. It doesn't take the students very long to realize that the structure is pretty corrupt when it has to bring in the cops."

Many Berkeley people who are well acquainted with the Free Speech Movement say that the most "political"—and some say the most influential—of the FSM leaders is Steve Weissman, a twenty-five-year-old graduate student from Tampa who has red hair and a pointed red beard and usually dresses in Ivy League style. Weissman told me he had considered becoming a full-time organizer for Students for a Democratic Society this semester but had decided to continue studying history instead. "I think we are arriving at a philosophy," he said. "There aren't many people, but it is a new voice. I think it represents the thinking of a lot more people, and thirty per cent of the student body bought our style. It's exemplified by SNCC in Mississippi: about the only other people working full time are forty or fifty Students for a Democratic Society people in the slum-organization projects. Politically, there's a feeling that while other groups may be necessary sometimes, there's no use celebrating coalitions. You take a direct line outside the normal arena and force the liberals to make a choice. What we're against is consensus politics—the idea of finding out what the regents will give before you ask for it. That's one thing. Something we're for is certain values for the future—a kind of democratic participation, letting people have some control over their lives, the way SNCC is organizing people in the Freedom Democratic Party right at the ward level, or the way students are asking for participation in the University, or the way we're trying to get poor people involved in the war on poverty, instead of just professors. In a way, the people we're closest to are the Populists, or the *narodniki*—the intellectuals in Russia who went out and worked with the peasants. Sure, we see connections from different issues. Our values are radical. We don't automatically accept the value of institutions, and we admit going beyond the normal American equality, because we include eco-nomic equality. We do accept the Socialist criticism of American capitalism, but that doesn't mean we buy any particular solution."

I asked Weissman about the charge sometimes made that many of the New Radicals have so profound a distaste for the society that the immediate goal of their action is less important to them than fomenting trouble or demonstrating the sickness of the society or, as some critics at Berkeley have asserted, attempting to under-mine faith in the democratic processes.

"You're not naïve enough not to realize that there's a grain of truth in that," Weissman said. "And I'm willing to grant that our alienation is deep enough so that we underrate the possibility of channels sometimes. But the conspiracy theory really comes down to Red-baiting or bed-baiting; it's either an attempt to make people think it's all a Communist plot or some Freudian theory that we're all just revolting against our parents. The criticism that it's a con-spiracy would be valid only if we didn't make any progress toward our ostensible goals, and I don't think they can show any place where we haven't."

I suggested to Weissman that one reason for the conspiracy

theory might be that there appears to be a gap between what one professor has called "working for liberal goals with radical methods" and changing the structure of society.

"It bothered me for a while that the end of radical politics seems to be increasing the welfare state," Weissman said. "Breaking down of hiring-policy rights with demonstrations just means some kind of federal fair-employment agency. Well, some changes are made and we're doing what has to be done. Maybe we're developing constituencies; that's more than the ideologists are doing. Maybe it means that the people are there to make a revolution if we ever decide that's what's needed."

It is generally agreed at Berkeley that the membership of the ideological clubs is more than matched by the students who fall roughly into the category of New Radicals. It is the New Radicalism, rather than the old, that comes near to expressing some of the dissatisfaction felt by students who would not consider themselves radicals, and it was the New Radicalism that led to the Free Speech Movement. Some professors were disturbed by what they felt was a tone of near anti-intellectualism in the FSM and this seems closely related to the New Radicals' tendency to emphasize action at the expense of theorizing, to explain themselves in moral rather than intellectual terms, to stress political rights rather than academic disciplines, and to insist that an issue is more important than an institution. Critics of the New Radicals have said that their style works best against liberals—who have a respect for institutions and for channels, and who also have a distaste for meeting mass action with force—and it is true that liberals seem to have extraordinary difficulty in communicating with them, or, to use a phrase often heard in Berkeley, "tuning in on them." For many observers, one of the ironies of the controversy lay in the fact that the chief villain was Clark Kerr, a man of widely praised liberal accomplishments, who had himself been given an award for liberalizing the regulations concerning free speech at the University of California, and who had himself—in a series of Godkin lectures at Harvard, later published as "The Uses of the University"—pointed out the elements of the modern American "multiversity" that would cause alienation and perhaps revolt among the students. But the FSM leaders seemed not at all surprised to find Kerr their bitterest opponent, for without some special effort at understanding a liberal would find that many of his tenets were handicaps in dealing with the New Radicals. A liberal's faith that wrongs can eventually be adjusted within the democratic processes is treated with contempt by people who believe the ends of channels to be tokenism or hypocrisy; the argument that a noisy free-speech controversy would serve the ends of right-wing opponents of the University is of no concern to people who have no great faith in institutions and consider such thinking the worst kind of "consensus politics." The style of the New Radicals is not to avoid controversy by compromise but to keep a controversy going until they have won their point. In December, Weissman told a gathering of graduate students that if Kerr had managed to carry the day at the Greek theater with a rousing speech, he would have taken the platform and used whatever oratory might have been necessary "to break the thing open again." He has told me that if the University had not itself broken the thing open again the week before the Greek Theater by its disciplinary action against four of the FSM leaders, the students would have acquired a print of "Un Chant d'Amour"—a Genet film that had been banned as obscene from a student film series that week—set up a portable projector and loudspeaker, and shown the film on the wall of Sproul Hall.

Although the campus is now comparatively peaceful, President Kerr is concerned about how a university is to handle people who, for instance, equate any compromise in negotiations with selling out. According to a young philosophy professor named John Searle, who has probably been the faculty member closest to the FSM, the problem should be stated another way. "The militants were forced into the leadership of the FSM because of the intransigence of the administration on an issue on which they were clearly in the wrong," Searle says. "Of course these people are absolutists. They are radicals. They perform a useful function in society as gadflies, but they have no loyalty to the structure, and once you've forced the population to adopt them as leaders, you have trouble. The problem is not how to handle them. The problem is how not to get in a position where a mass movement has to turn to them for leadership."

The only writer who was quoted consistently by the Free Speech Movement during the fall was Paul Goodman, a critic of American education who has long maintained that American college students are regimented rather than educated, and who said in a New York rally backing the FSM that "at present in the United States, students —middle-class youth—are the major exploited class." Three days after the Vietnam protest rally, Goodman became the first speaker invited by the Free University to address a rally on the steps of Sproul Hall—although, as it turned out, the rally had to be moved to the lower plaza of the Student Union, because the Free University had neglected to reserve the steps of Sproul Hall, and the Cal Conservatives for Political Action, who *had* reserved them, for a man named Jay Field to lecture on the dangers of Communism in Hawaii, were unwilling to move their meeting. As the Conservatives were setting up their sign—which said in one corner "Labor Extorted," a reference to the "Labor Donated" notice that usually appears on the literature of the FSM—the area near the fountain across the plaza was unusually active. Tables had been set up by the Students Against Nazi Amnesty, CORE, and the FSM, which was selling long-playing records of speeches and songs heard during the controversy. Nearby, Savio and Ed Rosenfeld were arguing about the value of sitting in at the office of the local United States Attorney to protest the federal government's failure to see to it that Negroes were registered to vote in Selma, Alabama. Art Goldberg entered the plaza carrying two cardboard boxes of FSM records, and after he had deposited them on the FSM table he approached the girl who was in charge of Goodman's schedule, to ask about the possibility of Goodman's making a statement on Vietnam, there having been several more retaliatory bombing raids since the protest rally.

"He's talking about the student in society," she explained.

"Vietnam *is* the student in society," said Goldberg. "The student should be in the streets about it."

"Look, he's made one of the best statments about Vietnam," she said.

"I know he's good on Vietnam," Goldberg said.

"Not just good," she said.

"He should be good out loud," Goldberg said. "Let him say it."

At the CORE table, where students were picking up leaflets about the next week's picketing in Jack London Square—an event that CORE leaders realized would have to compete with a demonstration on Vietnam—Jack Weinberg had been asked by one of the Students Against Nazi Amnesty to sign the club's petition.

"I usually sign all petitions, but I'm kind of hung up on this issue," Weinberg said, and walked over to discuss the German statute of limitations with two or three other students.

On the steps of the student union, under a sign that read "Wear White: Cal vs. Oregon Feb 12, Cal vs. Oregon State Feb 13 at Harmon Gym," Denis Mosgofian, of the May 2nd Movement, was holding a meeting of students who had volunteered to serve as monitors for a march to the Berkeley Selective Service Board which was to follow the Goodman speech. He handed out orange crêpe-paper armbands to the monitors and held up a hand-drawn map to show them the line of march. "What we do depends on the turnout," he said. "We'll definitely picket, but if there are five hundred or a thousand people and there's militancy, maybe we'll sit in."

A student had been walking around and around the plaza with a sign announcing the Goodman speech, and by noon, as the University bell tower began its midday concert, several thousand students had gathered in the lower plaza. As the first Conservative speaker began to talk on Sproul Hall steps about the right of minorities as well as majorities to free speech, Weinberg signed the petition against Nazi amnesty, and then he and the rest of the crowd around the fountain made their way to the lower plaza.

Goodman was introduced by Mario Savio. "This platform seems very official," began Savio, who had first come to attention by speaking from the top of a police car. "Tie it up like this: Mr. Goodman wrote a book, *Growing Up Absurd*. The situation we find ourselves in today punctuates the title. There's a war going on in Vietnam. Eight hundred people got arrested here for trying to secure rights that were supposedly secured almost two hundred years ago. Now we stand in lines signing up for courses where we'll write papers that should never have been written, reads books that should never have been read, hear lectures that should never have been given. Sometimes you want to strike out at these absurd things. Sometimes you don't think you can do anything about it. Sometimes you want to strike out even if it's not doing anything. I want to tell you about two instances of striking out today, even if they're both somewhat quixotic in nature. At four-thirty tomorrow, at the Federal Building in San Francisco, there will be a demonstration against the war in Vietnam. Even the Senate is now thinking about this, but while they're deciding people are dying. Cars leave from Bancroft and Dana from three-thirty to four. Right after this meeting, there's another meeting about Vietnam here, and after that a march to the Berkeley recruiting station, again perhaps with a quixotic flavor."

Goodman, after noting that Savio had given him the gloomiest introduction he had ever received, talked about the relation of the University to society, saying that he agreed with Kerr's observation that the university and the community had become more and more interrelated, but stressing the point that the university should be a leader rather than a servant of the community, with faculties speaking out as faculties on such matters as censorship cases, progressive legislation, and the cultural level of the society. The students listened attentively, and laughed when Goodman, applying his argument to the FSM, said, "You had a Free Speech Movement last fall, and I was rather astonished, considering the number of intelligent people who were involved, at the modest level of ideology." Goodman went on, "If that kind of movement grows—and it's not important whether it has the same name—you have to find out what university students can give to society that others can't give."

After Goodman had finished—to enthusiastic applause—the chairman reminded the audience that meetings of the Free University would be held in the various departments during the next week. Then a representative of the campus Friends of SNCC announced a meeting at which the club would "discuss some ways—all ways —to put pressure on the government to do something in Alabama," and Denis Mosgofian came forward to direct the march on the Berkeley draft board. "We, the students, have a responsibility," Mosgofian said. "It's the same kind of responsibility we had last semester. It's quite clear nuclear war is in the offing. I don't even know if we'll be here Monday. . . . We of the May 2nd Movement, along with the DuBois Club, the YSA, and other clubs interested in peace, are going to march to the Selective Service office to present our demands: one, that the United States get out of Vietnam, and, two, that we will refuse under all conditions to fight."

Weissman took the microphone to announce that Goodman had agreed to join the march, and said, "I think it's vital that we show

that we want those troops to get out of Vietnam and into Selma."
A line had already formed on the Bancroft Strip, led by three young
men carrying a banner that said "Get Out of Vietnam." As the
crowd poured out of the lower plaza, it seemed huge, but as it filed
down Bancroft Way—with Mosgofian and his monitors hastily
straightening ranks and directing traffic—it quickly thinned out, and
when the line reached the draft board, about two blocks away, it
contained only about two hundred people. Goodman had dropped
out to go to lunch, but Weissman was still in the front ranks, and
about halfway down the line Savio and Suzanne Goldberg were
walking together, accompanied by a young man who was simultaneously playing a guitar and blowing a harmonica. The draft board
occupied a corner storefront office that had windows on both
streets. On one window somebody had whitewashed the legend
"No War." The pickets marched past the office and circled the
block—a route that took them along the main business street of
Berkeley.

" 'Stop Johnson's Dirty War!' " a middle-aged shopper said to
her companion, reading the placard carried by Suzanne Goldberg.
"They should talk about being dirty!"

When the pickets returned to the draft board, they formed an
orderly line that curved around the corner and was kept moving by
monitors stationed a few yards up each street. At the corner, Mosgofian, who had decided against a sit-in, was holding a long scroll
—a declaration that he intended to present to the woman in charge
of the draft board—and the draft-age males in the demonstration
were stepping up to sign their names to it in marker pencil. Mosgofian eventually shouted that he had a hundred and eight signatures,
but some of the demonstrators didn't seem to be paying much
attention. Savio and Miss Goldberg passed the corner laughing and
chatting. A few yards away, Steve Weissman, walking with Marty
Roysher, was discussing the effect that a war might have on the
civil-rights movement.

PAUL GOODMAN

Berkeley in February*

The dominant system of society is critically dependent on the schools, especially the universities. Schools provide the brain-power for the scientific technology. They are wistfully expected, beginning with age three, to bring everybody into the mainstream of economic usefulness; and more realistically, they process the professional personnel to control the increasing scores of millions useless to the economy, the out-caste poor, displaced farmers, people over 65, unemployable adolescents who must be regimented. Just as part of the Gross National Product, I have heard the estimate that more than forty per cent of the cash is in the Knowledge business.

The organization of all this, however, is calculated by the powers-that-be amazingly without regard to the thoughts or feelings of those who are to be "educated." (Fifty per cent of the total population is under twenty-five.) Establishment forecasts of the future almost never mention the response of the young as a factor; yet that response, whether as anomie or as insistence on more freedom and meaning than the system allows will be crucial. And if we take it into account, we see that the dominant system is probably unviable. Simply, it is not moral enough to grow up into.

The education has become mere exploitation—the abuse of the abilities and time of life of school youth for others' purposes. As I have put it elsewhere, it is the first time in history that a dominant class has imposed on its free children the discipline of slaves. And the exploitation itself is of a peculiarly difficult and deadly kind, for it involves not merely forced time and labor, but active intellectual

* From *Dissent*, Spring, 1965.

participation by the exploited, in learning and even in being original and creative under duress.* This is not viable. There must be both breakdown and revolutionary break-through; and recently I have come to hope that *freedom and meaning will outweigh anomie.* Needless to say, I am in love with that, and with Berkeley in February.

In my opinion, the situation at Berkeley is historical and will not be local. The calm excitement and matter-of-fact democracy and human contact now prevalent on the Berkeley campus are in revolutionary contrast to our usual demented, inauthentic, over-administered American society. This ordinary freedom had to be won by risky commitment, finding solidarity, living through fear; and its ferment will spread not only to other campuses but finally to other institutions of society.

The movement of the Negroes and their wise white friends, mainly youth, has been encouraging to change; and probably our society cannot incorporate its outcastes without revolutionary changes in structure. Nevertheless, the shape of reconstruction cannot, in my opinion, appear among marginal groups; they do not have enough culture, science, and technique to work a good modern society, though plenty of spirit and justice. But the rising of students and of professors recalled to manhood occurs in the best of the middle-class itself and in the center of the economy; the shape of reconstruction *can* appear here. Not accidentally, the movement for the outcaste has sparked and energized this more central revolution, and we will finally come to the real issues: the revival of democracy, the human use of technology, and getting rid of war.

* I am using the word "exploitation" strictly. It is hard for people in the labor movement to understand this term as applied to students. Harry Bridges, e.g., seems to feel that the Berkeley students were pampered brats; they never had it so good. We would do well to recall Marx's description of the nine-year-olds picking straw, not because this was economically valuable but as training in work-habits. Besides, we must notice that nearly fifty per cent of the young are now kept in schools till twenty-one and twenty-two years of age; previously most of them would have been in the factories, etc., for four or five years by that age.

As a university man, let me put it this way: Our society has been playing with the fire of mass higher learning; it is our duty to let it feel the blast of university truth.

During their troubles last winter, Berkeley students kept phoning me—at three AM Eastern time—in various states of fever, alarm, and despair; but then after a single shout of "Victory!" after the Faculty Senate decision in their favor, I heard nothing further. (Except for a New Year's Eve visit from Steve Weissman, one of the most thoughtful leaders of the Free Speech Movement, who was now interested in "University Reform.")

My expectation, on visiting in February, was that there would be deep depression. They had won their demand to advocate political action, like any other citizen. The civil rights energy, which had obviously been strong, could hardly continue animating them, since it was not essentially a campus issue at all. The election being over, Senator Knowland had subsided. And most important, they seemed to have no future goal to grow toward, to inspirit them. Indeed, reading the FSM's voluminous broadsides and pamphlets, I was appalled at the low level of analysis by such bright people. There was little ideology—which was good—but there was also almost no economics, history, or philosophy. Rather, endless pages about the First and Fourteenth Amendments, gripes about the violation of due process, and proofs of the ambiguities of Clark Kerr, all relevant but not newsy.

I was wrong. Instead of depression, I found what I have called "calm excitement"—the phrase belongs to a youth in the establishment-oriented student government. (During the troubles, the Associated Students were rather unfriendly to the FSM, but part of the "calm excitement" is a *spreading* among the students of the insistence on freedom and meaning.) My error was that I did not realize that every step of the students' fight was desperately immediate, unchartered, and uncharted. But therefore the fruit of it was character-change, the first opening of new possibilities. Beautifully, a moral struggle has given the students a *habit* of good faith and commitment, and their solidarity has turned into community, like the auroral flush of a good society.

The existential language that I am beginning to slip into is entirely the students' own. It is the lingua franca of the revolutionary campus, and is used with simplicity and conviction. (When, on another campus like Ann Arbor, I listen to even a fine group like the Students for a Democratic Society, their talk of "strategy" etc. is grating by comparison.) At Berkeley, there is a sprinkling of neo-Marxist lingo but it is noticeably heavy and dispiriting, except for an occasional Maoism, which is Chinese.

On February 10 occurred a curious dialogue between Jerry Byrne, the special counsel of a committee of the regents of the University of California to investigate "the causes of student unrest," and a group of students from the government, newspapers, religious organizations, and leaders of the former FSM (now FU, movement for a Free University). Byrne is a frank and likeable guy, a lawyer, and I had previous evidence that he was earnest and somewhat unorthodox. He explained to the students his mandate and the questionnaire and interview methods that he intended to employ. He intended, he said, to be objective; he had chosen assistants from outside of Berkeley; he had no ax to grind; he meant business. He would present his recommendations to the regents in three months. Were there any questions?

A slim dark-eyed youth spoke up: "Mr. Byrne, we have been through an existential moment. A composite picture of 'public' student opinion will not reveal our meaning." I take it that this meant that so-called objective methods would get him nowhere. "Yes," another student said, "Ideas don't pop out of data."

Byrne did not seem to grasp this epistemological subtlety; he assured the young man that he had "found students able to dissociate themselves from events last fall and simply work to future improvement." Later, however, the counsel said to me privately, "When that boy looked up at me, his eyes pierced to the bottom of my soul—there was no use in trying to lie to them. The discussion rose to another plane."

Another student (Mario Savio) asked a down-to-earth question: "Was there any guarantee that the regents would release the Byrne recommendations?" "No," said Jerry, they were the regents' property. (But the regents, gasped somebody else, were notorious for *falsifying* scholarly work, specifically a report on *braceros* made by the University.) Savio persisted: "How can the students cooperate with a report for the regents, if the board of regents is

itself a morally illegitimate body? how can *it* be the judge?" The
bother was that the regents consisted almost entirely of multi-
millionaires in aircraft, oil, banks, shipping, etc., with Max Rafferty
representing Education!

The question now was whether they ought morally to be talking
to Byrne at all, since his mandate was inauthentic. It was not that
they questioned *his* integrity, a student assured him kindly. About
this time, the counsel's unfailing friendly smile began to tighten, so
that it became increasingly impossible for him to get into contact
with them, unless he wiped off the smile, which he couldn't do.
Unluckily, none of the students knew enough psychosomatic medicine to point this out to him, and I kept my mouth shut. "Yes,"
said a student, "it's the genius of administration to turn a nice guy
like you into a fink." "How do we know that the student opinion
we give you won't be subpoenaed for the trial?" somebody asked
ominously. Jerry firmly and believably declared that this would
not happen.

A bright idea suggested itself. They could publish the inter-
views in progress, while they were still the students' property, so
to speak; they could make tapes! Jerry vetoed this with alarm.
"Then what *can* you suggest for us to do, what *action,* beginning
right now, that will put pressure on the regents and guarantee
some results?"—a student asked this very earnestly.

"How was I supposed to answer that!" Jerry complained to me
later. "In one corner was a reporter from the *Chronicle,* in another
a reporter from the *Examiner,* and they ask me to suggest an action
to coerce the regents—" Some more *action* from the students of
Berkeley was not, exactly, what the regents were after! "Oh, why
didn't you just explain that to them, Jerry—with a smile? They're
hip kids."

"Why," asked a young lady, "is unrest something that must be
'remedied'?" "How far will the inquiry probe? Might the report
suggest that government of the University should be given over to
the students and faculty? Would the range of questions include
whether UCAL should accept war contracts?" "Why," asked a
young fellow, "not let a Thousand Flowers Bloom?"—to my ear
this question was entirely innocent, without desire to shock.

The counsel fielded the questions well and generously. But he
did not seem to satisfy. "Don't you see, Jerry," I said finally, they

want you to show a burning zeal to improve their school, and you're not showing it." "I don't feel any burning zeal," cried Jerry, "I just want to do a good honest job, and I intend to do it." "There you are," said Savio, "why don't you quit?"—but to my ear, this was said without hostility, even affectionately. It meant, quit them and join *us,* and put your talents to an authentic use.

My total impression, indeed, was that the students, including the stars of the former FSM, intended to cooperate with the counsel in his further study. They would follow the maxim of Gandhi: always cooperate. But they would be exquisitely simple in what they are doing and therefore far brighter than Jerry Byrne; and in the long run he would learn more from them than he, with his auspices, would be able to do for them.

It is vividly clear on the Berkeley campus that there has been a breakthrough into communication, community. The causation seems to have been classical: justified protest, risky commitment, surprising solidarity and the development of mutual trust, shaking fear met with uncalculating courage, and then the breakthrough into the joyous feeling that "we have a say in the University," "it is our home," "we are free human beings."

They even speak of a founding Event, presumably the Faculty Senate vote that "justified" the students. (Correspondingly, Professor Wolin speaks of the "faculty's finest hour," as if the faculty had been revived and "justified" by the students!) "There occurred on this campus the first human Event in 40,000 years," Michael Rossman assured me—I did not press him for the predecessor. Savio told me with scorn and amazement of a registrar who *after* the event still tried to enforce a petty rule: "Don't you realize, I told her, that something *happened* yesterday?" The existential theory seems to be that by acting in freedom they made history, and conversely, the historical event made them free. (In a letter to the new chancellor, Martin Meyerson, John Seeley of Brandeis speaks of the students' action as "the Boston Tea Party.")

An unknown professor came up to me and said, "Since those kids acted up, I feel twenty years younger."

So far as the essence of a community of scholars is the personal relation of students and teachers, Berkeley has already accomplished university reform and Jerry Byrne's inquiry need go no further.* But in fact, in freedom, there is a buzz of activity toward legislating new institutions. Let me give a few examples.

The "Free University" is a para-university of voluntary study-groups off-campus, in which the collaboration of a teaching-assistant or assistant professor is invited. (Typical subjects, Moral Responsibility and the Sciences, Marx and Freud, History of the Oppression of Women). At a session I attended (Anarchism), a young lady complained rather tearfully that if they invited a professor to the next meeting just because he knew a lot about the subject, it would be just like the ordinary university; but the others, who were mostly graduates and undergraduates in history, assured her that the professor was very young. FU plans also "to launch projects for the general welfare of the larger community," e.g., a summer project to organize migrant farm labor; and not least, "to look into the nature of the University of California's financial connections, controls imposed on funds, indirect pressures on Professors."

To lighten the student load, I asked the new chancellor—or acting chancellor, it is hard to know—if academic credit couldn't be given for the para-courses, if they met certain standards. He could see no objection. A regent, however, thought that the reactionaries in the legislature might balk at some of the titles. . . .

Faculty proposals for university reform—e.g., by Professors Tussman and Trow—tend to small voluntary colleges within the University. In one model, one hundred and fifty students and ten professors will agree to study some area or issue that transcends departmental lines (as a gimmick to get around the entrenched chairmen?). Professor Searle tells me that he had already tried

* A former student of mine at Sarah Lawrence explained to me: "When Amy and I first came out, we didn't know anybody, so we invited our professor to tea. The other students thought that we were simply weird. But now it wouldn't be unusual."—This illustrates, by the way, that student-faculty estrangement is a two-way street. The paranoia of the students toward the grown-ups is probably stronger than the indifference of the professors toward the young. (Since I wrote this, Kerr and Meyerson "resigned" and were retained apparently as a bid for a vote of confidence against the reactionary wing of the regents).

such voluntary seminars last year, but the *students* didn't come—
they needed the support of credits and the official syllabus; but
perhaps it would be better now.

I discussed these faculty proposals with a regent, who declared
that they would cost too much. I think he is wrong. In my opinion,
administrators misestimate by applying to a different, decentralized
system, the costs that belong to the present over-centralized system. At present the multiversity operates by tightly holding together essentially disparate parts; inevitably a tremendous amount
of money is spent on administrative cement. This process, as I have
shown elsewhere, usually leads to a mark-up of three hundred to
four hundred per cent over actual educational costs. Of course,
from the multiversity point of view, the inflation is more than
paid for by rich contracted research, no matter what, and government and foundation grants.

Professor Leggett, the sociologist, has already instituted (1
think) an ingenious form of democracy for a lecture course. Each
section elects two delegates who sit with him and the teaching-
assistants at fortnightly meetings that criticize the course and chart
its further progress. The little council is called a soviet.

Chancellor Meyerson told me a good idea. He is after some
Ford money for a community project in Oakland. This could be
manned by students for academic credit as well as pay. In turn
I proposed to him the following: Instead of discontinuing the
department of journalism, as seems to be in the offing, rather make
it for real by putting out a good daily newspaper which the Bay
area sorely needs. (It is interesting to speculate how Senator
Knowland, who owns the Oakland paper, would take this competition, while CORE, recruited from the University, pickets his door
for unfair labor practices!)

The chancellor's best idea for university reform, however, is a
kind of tacit understanding between him and the students—at least
so I have been told—that certain idiotic rules, which ought not to
exist, need not necessarily be enforced in every jot and tittle.

I was crossing the campus with a regent and he suddenly asked
me, "Do you notice much change since you were here a couple of
years ago?" "What are you driving at?" I asked. "Don't you think
it's—more lively, more interesting?" "Oh, Bill," I cried, "why can't
you say that publicly? The kids would be so proud." "How can I

say that in my position?" said the regent. (His name is William Coblentz.) "Don't call them kids!" he said, "they're students." *

I have been describing a very simple situation, a kind of Fourth of August when the French barons gave up their feudal dues. (Alas! it probably won't last much longer than the Fourth of August, but let's not yet look into the future.) It is a situation where people talk to one another, mean what they say and intend to act on it, and therefore could conceivably improve their common lot. Is this extraordinary?

It is said that there was a "breakdown of communication" in Berkeley. There was, but why? The failure of communication is not an isolated cause but is endemic in the structure of American society and in the multiversity as part of it. There is a limitless amount of information, polling, data-processing, and decision-making by objective computation; yet when the chips are down, it turns out that nobody has expressed himself or been understood. Given its exploiting motives, it is impossible for American education to take the young seriously, except as objects to manipulate.†

It seemed odd that Clark Kerr, who had made a reputation as a mediator in labor disputes, should have failed so badly precisely in communications. But indeed he acted impeccably as a professional mediator; he kept the parties apart in order to negotiate their demands. Unfortunately, good faith and commitment are in principle not negotiable; the students were not making "offers" with the intention of "settling" for something different. And in the context of a community of scholars, the technique suddenly appeared as obscene. When students and professors insisted that he, the mediator, was a party to the dispute and must confront them, Kerr's

---

* Something like calling a Negro "boy." In many a Town-Gown fracas, the analogy of student and Negro is pretty obvious. At present in the town of Berkeley itself, there is an urban renewal plan to clean up a street which, to me, seems very pleasant and lively, but it *is* occupied by students and their beatnik cronies.

† This can be so hypocritical as to be nauseating. For instance, while I am writing this there is a to-do at Cornell about a marijuana "ring." This comes under the rubric of paternal concern, yet girls are dragged out of classes and dormitories to be grilled by FBI-men without counsel.

behavior was sociopathological. There were cases when he would not speak directly to professors *by phone* but insisted on an intermediary. When the students were occupying Sproul Hall, he stayed at home and would not speak to them. Clinging to a petty ruling, he kept regents and professors in separate rooms at the airport.

More seriously, there is evidence that men whom he involved as his intermediaries became utterly demoralized.

Inevitably, the militant students were caught in the toils and became administrative. Dealing with probably benevolent professors, they had to bring lawyers and speak through them, and they became acute experts in their rights under various amendments to the Constitution of the United States. Yet what they ultimately wanted was just to be told the truth: E.g., if the tables were banned because of traffic congestion, why, when the aisles were kept clear, were the tables *still* banned? Instead they were told another lie.

Or so it seemed to them. But they were making a naïve metaphysical error. They imagined that a mediator, one who avoids conflicts and negotiates, is a human being like you or me and makes propositions that are true or false. Thus they felt lied to and tricked and they got enraged. But they were really dealing with a juggling robot. Now, for a spell, disabused of their error, they can be serene—armed.

To be fair to Kerr, I doubt that it is possible, with honor, to avoid conflict among the forces working at the University of California: Birchite legislators, racist newspapers, Max Rafferty, the Atomic Energy Commission, civil rights, professors who might suddenly recall the Western tradition, students who might be naïvely moral. The only honorable alternatives are to quit, as Buell Gallagher did, or sometimes to take a stand and fight.

A Cuban student, not a Castroite, said to me, "Kerr made the same mistake as the U.S.A. with regard to Cuba. By refusing to talk, he left a vacuum. The extremists moved into it. Through the extremists, the mass discovered it had a community."

Besides the calm excitement and community, there is a third property of Berkeley in February that I, at least, found overwhelming: the fantastically expert organization of the students, as if for instant action *en masse*. Yet there does not seem to be top-down domination. The "leading figures" are rather easy-going, there is no jockeying for position, there is no party-line, and it looks as if new faces easily come to the fore. But as soon as there is an activity, the guerrillas are out in force. There is an evident discipline to attend meetings—naturally many students lost academic credit for the fall term. The Free University sponsored a speech of mine and 3500 students attended. When it was known I wanted to write this report, at once I received a list of key names and contacts all arranged: "he will phone you at 3:45"—one expected 15:45. They have put out phonograph records: Joan Baez songs, *FSM's Sounds and Songs of the Demonstration,* and a remarkable long-player of the Sproul Hall sit-in and the meeting of the Faculty Senate. The quantity of printed material is simply appalling. And a related aspect is the careful sociological research —one can learn immediately that fifty-three per cent of students in FSM favored sit-ins before the movement started; there are precise political-science analyses of contending forces, legal briefs property-holdings of each regent. Never in history, I guess, has a spontaneous uprising been so meticulously polled. The students might object to the factory-university, but they have certainly mastered its arts and sciences.

It is a remarkable phenomenon, a kind of hyper-organized anarchy. Perhaps it is a way of creating a free university in the conditions of high technology; if so—I am speaking seriously—it is a major social invention. Myself, I find it oppressive. My opinion is that when they begin to reach for positive cultural goods, rather than engaging in resistance and defense, they will have to become shaggier. But maybe I am prejudiced against social sciences—a writer—from the twenties.

The proper function of such a disciplined student body, I think, is not to be the free university, which must consist in piecemeal voluntary associations between teachers and students, but to be the student government, responsible for social and political rules; collective bargaining agent on food, housing, tuition and other finances; guardian of *Lernfreiheit* against administrative encroachments like grading, excessive courses, unreasonable policies of admission and transfer; mutual aid and self-protection against the local police.

Let us turn to a broader question: what is the relation of a liberated university to social change in the general community?

It was evident in the fall that the movement for the Negroes was a major background cause for the Free Speech Movement. It was part of the immediate bone of contention, the banning of recruiting; and more important, leaders who had taken their risks in Mississippi were not afraid to sit in against Clark Kerr.

Yet in February I did not hear a *single* spontaneous mention of this struggle. Testing, I raised the issue provocatively and was routinely put right and turned off. One of the leaders, Rossman, then explained to me that interest in Civil Rights was simply part of one's commitment, and it was exactly equivalent to the problem of making a classroom for real. (Rossman himself is a section-man in mathematics; he teaches "intuitive" mathematics—I did not have the chance to pursue whether this meant school of Brouwer or something else.) "Don't get me wrong," he said, "I picket *seriously;* just the same, it's a place to see the girls and sometimes we have a great time. It's our way of living." * He had a thing about abstract values being entirely dead for his generation, though they had had meaning for "my father and grandfather." I tried to show him that, for some of us, Social Justice with capital letters was not abstract but a concrete property of a tolerable environment, just like unpolluted rivers; and he was visibly impressed by the idea that a three-year-old divides the candy bar with another child for symmetry. (Maybe this was "intuitive" mathematics.)

In my opinion, the matrix of a community in which political action is a custom, is essential for the American future. And it is different, in both genesis and meaning, from the solidarity engendered by fighting for political causes. Those hostile to FSM have emphasized the number of off-campus participants, who are then called outside agitators, Maoists, Castroites, etc.; contrariwise, the champions of the students then prove that the outsiders are mosly alumni, wives, temporary drop-outs. But historically, it is better

---

* None of this was news to me. Several years ago I noted that students of Fair Play for Cuba had no "political" interest in Castro, but were enchanted by a young leader who spoke to everybody on the street and wrangled on national TV with conspirators against his life. To speak proleptically, he was not like—Clark Kerr.

to consider these university-centered politically active communities in terms of a "withdrawal" from the absurd system and its problems, and a return on more authentic premises.*

Consider the history of beat youth as a type. The withdrawal into voluntary poverty, the community of the illuminati, kicks on the road, and finger-painting, did not provide much world. Yet almost from the beginning there were social needs that *were* taken for real, especially banning the bomb, thwarting the fuzz, and supporting Negroes and Spanish because they were friends and equally out-caste. In California specifically, it was hard not to join in the rage at HUAC; but even more important was the horror at the Chessman execution: here *was* the threatening machine literally destroying human life, just as Camus had said.

Inevitably, in this return to involvement, there was joining with proper politicals. But *the event has been not that the young exiles have been politicized but that politics have been "existentialized" and brought into the community, even containing the dreadful sex and hashish.* And this is not because philosophy and pleasure have seduced people from the realities of life, but because *the thoughts and feelings of the young have been more relevant to the underlying realities of modern times,* the drive to rationalize, the abuse of high technology, and the hardware GNP, statism and the bomb. These abuses occur in every modern country and ideology, whether U.S.A., U.S.S.R., China, or even the emergent African states; and Great Society, Neo-Marxism, and even moral Pacifism do not fundamentally address them.

Come now to the university. A basic trait of the young is that they don't know much, but also, beautifully, that they want to learn something and they hang around hopefully relevant teachers. The young beats, of course, made a thing of voluntary ignorance like voluntary poverty; and the young hippies boringly went in for tiptop expertise—they knew all about black boxes and motivational research—without knowing anything. But pretty soon young

* I suppose this is what these young people mean by their abuse of the word "Alienation." Certainly in Marxist or psychiatric terms they are less alienated than most other people. Hopefully, if they continue a path of commitment, they will discover they are "alienated" in Luther's meaning!

people were bound to gravitate, or gravitate back, to the university, as cronies of students, or as auditors, or unmatriculated students, or as diffident and choosy students. To have a chance to learn something was a great advance for the dissident community; and it was certainly a vast advantage for the university to be infiltrated by a new breed of students who demanded authenticity and practical application. Yet, genetically and persistently, this fringe university community—with its own readings and music, political actions, free sexuality and hashish—is not identical with the *in loco parentis* and late-adolescent American college community. And administrators, incidentally, have heightened the tension by dissolving the fraternity system. Some of the young are then penned up in rule-ridden dormitories (built with federal funds but rented at high rates); but the more spirited go off-campus and get lost in the fringe community.

The new community, returning to the University and magnetizing the collegians, is by its genesis and nature not simply economically exploitable, unlike the ordinary college community which is at the top of the sixteen- to twenty-year ladder of school-processing. In principle, it has dropped out and returned. And it resists in the University the identical organized system that it resists outside. It is suspicious of being "vocationally guided"—though unfortunately it does not yet have much sense of true vocation. Correspondingly, it is resentful of the jet-set faculty busy with contracted research; and it correctly interprets the so-called "orientation to the discipline rather than to teaching" as nothing but careerism. Unfortunately, again, however, there is not yet any sense of what a real university of professionals would consist in. (I shall return to this.)

In the circumstances, there is an uncanny re-emergence of the primitive medieval university, with its fat-cat professors lecturing in the central halls, a ragged student community living in its own neighborhood, and, astoundingly, a new student leadership by the graduates and teaching-assistants, the very masters of arts who used to cause all the trouble in 1200! One would have expected, in the era of the organization man, that precisely the bright graduate-students, the junior-executives, would be the most conformist, to protect their status and advancement; yet we see at Berkeley that the teaching-assistants provided leaders and almost unanimously went on strike.

But as well as being a medieval fringe, the students *also* want "personal contact" with the dignitaries, as in a small American boarding-school. On the one hand they distrust everybody over thirty; on the other, they want the professors to become part of the fringe community, to give it intellectual structure and self assurance. And finally, as American citizens, they want self-rule, not only of their own social life like the medieval student-government, but also to have a say in the administrative and curricular doings: that is, the distant regents are regarded as illegitimate. This novel amalgam, then, of a fringe community of the young and masters of arts; "personal relations" between the students and the professors; and student membership on the Board of Regents—this amalgam is the free university.

On the campus, this ramshackle constitution proved to have political power. The organized guerrillas sat in. Then, "when the teaching-assistants went out," said a professor, "it was all over, for we can't run the school without them, and if we fired them, we'd never get another good graduate in California." And then the faculty, as Professor Wolin has put it, "stirred to ancestral memories of the ideal of a community of scholars bound together in the spirit of friendly persuasion and pledged to truth rather than abundance."—So the governor had to send his troopers and for a couple of days Clark Kerr's multiversity ceased to exist.

The question is: if such a free university exists in the offing, to whom, to what government, will the federal government, the foundations, and the corporations channel all that money that is the fuel of modern education? It's as bad as dealing with Saigon.

The enigma remains the faculty.

Let me recall a scrap of conversation with the new chancellor. He was pointing out to me that the chief obstacle to university reform was the teachers, inflexible, narrow, specialist, status-seeking. I cut him short impatiently: "Administrators have parroted this story to me verbatim at fifty colleges across the country. The fact is that for a hundred years you have cut their balls off and now you say they are impatient. Delegate power!" Meyerson reddened; he is himself a strong and broad mind, a professor, and, I suppose, an excellent teacher. A couple of days later he said to the council of the regents, "Goodman is right. Administration turns them into eunuchs and then complains that they are eunuchs."

The overwhelming faculty vote for the students seems to have been a reaction of nausea at the administration's lies, its subservience to outside pressures, its pathological avoidance of contact, and finally the presence of the cops. This is the kind of nausea that recalls decent but self-centered people to their plain duty. Professor Wolin says, the Faculty was "shocked out of its shameful neglect of teaching, its acquiescence in the bureaucratization of the University," and it recovered its "collective conscience." These explanations must be substantially accurate for they lead to the evident February situation of friendly contact with the students and cooperation in "university reform" toward *Lernfreiheit,* student democracy, faculty resumption of counseling, and so forth.

Nevertheless, although this breakthrough is splendid for the teachers as human beings—if professors don't like to associate with young people, why in the devil do they hang around schools? —in my opinion it does nothing for them as men. The revival of manhood can occur only if they come on again in the world as the university, as the protector of civilized standards, the professors of truth that makes a difference, and, in our country, the blasting critic of social baseness and lies. Every division and department is falling short. For instance, the University of California has "classified research," but this is entirely incompatible with the tradition of western science and its theory as consensus. (Some great universities have refused such contracts.) There is, in the country, censorship and managed news in utter contradiction to the principle of the humanities. The sex and narcotics laws of the community are grounded in superstitions that it is the business of the biological and social sciences publicly to expose, just as the eastern professors exposed the hoax of the Shelter program. The engineers and architects do not speak as faculties about the community-destroying urban renewal; and the education department does not speak as a faculty about the compulsory miseducation, or at least Max Rafferty.

I don't think that the students can much help their professors to remember *these* ancient duties. The professors will have to come to their own resolve. But if they do, I think that the students of Berkeley will be proud of them, and I think the students will begin to understand what it is to have not only a free university but a university altogether.

I have tried to point out that the regents and the new chancellor could easily accept a more flexible, decentralized, and human "free university." (I don't mean that they *will*, for the Bourbons never learn and never forget.) But I don't think that university truth is acceptable in our society, any more than the democratic action of the Free Speech Movement is *finally* acceptable.

I mentioned these things to a couple of liberal regents and they turned pale. The new chancellor didn't seem to relish them either—maybe I am wrong. And since the students asked me to address them, I talked about them at a mass meeting on the campus. (It was an unnerving scene: the planes kept roaring over my head on their way across the Pacific to Vietnam.) To my judgment, the students did not dig what I was saying: they do not have much memory of the tradition of the West. They know what freedom is—yes, they do—but they don't really know what a university is. Kind of to encourage them, I told them of two ancient examples, where revolt in the university led to great social revolutions. First, the Averroists, the new science, the rediscovered Aristotle: this was squelched and "harmonized" after a fierce struggle at Paris, yet it persisted and brought on, at Padua, the heroic age of modern science; it took less than 400 years! And it took only 250 years for the university revolt of Wiclif and Hus to bring on the university-led Reformation.

The Berkeley students didn't much relish the thought of Hus at the stake, but they were crazy for the Wyclifites at Oxford standing on the ramparts and fighting off the king with bows and arrows.

TWO PERSPECTIVES
ON BERKELEY

Multiversity Lost

an abridged version of a travesty by
KEN SANDERSON

Of Civil Disobedience, Due Process
And Bureaucracy, whose IBM
Thought Strong into the World, and Beebe too,
With loss of Freedom, till one moral Man
Restore us, and regain the native Right,
Sing Joan Baez, that on the marble stairs
Of Sproul, or of Dwinelle, didst inspire
Eight Hundred, who first taught the Freedom School
In Civil Rights, a Chanukah service
Singing Hatikvah; Or if Weinberg's car
Delight thee more, and Rossman's mouth that flow'd
Fast—he the Oracle of God; I thence
Invoke thy aid to my blasphemous Song,
That with no prior thought intends to sing
About the FSM and its Revolt
Against the Holy Multiversity.
And I to fortify my Argument
Invoke the First Amendment Guarantee
To justify the ways of men to curs.

Say first, for Towle hides nothing from thy view
Nor newspapers over windows, what cause
Mov'd those Eight Hundred in that Police State,
Loath'd of Feuer so highly, to fall off
From their President, and transgress his Will,
The Lords of Student Government besides?
Who first seduc'd them to that foul revolt?
Serpent Savio; hee it was, whose guile
Stirr'd up with Alienation, deceiv'd

305

The Students of Berkeley; what time his Pride
Had called him to the stage, with all his Host
Of Rebel Students, by whose aid conspiring
To seize the microphone from Scalapino,
Chanc'llor-for-a-day, before the Holy
Departmental Heads; and say what time
The Adamantine Deans and Regents all
Omnipotent, Immortal, Infinite,
Eternal Kings, they Authors of all being,
Fountains of Light, thron'd inaccessible,
Richer than Croesus, timeless as Cronus,
More pious than Aeneas, more wrathful
Than Achilles, ever craftier than
Ulysses, more trusting than Abraham,
More patient than the righteous Job, rosey
Fingered as the Dawn, wine-dark as the Sea,
Midas Touch! Land Owners of the world,
Bomb makers, Buyers of wheat, Owners of
Railroads and Man-handlers of the nation,
Stormy, husky, brawling, refused to hear
Th' insolent petitions of th' screaming
Verminous, bearded Beatniks; tell how once
Thoughts of dry semesters and dreary midterms
Dismayed them; how Savio the Elder
Statesman of Godless Generational
Animus, round once threw his baleful eyes,
Sipping at his coffee cup upon the Terrace,
O'erpriced Cafeteria, Dungeon dank,
Such place Administration had prepar'd
For those Intellectuals, their Prison ordained
Across the hallow'd Plaza, just beneath
Th' Eternal Eye of Sproul, whose sight discerns
Abstrusest thoughts, the Terrace feeding all
Trots, Yips, Libs, Finks, Progs, Pinks and shades of Red,
A Universe of Pot, how Savio
To his alter ego Rossman thus spoke.

*Arch-Rebels Savio, Weinberg, Rossman, and Goldberg tell of their
Alienation, and with the battle-cry of "Freedom Now!" they violate
campus Law. Omnipotent Mediator Kerr surveys the uprising from*

the top of his High Holy Campanille; addressing His Administrators,
He predicts:

> Our students pure will hearken to their lies,
> And transgress our Multiversity's rules,
> Loyalty Oaths of true obedience.
> And fall they all shall, those faithless; whose fault?
> Whose but their own? ingrates, they had of mee
> All they could have; I made them just and right,
> Sufficient to have stood, though free to fall.
> I made them all safe for ideas, and not
> Ideas safe for them. Go get their Reg cards.

Defying the Discipline of Deans, the Serpent tempts the Children of
Kerr into Pride and Pseudo-maturity: "Ye shall be as Adults!" Saint
Joan, Maid of Carmel, is then invoked to aid the Poet in telling of the
captured police car.

> . . . All around the captured prize,
> Eyeless in Plaza, at the Hall of slaves,
> Sat the rebel students, taunting, laughing.
> Philosopher Savio, snickering
> To himself, gloated o'er his victory,
> Watched with dev'lish approval the long line
> Of insurgents who mounted on the car
> To speak, mounted off-campus action, and
> Mounted each other at night in sleeping
> Bags that lay littered about the cement.
> Hail Berkeley Love, unwedded Sex, true source
> Of parental despair, no propriety,
> Sexual revolt, lumpen coffee-house
> Morality, impure, defil'd, perverse.

Student Body President Charlie Powell calls for Reason, but the
unwashed Intelligentsia hoot him down; the Eternal appears to Charlie
in the Student Union and says, "Servant of Kerr, well done . . ." The
Father then sends for the Highway Patrol to disperse the mob; Loyal
Charlie sings Hossanahs to the Liberal Bureaucracy. The Rebels hold
the car in the embattled Plaza through the following day and night;
they are tricked into signing a deceitful "Pact"; it appears that Peace
has come at last.

> No peace, alas, in fact; for the Rebels
> Withdrew in silence sinister, withdrew

But to begin Stage Two of the hidden
Guerrilla War, withdrew into secret
Chambers, disguised Headquarters that they called
Panty-Radium; there in the darkness
Of Panty-Radium they all convened
And for the space of one weekend, talked, plann'd
And built the Free Speech Movement: FSM.
The FSM! Hardly are those words out
When a vast image out of the Godkin Lectures
Troubles my sight: somewhere in reaction
A shape with punch-card body, and the head
Of an institute, a mind blank, nursing
Its federal grants like the wolf-mother
Of Romulus, is moving its slow hand
Toward the telephone, Establishment
Liberal, CCNY Alumnus.
The darkness drops again; but now I know
That thirty years of New Deal apathy
Were vexed to action by a student movement,
And what old men, their hours of honor past,
Speak of Due Process in Berkeley, and warn?

Committees appointed according to the provisions of the "Pack"
collapse; Surly Savio and his Soviet of five thousand besiege the meet-
ing of the Regents:

But it is written: Tempt not Regential
Power. The Regents bargained not but stood.

The FSM Steering Committee returns to Panty-Radium in desperation,
plans the Sit-in. Poet has Apocalyptic Vision of the FSM Antichrist.

"Mystery Berkeley the Great, Mother of
Robots and Mechanizations of the Earth"
In blood-red writ upon the foreheads smooth
Of social engineers, Craftsmen, Draftsmen
Of Managerial Society,
The Millennium is at hand! Beware
The seven hundred seventy-seven
Rebels who prepare to punch seven holes
In seven punch-cards of Sproul's IBM
Numbers are a glorious thyng, certeyn,

For lettre sleeth, so as we Robots seyn.
O Clark, Clark, Clark, amid your praise too soon,
Over-compromising Clark, Total Eclipse
Threatens the Name of Multiversity!
You must advise, and to this hazard draw
With speed the Governor's Highway Patrol
To preserve the name of the Factory,
And protect these, your Light, Angelic Mills.

*FIAT LEX! The Serpent goes limp, his detumescent tactic terrifying
the Chancellor, but not the Police, who pounce on Savio; removing
their badges (for efficiency), the fierce Avengers from the Left Hand
of God, the Right Wing of Brown, attack the lumpen-limpniks. As
the arrests proceed, the graduates, inspired by the Rebels' courage
never to submit or yield, begin the Strike (O unexpected stroke, worse
than of Death!); classes are dismissed, picket lines are formed.*

Spawn'd of Anomie, Alienation
(That last infirmity of Noble mind),
Like Lumbrici out of th' earth after rain,
Like quail or pheasant flushed from the marshes,
Like termites out of fumigated walls,
So rushed the throngs of graduate students
Out of Libraries, out of Research Labs,
Out of their carrels, throwing down their tomes,
Crying joyous, "Life, Life, Eternal Life!"
Vengeance is mine, saith the Student Body,
And I shall repay Multiversity.
What is Kerr that I be mindful of him?
Rage, ye Children of Ludd, smite the Machine!

*The arrested students are shipped to Santa Rita prison, where the
Serpent moves the alienated inmates to stage a Sit-down in the War-
den's office; Rebels, bailed out by "Young Turk" faculty, return to
the campus to join the Strikers and to goad them on. Meanwhile,
Administrators and Faculty debate how best to retake the Campus;
Kerr, who has a third plan in mind, rejects plans for open war and
for outright surrender:*

O Progeny of Cal, Empyreal Thrones,
Must we renounce, and changing style be call'd
Janitors, street-sweepers, mere mechanics?

. . . Therefore I propose the use of Reason,
Reason whose name will win back student hearts,
For even as the dogs of Pavlov fame
Were taught to salivate at ringing sound,
So students of this Multiversity
Will en masse return when Reason they hear
Called upon in fine words which I shall speak.
If this be Reason, make the most of it!

Senate Academic, rotten with Rebel supporters, is to meet on Tuesday; to head off a faculty revolt, Kerr calls a Multiversity Convocation in the Greek Theater for Monday. The Convocation begins; Kerr's mighty Banner is applauded by White Guards, jeered by Bolsheviks; Kerr begins his Speech with sweet pronouncement, offering the Multiversity as the Final Solution to the Managerial-Society problem; He offers the Rebels redemption and homes in Suburbia if they refrain from political action. The Rebels are moved by His Mercy, but Savio seizes the microphone with hopes of winning back the wavering minds of his following; before he can speak, the Guards jump him, and he disappears into a sea of uniforms and flash-bulbs behind the Stage. The Rebels, stunned first by Reason's Voice, and stunned again by Unreason's Deeds, thunder their indignation; suddenly, the air becomes oily and the sky turns black—Bureaucrats and Rebels both tremble in fear at the Final Judgment. In the tar-pool sky, a burning Sign appears: MENE, MENE, TEKEL, EPHESEM. Kerr, his limbs loose with fright, bids Nobel Laureates to interpret the Sign, but they can not; at last, the Serpent, bound in a straight-jacket, is brought forth. He reads the judgment: History's God hath numbered Kerr's Kingdom and hath divided it in twain, returning it again to Faculty and Students. His interpretation is confirmed: the Sun its potent Ray reveals again, bathing the hills and shrines of Berkeley in splendor; distrust and malice are scattered in wafting winds.

Amaz'd were the multitudes with sudden
Joy they dared not feel or believe, so quick
Had come relief from War's extended blows,
So shaken as they were, so wan with care,
They gaped with disbelief such time for peace
To find; New Dispensation and New Law
Announc'd by music of crystalline spheres,

Midst brilliance played from Ludwig's Fountain clear
Redeeming waters, Pacem in Berkeley
Proclaimed in loud Hossanahs from the hearts
Of all who there were gathered, all but that One
Who seeing Fortune's wheel o'erturn did sense
The Idea of the Multiversity
Dissolve to vapor, and turning away
His face did mutter low "It is finished,"
And then he gave up the idea. At once
The fetters broken fell from off the feet
Of victor Savio, unbound he was
From buckles rude of his confining garb,
And smiling sweet he blessed the pilgrim throng
With V-for-Victory, Crusader's Sign
Of Benediction, Triumph sure and Grace.
O tremble Bureaucrats at Class Revolt
Of Collar White; hereafter learn with awe
To dread the Son of SNCC: hee all unarm'd
Shall chase thee with the terror of his voice
From Power Structure's position secure,
Thee and thy Legions, tremble at the thought!
Hail Son of Civil Rights, heir of New Worlds,
Saviour of Berkeley, on thy glorious work
Now enter, and begin to save mankind.
Thus sang the students hymms of praise. And while
The Colleges Laudamus weeping sang,
And erstwhile Rebels to the Fold returned,
Of Alienation purg'd, into Bliss
Eternal sworn, and to Obedience
Did vow themselves to build Utopia,
Hand in tearful hand extending all round,
The President, the chastis'd King, came down,
Down he came, no glistering Phaeton
Wanting the manage of unruly jades,
But modestly as a man might descend.
Some natural tears he dropp'd, but wip'd them soon;
His School was all before him, where to choose
His place of work, and History his guide:

Down from the platform, to his office bare,
There to enter with humble aspect low,
He text in hand with wand'ring steps and slow,
Through Berkeley took his solitary way.
And they lived happily ever after.

The Press and
The Student Revolt

by
COLIN MILLER

We need . . . to see to it that administration serves and
stimulates rather than rules the institution, that it be expendable when necessary and flexible all the time; to assure that
the university can do better what it does best: to solve the
whole range of governmental problems within the university.

Clark Kerr at Harvard,
April 25, 1963

It would be difficult to conceive of a university president adminis-
trating more remotely from this admonition than Clark Kerr as
president of the University of California in the fall of 1964. Instead
of stimulating he provoked. His flexibility was, generally, not negotiable. The governmental problems within the University were abated
rather than solved . . . but after the strongest and most sizeable
manifestation of civil disobedience ever seen on a university campus.

In one regard and one only did Kerr heed his own words: his
administration had an expendable chancellor, Edward Strong, who
was granted a leave of absence in time to avert a student demonstration that might have brought disaster to this great institution.

This sudy is to be concerned with the press and its presentation
of history as made at Berkeley in the last months of last year. Press
comment requires a point of view of its own arising from a knowledge
of the events involved. How fair was the press, one has to ask himself, in terms of what the commentator believes to be the facts? Of
necessity this involves opinions as to justifications, provocations, inter-
pretations; and these, in turn involve judgments as to the wisdom of
men.

Ordinarily the *San Francisco Chronicle* maintains a full time reporter to cover the campus. This man, Don Wegars, had been called
back to San Francisco for vacation relief, and was not in attendance
when the controversy began. Carl Irving, who covers the campus
full time for the *Oakland Tribune,* admits that he missed the im-

portance of these early events. No one seems to have seen the gradually mounting protest swelling from within the student groups, resentful of the administration's taking from them an area where they so long had had freedom of expression. Until the University took its first disciplinary action against the students for manning illegal tables, the press paid scant heed to the developing story.

So little understood was the importance of the Berkeley upheaval that *The New York Times'* two-man San Francisco bureau filed nothing for the first two months that the revolution was taking place at the University of California.

The first extended press coverage of the growing controversy was focused on the events of September 30, and October 1 and 2. The sit-in of September 30 was described by the *San Francisco Chronicle* as a "rebellion" in banner headlines, one inch high on page one. The carry-over in the *Examiner* used the term "revolt."

On the afternoon of October 1, concentrated, round-the-clock Berkeley coverage began with the thirty-two-hour sit-down surrounding the battered police car. Opinion-shaping headlines abounded. With but few exceptions the California press, particularly from the Bay area, dealt with the story as though it were a kind of academic Western. The *Chronicle,* for example:

BATTLE OF SPROUL HALL

UC STUDENT RIOT—

POLICE IN RETREAT

On the editorial page, the *Chronicle*'s comment was captioned:

TOLERANCE AT

BREAKING POINT

The *San Francisco Examiner,* again in inch high type across eight columns, said:

2000 IN UC SIEGE

While the local *Berkeley Gazette* in six columns on page one:

STUDENTS CONTINUE TO DEFY UC

OVERRULE ON CAMPUS POLITICS

This carried a subheading:

VIRTUAL

STATE

OF SIEGE

On the second, the *Oakland Tribune* first page story spread across three columns:

UC KERR WON'T

LIFT SUSPENSION

President stands firm in Face of Mob Action

Demonstrators Defy Police

This was in addition to another front page *Tribune* story:

3000 STUDENTS IN WILD NIGHT AT UC

The *Tribune* editorial comment was headlined:

UC STUDENT MOB DEFIES LAW, ORDER

Another news story in the *Tribune* reprinted quotations from a *Daily Californian* editorial which criticized the demonstrators and said, "Last night, the students became a near mob with a police car for their symbol. No one can rationally justify the simultaneous defiance of authority on the one hand and the expectation of protection on the other."

Newspapers like *The Sacramento Bee* sent their own men into Berkeley on October 2. But in order to understand the manner in which the story was generally handled over the country, the following Associated Press dispatch, as received in Philadelphia, Pennsylvania, the afternoon of October 2, is typical:

BERKELEY, CALIF., OCT. 2 (AP) —A MOB OF 3,500 STUDENTS CONTINUED TO DEFY UNIVERSITY OF CALIFORNIA OFFICIALS TODAY AFTER WRECKING A CAMPUS POLICE CAR AND REFUSING POLICE ORDERS TO VACATE THE ADMINISTRATION BUILDING.

THE DEMONSTRATION, WHICH STARTED YESTERDAY MORNING AND CONTINUED TODAY, WAS IN PROTEST OF A UNIVERSITY EDICT BANNING ON-CAMPUS SOLICITATION OF FUNDS FOR OFF-CAMPUS POLITICAL PROJECTS.

EXPULSION OF EIGHT STUDENTS TUESDAY FOR DISREGARDING THE UNIVERSITY RULE TOUCHED OFF THE DEMONSTRATION, WHICH SEVERAL TIMES THREATENED TO TURN INTO A FULL-SCALE RIOT.

THE CROWD BEGAN FORMING SHORTLY AFTER POLICE TOOK INTO CUSTODY A NON-STUDENT, JACK WEINBERG, 24, AND PREPARED TO TAKE HIM TO POLICE HEADQUARTERS ON CHARGES OF TRESPASSING.

POLICE SAID WEINBERG REFUSED TO STOP SOLICITING FUNDS DESPITE SEVERAL WARNINGS.

AS THE POLICE CAR CARRYING WEINBERG PREPARED TO DEPART AN AREA BETWEEN THE ADMINISTRATION AND STUDENT CENTER BUILDINGS, THOUSANDS OF STUDENTS GATHERED.

SEVERAL FLUNG THEMSELVES UNDER THE FRONT AND BACK WHEELS

OF THE PATROL CAR, WHILE OTHERS MOUNTED THE HOOD AND ROOF
TO MAKE SPEECHES AGAINST THE UNIVERSITY ADMINISTRATION.

POLICE SAID THE PATROL CAR WAS A TOTAL WRECK FROM STUDENTS
CLAMBERING OVER IT.

AT ONE POINT, 17 POLICEMEN ATTEMPTED TO EVICT HUNDREDS
OF STUDENTS WHO HAD JAMMED INTO SPROUL HALL, THE ADMINISTRA-
TION BUILDING.

THEY WERE MET BY A JEERING, SHOVING THRONG AND FORCED TO
RETREAT. ALL BUT FIVE OF THE STUDENTS LATER LEFT THE BUILDING.
THOSE WHO REMAINED WERE LOCKED IN FOR THE NIGHT.

DURING THE DEMONSTRATION, UNIVERSITY OFFICIALS SAID, SOME
25,000 OTHER STUDENTS REMAINED IN CLASSES OR AWAY FROM THE
DEMONSTRATION.

WEINBERG, A BERKELEY MEMBER OF THE CONGRESS OF RACIAL
EQUALITY (CORE) AND A 1963 GRADUATE OF THE UNIVERSITY, WAS
SOLICITING FUNDS TO HELP HIRE ATTORNEYS FOR THE EIGHT EXPELLED
STUDENTS.

UC CHANCELLOR E. W. STRONG ISSUED A STATEMENT ON THE CON-
TROVERSY WHICH NOTED THAT ON-CAMPUS SOLICITATION OF FUNDS
FOR POLITICAL PURPOSES WOULD THREATEN THE UNIVERSITY'S "FUTURE
AS AN INDEPENDENT EDUCATIONAL INSTITUTION."

STRONG SAID "THE ISSUE NOW HAS BEEN CARRIED FAR BEYOND THE
BOUNDS OF DISCUSSION BY A SMALL MINORITY OF STUDENTS.

"THE UNIVERSITY CANNOT AND WILL NOT ALLOW STUDENTS TO
ENGAGE IN DELIBERATE VIOLATIONS OF LAW AND ORDER ON THE CAM-
PUS."

HE SAID A CAMPUS POLITICAL ORGANIZATION KNOWN AS SLATE HAD
URGED IN ITS SUPPLEMENT REPORT THIS FALL, "OPEN, FIERCE AND
THOROUGHGOING REBELLION ON THE CAMPUS."

STRONG ADDED:

"INDIVIDUAL STUDENTS MUST ASK THEMSELVES WHETHER THEY
WISH TO BE A PART OF SUCH ACTION."

The AP story throbbed with the verve of Hildy Johnson. It was
exciting. It flowed easily. But how much understanding did it convey?

How much of what had happened at Berkeley since September 14
did it tell? Did it communicate an insight into the student mind in
uproar?

The University information office had repeatedly stressed to newsmen that the eight students had been suspended; the AP used the word "expulsion".

Was there editorializing by the AP in first calling Weinberg a "non-student" instead of an ex-student? The AP could not be expected to give a full explanation that Weinberg had taken time out from his graduate studies to work full time for CORE.

True, the police car was badly damaged but "total wreck" was an exaggeration. The students subsequently raised $350.00 for its repair.

The quote from Chancellor Strong about a student political organization's supplemental report which urged "open, fierce and thoroughgoing rebellion on the campus" was distortion for which the Associated Press could not be held responsible. The quotation was attributed directly to the chancellor. What Strong did not mention was the circumstance under which it had been printed.

The leaflet had been written by a California alumnus named Brad Cleaveland, known on campus as a "graduate drop-out." Strong implied that the Cleaveland supplemental report was official and endorsed by Slate.

To the contrary, the editor's preface to the report had said that all such "signed statements represented the views of the author and not necessarily the views of the editor. Those of the editor are expresed in signed editorials." The Slate supplement, therefore, fell into the category of a letter to the editor published by a newspaper. If Strong had read the supplement, it was impossible to have missed the Slate editor's disclaimer, published on the inside front cover.

How news can be editorialized in pictures was illustrated during the police car episode. While the police car was being besieged on the Sproul Plaza, a sit-in demonstration was going on in the foyer of Sproul Hall. In reporting it, the *Oakland Tribune* used a series of three pictures, the first of a student calling for help as the police started removing the demonstrators. The second photograph showed hands pulling at an officer about the legs as he stepped among the students. The third was of a policeman sprawling helplessly in the hands of students who were holding him.

Jan S. Winter of San Francisco, a student reporter and non-participant, who is a sophomore in English, was on the scene when the pictures were taken. He said the policeman was seized by student hands as he stepped on student bodies while he made his way across the Sproul foyer. The policeman was restrained but not harmed. Winter said that during the action portrayed by this sequence, he did not see any policemen being harmed, but he did see a policeman strike a student in the face with his fist.

The third picture in this sequence was published alone on the front page of the October 2 issue of the *Chronicle*. The other two pictures were not used or mentioned. Their elimination made the third picture carry a different meaning. The caption in the *Chronicle* read: "The brawling students dragged Berkeley policeman, Phil Mower, down the Sproul Hall steps. "I think one of them bit my leg!" .The same picture was used in the *Examiner,* with the caption "Police Officer gets bum's rush at Berkeley." It was widely carried by AP wirephoto across the country.

The *Oakland Tribune* on October 2 published a picture which was a shocking violation of ethical presentation. In the picture's background is a student on top of the besieged police car, and in front are numerous students. Directly before the camera is a girl with her back to the lens. On top of her pile of books is a volume with its face up. The only clear word on the cover is *"Marxism"*. The caption read "A textbook on Marxism was among the crowd." The intention of equating the demonstration with Communism was clear. Actually, the book's full title is *Essentials of Marxism,* a paperback published by Bantam Books. It is a textbook for Social Studies 1A, a freshman course. Obviously, the word Marxism in the photograph had been retouched. Every other word on the cover was blurred.

In the *Examiner* of October 2, there was a headline which read:
THE UC NON-STUDENT PROTESTERS
but the body of the story itself said, "Unlike many student demonstrations, yesterday's University of California protest was manned largely by bona fide students." The headline headed one way—the body another.

On October 3, the *Chronicle*'s Bob Robertson made the first reportorial effort to place the Free Speech Movement in perspective for his readers. In his lead, Elizabeth Gardner Stapleton, one of the eight persons suspended, pleaded, "Could you please tell your readers we're not a bunch of crazy beatniks?" Robertson responded, "All right, Mrs. Stapleton, it can be objectively stated that the people who precipitated this avalanche of protest are not a bunch of crazy beatniks. Beatniks don't care. These people care very much."

Robertson described Mrs. Stapleston as "the only girl among the first eight suspended . . . she is eighteen, a small, pretty, blond girl, the daughter of a Watsonville apple farmer and realtor, who was once, she said, 'a member of the Socialist Party—but no more.' "

Robertson quoted Mrs. Stapleton: "We did not attack that policeman. We people kept this thing very well disciplined. He walked over us. He kicked me and I've got water on the knee to prove it.

"I've got a B average here in the humanities and I worked for it. And I want to take what I learned out into the world and use it to help people."

Robertson described another of the eight, Brian Turner, as "a pleasant-faced quiet-mannered nineteen-year-old sophomore in economics. He has an A average. He said he was brought up in a liberal family but his previous commitment to liberal causes was secondary."

" 'I just joined SNCC a week and a half ago,' Turner told Robertson, 'Last year I promised myself that I had to study, but this year I felt I had a little more time to devote to my convictions.'

"The first time Brian was approached while manning a recruiting table he backed down because 'I didn't want to go it alone. I folded up the table and went home.'

" 'But I thought about it overnight and went back. When they came up to me again, my own principles prevented me from leaving. I had decided that the freedom of 27,000 people to speak freely was worth the sacrifice of my own academic career at Cal.' "

In another *Chronicle* article on the 3rd:

HOW THE DISPUTE
STARTED—SPARKS
THAT SET THE FIRE

In this story Chancellor Edward Strong was quoted: "The regulations represent the historic policy of the University as determined by the regents. The solicitation of funds for political purposes is also in violation of California Law, prohibiting such partisan political activity on state property."

Three months after Strong's statement the regents still had passed no liberalizing regulations. The California laws had not been amended. But by that time solicitation of funds for political purposes and par-

tisan political activity could be freely practiced. Chancellor Strong's
reasons of October 3 had become non-reasons.

The Hearst evening paper in San Francisco on the 3rd headlined:

KERR CITES ELEMENT
OF CASTRO-MAO REDS

On October 3, an Associated Press story, published in the Los
Angeles *Herald Examiner,* still had the eight students "expelled" instead of suspended. Its caption for the picture of Mario Savio announcing the signing of the truce: "Students Victorious at the University
of California."

A shred of hope seemed to be promised on October 4 with the
Examiner's headline

UNEASY CALM
SETTLES OVER
UC CAMPUS

but it was short-lived. On the 5th, the same paper carried a page one
story:

BROWN ORDERS UC
SIT-IN REPORT

with a carry-over on page twelve:

RIOT REPORT DEMANDED

In the southern part of the state the *Los Angeles Times* carried
a lead editorial October 6:

RULES AND RESPONSIBILITY AT UC

This commented on the accusation that Clark Kerr had been guilty
of "appeasement" in the pact to end the October 1–2 demonstrations.
Denying this, the *Times* said "The university did not capitulate to
student demands. At best, the demonstrators won a hearing for their
case, something they could easily have had anyway without recourse
to histrionics.

"Under difficult circumstances, school officials acted quite properly."

The *Times* described the demonstrators as "an irresponsible minority on the Berkeley campus."

The *Berkeley Gazette* on October 6 quoted the demonstrations'
leaders,

WE HAVE JUST BEGUN TO FIGHT

above a six-column story illustrated with four pictures on the Section

Page. The Palo Alto *Times* published a column on "Academic Anarchy" by its editor, Alexander Bodi, on the same day.

On the 7th, the *Examiner* published a column of letters to the editor captioned:

Berkeley Campus Riots

On the 7th, the *Oakland Tribune* story headlined:

KERR RAPS
OUTSIDERS
ON CAMPUS

The University's president was quoted as saying that "non-student elements were partly responsible for last week's demonstrations." "Up to forty per cent of the hard-core participants" came from off-campus. Kerr identified them "as very experienced and professional people tied in with organizations having Communist influence."

This interview with President Kerr had wide publication and lasting impact. As long afterwards as January 18, 1965, the Los Angeles *Herald Examiner* was being critical of the intrusions on the Berkeley campus. This editorial was headlined:

THOSE OUTSIDERS—
WHO ARE THEY?

The irresponsibility of these October statements attributed to Clark Kerr may have had more of an effect in shaping public opinion than any other factor. Typical of nation-wide misinterpretation was a letter I had from an old friend who writes widely syndicated editorials for many newspapers around the country. In January, he wrote me, "It seems . . . our New York area press covered this fracas quite thoroughly and enthusiastically. They were befuddled at first and inclined to make something of a hero out of the leader. But when they discovered very good evidence that agitators had infiltrated the 'rebels' and that the leader—if not actually a card-carrying Communist, was at least a fellow traveler or tool of the Commies, they jumped right on it, and wrote the stories for what they were.

"I think every man of good will today has to become something of a rebel himself against the tendency of the Reds and far leftists to paint every picture in their own colors and twist our bungling good intentions to their own advantage. I think the press here has been more than fair to their version of incidents so I feel that you can safely assume that they were not out to persecute anyone's right to dissent. Our universities, notably UC, with only two or three exceptions that I know, give the freest kind of reign to all shades of political opinion in seminars, speeches, writing."

Clark Kerr in an address before the San Diego Chamber of Commerce on October 7 said, "Diverse student groups ranging from the Young Socialists to the Young Goldwater Republicans are encouraged as never before by elements external to the university." He added that a few students, animated by world events "are becoming more addicted to direct action, even outside the law, than ever before." The "mob-action at Berkeley," spoken of by Kerr repeatedly in his San Diego address called up the vision of the "good guys" in the form of the administration trying to put down the "bad guys" in the form of the mob. Kerr did not refer to the constitutional questions involved in the student protest.

On October 9, Kerr won the praise of Jesse Unruh for "averting an ugly and potentially bloody riot," on the Berkeley campus the previous week. The *Oakland Tribune* headlined:

KERR PRAISED FOR
AVERTING   VIOLENCE

thus adding favorable shadings to the president's image.

The *People's World,* as was to be expected, on October 10, praised "free speech sit-down" under the headline

STUDENTS FOUGHT FOR
ANCIENT PRIVILEGE

The next day, October 11, the Los Angeles *Herald Examiner,* described the

RUCKUS ON CAMPUS

Said the *Examiner,* "The University of California at Berkeley . . . was the scene of disgraceful mob demonstrations by students and outside agitators attempting to dictate to University officials who had refused to allow a small group of students to engage in direct political activity on the campus."

On October 12, the *Chronicle* carried a Lucius Beebe column captioned "A dim view of the Berkeley Red Square," in which the demonstrators were described as "academic pan-handlers and moochers on the public bounty."

The *National Observer* on October 12 published an account of the October 1–2 "revolt." It quoted President Kerr who blamed the students for the disturbance: "It is very disappointing to find that the freedom we have sought to allow our students is not always matched by responsibility. There is no issue of freedom of speech at Berkeley."

The revolt, he said, resulted from a "nation-wide mood of young people—some of them just back from Alabama and Mississippi and full of ideas of direct action, and that you only get somewhere by direct action."

He added that many of the Berkeley demonstrators were not UC students, and "that some elements were impressed with the tactics of Fidel Castro and Mao Tse-tung. There are very few of these, but there are some."

Again no mention of the constitutional issues raised by the students.

All of the Kerr implications of Communist influence and outside intervention left a vivid and telling mark. Yet in his December 18 press conference at Los Angeles, President Kerr was quoted in *The New Leader* of January 18 as having "told a newsman that to the best of his knowledge, Weinberg was the only non-student among the FSM leadership."

On November 25, the *Examiner*'s Ed Montgomery began a series of three articles on what he called the "self-styled Free Speech Movement which has kept the University of California campus in turmoil for weeks." This was the most vigorous attack on FSM that had appeared.

Montgomery thought that of the 26,000 students "scarcely a pipers' guard" is involved in the disorder. "Dedicated students no longer evince even a passing interest. Serious scholars couldn't care less," Montgomery claimed.

In Montgomery's view, few of the students involved had "direct organizational ties of radical, extremist, or even Communist nature." Many were termed "dupes, unwilling or otherwise of trained agitators, some of whom are not even registered students."

Clark Kerr was quoted as having said, "The majority of the demonstrators were not students and that up to forty per cent of the hard-core leaders were adherents of the 'Mao-Red Chinese Communist Line.'"

It was Montgomery's belief there was "no doubt of Communist influence within the so-called Free Speech Movement."

In reply to the initial Montgomery piece, FSM sought to answer the charges. To the statement that FSM "involves only a minute faction of the student body," the answer was given that FSM was comprised of twenty-two organizations representing more than 3,000 students, these ranging in character from social action groups such as CORE and SNCC to political associations, like the Goldwater Conservatives and the Young Socialist Alliance; plus representatives from the Inter-Faith Council.

To Montgomery's assertion about the pipers' guard and the serious scholars, FSM pointed to the demonstration of 5,000 students at the regents' meeting of November 20.

The Executive Committee of sixty, FSM said, consisted of representatives from the twenty-two basic organizations who were meeting regularly three times a week. Montgomery's accusation that "the serious scholars were not participating" was refuted by the number of students with high scholastic averages in the leadership. Mario Savio, the spokesman, for example, had a 3.9 standing in philosophy. Chairman Henry F. May of the history department on December 4 offered faculty substantiation to the scholarly qualities of FSM memberships when he said that it comprised "large numbers of our best students, many never involved in politics in the past."

Of the sixty member Executive Committee, fifty-eight were students. Of the twelve on the steering committee, eleven were registered at the University. The twelfth, Jack Weinberg, graduated in June 1963 and was taking time out from his graduate studies for efforts on behalf of CORE. Montgomery claimed Mortimer Scheer, a one-time Communist party official, and Albert J. Lima, Communist party Chairman in Northern California, had participated in FSM activities. This was denied. Aside from pictures of Scheer and Lima on campus and an unsupported accusation, no evidence was given that they had actually participated in any decisions or activities of FSM.

Montgomery, FSM said, had not established times, places, or dates to substantiate his allegations.

The second of Montgomery's articles, published Thanksgiving Day, was similarly broad and unspecific. Guilt was established by association. The article said that suspect groups adhering to the Communist line were influential in the FSM leadership. "From within this coalition came the hard core advisers among the demonstrators. The hard core advisers operate among the façade of a steering committee, composed of representatives from nearly a score of campus organizations ranging in political line from the moderate right to extreme left."

FSM dismissed this charge with the statement that the steering committee members from the Goldwater group would not tolerate the outright interference Montgomery claimed existed.

FSM felt that in his second article, Montgomery concerned himself with only fragments of the background of certain individuals, but that only one, Betina Aptheker, daughter of an acknowledged Communist, was properly identified as an FSM leader. Miss Aptheker was on the steering committee. But, FSM pointed out, so was Mona Hutchin of the Conservatives for an Open Campus.*

In his third article, published November 27, Montgomery led provocatively: "The Marxist-dominated Free Speech Movement which has kept the UC campus at Berkeley in a turmoil for weeks—" Nowhere in his series had Montgomery proved the allegation of Marxist domination. In its letter of refutation to the *Examiner,* FSM said that "nowhere in any of his articles does Mr. Montgomery in any way substantiate the allegation which he makes here so blithely. To name names, take a few photos, and then make vague charges, is not sufficient for a good journalist. At no point does Mr. Montgomery explain what he means by "Marxist domination" and nowhere does he reveal specific facts to prove his case." FSM pointed to inaccuracies in his few specifics as prompting question as to the validity of some of his dubious "proof" of Marxist domination.

The long FSM letter to the *Examiner* concluded, "Within the Free Speech Movement we have represented political ideology from the left to the right, as well as religious beliefs from Christian to Judaic; but we have banded together to secure our rights as citizens and we'll continue to fight for these rights together. We struggle not for the right to hear merely what we want to hear but for each member of the University Community's right to speak his mind and act on his political conviction."

The FSM letter was never published by the *Examiner.* However true it may have been that justice was on the side of FSM, the fact

* On February 2, 1964, Miss Hutchin had a brief scuffle with San Francisco police. Wearing a button reading: I'm A Right-Wing Extremist, she was forcibly removed by three officers from a Powell Street cable car. Miss Hutchin insisted she had equal right to stand, as men are permitted to do, on the outside steps. Police disagreed. Six cars were backed up at the Market Street turntable. Miss Hutchin was taken to the Hall of Justice, remonstrated with and released.

was that the Montgomery series was given publication in a million newspapers through the San Francisco *Examiner* and the Los Angeles *Herald Examiner*. The latter publication took place after the Sproul Hall sit-in of December 2 and 3 and had large impact in Southern California.

On January 20, 1965, Mr. Montgomery stated, "You can rest on the facts in that series and go to sleep on them."

On November 27, with the University on vacation for the Thanksgiving weekend, the *Chronicle* carried an explanation from President Kerr of his press conference of October 6, fifty-two days before, in Los Angeles. This had been widely quoted regarding outsiders and off-campus elements with mention of the Communist Party and Communist causes. The Kerr explanation to the *Chronicle* also sought to explain what he had said on October 2 regarding Fidel Castro and Mao Tse-tung and the influence they had had on the tactics of the demonstrators.

In essence, the Kerr statement seemed to bring to light the statistics and facts for the purpose of a second misinterpretation rather than to correct an earlier false impression. However that may have been, the two intervening on the afternoon of December 2 the students occupied Sproul Hall. On December 3, the *Chronicle* front page bannered across eight columns

CAMPUS SHOWDOWN
THE BIGGEST UC SIT-IN

The students were described as having captured Sproul Hall. The *Chronicle* story was restrained, its strongest terms describing the insurgents as "rebels" and or "unwelcome overnight guests."

At the December 2 demonstration on the Sproul Hall steps preceding the actual invasion of the administration building, Stephen Weissman had told a crowd of 5,000, "There's absolutely no hope the University will accede to even one of our demands."

To which FSM's Martin Roysher added, "The administration has shown itself to be irresponsible and incapable of running a great University."

The *Chronicle* continued: "With a sort of efficiency not often found in the military, the demonstrators quickly designated the third and fourth floors as study areas, the second floor became the headquarters, the lobby a recreation room and first-aid station."

Another *Chronicle* story an page six:

SONGS AND SANDWICHES
BUSY NIGHT AT
BESIEGED HALL

The story was illustrated by a picture of a young mother, Ann Bratt, who was sitting-in with her seven-month-old-son, Christopher.

The *Examiner* was equally restrained, although underneath its front page banner:

UC LOCKS UP REBELS

The Hearst paper carried the subhead:

POLICE ALERT
IN BIG SIT-IN

In its last morning edition of December 3, the *Examiner* went all out:

BROWN ACTS—ORDERS
ARREST OF UC REBELS

This told the story of the police moving in on the 800 and more demonstrators in Sproul Hall. On this day too, the *Examiner* carried a two column box under the caption:

EXAMINER ASSAILED

in which it reported that FSM leaders had attacked the Montgomery series published during the Thanksgiving holiday. Mario Savio was quoted as having said, "It is a terrible imposition on the intelligence of the San Francisco Bay area that such a newspaper should exist and be circulated."

The same conservative approach shown by the two San Francisco morning papers on December 3 was also reflected in *The New York Times,* which carried a dispatch out of Berkeley by Wallace Turner. It quoted "reports . . . published in the San Francisco *Examiner,* a Hearst paper that called the Free Speech Movement "Marxist-dominated," thereby giving credence to the Kerr interview of October 7.

The New York Times story of the next day was published on page fifty under the headline:

BERKELEY STUDENTS STAGE SIT-IN
TO LATEST CURB ON FREE SPEECH

On December 3, the *Oakland Tribune,* an afternoon paper, carried its front page banner in fire red type:

MASS SIT IN ARRESTS
UNDER WAY AT UC

with subheads: "Sproul Hall captured for 14 Hours," and "Sproul Hall like a captured city."

A still later *Oakland Tribune* edition of December 3 changed the red type to a more ominous banner:

I WON'T TOLERATE U.C.

ANARCHY:

GOV. BROWN

Pictorially, the paper presented: "a howling coed and tight-lipped male students carried out of University of California Sproul Hall by Berkeley police officers." The *Tribune* also published an eight-column aerial photograph taken in the afternoon showing police blocking off embattled campus approaches while students picketed campus entrances.

Governor Brown was quoted: "As long as I am governor, there will be no anarchy and that is what has developed at the University of California." In the same story the *Tribune* quoted the telegram sent by 650 members of the Berkeley faculty to the governor: "Punitive action taken against hundreds of students cannot help to solve our current problems and will aggravate the already serious situation."

The Oakland paper also reported the arrest of Oakland attorney Robert Treuhaft: "District Attorney Jay Frank Coakley was informed that Treuhaft was advising students to 'go limp' so that police would have difficulty handling them."

(On December 17, Lawyer Treuhaft demanded a retraction from the *Tribune*. On January 5, the *Tribune* carried an apology: "Jay Frank Coakley has denied making the statement and the *Tribune* retracts.")

The San Francisco *Call Bulletin* that afternoon had an eight-column headline:

800 SIT-INS ARRESTED

This was in type an inch and a half high, the biggest used to date. The subhead read:

700 Police Ousting UC Rebels

The ratio of seven-eighths of an armed policeman to one unarmed student recalled Hemingway's description of the Italian soldier: "fearless while dispensing death when in no danger of suffering it."

The Berkeley *Gazette* bannered the story in red and published a picture of a girl being dragged down the stairs of Sproul Hall by two Alameda County sheriffs.

In Long Beach, California, the *Press Telegram* increased the number of jailed students:

POLICE BREAK UP UC SIT-IN
JAIL 900 'FREE SPEAKERS'

While the Fremont *News Register* reduced it:

POLICE ARREST 200
RIOTING STUDENTS

On the front page of the campus newspaper, *The Daily Californian*, and extensively quoted elsewhere throughout the state, was a long statement from President Kerr on the sit-in and Governor Brown's action. "Prominently stated in paragraph two was the charge that "as an early act of the occupation of this building, the office of President Emeritus Robert Gordon Sproul was broken into and the files were opened and the contents strewn about the room."

On the afternoon of December 4, President Emeritus Sproul emphatically denied his office had been broken into. Subsequently, President Kerr told how the report had reached him through the police, but there has been no formal withdrawal of the charge by the president, nor any expression of regret for having made it. Furthermore, the weekly issue of the University *Bulletin* dated three days later, December 7, and sent to every faculty member on all the campuses of the University, contained the charge intact.

On page eighteen, across eight columns, the *Chronicle* featured a story:

KERR CALLS IT 'ANARCHY'

by James Benet. This also contained the accusation that FSM had broken into President Emeritus Sproul's office during the sit-in.

The San Francisco *Examiner* had similarly been misled under identical circumstances. But *The New York Times*, with an earlier deadline because of the three-hour time differential, did not make the Sproul invasion accusation although it quoted from the Kerr statement in other particulars. The evening editions of the *Call Bulletin* came out with the vandalism charge hours after the first denial.

Likewise, the Berkeley *Gazette* repeated the denied declaration. This was carried through all editions, although the Kerr statement was dropped back to page fifteen from page one by the end of the day.

The third extra of the Berkeley *Gazette* had its now customary two-column red headline which said:

SIT-IN GROUP OUT OF JAIL
STUDENTS, FACULTY PICKET

The *Gazette* had a picture of a coed standing in an empty classroom before the notice of a class cancellation printed on the blackboard. On December 3, Professor Leon F. Litwack, a visiting professor of American history, from the University of Wisconsin, had dismissed his lecture with a memorable statement "It hardly behooves us to study, if not to celebrate, the rebels of the past while we seek to silence the rebels of the present."

The *Daily Californian* had an editorial signed by the editors from three campuses, Berkeley, Los Angeles and Davis, captioned:

WE NEED A LEADER

"Clark Kerr," the editorial said, "has shown perception and good will through his many statements to the press and the community. But to this day, he has not come down to the level of the students, down to the base court." The story continued to demand banner headlines in San Francisco. Said the *Examiner:*

BUT PROFS

ASK AMNESTY

801 ARRESTS

AT UC

POLICE SMASH

SIT-IN AT UC—

801 ARRESTED

The newspaper carried an hour by hour chronology from 2:30 AM Thursday morning until eleven hours later when the last "rebel occupant and the 801st demonstrator was arrested." One of the *Examiner's* stories was headlined:

PARALYZING UC
STUDENT STRIKE
SET FOR TODAY

On this day, the *Examiner* had more than 400 column-inches of coverage.

The New York Times front-paged the story across four columns with a picture captioned "University of California Students Face Line of Policemen Outside the Administration Building in Berkeley." The *Times* coverage, including a picture, ran to sixty-one-column inches.

The Hollywood *Citizen-News* published an editorial on December 4:

THE U. C. RIOTS

This editorial said, "The fuzzy-brained intellectuals of the University of California, the State Board of Education, and the regents are reaping the crop they have sowed. Rioters, insurrectionists, undisciplined and uncontrolled, set loose by the same breed of Communist agitators who have been invited to speak on campus, have defied all rules, regulations and authority of the University of California, Berkeley."

This was a union of incompatible bed-fellows. For one thing, the State Board of Education has nothing to do with the University of California or the regents; for another this was the first time the regents had been called "intellectuals," fuzzy-brained or not.

The editorial continued, "The University of California, its board of regents, the State School Board, AND THE GOVERNOR OF CALIFORNIA WHO APPOINTS THEM AND FOSTERS THEIR PROGRAM HAVE SEEN THE REAPING OF THEIR WILD OATS. Now do the governor and the regents and the school board have the intestinal fortitude to halt their egg-sucking and molly-coddling of Communists and set forth a code of practice and enforce it?

NO UNIVERSITY OR COLLEGE TEACHER OR ADMINISTRATION IS ESSENTIAL ON THE STATE PAYROLL; NO STATE UNIVERSITY OR COLLEGE IS INDISPENSABLE—THEY CAN BE CLOSED.

"All persons and portions of the University administration responsible for their complete dissolution of law, order and administration on the campus should be discharged and their credentials canceled." (Capital letters as published.)

The *Oakland Tribune* on the 4th had a two line eight column banner:

REBELS CALL STRIKE
TO PARALYZE CAMPUS

Its front-page picture was of a littered corridor in Sproul Hall after the arrests had been concluded. On an inside page was an eight-column nine-inch deep photograph of "friends and relatives of arrested UC demonstrators wait outside the Santa Rita Rehabilitation Center in pre-dawn darkness while prisoners are procesed for release." The story did not mention it, but at least two Nobel Laureates were there waiting for their students to be released.

On page two, there was a picture of a "demonstrator being hauled upstairs from the basement of Sproul Hall to a jail bus." The caption said:

U. C. DEMONSTRATOR
WINCES IN PAIN

Another picture was of a girl being dragged along the ground toward the steps of a patrol wagon. The *Tribune* estimated the cost to the taxpayer of the previous day had been $25,000.

The *Chronicle*'s coverage was similarly comprehensive. Its eight-column banner said:

THE FACULTY "REVOLTS"

below which there was a six column head:

U.C.'S WAR SPREADING

As enthusiasm for a strike mounted, Chancellor Strong issued a statement saying that such action of the teaching assistants would be a violation of "state law." That there was no such law fell into the same category of "non-reason" the Chancellor had employed in his support of the original Sather Gate ban in September.

On page two of the *Chronicle* three students described police brutality under the headline:

STUDENTS CALL POLICE BRUTAL

One of them, Michael J. Smith, said, "I was a guard at San Quentin for six months and I never saw a felon treated as these students were." Smith is twenty-three and a senior in political science. He is a member of Zeta Psi, the only fraternity member on the FSM Executive Committee. Former Senator William Knowland of the *Oakland Tribune* belonged to the same fraternity thirty-five years ago.

Although the charge of "outsider" was frequently found in news coverage immediately following the arrests, University records, taken from the police blotter following the 814 sit-in arrests, showed that 83.6 per cent were students, teaching and research assistants or University employees. The remaining 16.4 per cent were either husbands or wives of students or other non-student sympathizers. These statistics placed the charge of "40 per cent hard-core Mao-Castro sympathizers" in the same baseless category with McCarthy charges, more than a decade ago about Communists in the State Department.

A Fact-Finding Committee of Graduate Political Scientists published an analysis called "Preliminary Report of the Berkeley Free Speech Controversy." This broke down the political affiliations of the students arrested on December 3: 4.5 per cent belonged to radical groups; 18.2 per cent belonged to liberal groups such as the Young Democrats; 25.6 per cent were members of civil rights organizations such as NAACP and CORE; 1.2 per cent were affiliated with conservative groups; 7.3 per cent belonged to a religious organization; and 57 per cent had no political affiliation.*

According to the report, of the undergraduates arrested, 47 per cent had better than B averages; 71 per cent of the graduate students had averages between B and A; twenty were Phi Beta Kappa; eight were Woodrow Wilson fellows; twenty had published articles in scholarly journals; 53 were National Merit Scholarship winners or finalists; and 260 received other academic awards.

These were impressive statistics.

On December 5, there was conflict as to how successful Friday's strike had been. The San Francisco *Chronicle* said:

MASSIVE UC STRIKE FAILS
MOST STUDENTS GO TO CLASS

The FSM claimed the strike had been 75 per cent effective. There is no doubt that impact varied widely between departments—and that it was almost altogether ineffective in the conservative chemistry department. In the liberal history department, most classes were shut down. The *Chronicle* reported attendance of 6,000 at Friday's noontime rally on the Sproul Hall steps with a headline out of tune with the customary *Chronicle* objectivity:

SAVIO TAKES ON THE STATE

describing him as "unshaven, disheveled, but aflame as always with passion." The paper said the leader had trained his fire yesterday on a bigger target—the State of California.

The story continued: Savio told his cheering followers, "The Free Speech Movement should make general demands on the state."

These demands would include "total amnesty" for the hundreds of demonstrators arrested."

The New York Times reported: "About one-third of the school's 27,000 students stayed out of class, a spokesman for the University estimated. A student leader, however, said the strike was more than 75 per cent effective." Editorially, the *Times* commented: "Illegal occupation of the Administration Building at Berkeley was designed to give the rebels a synthetic martyrdom, to provoke the authorities into using force."

On Monday morning, December 7, classes were canceled so that

* A professor was asked if his student, Mr. Savio, was a communist. He reflected. "No, the Communist Party is too small for Mario Savio."

President Kerr and Robert Scalapino, chairman of the department of political science—and chairman of the recently formed Council of Department Chairmen—could address the students. The now famous convocation that took place at the Greek theater became a hot subject for news and debate, mainly because no one seemed certain as to whether Mario Savio tried to seize the microphone in order to speak or a policeman tried to seize him in order that he not speak.

On the afternoon of December 7 the *News Call Bulletin* headlined
REBEL LEADER
GETS HEAVE-HO
and said Savio had been grabbed by four policemen. There had been two. The story said, "He tried to grab the mike," but 18,000 had seen him walk to the podium to which the mike was attached. He hadn't tried to grab anything. On the contrary, he had been grabbed.

The San Francisco morning papers of December 8 bannered the events of the day before with the *Examiner's* front-page headline:
SAVIO HAULED OFF STAGE
CRITICAL DAY AT U. C.
Coverage of the previous day in news and pictures aggregated twenty-four full columns. On page seventeen there was a six-column story at the bottom of the page:
BIG NAMES BACK THE UC REBELS
It announced a statement by fifty-four Bay area educators and civic leaders who charged that University of California administrators "have consistently refused to recognize a fundamental constitutional question at the center of the school's current trouble." But this was lost in the overwhelming coverage given:
UGLY END TO
PEACE TALK
and intimations of legislative inquiries possibly to come. The text of Kerr's speech was carried. Inside there was an eight-column head:
200 PROFESSORS URGE LIMITS ON SPEECH RULES
which stated that a group of Berkeley faculty members had agreed there should be no regulation of off-campus political activities by the University.

The *Chronicle* was less thorough. Its emphasis was equally divided between FSM's rejection of the Kerr peace plan and a four-column photograph on page one of Mario Savio being ejected.

On page eighteen the *Chronicle* had a solid page of pictures and news coverage including three photographs of Savio, the first an instant before the police grabbed him from the rear, the second as they pulled him from the microphone and the third as the disheveled Savio spoke to announce there was a rally. Buried deep in this coverage was Kerr's expression of regret that Chancellor Edward Strong had been kept from the meeting by a serious internal ailment.

"There was scattered laughter," the *Chronicle* said.

During the afternoon of the seventh, the strike resumed. The *Chronicle* appraised its impact the next morning. "Steve Weissman, FSM strike leader, said two graduate students in mathematics had taken samplings that indicated student attendance was only 18 per cent of normal. The survey also showed only 42 per cent of the scheduled classes were in session.

"There was no doubt that many students and some instructors, particularly some young instructors in the category of teaching assistants, remained away from classes."

"But student picket lines intended to halt the delivery of food supplies and other materials to the University were ignored by union truck drivers."

At least two groups of students took positions in support of President Kerr. The *Chronicle* estimated the FSM noon rally drew a crowd twelve times the size of the pro-administration supporters.

On the eighth the Berkeley *Gazette* carried across eight columns:

WIDESPREAD COMMENTS ON CRISIS AT UC

The California Alumni Association deplored the threatened state of anarchy "imposed by relatively few agitators and malcontents and their misguided sympathizers."

Bertrand Russell in London was standing with FSM.

Jesse Unruh, speaker of the assembly, said he didn't think a legislative investigation was necessary at that point. Assemblyman Don Mulford said he was sorry Unruh hadn't begun it immediately.

CORE and SNCC were pro; the California Young Republican College Federation was anti. The Berkeley Chamber of Commerce commended Chancellor Strong.

The New York Times editorially supported Clark Kerr and commented that "Unquestionably part of the trouble has been fomented by left wingers from outside the student body." It was an easy accusation to make but a hard one to substantiate. The *Times* editorial closed with an observation that had been proven almost day to day.

"It is plain that there has been a breakdown of communication between the administration and large elements of the Berkeley community."

After the rally of the seventh, the FSM had decided to hold all activity in abeyance pending faculty action. During this period, faculty leaders had been meeting constantly trying to form a policy to set before the Academic Senate that would save the University. Out of one meeting came the proposal of the historic five-point plan, which the senate approved by a vote of eight to one. The senate proposal granted the students every important measure they had requested since September, and went a step further. The proposal to take discipline, in the area of political activity, from the hands of the administration and place it in the hands of the senate had not been part of the FSM platform. With the passage of the Academic Senate resolution FSM dropped all overt activity on campus pending action by the regents of the eighteenth.

On December 9 press criticism of the Academic Senate action began. The Berkeley *Daily Gazette* had an eight-column twenty-four point headline saying:

RAFFERTY SAYS UC PROFESSORS SHOULD RESIGN IF THEY DON'T LIKE THE RULES THAT ARE IMPOSED ON THE STUDENTS

In the same issue of the *Gazette,* the newspaper welcomed the Free Speech Movement's approval of the Academic Senate action with another three-column headline:

FSM STATEMENT TERMED THREAT
OF VIOLENCE BY LAW, ORDER UNIT

The *Examiner's* headline was:

Academic Senate Asks:
'TOTAL UC FREEDOM'

(This headline four-inches deep across eight columns occupied more than thirty column inches on page one.) The mood on campus was described as being "quiet but restive" by the *Examiner.*

"The hatchet was buried at the University of California yesterday —but as the old expression goes—in a shallow, well-marked grave."

In the *Oakland Tribune* this headline appeared:

RAFFERTY RAPS
PROGRAMS, WARNS OF
'BLACKMAIL'

The *Tribune* took time out from the upheaval to note an indicative election held by the student body on December 8. Candidates for the customary conservative student senate of the University had then been chosen. Those endorsed by Slate, the off-campus student political organization which had been endorsed by FSM were, without exception, swept into office. The final vote tally of 5,276 was the highest ever recorded in an ASUC election.

Rafferty's blackmail accusation was given front-page treatment in the *Oakland Tribune*. On the editorial page, the *Tribune* asked:

WAS FREE SPEECH
VIOLATED ON CAMPUS?

This column by Richard S. Wheeler answered the question: "Certainly much of the emotionalism now enveloping the Free Speech controversy at the University of California would evaporate with the application of hard mental discipline to the problem." Wheeler said, "To the question, then, if whether there was repression of any opinion or idea, the answer is a resounding no."

The afternoon *Call Bulletin* gave prominence to the Rafferty opposition to the faculty.

RAFFERTY WILL VOTE
AGAINST PEACE PACT

But immediately underneath the Rafferty story there were expressions of support from student groups at Brandeis, Harvard, Radcliffe, Tufts, Simmons, Reed, Fresno State as well as other UC campuses.

The *Oakland Tribune* published no comment of its own on the Academic Senate's measure. It did, however, reprint a vigorously anti-faculty editorial from the Los Angeles *Times*. This called the senate's vote "an apparent surrender to irresponsible student elements which arrogantly set out to wreck the University unless their demands were met."

The Oceanside *Blade-Tribune* said the *Times*'s editorial seemed to intimate "Friday's regents meeting would correct the error. Mrs. Norman Chandler, the wife of the *Times*'s principal executive officer is a member of the board of regents."

Editorial opinion was beginning to crop up in news columns across the country. On Thursday, December 10, the Philadelphia *Evening Bulletin* commented on

THE BERKELEY MADNESS:

"The real tragedy at Berkeley, where the University of California has been tearing itself to shreds over the most irrational and irrelevant questions of campus conduct, is in the failure of the faculty to display the leadership and maturity which the public has a right to expect from it. . . .

"A surprisingly large majority of the faculty appears to have condoned or supported lawless, senseless, unfair and vicious attacks on University discipline by a minority of students and campus hangers-on, of which Berkeley has many. . . .

"These professors have provided a dismal lesson in civic responsibility. They have so poisoned the air at Berkeley that this fount of scientific advance and scholarly endeavor may be crippled for years."

The *Bulletin* has a reputation for fairness and objectivity. It is probable that this editorial was the result of inaccurate information that reached the hands of its editors. There is no other justification possible for the description of 824 distinguished scholars as condoning or supporting "lawless, senseless, unfair and vicious attacks on University discipline."

Two days before, Jim Scott, sports editor of the Berkeley *Gazette*, had attacked the Free Speech controversy on the sports page of his newspaper. On a trip to New York as a guest of *Look Magazine* for the presentation of *Look's* All American Football Awards, Scott said he had found himself beset with inquiries about the Berkeley uprisings. He hinted that the high academic requirements at UC ought to be lowered so that more of the area's good athletes with low grades could get in. Scott suggested that better athletic standings would improve the University's morale. "The demonstrators have used their soiled bodies, their foggy intellects only to tear down the reputation of this citadel of learning, which helped build the bomb, produce a dozen Nobel award winners. New Yorkers retched in disbelief to see on TV their bodies, a mélange of beards and black socks, piled up like cattle across the corridors."

The sports editor of the *Daily Californian* on December 9 answered angrily, "How can you say that their bodies were soiled when you weren't even there? I was there and I know damn well their bodies weren't soiled. Foggy intellects? Since when do people who want constitutional rights have foggy intellects? It seems to me that the people who don't want to investigate both sides of the question and hear arguments from both sides are the ones with the foggy intellects.

"That the University helped build the bomb is nothing to brag about, but that it has had a dozen Nobel award winners is. Now I ask you, how many of those came off the football field?"

On December 10, the Santa Monica Evening Outlook editorial page sounded a dire note:

A FACULTY BOWS TO ANARCHY

The editorial began, "December 8, 1964, will henceforth be noted as a day of academic infamy in California. It was made so when the faculty of the University of California at Berkeley, in effect, replaced the rule of law with a license to practice anarchy.

"The Academic Senate's action in yielding to the rioting mob of students and non-students is disgraceful.

"It is to be hoped that Governor Brown will not retreat an inch from the tough stand he took recently . . . to crack down on the rioters. The Governor was dealing with subversion then, and the situation has not changed an iota.

"It is subversion when faculty members succumb to demands of anarchists. . . .

"The organizations involved in the student riots at California are of such sinister repute that a complete investigation is in order. Unruly behavior by students is shocking enough, but when it is given aid and comfort by such as the DuBois Club, the Young Peoples' Socialist League and the Young Socialist Alliance, it becomes a matter for agencies investigating un-American activities.

"There would appear to be dark and dangerous alliances at work in the disorders at the Berkeley campus. What they are is unknown. What is known is that the rule of law has been the first casualty."

The Los Angeles *Herald-Examiner* asked if the Academic Senate's resolution had been

ABJECT SURRENDER?

The editorial said the faculty's recommendations regarding disciplinary measures had been "high handed procedures indeed."

The editorial asked, "Can planning and politicking on the campus be allowed to deteriorate to a point where Communist-front recruiting is allowed? Can students be allowed to violate civil laws on campus, such as the recent mob sit-ins for which they would face civil arrest off-campus?

"These are some of the questions that face the board of regents at their coming meeting on December 18. That and the bigger question, 'Do the people of California, the taxpayers who pay for the University and their representatives at the head of the University's administration run the University or is it to be ruled by the teachers and the students?' "

The *Christian Science Monitor* was more moderate but nonetheless critical: "We feel that students should feel responsible to their university even when off-campus. When they step off the campus they do not certainly cease to be members of the group they have chosen to join.

"Student demonstrations at Berkeley—like those at Saigon and points east and west—have had irresponsible elements within them."

Then more tolerantly, "But they have also shown evidence of student interest in causes beyond themselves."

"The turmoil on the Berkeley campus says something not only about the present student generation but about the learning conditions with which they are confronted within the multiversity."

The Long Beach *Press Telegram* editorialized

TIME TO END THE FARCE:

"The patience of the people is exhausted. The time has come to quit pampering troublesome children and start applying the flat of the official hand to that of the recalcitrant bottom."

The San Francisco *Chronicle* was alarmed:

A GREAT SCHOOL
IS IN DANGER

The *Chronicle* said, "It is a terrifying sight to watch a great university disembowel itself in the public squares.

"Yet in Berkeley the University of California is hell-bent on tearing itself apart."

The Berkeley *Daily Gazette's* red, two line banner across page one on December 10:

UNRUH EXPECTS UC REGENTS
WILL REJECT FACULTY PLAN

The *Oakland Tribune* had a three column page one headline:

FUTURE UNCERTAIN
FOR U. C. REBELS

with a subhead:

Rebel 'Victory'
Calms Campus—
Will it last?

The San Francisco *News Call Bulletin* asked a front-page question under a six-column headline:

UC POWER TEST SHAPES UP

Regents in
Charge? Or
Faculty?

Editorially, the same edition of the *Call Bulletin* decried the Academic Senate's resolution for the assumption of some disciplinary supervision by the faculty. "The University faculty traditionally has a voice in management and properly so. A university is a special academic community and the academicians should be heard but that voice must have certain limits." The writer of this editorial obviously was unaware that from 1920 until 1938 the faculty at Berkeley had been in complete control of student discipline. The faculty, in the latter year had turned discipline over to the administration because it had found the problems coming before it were petty and uninteresting. That was in another era.

On the tenth, the chairman of the California board of regents, according to a story in the *Examiner,* sounded a warning. Edward W. Carter of Los Angeles, the story said, "served terse notice on faculty members and rebellious students yesterday that the regents and not the Academic Senate run the huge institution."

On the tenth, *The New York Times* admitted there was some justice on both sides of the controversy. On its editorial page, the *Times* commented, "It is plain, as we have previously observed, that there has been a serious breakdown of communication between the administration and the students at Berkeley. It is also plain that there is no monopoly of right on either side. The task for the regents is to establish rules that will permit a maximum of political freedom without eliminating a concern for legality and for the responsible exercise of discipline. Repression cannot rule any campus, but part of the function of education is to build a respect for law through the free exchange of ideas."

The *Tulare Advance-Register,* like many other small California newspapers, attacked vigorously: "A handful of misfits, blessed with above average intellects but apparently bearing a grudge against a world which has gotten along without them so well up to this point, had stirred up an almost incomprehensible mess that has transcended the boundaries of the Berkeley campus.

"These young men who travel under the guise of fighters for free speech but whose followers would deny those who disagree with them a civil hearing, have gathered around them several thousand students— and, most astonishing of all, a long list of faculty members whose most distinguishing mark should be maturity—to disrupt the University to the point where the job of educating young people has almost been shunted aside.

"The *Advance Register* takes a back seat to no one in its advocacy of the right of freedom of speech. But that is not the issue in Berkeley —and neither is academic freedom. . . .

"The real issue is whether the University is going to be run by the administration which is the duly constitutive representative of the people of California or whether it is going to be run by an immature but loud-voiced minority of students."

Some of the editorials were too eloquent to need comment.

On December 17, the San Francisco *Chronicle* headlined its editorial:

THE OPPORTUNITY
OF THE REGENTS

"The moment has arrived when the regents of the University, meeting in Los Angeles today and tomorrow, must lead the way to a resolution of the torment and dissention, the disruption and misunderstanding which have torn the campus apart.

"It is the role and the opportunity of the regents to solve the crisis at UC in such a way that next day's papers will not be able to headline either as, 'Regents Bow to Faculty and Students' or as 'Regents Crack Down on Faculty and Students.' "

On the same day, the *Chronicle* listed the expressions of opinion on the controversy which had piled up before the University and the regents.

Among them, the Rockefeller Institute for Research in New York supported the student-faculty position in a telegram to the regents signed by forty-two professors including Nobel Prize Winners Edward Tatum and Fritz Lipmann.

Coverage, over the state, of the open regents' meeting, was thorough. The regents denied the Academic Senate jurisdiction over student discipline. This matter was declared not subject to negotiation. The regents proposed a comprehensive review of the University's policies with the intent of providing maximum freedom on campus consistent with individual and group responsibility. A committee of regents was appointed to make recommendations to the board.

The final regent action said there was no contemplation that "advocacy or content of speech shall be restricted beyond the purview of the first and fourteenth amendments to the constitution."

An Associated Press story about the regents' meeting expressed concern about the fourth point which involved the two constitutional amendments the regents said would be observed. Regents' Chairman Edward Carter had said at the press conference that the regents had not changed position and that they had "never intended to limit advocacy."

Members of the Emergency Executive Committee of the Academic Senate elected a few days before, had met privately with the regents during the Los Angeles session. They were distressed that their disciplinary recommendations had not been accepted but felt progress had been made.

The matter of amnesty was not touched upon by the regents in any public announcement but there were rumors the matter had been hotly debated inside the closed sessions. President Kerr, in a press conference held after the regents' meeting, said that his amnesty promises made on December 7 were still in full force and effect. "My commitment stands," Kerr said, "I feel personally bound by it."

But as the session ended, the Associated Press observed, "Exactly how University of California Administration will move against future student political demonstrations was unclear, despite the action of the board of regents."

In its coverage of the December meeting, the Oceanside *Blade Tribune* pointed to a fact that seemed to presage future difficulties. The regent action promised no more than an "uneasy peace." "The regents have again reposed authority in the hands of the Berkeley administration of President Kerr and Chancellor Strong, the men under whom all the difficulties began in the first place."

The *Blade-Tribune* continued that the proposals approved by the regents "failed to endorse, or even mention the recommendations made December 8 by the Berkeley Academic Senate and approved by an 824–115 vote." This was done by avoiding any reference at all to the Berkeley division and commenting upon a proposal of the Academic Council, drawn from all the state-wide campuses of the University.

The San Francisco *Chronicle* on December 20 carried an exclusive story by James Benet forecasting:

CHANCELLOR AT UC
WILL BE REPLACED

The story which had clearly come from inside the closed regents' meeting said there had been "bitter dispute" among the regents over whether there should be further student penalties by the University, with Clark Kerr standing firmly against them.

Editorially, the regents' action of the eighteenth was uniformly praised. "The Calm Voice of the Regents," said the *Examiner,* "has brought to the Berkeley campus controversy . . . the calm voice of reason expected from that distinguished body of citizens.

"Pending final resolution of the controversy existing regulations remain in effect. These regulations do not countenance on-campus mounting of unlawful off-campus actions. This is one of the hard cores of the controversy. The only way it will ever be resolved satisfactorily is the way the regents are now showing; through the use of the rule of reason."

The *News Call Bulletin* commended the "Regents Good Faith." The editorial said: "One would have to look pretty hard on the position of the UC Regents to find any but the strongest desire to guarantee freedom of expression on the campus."

The *Oakland Tribune* said the regents were *"Putting Things in Order"* and added, "The decisions made last Friday by the University of California regents will do much to restore academic meteors to their proper orbits. . . .

"There still remains the problem of resolving the state's constitution's flat ban on campus political activity with the freedom granted to students and faculty. And there remains the problem of disciplining the ring leaders of the revolt."

The San Diego *Evening Tribune* commented:

REGENTS SPUR RESTORATION
OF CONFIDENCE IN UNIVERSITY

The Los Angeles *Herald-Examiner* said the regents' action "was reassuring to the people of the state." But it warned, "There should be no backing down. Mob threats should be met with legal force and, as Governor Brown has declared, 'anarchy' should not be tolerated on state university campuses. If the regents and the University administration remain firm and determined in this policy, they will gain the whole-hearted approval of the people of California."

The Monrovia *News-Post* said the regents had spoken for the people in their decision "not to compromise with the demands for licensed and privileged violation of discipline demonstrated by the so-called Free Speech Movement at Berkeley.

"The regents have spoken—now let's get down to the business of serious education for the benefit of present and future generations of California."

The identical editorial appeared in the Pasadena *Star News*.

The Bakersfield *Californian* commented editorially: "There will be wide-spread satisfaction with the statement of policy issued by the University of California board of regents after its deliberations over the recent 'political freedom' issue at the University's Berkeley campus."

Most of the editorial praise heaped upon the regents for their December 18 action arose from their refusal to grant disciplinary supervision to the faculty. The measure passed at the December 18 meeting said, "Ultimate authority for student discipline within the University is constitutionally vested in the regents, and is a matter not subject to negotiation."

So the regents were praised for their refusal "to surrender." This was a neat, but deceptive maneuver that had no real bearing on what the Academic Senate had asked. The senate, in its recommendation, had not requested that the regents give up their "ultimate authority for student discipline"; they had asked that the regents repose that part of it concerned with political action in the hands of the faculty instead of the administration. The "ultimate authority" would still belong to the regents.

From the end of the so-called "Wheeler Regime" at Berkeley in 1919 until 1938 all student disciplinary supervision was vested in the faculty. It had been voluntarily surrendered to the administration in the latter year. Now the faculty was suggesting it might be well for them to have a portion of it back.

On January 6, after the appointment of Martin Meyerson as acting chancellor the San Francisco *Chronicle* published what was headlined:

A CANDID
INTERVIEW
WITH KERR

It was written by William Trombley of the Los Angeles *Times* and carried to the *Chronicle* and forty-four other cities by the *Times'* own leased wire service. It said:

"As peace settled—at least temporarily—over the Berkeley campus, University of California President Clark Kerr yesterday traced the frenzied events of the last few months.

"In an interview, he told with characteristic precision of the 'free speech' rebellion from September 14 to the present, when a new set of campus political rules, enforced by a new chancellor, appeared to have brought peace.

"He admitted he had made mistakes in judgment and tactics during the early stages of the uprising. When Kerr returned to the campus September 15, following a seven week trip to Europe and the Far East, he found that the day before, Berkeley administrators had closed the traditional Sather Gate political area.

" 'I thought that was a mistake and that we should return this area to the students,' Kerr said, 'but that was difficult. It had just been taken away—we could hardly turn around and hand it right back.' "

But the greatest damage of the Kerr interview was caused by his reflections on faculty character.

"Kerr traced a series of developments which he believes have played an important part in creating faculty sympathy for the Free Speech Movement. He pointed out that Berkeley is now challenged for supremacy by other branches of the University . . .

" 'Berkeley now finds itself merely the brightest jewel in a crown that has many other jewels and this had a traumatic effect on the Berkeley faculty.

" 'This trauma had led Berkeley professors into several actions against the statewide administration,' Kerr added, 'the latest of which is the sentiment expressed for FSM.' "

Members of the faculty were shocked by this accusation. One professor asked, "Where does he think those 'many other jewels' have come from? Doesn't he realize the professors at Berkeley have been trying to persuade their friends at other colleges to come to the new UC campuses? It's unbelievable."

Another professor said in response to the comment, "The faculty has not answered the Kerr charge because to do so would be to dignify it."

President Kerr's press representative said nothing to deny this portion of the Trombley interview when questioned as to its accuracy.

Berkeley, from September 14 on, has been the biggest education story of 1964. By the end of the year what had happened there should have penetrated the consciousness of every literate reader in the country.

It has been difficult to reach a comprehensive understanding of the Berkeley controversy from the mass of printed and spoken misinterpretation and actual distortion. The California Poll, published in the San Francisco *Chronicle* for February 2, is proof of such an indictment.

The poll found "92 per cent of the adult public has heard or read something about the demonstrations, and 74 per cent takes a disapproving attitude toward them."

The poll had interviewed a cross-section of people in mid-January: "When asked about what they remembered seeing or hearing about the demonstrations, many people characterized them as 'riots,' 'mobs,' 'strikes,' and a significant number spontaneously mentioned they believed the whole thing was Communist-backed or influenced by other outside sources."

The poll listed twelve broad classifications into which the public's comments fell. Not one included the real issue that has been at stake since September 14: the constitutionality of the University's restrictions. The poll revealed shadow not substance. It was a measure of the failure of the press to convey information.

How, one must ask, could the public believe otherwise when, for so many months, they had been subjected to half-truths or unsubstantiated accusations?

Both Hearst newspapers in San Francisco, for example, had been the first to unite the Berkeley troubles in headlines with "Reds on Campus" as the *Examiner* did on October 3 in a page one attribution to Clark Kerr. On the same day the *Call-Bulletin* quoted the president as saying the "University was contending with a hard core of Castro-Mao Tse-tung line communists during the . . . demonstrations."

And that "49 per cent (*sic*) of the hard-core group are followers of the Castro . . . line."

Such as these, associating a student movement with enemies of the state, lifted the movement into the area of violent attack—which it never was.